Assessment of Research on Natural Hazards

The MIT Press Environmental Studies Series
Gordon J. F. MacDonald, consulting editor

Man, Materials, and Environment, National Academy of Sciences
and National Academy of Engineering, 1973.

Citizen Groups and the Nuclear Power Controversy: Uses of
Scientific and Technological Information, Steven Ebbin and
Raphael Kasper, 1974.

Assessment of Research on Natural Hazards, Gilbert F. White
and J. Eugene Haas, 1975.

Assessment of Research on Natural Hazards

Gilbert F. White
J. Eugene Haas

with the collaboration of
members of the project staff

The MIT Press
Cambridge, Massachusetts, and London, England

Library of Congress Cataloging in Publication Data

White, Gilbert Fowler, 1911-

   (The MIT Press environmental studies series)
   Bibliography: p.
   Includes index.
   1. Natural disasters--United States. 2. Geology--United
States. I. Haas, John Eugene, joint author. II. Title.
GB121.W4   363.3'4'0973   75-2058
ISBN 0-262-08083-4

Printed in the United States of America

PUBLISHER'S NOTE

This format is intended to reduce the cost of publishing certain works in book form and to shorten the gap between editorial preparation and final publication. The time and expense of detailed editing and composition in print have been avoided by photographing the text of this book directly from the author's typescript.

The MIT Press

Prepared with the Support of the
National Science Foundation
Research Applied to National Needs
Washington, D.C.   20550

NSF Grant Number GI-32942

Any opinions, findings, conclusions or recommendations expressed
in this publication are those of the authors and do not necessarily reflect the views of the National Science Foundation.

Contents   viii

In undertaking an Assessment of Research on Natural Hazards we
had two broad aims. The first was to provide a more nearly
balanced and comprehensive basis for judging the social utility
of allocating funds and personnel for various types of research
on geophysical hazards. The second was to stimulate, in the
process of that analysis, a more systematic appraisal of
research needs by scientific investigators in cooperation with
the users of their findings.

The decision to initiate the analysis stemmed from recognition of several characteristics of response to extreme events
in nature in the United States. By 1972 the increasing national
costs of damages and social dislocations induced by extreme
events such as hurricanes and earthquakes were apparent. Serious doubt prevailed as to whether or not the measures the nation
was taking to cope with these hazards were yielding the expected returns. The numerous city managers, relief directors, design engineers, and others responsible for emergency or corrective measures communicated only in a very limited way with
scientists carrying out research on the basic problems. In
particular, there was relatively little transfer of information or experience from those who were coping with one hazard
such as floods to those who were confronting another hazard
such as earthquakes.

It seemed likely that by adopting a broader view of the
whole range of ways in which individuals, communities, and
national organizations deal with these extreme events, it
would be possible to arrive at more discerning judgments of
measures to take or avoid in the national interest. We did
not wish to initiate new lines of research ourselves. We did
wish to provide a basis for evaluating the prospective impact
of either continuing the prevailing research activities or
reallocating resources to new lines of scientific investigation.

To this effort we brought different and complementary experience in investigation of natural hazards. One of us (Haas) carried out studies of community response to disaster, and had enlarged this to investigations of complex social organizations and of social reactions to alterations in the environment, as in the case of weather modification. The other one of us (White) had made geographic studies of adjustments to floods and, with other collaborators, had broadened this to comparative investigations of ways in which individuals and communities adapt to or cope with the long-run probabilities of extreme events in nature. We supplemented these sociological and geographic modes of approach with the insights and methods of climatologists, economists, engineers, lawyers, meteorologists, and social psychologists in assembling an interdisciplinary team to carry out a critical appraisal of 15 interrelated hazards.

It was far easier to bring together the methods of a variety of disciplines than to integrate them. With various degrees of success we tried to provide a more solid groundwork for examining opportunities to improve the national situation by research in many relevant fields ranging from geophysical measurements to studies of personality and community response to stress situations.

We were able to build upon the landmark reports of the Office of Emergency Preparedness which had reviewed the situation with respect to natural disasters in the United States (1972). We had the benefit of the effort to recognize research priorities initiated by the Office of Science and Technology during 1971. During the course of our investigation, we participated in the review of research priorities prepared by the Committee on Public Engineering Policy (1973), and contributed to and learned from that exercise.

Although the final responsibility for the recommendations
and findings of the assessment as summarized in this volume is
ours, we drew heavily upon the numerous contributions of individual members of the staff, in some instances taking wording
from supporting reports. It is difficult to assign specific
responsibility for many of the ideas which emerged during the
course of the two-year investigation. Our staff meetings often
were times of lively and frank expression of views. In incor-
porating the ideas and insights which came from those meetings
and from the individual staff reports, we are happily aware of
our debt to all of those who participated in the project. The
names of the staff are given in the section on Participants at
the end of this volume, and their names also appear as authors,
coauthors, or contributors to the more than 15 supporting
reports which are listed at the end of the Bibliography.

We wish to give special mention to members of the professional staff who made distinctive contributions to the mode of
analysis in the project. These included Robert S. Ayre, Earl
J. Baker, Waltraud A. R. Brinkmann, Harold C. Cochrane, Neil
J. Ericksen, Paul C. Huszar, Brian A. Knowles, Gordon McPhee,
Dennis S. Mileti, John H. Sorenson, and Richard A. Warrick.
To a remarkable degree, Janice R. Hutton was responsible for
the cordial and effective management of the whole operation
with the assistance of Karen K. Bird and Madalyn M. Parsons.

Much of the stenographic burden during the project was
carried by Karen K. Bird and Doris Knapp; Judy Fukuhara, Holly
Hollingsworth, Jacque Myers and Deanna Nervig assisted in the
typing of this volume. Richard Nervig drafted many of the
illustrations. Sarah K. Nathe had general editorial responsibility for project publications. Anita Cochran did much of
the proofing and assisted with the bibliographies.

W. J. D. Kennedy and Henry Lansford edited Chapter 11,

using summaries of the individual hazard reports as their primary source material. They also served as consultants on some other aspects of the writing and editing of this volume.

Roy Popkin fashioned the executive summary out of preliminary drafts by the authors, and added felicity of expression to his earlier contributions to the ideas in the report.

We are warmly appreciative of the advice in the conduct of the investigation which we have had from members of our Advisory Committee:

George W. Baker, Kenneth E. Boulding, Earl Cook, Charles H. W. Foster, George Housner, Thad McLaughlin, Daniel Price, E. L. Quarantelli, Will Reedy, Robert Schnabel, Herbert Temple, Jr., Joseph Tofani (represented by John R. Hadd), John Townsend, and Neil P. Woodruff. Bruce Hanshaw was of special assistance in the early stages.

Three consultants gave especially discerning advice throughout the study: Ian Burton, Don G. Friedman, and Robert W. Kates. On problems of insurance Howard Kunreuther was consistently helpful.

A large number of experts in various fields of natural hazards participated either in workshops or in the National Conference on Natural Hazards Research which was held midstream in our project. In addition, others served as special consultants and reviewers of reports. The names of project participants are given in an appendix to this report. We appraised our draft findings with key administrators of Federal and state agencies responsible for activities in the field and benefitted from their reactions; however, we do not hold them responsible for the specific conclusions which have emerged.

The entire project was made possible by the solid support of the National Science Foundation through its Directorate of Research Applied to National Needs under grant number GI-32942.

Alfred E. Eggers, Jr. and Harvey Averch were responsible for the program of which this effort was a part. George W. Baker gave understanding support and critical appraisal to it from its inception.

It was expected in making the original project proposal to the National Science Foundation that the analysis would: 1. estimate the significance of the hazard in the national life; 2. examine the social and economic consequences of adopting each of the possible adjustments to each hazard; 3. judge the likely effects on choice of adjustments of current and possible new public policies; 4. identify those points at which new research or technical development would be desirable in terms of reducing social losses or increasing net productivity; and 5. conclude with a proposed national program for research and development. All these steps were taken with more or less success; evidence in some cases was lacking or difficult to obtain, and the analysis was deflected by imprecision in judgment. The findings are far from uniform in quality of supporting study.

At the outset it was thought that the principal contribution of the study would flow from a comprehensive review of research emphasis related to natural hazards. Until all the findings have been exposed to critical review and possible action, no fair appraisal can be made of their effects. Meanwhile, it is evident that the process of preparing them has spurred serious discussion of what the major gaps are in knowledge about hazards, and when the funding level is appropriate. The Federal policy-makers and administrators have taken part in the analysis and have given serious thought to the significance of the recommended program for their activities. A framework for systematic evaluation of individual research proposals now is available. A pattern for cooperative effort

in the United States has been outlined and tried. What influence it may have upon United States policy in dealing with
disaster situations in other countries is not yet apparent.

If we achieve our aims, there will be readjustment in think-
ing among research workers and administrators in government
agencies and universities on what needs to be done in dealing
with geophysical hazards. There also will be keener recognition
within the legislative halls of the nature of those needs as
they affect authorizations and appropriations. This summary
volume is not intended to be a precise blueprint for specific
action by government agencies. Rather, it should be viewed as
a reconnaissance map sketching the lines along which reallocation of research on those growing national problems may proceed
more fruitfully.

Gilbert F. White
J. Eugene Haas
Boulder, Colorado
February 1, 1975

Chapter 1

SUMMARY OF FINDINGS

Disaster research in the United States must move in new
directions.

Although our nation is becoming increasingly vulnerable to
natural hazards, disaster-caused losses are rising and Federal
assistance programs expanding, the preponderant Federal investment in natural hazards research is in studies which enforce
rather than reduce the likelihood of catastrophe.

Redirection of Federally funded natural hazards activity
could sharply reduce human suffering, substantially curb the
nation's annual billion-dollar disaster-caused economic losses,
and bring about a marked reduction in Federal and state expenditures required to cope with such losses. It could halt the
rising trend in property damages, and also reduce the social
disruption and secondary losses to the total economy caused by
interruptions in production, transportation and communications
facilities.

This can be accomplished without creating new agencies or
programs and without initially heavy increases in funding.
Over a period of years, the total amount invested in natural
hazards research would probably increase by less than the
roughly $40 million currently being spent, but the savings to
the government and the economy would be greater.

Research today concentrates largely on technologically
oriented solutions to problems of natural hazards, instead of
focusing equally on the social, economic and political factors
which lead to nonadoption of technological findings, or which
indicate that proposed steps would not work or would only
tend to perpetuate and increase the problem. In short, the
all-important social, economic and political "people" factors
involved in hazards reduction have been largely ignored. They

need to be examined in harmony with physical and technical
factors. It is not a question of more technology or less technology, but of technology in balance.

Today is the most opportune time for redirection of the
government's natural hazards research investment. In the
Disaster Relief Act of 1974, the Congress provides two important vehicles for implementing the findings of meaningful
research: 1. the Act provides funds for the states to develop
and maintain predisaster prevention and preparedness plans; and
2. the Act provides for establishment of Recovery Councils to
carry out plans for postdisaster restoration and development
along lines which will not repeat past mistakes.

The findings from redirected research will provide basic
guidelines for public officials at the Federal, state, county
and municipal level as they develop preparedness or hazard
mitigation plans, or make crucial decisions on the rebuilding
of disaster-stricken communities. Today, such planning and
redevelopment decisions are all too often based on the
exigencies of the moment, public and political pressures (for
the rapid restoration of a vote or tax base), or on a hodge-
podge of programs and traditional policies. Many of those
policies have existed for years and long since were outmoded
by population shifts, economic developments, uncontrolled and
potentially dangerous use of hazardous areas, and the availability of new scientific knowledge about natural hazards.

To provide guidelines and make them realistic, it is necessary to know not only what can be done, to prevent or mitigate
flooding, but also, for example, what factors were involved in
Rapid City's decision to rezone the area in which 238 people
were killed, and over 1,000 homes destroyed or damaged in 1972,
as compared to earlier decisions against flood mitigation steps
which would have prevented those tragic losses. And it is

necessary to know the factors governing decisions that created
protective works which were inadequate to prevent the flooding
of Wilkes-Barre, Elmira, Corning, and other cities after
Tropical Storm Agnes, and the postdisaster decisions which to
some extent enhance the probability of a future disaster in the
same places by allowing the rebuilding of flood-ravaged areas
and development of additional flood-prone areas along the
Susquehanna River.

It is necessary to know what social, economic and political
tradeoffs are placing millions of people in coastal areas
where one day they will be hit by hurricane wind and storm
surge, and why much of this building is done without also providing adequate means of evacuating the area efficiently when
a storm warning is issued. Money spent on warning system
development is wasted if people are allowed to live in vulnerable places without adequate means to escape when danger
threatens.

It is necessary to know to what extent current insurance
programs, relief and rehabilitation programs, the availability
of recovery funds, and protective construction create complacency about potential hazards and mitigate against adoption
of desirable land use controls, building codes and other
disaster-prevention measures.

It is necessary to know how technological advances in
development of detection and warning systems for hurricanes,
floods, earthquakes and other hazards can be more effectively
translated into official and public actions to protect life
and property.

It is necessary to know more about the economic gains and
losses involved in decisions for or against rezoning hazard
areas, implementation of insurance programs requiring land use
controls, the utilization of flood-proofing, mobile home

tiedowns, windstorm and earthquake-resistant construction, and strengthened building codes and comparable hazard mitigation efforts. What are the cost-benefit considerations, the relationships between the economic costs or investments involved and the potential risk and loss? Who in the affected population gains and who loses? How does the economic choice for an individual property owner differ from the prudent choice for a community which takes a longer view?

It is necessary to know what constrains implementation of such efforts--why earthquake engineers come up with new construction requirements, but communities fail to include them in their building codes; why building codes or land use ordinances are adopted, but not adequately enforced.

In other words, future research needs to focus on what can be done usefully from a technological and regulatory sense, as well as how to help local governments and the public-at-risk to implement new approaches.

Historically, changes in public policy related to natural hazards were made sporadically, usually after a major disaster. Steps should be taken to see that the findings are available to responsible public officials when such incidents create a climate for the readjustment of public policy. More than research, per se, is required. Along with redirected research efforts must come a system for making the findings available to public officials and agencies so they are prepared to take administrative or legislative action once a disaster makes such actions propitious. While to some extent this is locking the barn door after the horse is stolen, it will prevent future deaths and economic and social losses by eliminating repetition of earlier mistakes.

Right now, only a small proportion of all hazard-related research findings ever reach the general public. This needs to be corrected if wise action is sought.

Current Status of Natural Hazards Research in the United States

Natural hazards research in our nation is spotty, largely
uncoordinated, and concentrated in physical and technological
fields. While there has been and is a great deal of research
effort directed at fields such as hurricane and tornado detection, weather forecasting and modification, flood control,
earthquake engineering and prediction, hailstorm modification,
water supply augmentation, forest fire control, snowstorm prediction, and hazard-resistant building design, relatively little
is done in relation to the economic, social and political
aspects of adjustment to natural hazards.

The social research stimulated over the years by the
National Academy of Sciences Disaster Research Committee, the
Institute for Defense Analyses, the Ohio State University
Disaster Research Center and other groups only occasionally
results in application of findings by public and voluntary
agencies involved in disaster prevention or recovery.

Unfortunately, much of the social research has been sporadic
and limited to an investigator's interest in local problems and
narrow theory. No broad body of knowledge has been created,
nor have earlier research findings been updated in terms of
underlying social and economic changes in the United States.
A classic example relates to the psychological effects of
disaster on its victims in a stricken community. On the basis
of a handful of research reports, it was believed for years that
such effects were minimal. It was only after the San Fernando
earthquake in 1971, the Buffalo Creek, Rapid City, and Agnes floods
of 1972, and the Mississippi Valley floods of 1973 that the
great need for crisis intervention and mental health counselling
became apparent. Few resources were available to provide such

help because the needs had not been anticipated. Yet an out-of-court settlement of a lawsuit brought against Pittston Coal after the Buffalo Creek dam disaster paid millions of dollars to survivors for long-term psychic impairment caused by the flood. The Disaster Relief Act of 1974 provides funds for psychological services to disaster victims, and only now are agencies such as state mental health units, the Red Cross and church groups cranking up to meet needs which went sadly unmet in earlier disasters.

There have been less than half a dozen research efforts related to the economics of disaster, and only one major project related to disaster insurance. The Ohio State research efforts concentrated primarily on organizational response.

Much time and effort properly goes into studying the physical mechanisms and properties of a hurricane, tornado, landslide or earthquake, but relatively little goes into studying the human aspects of such geophysical phenomena.

Most hazard research is conducted by agencies with ongoing missions directly or indirectly on one or more hazards. The agency itself is the main user of the research and finances the studies; the research is geared to the agency's particular needs. While an agency may have an ongoing, annually funded research program, the funds are not necessarily adequate and the agency research staff is usually limited to a range of specialities relating to the primary mission. On occasion, such staffs undertake research for which they are not qualified. Sometimes, research is farmed out to academic groups or research and development firms, with mixed results.

However, most organizations responsible for dealing with natural hazards cannot afford to sponsor any kind of research. This is especially true of state and local agencies and voluntary agencies. At present, no agency provides basic funding or coordination for natural hazards research.

The Defense Civil Preparedness Agency (DCPA) of the
Department of Defense confines most of its research to enemy-
attack related problems. The Department of Housing and Urban
Development (HUD), under which comes the Federal Disaster
Assistance Administration (FDAA), refuses to provide leadership
in the research field. The Red Cross Disaster Services has no
research funds.

The National Science Foundation (NSF) may be the key to how
much natural hazards research gets done, although NSF tends to
emphasize engineering and physical science research, and currently funds only a little work in social science fields. For
example, NSF invests more than $5-7 million in earthquake
engineering research, but allocates only a small sum to the
social and economic aspects of earthquake prediction. The
Research Applied to National Needs directorate within NSF has
moved to determine the research needs of "user agencies", but
has not translated those needs in a major way into project
funding.

HUD is funding a few projects related to emergency housing
and earthquake damage, but again these are largely technically
oriented.

The National Oceanic and Atmospheric Administration (NOAA),
the U.S. Geological Survey (USGS), and other comparable agencies
conduct a good deal of technically oriented research. The
FDAA is now engaged in earthquake response planning. That
planning effort, involving 22 Federal agencies, the Red Cross
and the State of California, is based on damage potential surveys made by NOAA and the USGS, but the plans reflect needs for
response as *seen by the action agencies,* and involve little
consideration of long-range public policy related to prior
development, rebuilding and recovery.

How Research Can Improve Our Current Situation

It may seem foolhardy to recommend new directions and perhaps
increased funding for natural hazards research at a time when
intensive efforts are made to restrict Federal spending because
of the nation's economic problems. However, a redirection of
national disaster research efforts and funding will yield
benefits in several directions without adding materially to
the total cost of the research. Current research with minimal
economic payoffs must be replaced with research that ultimately
will produce a stronger nation and lower catastrophic losses.

The present situation finds losses and potential losses
from natural hazards rising. The nation's vulnerability to
natural hazards is being increased by the following factors.

1. Shifts in population from country and city to
suburban and exurban locations. More and more people
live in unprotected flood plains, seismic risk areas
and exposed coastal locations.

2. More people live in new and unfamiliar environments where they are totally unaware of potential risks
and the possible ways of dealing with them.

3. The increasing size of corporations enlarges their
capacity to absorb risks, which may result in plants
being located in high risk areas, or failure to adopt
hazard-resistant building methods. The location of
these firms attracts job-seekers and housing development to the same dangerous locations.

4. The rapid enlargement of the proportion of new
housing starts accounted for by mobile homes means
more families are living in dwellings which are
easily damaged by natural hazards.

On the other hand growing emphasis upon consumer protection
as it affects building location and design standards and the
need for adequate information on location and design works
against unwisely selected criteria. The very existence of
"consumerism", however, may create a false sense of security.

Research could help reduce potential vulnerability to, and

costs of natural hazards by:

    1. increasing national economic efficiency through
heavier reliance upon individual choices within guidelines intended to prevent vulnerability to greater
catastrophes;

    2. enhancing human health through better warning sys-
tems, consumer protection and increased preparedness
for emergency action;

    3. avoiding national disruption by focusing on ways
to reduce catastrophe potential;

    4. creating more equitable distribution of costs and
benefits of recovery through programs which provide
benefits more equally among various economic and social
groups; and

    5. slowing down further modification of ecosystems and
atmospheric circulation to maintain environmental quality
and preserve broad options in further use and protection
of natural landscapes.

Much recent research related to natural hazards had no
significant effect on the national impact of unusual natural
events. This is partly because of its spottiness, partly
because the results do not facilitate a change in the
present mix of adjustments to natural hazards even if such
change is desired, and partly because inadequate provision
was made to translate the research findings into action.

The research recommended in this report will have maximum
benefit if there is early consultation and involvement of
"users" in the design of research projects, the ways in which
people use new information is studied, and explicit provision
is made for transmitting research findings to action agencies
and the general public.

Recommended Research Efforts

In estimating the value of the various opportunities which
follow, the Assessment pursued a series of questions which
began with the present state of knowledge about hazards, and

ended with practical considerations of what kinds of study
would bear fruit and what the possibility would be of translating new information into action (see Figure 1-1). This
required examination of how the nation now responds to each
hazard and what affects the mix of adjustments and level of
risk that are acceptable. In asking what difference it would
make if new adjustments were adopted and how research might
lead to improvement, the Assessment drew heavily upon the
experience and judgment of people carrying out research, as
well as officials responsible for using the results. It
employed a variety of analytical methods, including simulation
models and scenarios. Finally, it arrived at evaluations in
terms of national aims.

To begin with, five new research strategies are called for.
Three of them relate to the way the research is done, the
others to the way in which the research findings are applied
and disseminated.

Postaudits - A systematic program is needed to examine what
happens when a major disaster occurs. The present emergency,
catch-as-catch-can appraisals by hurriedly assembled groups,
often unsuited to the tasks, should be replaced by predesig-
nated interdisciplinary teams prepared to make intensive
studies of common factors in a number of disaster situations,
covering perhaps ten each year. This would make it possible
to examine the reaction to warnings under a variety of circumstances, to determine what factors enable one community to
organize for recovery more effectively than another, the
similarities and differences involved in making comparable
decisions about relocation of families, rebuilding, repair
of public facilities, and similar actions. This effort should
be organized as a collaboration of the principal Federal and

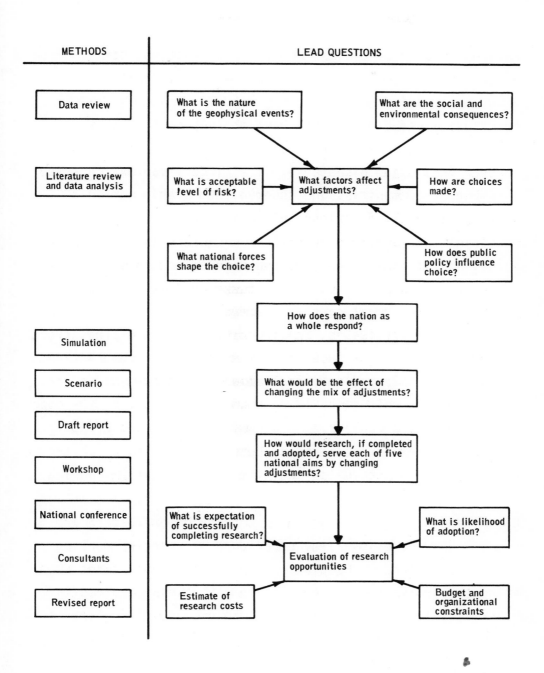

METHODS | LEAD QUESTIONS

Data review

Literature review and data analysis

Simulation

Scenario

Draft report

Workshop

National conference

Consultants

Revised report

What is the nature of the geophysical events?

What are the social and environmental consequences?

What is acceptable level of risk?

What factors affect adjustments?

How are choices made?

What national forces shape the choice?

How does public policy influence choice?

How does the nation as a whole respond?

What would be the effect of changing the mix of adjustments?

How would research, if completed and adopted, serve each of five national aims by changing adjustments?

What is expectation of successfully completing research?

What is likelihood of adoption?

Evaluation of research opportunities

Estimate of research costs

Budget and organizational constraints

FIGURE 1–1

QUESTIONS AND METHODS

voluntary agencies, the Council of State Governments, the
National League of Cities, and university scientists. An
annual funding level of 20 person years is indicated.

Longitudinal studies - Never have there been long-term
studies of how communities and families prepare for, and
recover from major disasters. It will be important to select
a number of communities and observe them over a period of
years if the full experience of families and communities in
preparing for, and recovering from disasters is to be understood, and if their likely response under new conditions of
information and public policy is to be predicted. Such an
effort requires great care in sampling, concentration of data
collection on key issues, and ingenious testing of the effects
of new information or incentives. A network of observation
communities, selected in consultation with the agencies likely
to apply the findings, could be examined in light of the major
themes mentioned earlier. An annual funding level of up to
60 person years is recommended, but a detailed research design
exercise should precede any commitment to long-term funding.

Clearinghouse service - Agencies working on one hazard are
usually unaware of parallel experience of agencies working
with other hazards. People involved with an adjustment such
as control works rarely communicate with those involved in
other activities such as land use management. This lack of
communication becomes particularly acute when it is recognized that if changes in research emphasis are to be accomplished, large numbers of new investigators will have to be
drawn from other fields. It also leads to duplication of
effort, studies for contradictory purposes, and a waste of
limited research funds. A simple method should be devised to

assure rapid and wide circulation of information and judgment
among the producers and users of research on natural hazards.

A clearinghouse could also provide immediately available
information on current research findings for local and state
planners and for Recovery Councils established after a disaster's
occurrence under the Disaster Relief Act of 1974.

Such a clearinghouse could be established at an annual cost
of two person years.

An immediate strategy for the states - Inasmuch as the Disaster
Relief Act of 1974 authorized appropriations up to $250,000 to
each state to enable it to prepare disaster preparedness and
prevention plans, it is important that in the next two years
the responsible state agencies be made aware of currently
available research findings, the nature of research most likely
to have future relevance for the state's individual disaster
problems, and the ways in which plans prepared for the state
may be made harmonious with those of Federal agencies, voluntary groups and neighboring states. This could be done through
immediate strengthening by NSF of scientific advice to state
agencies and to workshops organized by FDAA, and through the
clearinghouse, as well as through direct sharing of research
findings and plans by appropriate Federal agencies, or
through the Council of State Governments and NOAA's Community
Preparedness staff. No long-term cost is envisioned here, but
expenditures over two years might reach $500,000.

Congressional overview - Responsibility at the Congressional
level for Federal activities in the natural hazards field is
divided among a number of House and Senate committees according
to the principal function of the agencies with which they deal.
Congressional review of studies of meteorological phenomena

and hydrological hazards, for example, are divided among the
NSF, NOAA, the Corps of Engineers,and HUD, among others.
Earthquake studies rest in the USGS and NSF and may come under
one group of committees. Disaster relief and insurance may
come under different ones. It would be impractical to combine
all of these activities under a single agency responsive to
one committee in each house. Hence, there should be a bian-
nual review by a Congressional committee or committees which
would examine the whole range of activities in the Federal
sphere, ask how they relate to state and local activities, and
note activities that are neglected or deserve closer integration. This would help coordinate the efforts and assure that
the sparse Federal funds available for natural hazards research
come close to achieving maximum net returns to the nation.

Research Needs Common to Most Natural Hazards

In the United States there are five major methods of adjusting
to natural hazards common to all or most of the hazards covered
in this study. Sometimes they are used in combination, but the
utilization of one adjustment, such as insurance or relief and
rehabilitation, may work against utilization of another, such
as land use management even though the latter may hold a
greater long-term potential for reducing danger and loss. These
five adjustment methods are:
1. relief and rehabilitation;
2. insurance;
3. warning systems;
4. technological aids (protective works, etc.); and
5. land use management.
Depending upon local conditions, it may be most productive
to promote protection works in one area while planning open
space in another, or to mix warnings with a scheme for widened

insurance coverage.

With the currently increasing natural hazard losses and loss potential, and the move towards national and state-wide land use management efforts, the nation would benefit substantially from comparative investigations of these adjustment processes and of the effects of different mixes. There is much to gain by examining insurance experience across the whole range of hazards, or by asking why land use regulations are acceptable in some flood plains but not in an earthquake zone, or why people will vote for a levee construction bond issue in one area while in another they will walk through the aftershocks of an earthquake to vote down a bond issue for strengthening the earthquake resistance of a local school, even though such strengthening is required by law.

It is recommended that the National Science Foundation be authorized to support research in each field at a level similar to its present program on earthquake engineering. It hardly makes sense to fund earthquake engineering research if the adoption of engineering findings may be inhibited by community preference for Federal relief programs or insurance premiums which may cost less at the time.

Remarkably little is known about why people choose among the various possible adjustments. It is often assumed without investigation that people will act in a certain way, but when a disaster occurs or preventive steps are proposed, they act differently. Historically, changes in public policy which follow in the wake of disaster, such as the Alaskan earthquake of 1964 or Tropical Storm Agnes in 1972, have been hurried and sometimes self-defeating because they were not based upon solid research initiated well ahead of the disaster triggering the subsequent policy changes.

The nation's willingness to accept the risk of major

disasters differs markedly between hazards, but appears to be
moving toward less tolerance for catastrophic episodes and
loss of life. At the same time, on the Federal level there
is a broad effort, particularly through the National Flood
Insurance Program, to make those individuals and municipalities
who knowingly occupy vulnerable zones pay for a larger part of
whatever damages they incur.

An investment by the NSF in broad-based research into the
various adjustments would help establish effective ways to
harness public concern about natural hazards with the Federal
approach and achieve a more economic and, in the long run,
productive mix of adjustments.

Research Opportunities for Specific Hazards

Distinctive research opportunities in relation to the 15 different hazards are described in the following brief descriptions. Some of the recommended work on possible adjustments
could be combined with the more general studies recommended
above. Table 1-1 sums up the costs involved. The suggestions
are made in terms of professional person years to avoid problems raised by changing dollar values and by differences in
type of required facilities. More detailed descriptions are
given in Chapter 11, and supporting materials are provided in
the reports listed at the end of the Bibliography.

Hurricane - Current research concentrates chiefly on hurricane
dynamics as a basis for improved forecasts and possible modification. Continuing work along these lines is desirable, but
greater returns over the next decade can be achieved from
research on land use management, insurance and warning systems.
The heightened pace of invasion of vulnerable coastal lands,
the opportunity to combine land use measures with new insurance

and relief policies to reduce uneconomic development and promote
safe construction, and the incomplete character of the present
warning system require a major shift in emphasis and expenditure.

Research is needed to lay the groundwork for sound land use
management of vulnerable coastal zones and to guide new development and renovations so they will avoid catastrophe breeding
and uneconomic changes. Such research should include finding
methods to speed the pace of hazard mapping; appraising conditions in which local communities can adopt land use regulations
and building codes which take into account hurricane risks;
analysis of the socioeconomic effects of such management; and
methods of promoting adoption of hurricane-proofing measures
where technically and economically feasible.

Continued research on warning systems is an important
corollary of land use management studies, but these studies
would be facilitated by an accelerated program of hazard area
mapping, by illumination of factors affecting insurance pur-
chases, and by investigation of public response to hurricane
forecasts. The elements of a fully effective scheme, combining private insurance against wind with federally subsidized
insurance against storm surge losses, remains to be formulated.
There is a need, too, for a critical appraisal of possible
evacuation methods in densely populated coastal urban and
resort areas.

Hurricane modification capability can be advanced through
basic studies of hurricane dynamics and experimental cloud
seeding, but whatever its long-range success, its advancement
should not be permitted to create the same kind of false sense
of security that is inspired by flood protection works, and
which could generate larger losses by preventing adoption of
land use controls or purchase of insurance.

The estimated cost of desirable additional hurricane research is 258 person years.

The estimated cost of all research recommended as especially promising is summarized in Table 1-1 at the end of this chapter.

Flood - In dealing with floods, the United States is in a uniquely flexible position. Past national policy concentrated on flood control and protection works, including land treatment in rural areas. In 1968, the policy expanded to provide for a comprehensive program of flood insurance. As the result of this and new disaster relief and rehabilitation policies, Federal agencies now give increased attention to the management of flood plains. The system of flood warnings is enhanced by expanding flash flood forecasting services. New emphasis is placed on flood-proofing.

Against this background, research leading to new knowledge of possible flood plain adjustments and their application may have greater influence upon the national flood scene than at any time since 1936, when the now-outmoded Federal policy was established.

It is clear that the present mix of aims and methods in coping with floods will change, but its direction is uncertain. The changes will be influenced in part by short-term public policy decisions, and in the near future by research undertaken in the next few years. Research related to engineering design of flood control or flood protection works is unlikely to reduce the level of flood damage, although it may result in more efficient use of construction materials and will increase assurance of structural safety. Indeed, further work on protection and insurance may build greater potential for catastrophes, by inducing a buildup in vulnerable property and by creating both a false sense of security and protection.

The more promising studies with respect to flood protection

and control designs are those related to improving urban high-way, sewer, storm drainage, and hydraulics of control structures and flood channels.

Warning systems and flood-proofing require refinement and extension of forecasting methods. These must be linked to accelerated local information gathering and heavier attention to methods of perfecting warning and evacuation programs in local communities. To have major long-run impact on property losses, the warning systems should be closely correlated with basic improvements in flood-proofing technology, and by examination of the social and economic aspects of flood-proofing as it is adopted or rejected by property owners.

The most promising short-term research thrust is testing and refining new approaches to land use management by studying ways to speed up the adoption of sound land use schemes and to measure their social effectiveness. Land use management can be significantly advanced by coupling relief and rehabilitation efforts and insurance regulation with plans for community preparedness and long-term reconstruction.

All of this work is dependent to some extent upon improving methods of estimating flood hazards. These activities should be accompanied by basic research on variables affecting flood damage. Fresh analysis should be made of public participation in project choice with an eye to helping communities arrive at workable methods of choosing the optimal mix of adjustments for their particular locations.

Such research will require a major shift of emphasis. Today's needs require a larger concern for adoption of flood warnings and for land use management in relationship to improved insurance and relief and rehabilitation policies. (A change is already under way in allocation of Corps of Engineers funds.)

The additional research will cost 893 person years.

Tornado - Because the practicability of modifying tornadoes is
remote, research on how to improve warning systems by making
the nonvisual detection of tornadoes more accurate, by speeding and widening dissemination of forecasts, and by finding
out what factors affect social response can substantially
affect the death and injury rate. One example would be to
find out why some school systems in tornado-prone areas hold
regular tornado drills, but most do not. If the tornado which
hit Xenia, Ohio, in 1974 had occurred earlier, hundreds of
children would have been killed; Xenia had no in-school tornado
plans. However, when a tornado hit two schools in McComb,
Mississippi, during school hours, injuries were minimal because
the children had taken cover according to plan. Studies of
improved building codes and schemes for community preparedness
offer promising possibilities for reducing property losses.
Research should also be done on the relationship of insurance
and relief and rehabilitation to the strengthening of building
codes and tornado warning systems.

The cost of the promising research is 260 person years.

Lightning - Property losses from lightning strikes could be
reduced with the aid of research in two directions. Technical
studies of ways to protect power stations, power lines, and
other electrical and electronic equipment from interruption
should be supplemented by examination of factors affecting
the adoption of new techniques and how they are influenced by
the use of insurance or alternative power sources. Forest
fire management could be improved by giving more emphasis to
a combined program of research on presuppression, detection,
and suppression techniques. Increased understanding of

atmospheric electricity is a desirable, long-term goal, but
drastic change is not in prospect for that or for work on protection of electrical equipment or forest management.

The cost of promising research is 85 person years.

Hail - Research leading to more effective adjustments to hail
damage involves both physical studies of hailstorm physics
and dynamics and socioeconomic analysis of effects and constraints associated with hail suppression. The question of
why there is not more nearly adequate use of crop insurance
to reduce hail-caused disruption of agricultural activities
needs to be related to research on the possibility of alternative land use systems in highly vulnerable areas.

The cost of additional research is 175 person years.

Windstorm - Windstorm investigation now centers largely on
building technology and a meager collection of wind damage
data. Beyond a modest increase in studies to improve wind-
resistant building and mobile home design, research is
recommended to find out what affects the adoption of such
techniques and why owners respond as they do to windstorm
insurance offerings.

The cost of promising research is 62 person years.

Frost - A basic need is to determine the exact character of
frost-caused losses and the processes by which farmers decide
to heed warnings or to adopt new methods of crop protection.
These studies should be closely linked to investigation of
crop insurance and the economic conditions under which it is
bought. Although the potential savings from protective
measures may be large, they may be difficult to achieve
because of farmers' reluctance to change crop practices. At

a time when food production is critical, research on how to motivate changed practices is of great importance.

The cost of promising research is 140 person years.

Urban snow - With changing population and travel patterns creating circumstances under which heavy snowstorms are extremely disruptive, there is a need for pilot studies of damages and costs involved in adjusting to snow hazard. As a supplement, studies on a modest scale of the "snowfest" response and of insurance against disruption would be in order. Until significant improvements are made in the forecasting of heavy rapid snowfall, there is little point in pursuing more sophisticated studies of warning systems.

The cost of promising research is 15 person years.

Earthquake - The threat of very large earthquake disasters grows rapidly, the relatively low recorded losses in recent years notwithstanding. (Tropical Storm Agnes, the nation's worst disaster, did $4 billion in damage; a repeat of the 1811 Mississippi Valley earthquake could cost over $100 billion.) The twin goals of reducing and predicting earthquakes by geophysical means already receive substantial research atten- tion, but may yield low or negative benefits unless accompanied by studies of how they would be applied and how warnings could be effectively disseminated. The social and economic problems inherent in earthquake warnings are much more severe than those for floods or hurricanes because the potential damage impact is much greater, and the time periods involved may be longer. Research on the socioeconomic and political conse- quences of earthquake prediction deserves urgent and sustained support.

Of great immediate significance in terms of damage reduction

and lives saved are acceleration of studies of suitable building codes in hazard zones, methods of earthquake-resistant construction for old buildings, and understanding the processes by
which codes are implemented and enforced and new designs adopted.
Risk zoning and land use management for community development
are at the heart of improving our earthquake defenses. Research
on these subjects needs to be correlated with appraisals of
factors affecting insurance purchase and the community support
of preparedness plans.

The cost of promising research is 780 person years.

Tsunami - The rarity of tsunami disasters argues for a modest
program of research on problems of tsunami-resistant construction and community preparedness. However, more work is needed
on the identification of vulnerable coastlines--there are
warning systems for the Pacific Coast and Alaska and Hawaii,
but none whatever for earthquake-generated tsunamis along the
densely populated Atlantic coast--and of the process of land
use regulation in all vulnerable zones and the effective
implementation of warning systems.

The cost of promising research is 35 person years.

Landslide - With the expanding construction of new residences
upon hazardous slopes, the time is ripe for a national research
effort to help curb dangerous and uneconomic location of homes
on sites subject to land or mudslides. This effort needs to
combine studies of possible protection measures with development of a national information program that would facilitate
prediction of hazard areas. Required new activity includes
both case studies of recent slides and delimitation of hazards
in specific sites. It requires appraisal of experience with
land use management and the relation of that activity to

community preparedness, insurance, and relief and rehabilitation.

The cost of the promising research is 158 person years.

Snow avalanche - In high altitude areas where winter recreation
is exposing more people to snow avalanches, one need for
research is to improve forecasting by better understanding of
the mechanics of snow. More immediately, the magnitude of the
problem should be recognized by establishing a resources
archives program, and by studies of information dissemination, model land management codes and alternative control
technology.

The cost of the research is 100 person years.

Coastal erosion - The current heavy reliance of Federal coastal
erosion control efforts on conventional public engineering
works, many of which are of doubtful efficiency, has serious
environmental effects and does not curb coastal encroachment.
This necessitates a redirection of research efforts. The
situation calls for heavier emphasis on studying basic shore
processes, long-range erosion forecast, factors affecting
community adoption of land use programs, possible expanded use
of hazard insurance, and application of more sophisticated
technology by private property owners.

The cost of promising research is 238 person years.

Drought - As the nation contemplates the possibility of another
serious drought when world food stocks are low, research
activities different from those that curtailed national disruption during the 1950's drought are required. Taking recent
social changes into account, heavier emphasis should be placed
upon long-term alternatives in land use regulation, increased

operational flexibility and water use efficiency, and the
modelling of climate in probability terms. The justification for a broad attack on rural drought questions is
especially urgent.

The cost of promising research is 547 person years, of
which the major part is for rural studies.

Volcano - Although the United States has active or potentially
active volcanoes in Hawaii, Alaska and the Pacific northwest,
knowledge about the physical characteristics of the volcano
hazard is insufficient to define many continental hazard areas
clearly. Nor has enough attention been paid to the social
implications of great eruptions so that public policies can
be designed with confidence. Special studies of human response
to volcanic action, including land use management and possible
warning systems, should be expanded in an integrated program
by building upon previous geological studies.

The cost of promising research is 381 person years.

There are other natural hazards, some partially man-made,
which need to be investigated. They include land subsidence,
as in the Houston-Galveston area, and the costly nationwide
problem with expansive soils, but these were not included in
this Assessment. It is our belief that carrying out the
research recommended in this volume will provide a basis for
some adjustments to these and other possible hazards.

The full cost of these new lines of research if pursued
over a ten-year period is estimated in Table 1-1 in terms of
person years. The dollar cost would be on the order of $250
million annually. Many of the recommended innovations are
for short periods of two or three years with the thought that
after a trial period they would either be abandoned or continued.

Specific details about how the foregoing recommendations were arrived at, and how they can be expected to curb sharply national losses caused by natural hazards will be found in the succeeding chapters, and in the series of supporting reports issued by the Assessment project.

TABLE 1-1

SUMMARY OF RESEARCH OPPORTUNITIES

Topic	Estimated Person Years Over Ten Years	
New Research Strategies		
Postaudits of hazard experience	200	
Longitudinal investigations	600	
Clearinghouse services	20	
Immediate assistance to states	10	
TOTAL		830
Common Adjustment Themes		
Relief and rehabilitation		
Insurance		
Warning systems	200	
Technological aids		
Land use management		
TOTAL		200
Investigations of individual hazards		
Hurricane	293	
Flood	893	
Tornado	260	
Lightning	85	
Hail	175	
Windstorm	62	
Frost	140	
Urban snow	15	
Earthquake	780	
Tsunami	35	
Landslide	158	
Snow avalanche	100	
Coastal erosion	238	
Drought - Rural	477	
Urban	70	
Volcano	381	
TOTAL		4,162
Total - All types of research		5,192

Chapter 2

FUTURE DISASTERS

One sobering lesson from past experience with hazards is that
the nation has difficulty visualizing the human suffering and
economic disruption which will result from events whose coming
is certain but whose timing is completely uncertain. The
magnitude of some of those events which will shake the nation
at some unknown time and the ways in which their severity
could be reduced by taking action in the years immediately
ahead are suggested by three scenarios of hypothetical events.

Such scenarios require a good deal of conjecture even
though description of the basic physical and social parameters
is as accurate as possible at present. Whether or not the
hypothetical disaster occurs at the designated place, a
similar situation is likely to occur some time over the course
of the next few decades. Such an event is as likely to occur
next year as in any year thereafter. Each of the three is
outlined in a somewhat different fashion to illustrate individual lessons that have wider application. Together, they
emphasize the urgency of research which would lay the groundwork for curbing future disaster.

Miami, Florida

The threat posed by hurricanes at many points along the South
Atlantic and Gulf coasts is dramatized by an account of vulnerable population and property in dynamic interaction in
Miami, Florida. The following is a current judgment of the
probable results of a hurricane of a given strength striking
a sector of the Florida shore where the parameters of occupance and adjustment are known. It concentrates on threats
to life and does not estimate total property losses.

The meteorological catalyst is a large, slow-moving, wet
hurricane making landfall south of Miami. Specifically, it is
a hurricane with a central pressure of 925 mbs and radius of
maximum winds of 15 miles. This is equivalent to Donna (1960),
Carla (1961), and Betsy (1965), and much less severe than the
Keys storm of 1935, which drowned 730 people in that relatively
low density population area. It passes just south of Key
Biscayne and moves onshore at 15 mph at the new residential
community of Saga Bay (see Figure 2-1).

Under these conditions, the National Hurricane Center in
Coral Gables issues a warning for residents of Key Biscayne,
Virginia Key, and south Miami to evacuate. Such a warning is
normally made with at least 12 hours of daylight remaining
before the predicted landfall of the hurricane.

Key Biscayne and Virginia Key are about five miles off the
coast of south Miami. Virginia Key is occupied by a sea
aquarium, the oceanographic laboratories of the University of
Miami, and research facilities of the National Oceanic and
Atmospheric Administration. Key Biscayne, a large residential community of mostly wealthy residents, is attractive
for residential location due to the close proximity of the
water and its distance from the more congested mainland. The
elevations of these areas above mean sea level range from two
or three feet to about ten feet, with an average of approximately five feet. Rickenbacker Causeway, a two-mile bridge
across Biscayne Bay bisected by a drawbridge, connects Key
Biscayne and Virginia Key with the mainland. At best, it
requires at least nine to ten hours to evacuate the approximately 10,000 inhabitants.

A number of possible events could preclude successful
evacuation of the entire population. First, not all of the

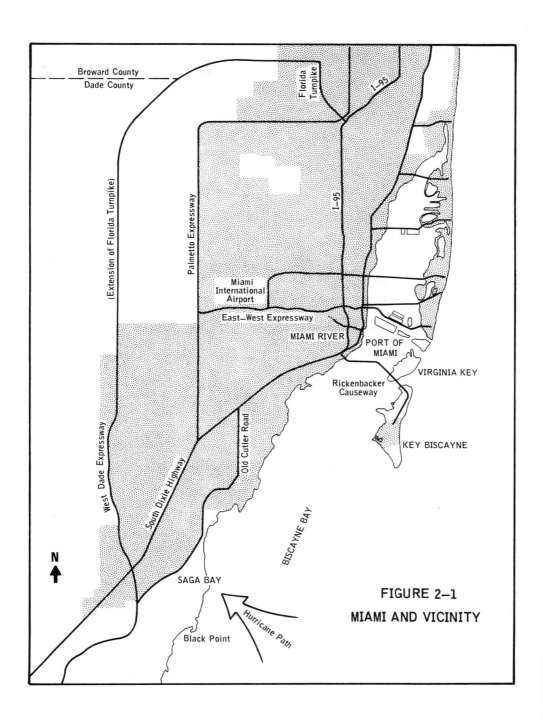

FIGURE 2–1

MIAMI AND VICINITY

12 hours of warning are available for evacuation. As much as six hours prior to a slow-moving hurricane's landfall, storm surge may cause tides to begin rising, thereby flooding some low points on roadways used for evacuation, and bringing automobile traffic to a halt. Even before the storm surge hits its peak at the coast, traffic is snarled by a combination of congestion, weather, flat tires, and automobile accidents. Residents of Key Biscayne and Virginia Key must act swiftly to evacuate once the warning is received in order to avert a major disaster; those not promptly heeding the warning are trapped by the time the magnitude of the hurricane becomes visibly apparent. Since a large proportion of Florida's population has never witnessed a severe hurricane, a warning response rate of less than 50% can be expected.

The drawbridge represents another weak link in the escape route. With the onset of a major storm, marine traffic through the drawbridge increases as vessels seek the shelter of the Miami River and other havens northward. Commercial marine traffic is normally heavy, and several times in past years, barges (which are now pushed rather than pulled by tugboats) have jack-knifed while passing through the raised bridge and jammed its mechanisms. Rising winds and heavy seas contribute to the probability of such an event. Even without such an accident, drawbridges periodically fail and lock in the up position.

Severing of the causeway for any reason means large fatalities from storm surge in the trapped population. Alternative escape routes are severely limited by time and geography. No large boat landings exist on either Key Biscayne or Virginia Key, so only small craft can be utilized for an evacuation by sea. Only a handful of people can be

transported at a time, and organizing and carrying out such an
operation consumes much precious time. Moreover, the danger
to those in boats increases rapidly as the hurricane approaches.

Evacuation by air is precluded by the lack of an airport
and the danger of utilizing helicopters in high winds. Vertical evacuation into high-rise condominiums is an increasing
possibility with new construction, but is limited by space
and the willingness of owners to allow public access to their
private property. (The problem is analogous to that for
private atomic bomb shelters during the 1950's.) The five-
to ten-foot land elevations afford minimal shelter from the
wind-driven storm surge waves of 10-15 feet along the right
side of the hurricane.

Mainlanders also experience severe difficulties in their
attempts to evacuate. A storm surge six hours in advance of
the hurricane's center catches many residents still preparing
to leave. Heavy rainfall and high winds also hamper evacuation attempts.

Saga Bay is an excellent example of how the hurricane
disaster potential is exacerbated by coastal development.
The area is located south of Miami in the area below Old
Cutler Road and above Black Point; it is anticipated to house
a population of approximately 100,000 to 150,000 initially.
Feasibility of the development was enhanced by construction
of the West Dade Expressway, which is connected to Saga Bay
by the Old Cutler Road. Elevation of the Saga Bay area varies
from sea level to five feet above mean sea level.

In order to meet Federal housing regulations, houses are
elevated five feet above mean sea level on fill dug from
nearby man-made lakes. The Saga Bay developers, however,

also tore out the mangroves along the coast, which are un-
sightly and ill-smelling. These mangroves formerly provided
one of the few effective barriers to storm surge, and the
smooth, cleared beaches that are being built invite the un-
restrained sweep of storm surge across the entire area. Storm
surge accompanying a hurricane of magnitude postulated cannot be deterred by the slight elevation of the houses.

The evacuation route for Saga Bay residents is along Old
Cutler Road to the expressway and then north. While Old
Cutler Road generally has an elevation of five to ten feet
above sea level, and might not initially be affected by storm
surge, heavy rainfall swells Black Creek beyond its banks
and cuts the shortest route to the expressway.

Travel north on Old Cutler Road carries evacuees to the
already overburdened and inadequate Dixie Highway, and into
the congestion of evacuees from Key Biscayne, Virginia Key,
and Coral Gables at the intersection of the Rickenbacker
Causeway, Dixie Highway, and Interstate Highway 95. Regardless of the direction of travel on Old Cutler Road, evacuees
from Saga Bay encounter serious congestion and slow-moving
traffic as the capacity of the road is exceeded and the
weather deteriorates. Time runs out for many as they find
themselves trapped in their automobiles when the hurricane
hits.

Reaching the West Dade Expressway does not mean safety,
however, and further obstacles must be overcome. The expressway connects with the Florida Turnpike, which is located west
of most residential development in the Miami area. It too
becomes severely overburdened as Miami residents evacuate.
The Palmetto and the North-South (I-95) Expressways have
major tie-ups, as do all northbound streets, and travel is
induced westward to the turnpike extension.

The severity of traffic jams in Miami is made worse by the
interaction with two evacuation operations, those for boats,
and those for people by automobile. Slip lease agreements
between boat owners and the marinas normally stipulate that
owners will evacuate their boats when a hurricane warning is
received. At the time of evacuation, these boats are instruct-
ed to proceed to the mouth of the Miami River to be escorted
up the river in flotillas. Other than the expressways, all
of the major north-south arteries in Miami cross the Miami
River and, therefore, have drawbridges. The use of flotillas
is designed to minimize the raising of bridges, but major
automobile tie-ups occur; once the flow of traffic is interrupted it takes considerable time to return to normal.

In addition, the evacuation of boats poses a serious threat
of a catastrophe at sea. There are roughly 10,000 small craft
registered in Biscayne Bay, but only 1,000 of them can be
accommodated up the Miami River. When the river is full,
boats are turned away to seek another refuge. No other shelter is close at hand, however, and many boats are caught in
open water by the hurricane.

Flooding hampers evacuation operations, as well as severely
damaging property. Much flooding is caused by the South
Florida Water Control Conservation Project, which is a large
network of canals constructed by the Corps of Engineers to
prevent flooding of agricultural land in south central Florida.
These canals flow to the sea through most residential communities in Dade and Broward Counties and, in fact, provide high-
priced, waterfront sites. With the onset of storm surge,
however, their flow to the sea will be blocked and with heavy
rainfall they can be expected to flood both streets and
property.

In sum, the total loss of life is high. A storm surge well

in advance of the hurricane's center catches many still preparing to evacuate. Flooding of escape routes due to heavy
rain exacerbates the severe traffic tie-ups which are normally expected with a large number of automobiles. (Rush
hour traffic probably represents less than 25% of the traffic
which could be expected with a warning to evacuate, and even
this amount cannot be accommodated without major delays.)
Warning and evacuation as they now are planned and proceed are
inadequate responses to the posited threat.

Boulder, Colorado

An historical review - Attracted to the foot of the Rocky
Mountains by the discovery of gold and silver in the rocks
and streams of the Front Range, early settlers established
the town of Boulder in 1859, just one mile east of the mouth
of Boulder Canyon, some eight hundred feet north of Middle
Boulder Creek (Figure 2-2).

Reflecting the prosperity of mining operations and the
diversification of the local economy, the original urban
nucleus continued to expand, eastward at first and, after the
opening of the University of Colorado in 1877, southward
along the two principal arteries of travel, Pearl and 12th
(Broadway) streets. Initially, development of the low-lying
floodable land adjacent to Middle Boulder Creek was limited
to industry dependent upon rail transport and water power.
However, at the close of the 19th century, the growth of
built-up area in relation to the 100-year flood plain had
resulted in an increasing exposure of industrial as well as
commercial and industrial structures to flood hazard, a fact
of which Boulder residents had been dramatically reminded by

FIGURE 2–2

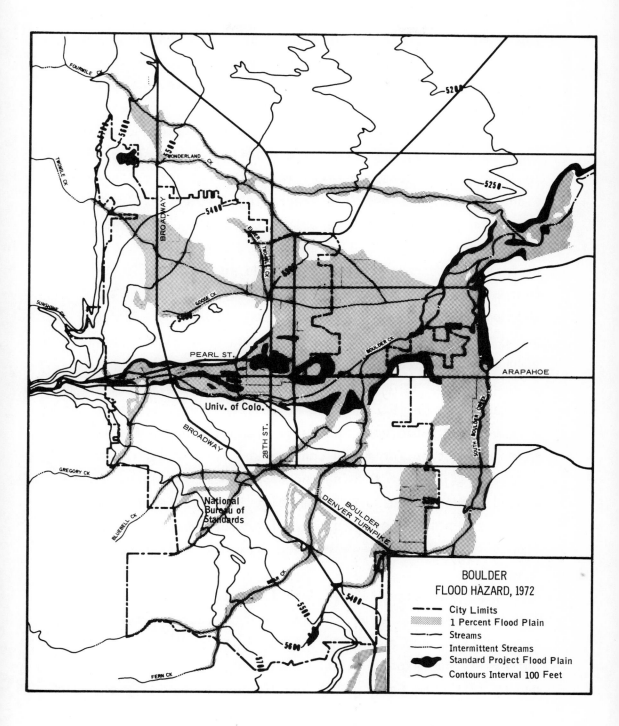

(adapted from City of Boulder, 1972)

the floods of June, 1864; May, 1876; and June, 1894. Following these floods, measures were taken at the municipal level
to provide funds for the repair of bridges and streets. Suggestions for flood protection and control works, however,
were never implemented.

Six more floods occurred during the first two decades of
the 20th century, but a policy of limited growth, established
in 1907, had temporarily decelerated the rate of urban expansion and had succeeded in discouraging further development of
the flood plain. In his report to the Boulder City Improvement Association in 1910, Frederick L. Olmstead, Jr., a
prominent landscape architect, warned against the dangers of
encroachment on the flood plain and proposed that, after a
thorough flood hazard survey had been conducted, a flood
plain management plan be adopted in conjunction with protection and control works along Middle Boulder Creek.

A detailed engineering survey was subsequently carried out
and resulted, in 1912, in the Metcalf and Eddy Report to the
Boulder City Improvement Society. Despite these efforts to
stimulate action for flood control and limited land use
management, lack of funding and disinterest in planning prevented effective measures from being taken. The only note-
worthy exceptions were a number of privately donated tracts of
floodable land which were removed from high loss potential
development.

The period between World Wars I and II--and between the
floods of 1921 and 1938--was marked by relative growth
stabilization and development towards the south, where the
University was expanding at a rapid rate. Although Boulder
had by this time become both legally and financially equipped
to deal more effectively with flood aftermath, no protective

measures were taken.

By 1940, the town of Boulder, with 12,000 inhabitants,
witnessed the close of three decades of limited growth and
entered a period of rapid demographic and areal expansion
which continued vigorously into the 1970's. By 1974, the
urban population had increased more than fivefold, as had the
total developed surface area. Other than the city's pleasant
natural setting in the shadow of the Front Range, many local
poles of attraction could be listed as factors encouraging
this rapid surge in development, not the least important
among them being the University of Colorado, the National
Bureau of Standards, Boulder Industrial Park, and the National
Center for Atmospheric Research. The Denver-Boulder Turnpike,
completed in 1952, also contributed to growth.

As shown in Figure 2-2, the expansion of the urban unit
was accompanied by an invasion of the 1% flood plain. The
sequel to this encroachment was a tremendous increase in the
flood damage potential to which high-value industrial and
commercial land use in the south and east, and residential
units in the north, have become exposed. By 1973, the flood
problem in Boulder had already acquired potentially catastrophic dimensions.

Of the more than 20 flood plain surveys carried out in
Boulder from 1945 to 1973, two-thirds recommended structural
adjustments to the hazard and only one-fifth advocated nonstructural measures to reduce the risk. In either case, however, only rarely were proposals adopted and funded. In
1945, the Corps of Engineers submitted to the municipal
authorities recommendations for protective construction works,
but envisaged costs and widespread skepticism with regard to
the very existence of the hazard prevented these proposals

from being implemented. Not only had the perception of the flood hazard been dulled, but a general sense of security prevailed since it was widely believed that the flood hazard was a problem of the past that no longer existed. That attitude gained considerable ground after the construction by a public utility of Barker Dam, a storage reservoir 15 miles upstream from town.

This skepticism soon became active. In 1956, effective opposition succeeded in defeating efforts to create a Flood Control District for Boulder; until the late 1960's, opposition and apathy managed to frustrate every attempt to enable Boulder to come to grips with the increasingly catastrophic potential hazard to the lives and property of occupants of the flood plain.

On June 16-20, 1965, and again on May 4-8, 1969, flooding on Middle Boulder Creek and its tributaries supplied the motivation necessary to break the long pattern of apathy and inaction. Damages were considerable, particularly those resulting from the 1969 event which, in addition to inflicting almost $3 million in property damages, claimed three lives. It was after this that flood plain management and emergency planning began to receive the priority that previously only the experts had acknowledged.

Although the formulation of flood plain regulations was a step towards more rational use of floodable land, the regulations proved to be quite flexible and, providing certain flood-proofing measures were taken, authorization could be obtained for the construction of permanent structures on the flood plain.

At the close of 1973, a mere 3-4% of potential insurers had purchased federally subsidized flood insurance premiums. The reasons for this are multiple, but certainly one of the

most prevalent was the prevailing judgment of the true flood
risk.

In 1969, following widespread flooding throughout the
eastern part of the State of Colorado, the State Legislature
created an Urban Drainage and Flood Control District to
coordinate flood damage abatement programs and to provide
financial and technical assistance to participant communities.
Boulder was the subject of a pilot study undertaken by the
District, and this and subsequent surveys served as the basis
for a series of recommendations for structural and nonstructural adjustments which were submitted for municipal consideration. They were the object of great scrutiny in terms of
their cost-effectiveness and their possible environmental
impacts.

By 1969, it had become evident that the choice between
structural and nonstructural approaches was not going to be
a clear-cut one, but a compromise between the two. It was
with the intention of providing Boulder with an organ capable
of implementing a unified flood plain management program combining structural and nonstructural adjustments to the hazard
that, on August 21, 1973, the City Council passed an ordinance
creating a storm drainage and flood control utility. At long
last the search for a truly comprehensive flood plain management program had begun.

To suggest what could happen at that stage in the city's
life were a flood to strike the valley, a hypothetical event
is described.

The hypothetical 1975 flood - The accumulation of massive
thunderheads over Boulder and the foothills to the west was
not sufficient cause for alarm to the residents of Boulder
on the warm and still evening of Saturday, August 31, 1975.

By 5:00 pm, the sky had blackened and over the mountain
flanks rain had begun to pour. Within a half hour torrential
rains were falling over the mountain ridges south of Salina,
and by 7:00 pm the storm had unleashed its full fury over the
entire Boulder drainage basin. The Director of Operations had
by this time become concerned and was beginning to dispatch
personnel to evaluate the extent of the danger of flooding.

For mountain dwellers along the upper reaches of tributaries to Middle Boulder Creek, the danger had already become
disaster. Warnings phoned to valley residents by observant
neighbors on the canyon rims above arrived too late to prevent
catastrophe. Gushing stream waters left their banks to inun-
date Wallstreet and Salina, ripping homes from their foundations and sweeping five persons to their death. At the con-
fluence of Fourmile and Middle Boulder creeks at Orodell,
debris-laden water smashed through 11 houses and a motel after
having cut a transmission line and causing the collapse of a
pylon a few hundred yards upstream. Only the clogging of the
conduit under Boulder Canyon Road brought a temporary halt to
the onrush of flood waters. This obstacle, however, soon collapsed, sending a great wall of water downstream towards
Boulder.

Meanwhile, the first crashing wave of flood water on Middle
Boulder Creek had arrived at the west end of town, where it
ruptured a water supply line and, after an initial clogging
and back-pooling, overcame and finally smashed through the
Arapahoe Avenue bridges. A gas line anchored to one of the
latter snapped under the great surge of water, and explosions
could be heard by nearby residents who had already begun to
evacuate hastily.

As flood waters spread laterally across the flood plains,
flow velocities decreased, but the rampage continued. Trees

were uprooted, and hundreds of automobiles were juggled about
in the advancing waters. Older buildings in the center of
town were rent from their foundations as flood waters deepened.
Newer structures too suffered damage as flooding approached
its peak. Private homes, University housing units, the
Municipal Building, the Chamber of Commerce, the Public
Library, the First National Bank, and the Arapahoe and Cross-
roads shopping centers were all severely damaged. At the
University's Physical Science Research Buildings, Behavioral
Genetics Laboratories, and Cyclotron, expensive equipment
and irreplaceable research materials were destroyed.

By 10:30 pm, the flood had reached its peak. Flooding on
Middle Boulder Creek and its tributaries had already claimed
dozens of lives and the destruction of property had amounted
to millions of dollars. The disruption rendered emergency
rescue and evacuation operations extremely difficult and, in
some areas, impossible.

Fires were flaring up throughout the city, telephone communications were cut, water, sewage and gas leaks were widespread; and the supply of electricity had been minimized by
the collapse of the Public Service pylon near Orodell and by
the inundation of substations in Boulder. All 140 patients
at the flooded Community Hospital had to be evacuated to
Longmont.

Earlier, before the event had reached disaster proportions,
the Director of Operations had begun to receive reports of
flooding on mountain streams and had set in motion the
Emergency Plan for Floods. As information continued to flow
into the Office of Emergency Operations, the alert was transmitted to all agencies responsible for rescue and evacuation.
Emergency crews were dispersed to prearranged quadrants of the
city and, amid the blare of sirens and repeated radio

transmission of evacuation instructions, search and rescue
commenced. For many of the flood victims, particularly those
in the flooded mountain communities, it was already too late.

The Red Cross, while maintaining radio contact with the
Emergency Operations personnel, had opened its shelters at
Centennial and Southern Hills junior high schools. To supplement the insufficient shelter supplies, a request was phoned
to the Denver Red Cross for extra medical and feeding units,
beds, blankets, and other necessary equipment. However, the
delivery of these supplies was delayed by flooding on the
southern and eastern highways. Adding to the chaos and congestion were hundreds of curious spectators whose convergence
upon the flood area hindered rescue operations.

Although from the very earliest stages of the flood repeated warnings and evacuation instructions had been broad-
cast over radio and television, the skeptical public initially
paid little attention to these messages. Many of those who
did heed the advice found that, after having left an area of
immediate danger, they had brought themselves to an even more
perilous site. Brash response to warnings and lack of precision in evacuation instructions complicated the situation
even further.

The coming of dawn revealed the extent of destruction on
the devastated flood plain. A postdisaster survey revealed
that in the city of Boulder, 50 lives were taken and $38
million in property damage had been caused by the flood.
Lives lost in Boulder County totaled 95, and damage there
exceeded $43 million.

The disaster-stricken community had now to channel its
energies into a massive effort to rebuild and, especially, to
prevent the recurrence of the catastrophe. One month after
the flood, a report was submitted to the City Council calling

for an application to the U.S. Department of Housing and Urban
Development for a grant of $25 million to enable the city to
carry out reconstruction within the framework of an integrated
flood plain management program.

After 80 years of inaction, the city had finally engaged
itself in an effort to create a comprehensive flood plain
management program which would prevent a disaster of such
magnitude from occurring. When the great flood did occur,
the city found itself unprepared to prevent the tragic loss
of life and destruction which the raging waters inflicted
upon the community.

San Francisco, California

The San Fernando earthquake of February 9, 1971, was a shocker
to many Californians. It wasn't that they didn't know about
earthquakes; every year they felt some mild temblors. But
it had been almost 20 years since a significant earthquake
had occurred in California and 8,367,000 (42%) newcomers
had appeared in the state in the meantime. Few of them had
much of an idea about what an earthquake can do, although
some remembered television news coverage of the Good Friday
earthquake in Alaska in 1964. It had been almost 40 years
since an earthquake had disrupted either of the largest population centers--the Los Angeles and San Francisco areas.
The shocking thing was that important buildings such as
hospitals, which were supposedly built to withstand earthquakes, failed to do so successfully. The sight of fallen
overpasses and a dam about to collapse and flood 80,000 residents was a jolting experience.

The San Fernando earthquake not only shocked many Californians, but spurred some into action. The Governor's
Earthquake Council brought out its first report the next year.

The California Legislature's Joint Committee on Seismic Safety
moved even more quickly. It conducted a conference on earthquake risk in September, 1971, and published an analysis of
what the San Fernando earthquake implied for changes in public
policy. Its work led to legislative changes designed to insure the functioning of hospitals in an earthquake event and
required inundation mapping for areas below dams and reservoirs so that property owners would be adequately informed of
their risk in the event of a damaging earthquake.

Taking a lead from the Governor's Earthquake Council report,
the Region IX Federal Regional Council, a loose association of
Federal agencies, contracted in 1973 with some experienced
social science disaster researchers for an analysis of the
most critical socioeconomic problems that would have to be
faced following a major earthquake in California. The
agencies wanted to know in capsule form what types of information they should have readily available in order to make
prompt, informed decisions following a major earthquake.

During the first few years following the San Fernando
earthquake, comprehensive analyses were made of probable losses
in the San Francisco Bay area and the Los Angeles area following large earthquakes in those areas.

Time was the enemy of action. With a few exceptions, the
urge to "do something" following the San Fernando earthquake
was satisfied by some fact gathering and the preparation of
recommendations. Conferences continued to be held and research
on the earthquake problem continued. For the most part,
needed policy decisions followed by programmatic changes did
not take place.

By 1974, serious talk of reliable earthquake prediction in
the near future became prevalent. In September, the Wall

Street Journal carried a front page article trying to sum-
marize the state of the art and prospects for the future. The
leaders in the field of earthquake engineering and a few
social scientists began to wonder aloud if earthquake prediction might be more of a curse than a blessing by giving community decision-makers and citizens a false sense of security.
There was even some talk of earthquake control within several
generations.

How much the anticipation of reliable earthquake prediction
contributed to inaction in the Bay Area, in Sacramento, and
in the Federal agencies will probably never be known. What
is clear is that the impetus for action produced by the San
Fernando earthquake and, to a lesser degree, by the 1972
Managua earthquake, slowly subsided.

By the 200th anniversary of the nation, things had re-
turned to normal in the San Francisco Bay Area. The upcoming
Presidential election was the focus of much attention.
Earthquake risk was once again a matter that only a few professionals expressed concern about. The policy-makers were
not listening. It had been 70 years since San Francisco had
been shaken and burned. There was only a modest residue of
action to suggest that that earlier catastrophe existed any
longer in the collective memory of the Bay Area populace.

The 1976 earthquake would not be forgotten quite as easily.
This time highly prestigious persons were involved. As fate
would have it, a huge motorcade was snaking its way through
downtown San Francisco. The Republican presidential nominee
and his running mate were in separate cars leading the parade.
Thousands of office workers and school children had been freed
from their daily routines to view the carefully planned spec-
tacle. The event was well-covered by the television cameras.

At the corner of Grant and Market the crowd was especially large and friendly. Without giving any prior hint of his intentions, the nominee ordered his limousine to stop. He got out of the car, walked briskly to the sidewalk where the crowd was being restrained, and started shaking hands as he walked along. His running mate went to the other side of the street to engage in some quick handshaking.

With an intensity on the Mercalli scale of the 1906 tremor, the earthquake struck. With one massive convulsion the sidewalks seemed to bolt in one direction as if a carpet were being jerked out (Figure 2-3). Hundreds of persons, including the two nominees, lost their balance and in falling, toppled others with them. Almost instantly parapets and cornices rained down, mingled with flying glass. More than 50 persons were killed within the first 30 seconds in the vicinity of the corner. Among them was the handshaking presidential nominee. Almost a thousand persons were seriously injured in the vicinity, including the vice presidential nominee.

The shock to the nation was so great that other dimensions of the disaster were overlooked for a time. All told, immediate direct damage to structures and utilities would be assessed at something over $10 billion, about half of that taking place within San Francisco proper. But that was small compared to the human toll.

Aircraft headed for the San Francisco International Airport saw dozens of large dust plumes rise through the haze of the Bay Area shortly after all radio contact with the airport control tower was broken. Within five to ten minutes huge columns of smoke also became visible to aircraft passengers. Much of the smoke seemed to be coming from the refinery areas. Only the flight crews knew at first what produced the smoke and dust columns. The Oakland Airport control tower managed

FIGURE 2–3

ESTIMATED DISTRIBUTION OF DAMAGE TO RESIDENTIAL PROPERTY IN THE SAN FRANCISCO BAY AREA FROM AN EARTHQUAKE OF AN INTENSITY ON THE MODIFIED MERCALLI SCALE OF THE 1906 EARTHQUAKE (COCHRANE, 1974)

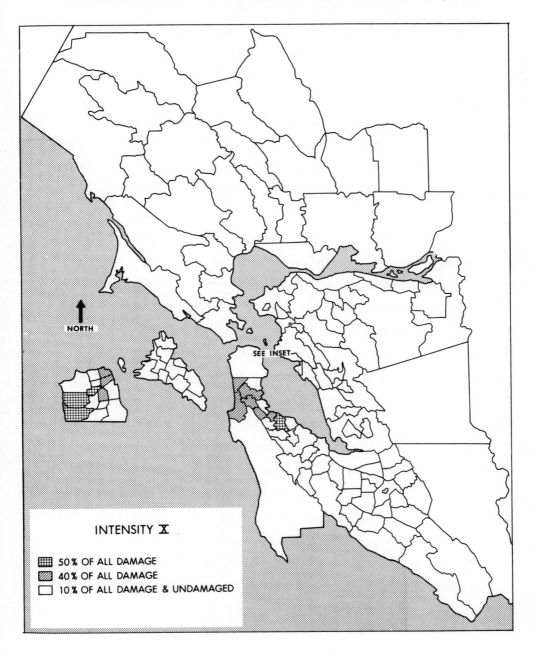

NORTH

SEE INSET

INTENSITY X

▦ 50% OF ALL DAMAGE
▨ 40% OF ALL DAMAGE
□ 10% OF ALL DAMAGE & UNDAMAGED

to stay in operation and it gradually took radio control of
all aircraft which had been headed for San Francisco and San
Jose. All aircraft were informed that because of the earthquake the Oakland runways could not be assumed to be service-
able until examined. Flights were detoured to Sacramento and
Fresno.

The dust plumes were from large buildings that had collapsed. Fifty to sixty major fires broke out within the first
hour. Of the 8,750 persons who died, about one-third were
killed in collapsed buildings or from falling debris. Most
of the others died from the heat, smoke, and fumes of the
fires that burned out of control in most instances. Only near
the periphery of the heavily damaged area was normal water
pressure available to fight the fires. The largest losses
came in tall buildings, where fires erupted on lower floors
and the smoke and fumes moved upward to where hundreds of
employees were trapped.

The toll of some 22,000 injured was staggering. All hospitals within 75-100 miles were overwhelmed. Almost everything
that could have gone wrong did. Dozens of cars parked along
the steep hills of San Francisco bounced free of the curb and
careened down the streets knocking down confused pedestrians,
bouncing off other vehicles, some of which were then set in
motion, and slamming into store fronts and apartments. Hundreds of other persons were injured as they tried to scramble
down outside fire escapes and internal stairwells. The violent
shaking that continued for some two to three minutes made it
all but impossible to avoid falling while going down stairs.
Thousands were injured by falling ceilings and light fixtures.
Others were injured by sliding furniture--desks, filing cabi-
nets, refrigerators, bookcases. In the end the largest

single class of injuries came from the most obvious sources of
all--flying debris from hundreds of thousands of shattered
windows and falling masonry.

It was estimated that more than 500,000 persons were home-
less during the first three to five days. In the majority of
instances the dwelling units suffered only minor damage, but
the water and sewer systems were so badly damaged that more
than 100,000 dwelling units were unusable. Fortunately there
were surrounding cities which could absorb half a million dis-
placed persons. Schools and churches by the hundreds were
quickly turned into makeshift shelters. In many instances
there were no beds or even mattresses to sleep on. On the
first and second day many of the victims went hungry simply
because mechanisms for food distribution and preparation for
quantity feeding had yet to get into operation.

There was the usual problem of convergence on the stricken
area. Airports on the periphery soon became jammed with
planes unloading every manner of material. Incoming highways
became clogged by "volunteers" within 24 hours. And along
the coast almost every yacht within 100 miles came to "help."
News media helicopters hovered over the city like vultures.

Perhaps the most basic problem of all was the least visible
--a lack of adequate communication. Hard facts were exceedingly difficult to come by, at first because there weren't
any and later because those who needed them didn't know who
had them, or if they knew, were unable to reach the right
sources. Many activities ground to a halt. Within the heavily damaged area industrial and commercial output approached
zero. Formal educational and recreational activity disap-
peared. Most standard functions of city government were not
performed. Neither payroll nor welfare checks were processed

or, if processed, remained undelivered.

The California National Guard, supported by United States military personnel, held a tight grip on the city. They saw to it that looting was rare. But that same tight cordon also made it all but impossible for legitimate search and clean-up activity by the average citizen to get started.

Enlarging the View

The Miami, Boulder, and San Francisco scenarios may not be realized in this century, or they may be validated in tragic detail next year. Without doubt, events like them will un-fold in the years ahead. It is important for the American people to recognize that such occurrences are inevitable and will extend to other areas and other hazards.

The number of scenarios could be enlarged immensely without doing violence to physical possibilities or social constraints. Among the numerous situations which might be described in that larger picture, a few commend themselves for the message they might convey.

1. Juneau, Alaska--a massive snow avalanche will one day obliterate a segment of the residential area that now is carefully charted as lying in its path.

2. Columbus, Ohio--a tornado of the violence of those of April 1974 could cut across one side of the city.

3. Pacific Northwest--a volcanic eruption could shower large sections of the Portland region with ash, trigger changes in water and ice flows, and level nearby settlements.

4. Great Plains--a drought of the magnitude of those of the 1930's and 1950's could drastically reduce crop and livestock production over several years when world food stocks are perilously low.

Each of these is possible. Some, like the Great Plains drought, may be highly probable within the next 20 years.

When they or similar disasters take place there undoubtedly
will be generous, quick and often efficient public relief.
They will build up pressure for new Federal activity, and they
will challenge the prevailing complacency.

The disasters will emphasize conclusions which already are
apparent: that detection and forecasting proficiency will not
alone prevent catastrophe; that slowness to plan with land use
will build up the catastrophe potential; that reliance upon a
few technological improvements such as earthquake resistance
in buildings will not avert broader disaster; that sustained
local awareness and responsibility is essential to prevent invasion of new vulnerable zones; that provision must be made
to deal in an integrated fashion with the extremely rare volcano as well as with the doggedly returning drought. Details
of the research that would help these observations into action are given in chapters 9, 10 and 11.

To state these and other conclusions emerging from the
assessment of natural hazard research is not to suggest that
heavier or different inputs of research will dispel all of
the problems they bespeak. However, a research effort with
a different balance is required if the Congress and the nation
are not to be caught unprepared when the next great disaster
strikes, and if the slow process of preventing undesirable
losses is to be speeded up.

The following chapters outline the ways in which the nation
now copes with such extreme geophysical events and arrives
at levels of risk it tolerates in choosing among the many
types of action open to it. The possibility that national
aims would be advanced by changes in policy and that new research would, in fact, bring about helpful changes then is
examined as a basis for describing the lines of research which
appear more promising.

Chapter 3

THE NATION'S RESPONSE TO EXTREME GEOPHYSICAL EVENTS

Need the United States continue to suffer heavy annual losses
from the extreme events in nature which come at uncertain
times and with great variation in magnitude? Is the toll of
property damage, deaths, damage to health, and disruption of
the social process an inevitable part of the life of a healthy
country? Would the country gain or lose from new steps to
reduce these losses and disruptive effects? Could research
contribute constructively to such reduction and to the enhancement of the nation's use of its resources of land, air,
and water? As listed in Figure 1-1, a series of leading questions is intended to explore the evidence which bears on promising research opportunities.

Those questions are of undoubted importance to the welfare
of the country. The answers to them are far from clear. Relatively precise and comprehensive understanding of the way in
which the nation and its subdivisions respond to rare geophysical events is not available. There is even less
authoritative evidence on the social response to the physical
phenomena than on the natural events themselves. The range
of response includes the kinds of adjustments that are
adopted to deal with hazards, and the consequences borne by
various sectors of the nation.

A critical examination of available evidence shows that
only crude estimates can be made of what direct losses in
lives and property are suffered by the United States each
year. The figures on casualties are deceptively precise;
there are few checks on the specific causes of reported death
and injury or on the ways in which they are linked with the
disaster. For most of the calculations of property losses,
the figures may be in error by a factor of two or three. For

example, the estimates of mean annual loss due to hail range
from $400 million to three times that figure, depending upon
what allowance is made for secondary effects. It is even more
difficult to deal with the systemic effects of economic and
social disruption caused by the extreme events.

Thus far there is no adequate way of weighing the psychological consequences of populations exposed to the
violence of the event, the enduring dislocations of family
life, and the frustrating periods of rehabilitation which
follow. The costs and benefits of prevailing means of coping
with hazards are extremely hard to estimate. All of these
qualifications need to be in mind when tallying the national
effects of hazards.

A further notion of how the nation responds to extreme
geophysical events may be gained from asking what mixes of
activities are adopted by the nation, its communities, and
their individual citizens to cope with these disrupting events.
What is done with regard to one hazard may influence the impact of other activities on the hazard, or the exposure of
population to other hazards. For example, the kind of insurance which is offered homeowners against wind damage may
influence the extent to which house construction is earthquake-resistant because it could specify, as do building codes,
a design that is resistant to both earthquake and wind. It
may also affect the readiness of the occupants to respond to
warning of a high wind.

The consequences to the nation as a whole can be judged in
terms of the net effects on deaths, casualties, property, the
functioning of economic and social systems, the mental health
of individuals, the equilibrium of the environment, and the
resulting distribution of costs and benefits.

Adjustments

The nation and its component parts respond to extreme natural events either through adaptation in the organization and processes of the social system, or in specific and conscious adjustment intended to reduce the costs or increase the net benefits of the hazards. By *adaptation* is meant long-term arrangement of activity to take account of the threat of natural extremes. It is illustrated by farming systems in arid regions which endure a persistently dry climate, or the patterns of land use in flood plains which avoid unprofitable exposure of especially sensitive crops to recurrent inundations. Adaptations embrace a wide variety of other kinds of allocations of land use and investment.

By *adjustment* is meant all those intentional actions which are taken to cope with the risk and uncertainty of natural events. These fall into three major classes:

1. *Modifying the causes of the hazard,* as in the case of reducing the velocity of a hurricane by cloud seeding, relieving the seismic stresses in an earthquake zone to prevent high-intensity movements, or heating an orchard to prevent freezing from cold air;

2. *Modifying vulnerability* to the natural event, as through constructing flood control dams, warning systems, building earthquake-resistant houses, or prohibiting construction in the path of a snow avalanche; and

3. *Distributing the losses,* as in the case of insurance, relief and rehabilitation operations, or individual loss-bearing.

Under each of these general categories of adjustments there is a variety of activities. Examples of some common adjustments are given in Table 3-1. This table is not intended to be inclusive: it merely illustrates activities

TABLE 3-1
EXAMPLES OF ADJUSTMENTS TO NATURAL HAZARDS IN THE UNITED STATES

Types of Hazards	Types of Adjustment		
	Modify Event	Modify Vulnerability	Distribute Losses
Avalanche	Artificial release	Snow shields	Emergency relief
Coastal Erosion	Beach nourishment	Beach groynes	Flood insurance
Drought	Cloud seeding	Cropping pattern	Crop insurance
Earthquake	Earthquake reduction (theoretical)	Earthquake-resistant buildings	Emergency relief
Flood	Upstream water control	Flood-proofing	SBA loans
Frost	Orchard heating	Warning network	Crop insurance
Hail	Cloud seeding	Plant selection	Hail insurance
Hurricane	Cloud seeding	Land use pattern	Emergency relief
Landslide	--	Land use regulation	--
Lightning	Cloud seeding	Lightning conductors	Homeowners insurance
Tornado	--	Warning network	Emergency relief
Tsunami	--	Warning network	Emergency relief
Urban Snow	--	Snow removal preparations	Taxation for snow removal
Volcano	--	Land use regulations	Emergency relief
Windstorm	--	Mobile home design	Property insurance

(Burton, Kates and White, 1975)

which are reviewed more comprehensively in Chapter 11.

Each adjustment carries a specific set of social benefits and costs. In most cases an adjustment yields returns to the society as a whole or to sectors of it. For example, flood plain use in many areas benefits from flat terrain which favors it in building costs over adjoining higher areas. Many coastal areas subject to hurricane storm surge enjoy ready access to beach or salt water.

At the same time, an adjustment carries definite costs to society. These may include:

1. *Losses* caused by the occurrence of the event, as in the case of property damages, injuries to physical and mental health, deaths, and social disruption; and

2. *Costs* of undertaking the adjustment, as in the case of building a flood control dam, seeding a hurricane, operating smudge pots in an orchard, or operating an insurance system.

It is possible to put together a moderately accurate picture of the magnitude of losses to life, a less accurate estimate of property damages and injuries to physical health, and a far less satisfactory set of estimates on the degree of social disruption and injuries to mental health caused by hazards. One of the crucial dimensions--the capacity of the hazard to develop truly catastrophic disruptions within society--can only be captured in a crude fashion.

There are much less adequate measures of the costs of carrying out the various adjustments. For example, a farming area may suffer relatively few damages from drought, but it also may embody a heavy investment in operating expenses to prevent drought damages in the form of supplementary irrigation systems and cloud seeding operations.

In gross form the social effect of any given adjustment may be expressed as:

> Net Social Effect = Total Benefits - Total Damages -
> Total Costs of Instituting the Adjustment

The net effect of adjustment to hail by cloud seeding in a
Kansas wheat farming area could be shown as:

> Net Social Effect = Benefits from wheat farming
> operations - Residual hail damage - Cost of hail
> suppression operations - Other operating costs -
> External costs in other areas

A wheat farmer, in estimating the cost of a cloud seeding venture to suppress hail (it may run only a few cents annually
per acre), usually takes into account his prospective net income from the total crop operation and the probability of
suffering hail damage with and without cloud seeding.

The customary estimate of such effects is on a static basis.
That is, estimates do not take account of the major trends in
benefits and costs. The land use pattern on an eroding shoreline in 1975, while involving little damage to the residents
at the time, may generate new buildings and new shore currents
that cause bitter losses in 1985. The situation is dynamic
because particular mixes of adjustments are apt to change over
time, and because outside factors influence the acceptance or
rejection of particular adjustments. For this reason, trend
lines should be inserted in any presentation of the level of
impacts. These need to be read along with the absolute figures. While the total damages for avalanches are relatively
small, the trend in damages is sharply upward. Conversely,
although the loss of life in tornadoes is on the order of
100 annually, the current trend seems to be downward, or, at
worst, stationary.

The changing characteristics of the adjustments available
to individuals in dealing with a hazard are illustrated in
Figure 3-1. At Stage 1 in time, residents of a hurricane
coast were obliged to bear their losses in the face of rising

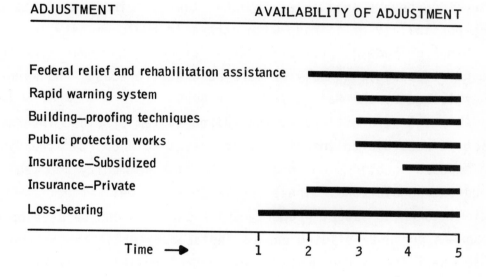

FIGURE 3-1

CHANGES IN AVAILABLE ADJUSTMENTS TO RESIDENTS IN A
REMOTE HURRICANE HAZARD ZONE

winds without knowledge of how severe the wind would be or when
the peak would strike. They had the opportunity to build their
houses to resist wind and storm surge only on the basis of
their individual experience. If losses were suffered, they
expected to bear those losses. At Stage 2 it became possible
to insure against certain losses, principally wind, with private insurance companies. At Stage 3, the possibility of
engineering works to deflect or reduce in some measure the
effects of the hurricane was offered through a Federal construction program. Technical advice on wind-resistant construction became available. By that time the individual had
the possibility of joining with others in the community in
pushing for Federal protection works at about the same time he
found it possible to rely on more accurate forecasts and warnings issued by the National Weather Service.

At Stage 4, a nationally subsidized system of flood insurance
made it possible to insure against losses to property already
in exposed locations on condition that the community adopted
land use regulations. These regulations may well affect the
extent to which vacant property which one owns can be developed
or one's present building can be replaced after it has become
obsolete. The extended system of Federal relief and rehabilitation then covers some of the losses which earlier he would
have had to bear alone. By Stage 5 he was able to rely on
any one of a rather complicated mix of adjustments, and his
choice of a particular mix may have been influenced by the
availability of others. For example, he may have been less
interested in building a wind-resistant house if he knew that
he could be partially reimbursed for losses through a subsidized insurance program or through more generous relief and
rehabilitation. The same kind of change in mix in adjustments
can be charted for other hazards and other groups of people.

It should be recognized that people occupying similar sites in hazard zones may adopt radically different mixes of adjustments. Some owners may avoid building in a seismically unstable terrain, others may insist upon highly resistant designs for new structures, and still others may take no special precautions. Whatever the resulting mix, it may change over time as the available options shift.

More important than the immediate trends are the factors producing them. These can be examined in terms of the interaction of adjustments, of changes in public value criteria, and of the conditions of choice.

Interactions of Adjustments

Only a little is known about how one adjustment encourages or inhibits another. For example, there is evidence that the construction of upstream flood storage works encourages people to move further into the flood plain (White, *et al.*, 1958). Levee protection works may change the flood plain by expanding the overflow area from a flood of specified flow (see Figure 3-2). In some instances, the possibility that upstream works might be constructed induces people to take larger risks than if they were to think no protection works were in prospect. On the other hand, there are only speculative notions on the extent to which the provision of insurance against flood losses will influence the degree to which homeowners will adopt floodproofing measures. Similarly, it is guesswork how much the yet unrealized prospect for practicable hurricane modification by cloud seeding along the Atlantic Coast of Florida will stimulate developers to move further into areas subject to storm surge with a 2% probability. The social system sets limits within which different adjustments are selected, but it, in turn, is influenced by the resulting activities.

FIGURE 3—2
HAZARDS, ADJUSTMENTS AND EFFECTS

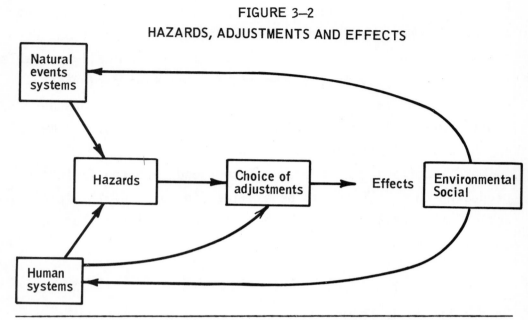

Figure 3-3 indicates the present state of understanding of the static interaction of adjustments for one hazard, floods. Evidence reviewed in the supporting report on flood (White, 1975), suggests that some are closely linked, some are only weakly linked, and that there are others for which there is no solid ground for estimating the relation. If a community adopts land use regulations in flooded areas, it is less likely to seek control and protection works for the same area. On the other hand, field studies suggest that if the community has already benefited from a levee or an upstream flood pro-tection work, it shows less disposition to support land use regulations in the remaining vulnerable zones of the flood plain. Insurance coverage with annual payment of premiums may be expected to stimulate interest in warnings if there is a substantial deductible item. There is little experience and only weak theory upon which to base a judgment on the extent to which adoption of land use regulations inhibits or encourages flood-proofing by owners of exposed buildings.

FIGURE 3–3

MATRIX OF INTERACTION OF ADJUSTMENTS TO FLOODS

Initial Adjustment	Other Adjustment Affected					
	Control and Protection	Flood-Proofing	Land Use Planning	Warnings	Insurance	Relief and Rehabilitation
Control and Protection		○	○	○	○	○
Flood–Proofing	○		○	●	?	○
Land Use Planning	○	?		●	●	○
Warnings	○	●	●		?	○
Insurance	○	?	?	●		○
Relief and Rehabilitation	●	○	○	○	○	

Stimulated by the initial adjustment:

● — High stimulation

○ — Little or none

? — Doubtful

Certain of the adjustments probably are linked in a causal fashion over time. Judging from testimony at flood insurance hearings, loss-bearing experience of developers in some hurricane coastal zones encouraged the provision of Federal subsidies for insurance against hurricane losses. Insurance was contingent upon requirements for local land use regulations. Once the local land use regulations are enacted, they become a deterrent to further development of the hazardous area; this leads either to a reduction in the rate of development, or to steps on the part of developers to either modify the insurance provisions or eliminate land use planning and accompanying insurance guarantees in the community.

Some of the interactions may be observed over a relatively short period of time--a year or two--whereas others become effective only over much longer periods. Linkages that affect decisions about house construction and repair have their full effects over amortization periods of 20 years. Certain linkages will not become strong except over periods of two or three decades.

The approach taken here differs in two ways from that ordinarily taken in appraisal of research needs or planning policy with respect to natural hazards in the United States. First, it recognizes that action taken with respect to one adjustment, such as hurricane modification, flood protection works or hail insurance, may have a profound effect upon the kind of response which society makes to any one of the other adjustments. Second, it regards those interactions as dynamic and prudently holds that the relationship will change. This means that planning must provide not only for shifts in the relative importance of different adjustments, but also for research to identify the trends and to explore ways in which they may be guided to yield greater social utility to the individual, community and nation.

The Consequences

The most direct and poignant consequence of natural hazards is
loss of life. For all geophysical hazards for the country as
a whole, the total deaths are modest indeed when compared with
highway deaths at 50 times that rate. On the average they
probably are less than 1,000 a year, recognizing that the data
base is very weak. A few of the hazards, such as coastal erosion, frost, hail and landslide, rarely cause death; for a few
of them, principally drought, it is not practicable to distinguish long-term effects of deprivation in the path of the
hazard from other factors at work (see Figure 3-4). The
estimates are for historical periods of greatly different
lengths.

There is no linear relation between the total number of
deaths and the *number of injuries.* In the case of snow avalanches, the two are about equal. At the other extreme, the
ratio of deaths to injuries for hurricanes is about 1 to 50.
For lightning it is approximately 1 to 2.

Lightning causes as many deaths as does tornado; urban snow
and windstorm have about the same magnitude of fatality rate.
The fatal coronary arrests in the midst of snow shovelling
equal the violent deaths in tornado debris. Hurricane deaths
on the average are about one-half as great as those from
lightning. In terms of the historical record, deaths from
earthquake are very small and about equivalent to those of
snow avalanches. The tornado and hurricane deaths typically
command more public attention because they are concentrated in
place and numbers and come at times of dramatic atmospheric
violence. The scattered and less dramatic losses through
lightning, windstorms, and urban snow attract little attention.

FIGURE 3–4
MEAN ANNUAL LOSSES

HAZARD	DEATHS per 10 Million	INJURIES per 10 Million	PROPERTY DAMAGE 1▭▭▭▭6 $ PER CAPITA
Avalanche	.35	.48	▪
Coastal Erosion	–	–	▬
Drought	–	–	▬▬
Earthquake	.38	?	▪
Flood	3.90	?	▬▬▬
Frost	–	–	▬▬▬
Hail	–	–	▬
Hurricane	2.52	119.52	▬
Landslide	–	–	▪
Lightning	5.43	10.95	▪
Tornado	5.24	90.48	▬
Tsunami	1.57	?	ı
Urban Snow	5.19	3.19	ı
Volcano	NA	NA	NA
Windstorm	4.65	29.42	▬

NA – Not Applicable

Mean earthquake losses in both property and life are
extremely small by comparison with several other hazards.
When they do occur, earthquakes characteristically generate
large public anxiety. The possibility of massive losses when
another San Francisco or Los Angeles or Boston earthquake does
occur is immense, and is not ignored in some quarters.

The information concerning *direct property losses* is somewhat more full, but for none of the hazards, as indicated
above, is it comprehensive and thoroughly accurate. In absolute figures the larger sources of direct property loss are
flood, frost, and drought. In an intermediate group are hail,
hurricane, landslide, lightning, tornado, and windstorm (see
Figure 3-4). At a lower magnitude, ranging between 10 and 20
million annually, are earthquake, tsunami, and urban snow. The
volcano events are so rare that it is impracticable to offer an
average annual estimate. On a per capita basis, these figures
show that average losses per person in the United States for
each of the hazards ranges from a minimum of two-tenths of a
cent for snow avalanches to more than $5 in the case of flood
and frost. Aggregating all of the losses, the total per capita
figure is on the order of $23 per capita, or .05% of per capita
income.

Losses of lives and property are shifting over time, as shown
in Figure 3-5. For all of the hazards except lightning there
is evidence that the trend is stable or upward in property
losses. The estimates are made for the past two or three
decades. The trend in loss of life is upward for earthquake,
windstorm and avalanche. For most other hazards the
casualties are stable or declining. The more conspicuous
shifts are in the case of tornadoes, where the decline is of
long duration.

Inherent in public appraisal of much of the geophysical

FIGURE 3–5
TRENDS IN DEATHS AND DAMAGES

HAZARD	DAMAGES	DEATHS
Avalanche	↗	↗
Coastal Erosion	↗	NA
Drought	?	NA
Earthquake	↗	↗
Flood	↗	↘
Frost	↗	NA
Hail	↗	NA
Hurricane	↗	↘
Landslide	↗	⇨
Lightning	?	↘
Tornado	↗	↘
Tsunami	NA	?
Urban Snow	↗	⇨
Volcano	NA	⇨
Windstorm	↗	↗

NA — Not Applicable

hazard is some estimate of the possibility of a major
catastrophe. *Catastrophe* is defined as a situation in which
damages to property, human health, social structure or
processes are of such severity that recovery and rehabilitation is a long and trying procedure. Six of the hazards have
high *catastrophe potential*. They are earthquake, flood,
hurricane, tornado, tsunami, and volcano. Those with low
capacity to create major disruption are snow avalanches,
coastal erosion, frost, hail, landslide, lightning and urban
snow. In the intermediate group are drought and windstorms.
Drought has wide systemic effects, but it comes on so slowly
that many emergency adjustments are made as it progresses.

For all of the hazards except drought there is evidence
of a trend towards heightened catastrophe potential. This
is illustrated in the individual hazard reports in Chapter
11, and is even the case with airborne electronic systems
and surface power transmission systems becoming more vulnerable
to damage from lightning, where damages seem to be declining
(see Figure 3-6).

The costs of adjustments taken by individuals and public
agencies to cope with these several hazards include the cost
of all direct protection works such as those for coastal
erosion, flood, hurricane, landslide, and tsunami. In addition, they cover the costs of measures to reduce the loss
potential in properties and lives, such as the extra 5% often
estimated to be involved in making buildings resistant to
earthquake, flood, or high wind, or the cash payment for
installation of lightning rods and tiedowns for mobile homes.
There is no comprehensive tally of these costs, but some estimated trends are given in Figure 3-7 for the past three
decades.

Expenditures for flood protection, flood warnings, flood

FIGURE 3–6
CATASTROPHE POTENTIAL FROM NATURAL HAZARDS

HAZARD	CATASTROPHE POTENTIAL
Avalanche	Low
Coastal Erosion	Low
Drought	Medium
Earthquake	High
Flood	High
Frost	Low
Hail	Low
Hurricane	High
Landslide	Low
Lightning	Low
Tornado	High
Tsunami	High
Urban Snow	Low
Volcano	High
Windstorm	Medium

Low   Medium   High

FIGURE 3-7

TRENDS IN ADJUSTMENT COSTS FOR NATURAL HAZARDS

HAZARD	ADJUSTMENT EXPENDITURES
Avalanche	⇨
Coastal Erosion	⬈
Drought	⇨
Earthquake	⬈
Flood	⬈
Frost	⇨
Hail	⇨
Hurricane	⬈
Landslide	⬈
Lightning	⇨
Tornado	⬈
Tsunami	⇨
Urban Snow	⇨
Volcano	⇨
Windstorm	⇨

insurance, and building modification are at least 60% of the
estimated damage to flooded property. To these must be added
the relief expenditures, recognizing that some are merely ways
of reallocating the distribution of losses.

Calculating the direct costs of relief and rehabilitation
on the part of the Federal government is straightforward.
However, other costs sustained at the Federal level, over and
above the transfer of losses through direct assistance,
include: Federal income tax deductions for casualty losses
claimed as a result of natural disaster; losses sustained by
the Veteran's Administration from foreclosures on home loans
induced by natural disasters; uncollected principal on disaster
loans; and indirect charges for salaries and services by the
staffs of numerous governmental agencies that participate in
or advise on the relief and rehabilitation activity. There
also is a substantial interest subsidy by the Federal government for all loan commitments. The administrative costs
involved in such activities are large by comparison with the
direct payments. Under the 1974 Disaster Relief Act, the
number of Federal agencies involved is enlarged and heavier
responsibility is given to the states. The total number of
personnel concerned with action following a disaster is increased and made more complex in organization.

In the aggregate, the adjustment costs may account for at
least 50% of the direct property losses. As already noted,
it is 60% or more for floods.

In no instance is the annual cost of such adjustments,
including losses, showing signs of decreasing at the present
time. In some instances, such as coastal erosion, landslide
and tornado, the costs are increasing at a substantial rate.
In others, such as flood, frost, urban snow and windstorms,
the per capita costs seem to be at about the same level, in

constant dollars.

Some of the adjustments lead to *modification or deterioration of the environment.* This is the case with coastal erosion, flood, and hurricane control structures. Tallying up their relative benefits and costs is practicable for selected small projects, but not on a large scale. The Council on Environmental Quality study on stream channelization (1973) illustrates the complications in judging the net effects of only one type of work. Tracing out the full consequences of drainage projects proved extremely difficult. Adjustments may be accompanied in some degree by benefits beyond those from reduction in hazard-related losses, as in the case of recreational use of water above the detention storage in flood control reservoirs. A full balance sheet for environmental costs of adjustments to hazards would require explicit appraisal of the environmental impacts of coastal erosion works, flood control works, land treatment practices, cloud seeding, forest fire control, and shifts in land use. A few efforts have been made to anticipate such consequences, as in the case of cloud seeding in relation to ecosystem stability in the Southern Rockies (Weisbecker, 1974), but the number is still small.

Perhaps a more significant aspect of the shift in adjustment costs is that a substantial proportion of them appear to contribute to the enlargement of catastrophe potential as a result of strengthened reliance upon technological measures. The technological devices, in turn, hold greater implications for environmental modification.

The general distribution of the disruptive effects of an extreme event is suggested in Figure 3-8. Ordinarily, the larger the population affected, the smaller are the per capita losses, with the ultimate loss being death to a very small

FIGURE 3–8

IMPACT OF DISASTER: A CONTINUUM OF EFFECTS

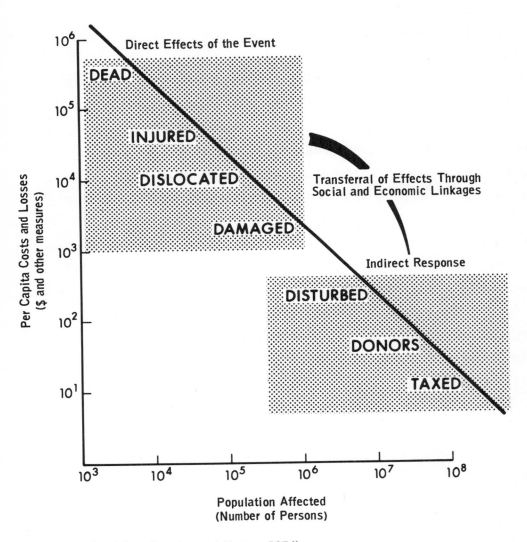

(adapted from Bowden and Kates, 1974)

number of people. For any disaster it is possible to estimate
the number of dead, injured, dislocated, damaged, disturbed,
and those who must pay for the event as donors of relief
funds, services, or as payers of taxes to take care of relief
and rehabilitation and research. Cochrane (1975) has estimated
this distribution curve for four major events--high winds in
Boulder, a tornado in Lubbock, Texas, a long sustained drought
in the Great Plains, and a high frequency earthquake in San
Francisco. These are shown in Figure 3-9. Taking somewhat
arbitrary figures for the costs of lives and injuries, the
curve for Lubbock shows hundreds of lives lost, thousands of
injuries, about 10,000 people dislocated, somewhat more disturbed, and perhaps a million people sharing in donations to
the relief operations. In the case of a Great Plains drought,
it is expected that about half the nation would be involved
in tax payments of about $10 per capita. The number of lives
lost from a drought is highly conjectural.

These effects not only differ for the nation as a whole for
any one event, but differ in the ways they affect various income groups in society. While some general figures can be giv-
en on the value of a human life ($300,000 is a current one),
or on the cost of an injury ($10,000 is a frequent figure from
insurance claims), the distribution of losses from a disaster
frequently is highly skewed. Those in the lower income
brackets have more dilapidated housing and therefore are more
subject to the ravages of wind or water. The ratio of deaths
to structures totally destroyed varies according to the hazard,
with the largest ratio occurring in floods, hurricanes, and
tornadoes in extreme situations. It appears that deaths in
floods may be higher for those in the age bracket over 64.

The extent to which <u>mental health</u> difficulties result from
disasters is unknown. There has been an increasing tendency

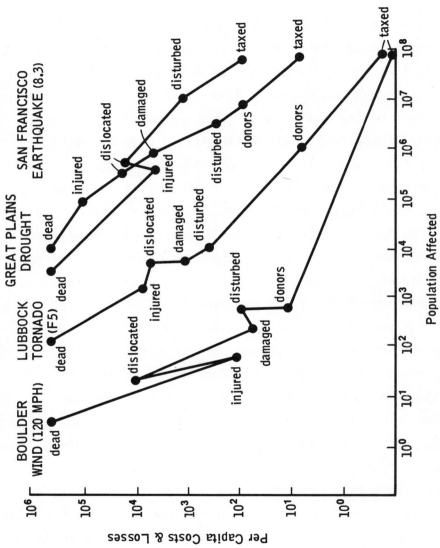
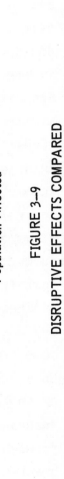

FIGURE 3–9

DISRUPTIVE EFFECTS COMPARED

in both the journalistic and professional literature to
describe psychological problems of everyday living coming
directly or indirectly from natural disasters, and the
Disaster Relief Act of 1974 authorized delivery of mental
health services after disasters. This may reflect better and
more sensitive reporting or more effective means of identifying such problems, or it may reflect changes in capacity to
respond to disasters or in willingness to seek and benefit
from public assistance. Evidence is conflicting on the consequences for children as well as for adults.

The broader *systemic effects* of a natural disaster on the
economy appear to be significant only for very large earthquakes, tornadoes, hurricanes, floods, and perhaps droughts.
A Betsy-type hurricane in Dade County, Florida would have
relatively small systemic impacts, whereas a Camille-type hurricane in the same area might be expected to affect a large
number of families and a much broader area. For a long time
a rough rule of thumb in estimating disaster losses was that
direct property damages often are equivalent to indirect and
systemic effects. A more careful study by Cochrane of the
San Francisco situation (1974) suggests that this is true as
a minimum where an entire metropolitan area is affected (see
Figure 3-10).

Every one of the hazards presents the dilemma that in
planning for its amelioration, the *future is predicted in terms
of recorded performance,* but with knowledge that lurking on
the near or distant horizon is an event which will exceed in
magnitude any previously recorded. There always is the
possibility that a hurricane will generate a lower pressure
than any experienced in the previous 70 years; that a snowfall will exceed by several inches any known to have occurred
in a similar section of the United States; that an early

FIGURE 3–10

BREAKDOWN OF LOSSES FROM A REPETITION OF AN EARTHQUAKE
IN SAN FRANCISCO OF THE SAME MAGNITUDE OF THAT IN 1906

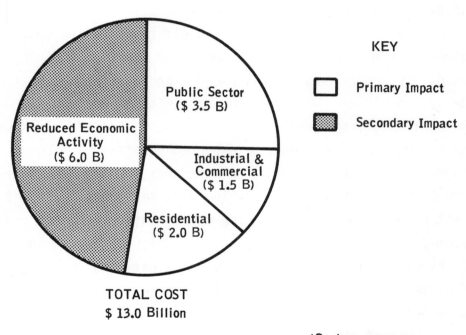

TOTAL COST
$ 13.0 Billion

(Cochrane, 1974)

killing frost may reach farther south into croplands of the
United States than any on records or that a sustained drought
of the magnitude of the one which drove early inhabitants out
of the American Southwest in the 13th Century A.D. may one
day return.

Some events of lesser magnitude carry the seeds of catastrophe. One of the classic cases was the Tropical Storm Agnes
flood disaster of June, 1972. In that event more than 40% of
the damage to property in urban areas occurred in lands which
had been protected by carefully designed engineering works
intended to curb streamflows of a specified magnitude and
recurrence interval (National Advisory Committee on Oceans and
Atmosphere, 1972). The works did not fail through any deficiency in engineering design. They were overtopped because in
planning the original works it was decided as a matter of engineering feasibility and economic justification that the expenditures required to cope with floods of larger magnitude would
not be provided at a later time by upstream storage. The over
overtopping of the levees at Wilkes-Barre and Corning was
foreseen. What was more difficult to anticipate was the
character and magnitude of the social repercussions when the
rare event did take place.

Other Hazards

Other geophysical events may impose serious losses and disruption on the nation. One extreme event is the possibility of a
large *meteorite* fall which, if it were to reach the proportions of some of those recorded in recent geological history
and if it were to strike a populated area, could cause tremendous havoc. Its probability is so small and the difficulty
of predicting where it might occur is so great at this time

that no effort has been made to take this into account as a
major hazard.

Of possibly far greater significance is a *shift in global
climatic patterns*. The question of whether or not climatic
shifts, as distinct from roughly cyclical fluctuations discussed under the heading of drought, are in progress or in
prospect is now receiving serious scientific examination.
Opinions on the significance of change, if any, are far
apart. If some of the investigators are correct, a new ice
age is on the way. There also is dispute as to whether or not
human intervention such as grass fires and fossil fuel consumption may trigger a change. The Assessment analysis assumed
that a large climatic change is not impossible, but does not
attempt to speculate on its consequences. However, the mode
of analysis applied here to social response to lesser hazards
would also be suitable to examining how the nation might
respond to a momentous climatic change.

At the other extreme in terms of frequency is the hazard of
expansive soils, a widespread threat that rarely attains dramatic proportions. Montmorillonite clays may account for
swelling to as much as one and one-half or two times the dry
volume. Upon expansion, the clay loses a good deal of its
strength and tends to become a lubricant for soil movement.
If construction takes place on such soils when wet and they
subsequently are drained, the shrinkage involved in drying may
cause severe cracking in structures. Contrariwise, saturation
of soil from lawn watering or sewer leakage may cause major
damage through expansion of sidewalks, highways, utility lines,
and foundations.

Jones and Holtz (1973) estimate that the average annual
damage to structure from soil movements amounts to more than
$2.2 billion, of which $300 million is estimated for single

family homes; $360 million for streets and highways.

The problems raised by expansive clay soils are spread over large sections of the country, particularly in the Southwest. They are not analyzed in this report because they do not involve the difficulties of the recurrent extreme event of unpredictable timing. Expansive soils are more akin to rust and corrosion of metal structures or to the difficulties caused by shifting and insecure foundations. Their omission from this analysis does not constitute a judgment that they are unimportant, only that they belong in a different category of analysis, as do a number of other factors contributing to the deterioration of buildings.

Likewise, no consideration has been given to soil erosion on agricultural land on the basis that this is covered as a part of research on agricultural land use management.

Conclusion

The severity of catastrophe, like the amount of damage to which any given land use is susceptible, is a partial function of the preparations for the happening and its aftermath. If the nation were to take enough pains, it could prevent most severe natural disasters. Conceivably, it could be so well prepared for the treatment of the injured, the rebuilding of destroyed property, and the reallocation and substitution of resources that it would make up for systemic disturbances: what might otherwise be a catastrophe would be a lower order dislocation.

The unfolding situation with respect to natural hazards is akin to some other aspects of industrial society. With increasing complexity of technological tools and organization, the nation becomes more vulnerable to the interruptions caused by events of low probability but highly disruptive capacity.

One lesson that emerges from a review of the nation's experience is that the United States is becoming more vulnerable
to catastrophes caused by natural events.

Closely related to this finding is the observation, supported in Chapter 11, that the preponderant investment in
research at the Federal level is in studies which reinforce
rather than reduce measures that increase the likelihood of
catastrophe. Commonly, research tends to concentrate on a
few technologically oriented solutions. The alternative would
be to place greater emphasis upon a variety of solutions.

In this situation, steps to provide greater flexibility
not only in responding to those catastophes now foreseen, but
in averting them as they are shaped by shifts in social
orgnaization and technology, are needed. For example, the
improvement of communication systems makes it possible to
experience less frequently, but in far larger magnitude than
ever before, the social effects of a massive disruption in
information flow and storage. The more intricate the network
of computer-monitored operations, the greater the confusion
when the whole system comes to a halt during a rare but
possible power outage. The capacity to modify hurricane
wind velocities by cloud seeding could lead to the possibility
that a large city such as Miami might be less, rather than more
prepared to deal with a great hurricane in the event that
activities of expected efficacy were to fail in some special
circumstance.

To assist in maintaining flexibility is there a research
strategy to assure examination of alternative measures for
dealing with natural hazard and to cultivate a systematic
variety of measures so that the society is never completely
dependent upon one form of adjustment? The nation can set
its activities either to reduce or to enhance the severity of

catastrophe. Sometimes by conscious choice, but usually by
a series of casual and partial decisions, the nation decides
how much average loss and how much catastrophe it will bear.
This leads to the question of acceptable levels of risk.

Chapter 4

ACCEPTABLE LEVELS OF RISK

A few elementary points should be stated about acceptable
levels of risk before dealing with the choices made by
individuals and government. The risk which is tolerable varies
among hazards and social groups, and it changes over time. A
major generator of change is a crisis situation.

The Level of Social Tolerance

Many people who live in hazardous areas, such as the residents
of seismic risk zones in Memphis, Tennessee, or Boston, Massachusetts, are unaware of the risk. Others are conscious
of the risk, but do not judge it to be of sufficient magnitude
to warrant explicit adjustments by them or by public agencies,
as is the case with dwellers on Alaskan coasts where tsunamis
may strike. Still others, such as the inhabitants of the
Missouri River flood plain, are acutely aware of the risk and
promote vigorous steps to cope with it. Responsible officials
in those areas may also differ in their awareness of the
threats presented by the natural occurrences.

Public groups are extremely sensitive to some risks and go
to considerable expense and organizational trouble in order to
reduce social impacts from a possible disaster. However, they
are more alert and committed to the reduction of loss of life
from certain hazards, such as tornadoes and floods, than from
others, such as lightning and earthquakes. If Federal agencies
were to put effort proportionate to potential catastrophic
losses into reducing deaths from earthquakes--as they do for
tornadoes--the nation now would have a huge system for identification of seismic areas and explicit provision of a variety
of adjustments to hold down the deaths which surely will come
if earthquakes of a magnitude of 7 on the Richter Scale strike

those zones.

Starr (1972), in examining risk to health, classifies natural hazards as being "involuntary" risks which are borne by people without conscious choice, as with the use of electric power or automobiles; and "voluntary" risks, such as motorcycling, tobacco smoking and general aviation, which are consciously assumed. In fact, natural hazards have a strong component of the voluntary. They always result from an interaction between a human activity and a destructive event in nature. As will be discussed in the following chapter, they result from unconscious or conscious choice at either the individual or the public level. It is well recognized that while the level of risk to life per hour of exposure to certain natural hazards is low relative to the risks of some other activities such as mining, public agencies place a relatively high value on reducing the incidence of loss of life from natural extremes.

The acceptable level of loss varies from one hazard to another. It is affected by other factors whose weights are not well understood. Considerations of who bears the costs and gains, as noted in the preceding chapter, may be influential. Awareness of the likely impacts may be significant. National agencies may go to pains to cut down the losses from tornadoes, while any one community chronically facing the low probability of a tornado may be more complacent. A city may tolerate new building in a seismically unstable zone, while curbing development in a flood plain.

A third significant fact about the nation's acceptance of risk, in addition to the differences from one part of the social system to another and from one hazard to another, is that the criteria of acceptable risk may change, sometimes slowly, sometimes abruptly. It would be whimsical to expect

a radical shift in risk-bearing over a short period of time
unless there is a sharp change in the political process. However, the criteria appear to move by steps in the direction
of reducing the level of risk which the nation as a whole is
prepared to bear.

The trends are not all in the same direction. While the
tolerance of public agencies to disaster dislocations has
decreased in a few fields of natural hazards, the willingness
to incur risks for others seems to have increased. This is
the case with the willingness of private developers to invade
flood plains, to build residences in unstable landslide areas,
or to locate within the reach of hurricane storm surge. In
assessing future needs, to the extent that the present trends
prevail, the nation may be expected to become more discrimi-
nating in seeking to reduce risk.

It has been argued that the nation's tolerance to natural
risk is shaped by the aggregate of choices by affected
individuals. Their choices, as will be shown in the following chapter, are affected by both explicit policy and by
national forces. In asking what contributes to the prevailing situation, it is helpful to recognize a basic difference
in perspective toward risk, and then to note the special conditions in which public policy usually changes.

Starr (1972) states the problem as, "How safe is safe
enough?" The number of people who lose their lives annually
from tornadoes or tsunamis may be viewed as a function of the
preferences of all the individuals affected, the policies of
public agencies governing risk-bearing, and other policies
and factors which develop quite independently of the risk, but
affect its incidence and intensity. These combine to set the
threshold of risk which the nation accepts at any given time.

One way to describe that level is to show two major

parameters for a hazard: 1. the average flow of costs and
benefits, and 2. the potentiality for a catastrophic event
as defined in the preceding chapter. For reasons reviewed
in that chapter, it is difficult to compute the aggregate
national balance for the net benefits or costs. However, it
is practicable to estimate the direction of change that would
be generated by a shift in the mix of adjustments (see Figure
4-1). Ideally, a shift from the present level at point A
would move toward E by reducing catastrophe potential and
reaping net gains in benefits. Much of the effort to modify
vulnerability through protection works is in the direction
of D. Some well-intentioned attempts to ward off disasters
at very high cost would move toward C. The least promising
shift would be toward B.

Why the Level Changes

In American society the level of acceptable risk appears to
change as a consequence of interaction of two sets of conditions. Experience accumulates over the long run on the consequences of extreme events. Individuals and communities make
adjustments to these consequences. Trends in the activity are
discernible. For example, the willingness of municipal governments to permit construction which would leave mobile homes
and residences vulnerable to damage from high winds has pro-
gressively declined, partly in response to mounting experience of insurance companies in indemnification of losses, and
partly as a result of municipal troubles in cleaning up after
high winds--coping with materials blown from construction
sites, and with the interruption of municipal utilities.
     This accumulated experience often finds its most vigorous
expression after some severe event of catastrophic or near
catastrophic proportions. The great proportion of changes in

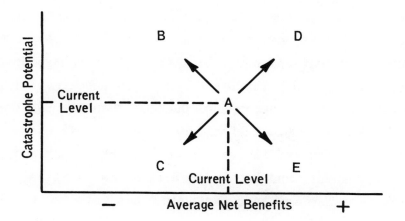

FIGURE 4–1

ACCEPTABLE LEVELS OF ECONOMIC BENEFITS
AND CATASTROPHE POTENTIAL

Federal legislation on natural hazards follows within a few
months or a year of a major disaster. The record for Federal
flood control legislation since the great Mississippi flood
of 1927 mirrors in an exact fashion the occurrence of severe
flooding in the preceding year.

Changes in Federal policy affecting relief and rehabilita-
tion are inevitably linked with major events such as the
Alaskan earthquake of 1964, Hurricane Camille in 1969, and the
Tropical Storm Agnes floods of 1972.

A disaster which at one stage in the nation's history commands major individual and public action would not have done
so at an earlier period. The San Fernando Earthquake of 1971
was far more mild in its human consequences than the San Francisco Earthquake of 1906: the toll of property loss was
approximately 37% that of the earlier earthquake after adjusting for price changes, and the loss of life, comparatively,
was only 9%. The San Fernando Earthquake was followed by
generous Federal assistance to earthquake sufferers. The San
Francisco earthquake had spurred no major Federal relief outlay.
The nation had become wealthier, less tolerant of massive local
losses, and local agencies were more ready to turn to Federal
sources of support immediately afterwards and for long-term
reconstruction. Likewise, the proportion of private property
owners who were ready to insure themselves against future damage from earthquakes was very small following the San Francisco disaster, but larger following San Fernando even though
there was no Federal subsidy to the offered insurance.

The 1972 disasters in Rapid City and the northeastern states
were followed by an increase in foregiveness allowance for SBA
loans from the previous $2,500 to $5,000. The record is one
of sporadically expanding Federal assistance until 1974.

The enactment of the Disaster Relief Act of 1974 was partly

a confirmation and partly an exception to the rule. The new
legislation was prepared with considerable care by the Congressional public works committees which had worked on the
problem over a period of a year and one-half, sorting out the
lessons from the disasters of 1972. Early action on the floor
was deliberate. However, final enactment came precipitously
and far more rapidly than had been anticipated by the sponsors.
The speedy conclusion was linked with the occurrence of the
April, 1974, tornadoes in portions of the Ohio and southeastern
drainage areas. Instances in which changes occur independently
of crisis situations are few.

The implication of this process for any review of research
opportunities is that changes in public policy may be expected
to come usually in sporadic actions, and on the heels of major
disasters. Research programs need to be developed over longer
periods of time so that the findings are available when and
if disaster induces reconsideration in public policy. An
essential strategy for carrying out research in the hazards
field is to assure that the findings are made available to
agencies that will be prepared to act at either the administrative or legislative level once the situation is made propitious by disaster. Their action is more likely to be beneficial if they understand how alterations in policy would
advance public aims by affecting the ways in which choices are
made among the many alternatives that are open to the nation.

Chapter 5

ADJUSTMENT CHOICES

If there were a thorough understanding of the factors which affect the choice of adjustments to hazards at both the individual and community level, it would be relatively easy to identify the lines of action which would be likely to have a significant effect upon future benefits and costs of hazard adjustment, and upon changes in levels of risk acceptance in the United States. As indicated in Chapter 4, ignorance of those forces reflects a major bias in past research on natural hazards and presents two major problems. One problem is a lack of dynamic analysis of the way choices are made, the other is a neglect of external forces that shape the choices.

The prevailing tendency in analysis of natural hazards is to assume that the situation will remain static. For example, it is assumed in planning for snow avalanches that there will not be a major shift in the demand for or use of snowy areas. In planning for flood control for agricultural areas it is assumed that the factors which have affected farming use of flood plains will continue over the next 30 years in the same fashion as in the preceding 30.

Given this static orientation, there is little incentive to find out how the adjustments or conditions of choice change, and what accounts for those deviations. Investigations of warning systems, for example, tend to focus upon the operation of the forecast and on calculations of likely benefits. They pay only slight attention to the way in which the forecast is employed in actual conditions, and they rarely ask how shifts in society or in forecasting technology might be expected to change the way in which people design structures, engage in management of land, or participate in community preparedness planning.

One result of this deficiency is a weak base for estimates of the full social effects of changes in adjustments. There is every prospect that it will remain weak for a long time. Most of the appraisals presented in this report are grounded upon partial information and upon speculative judgment of what shifts may be expected in the future. A further corollary of the sobering lack of information on adjustment choice is that if public policy in the field is to advance fruitfully in gaining larger national benefits from the management of the extremes in nature, new emphasis is needed upon understanding the choice process. This accounts for the heavy weight placed in this report on social and behavioral research. It is essential to the proper evaluation of the benefits from physical and biological research, and it is required to make up for a long period of neglect, but it also will be extremely difficult to achieve.

In arriving at particular mixes of adjustments which are satisfactory to individuals, to communities, or to the nation, the process of choice is sometimes unconscious and sometimes highly explicit. New mountain cabins are built on slopes by people who do not recognize the terrain as unstable. In contrast, certain choices are plainly recognized, as in the case of public decisions to build a coastal revetment, or of the private decision to buy earthquake insurance. It would be a mistake to suggest that all of the decisions are irrational and the result of random choice by individuals, but it would be equally misleading to assume that all individuals act in a rational fashion with ready access to currently available information.

The process of decision always involves a consideration of the types of costs and benefits which have been indicated. It also may be affected by factors that work toward change in

social structure and are of sufficient magnitude to overshadow the immediate situational considerations. For example,
in the early days of soil conservation and watershed protection (during the 1930s), it was commonly assumed that if land
use and watershed-treatment measures were taken upstream, the
farmers with downstream bottom lands less subject to floods
would then proceed to use the soils more intensively. In
some drainage areas exactly the opposite result occurred
following the installation of upstream watershed protection
works. Although flood levels were reduced and therefore the
mean annual losses from flooding were diminished for the same
kind of crops, the farming system in these areas was subject
to economic inducements, including the development of part-
time employment for farmers, that led to increase in size of
farms, a shift from intensive crops to pasture cultivation,
and a progressive diminution in the amount of intensive cultivation in the bottom lands. Those changes had no direct connection with the reduction in flooding.

Similarly, the risk of soil erosion on farming lands was
greatly reduced by changes in cropping patterns that resulted
from movement of farm labor to the cities during and after
World War II in response to the attraction of urban employment. Soil conservation practices in some areas were adopted
as a result of those forces, rather than because of any
changes in conservation techniques.

In considering the actions that are taken by individuals
or public agencies in dealing with natural hazards, it is important to recognize that society commonly has a set of built-
in long-term adaptations to hazard which may not reflect conscious choice. It is essential to recognize, as suggested
in Chapter 4, that a large number of exogenous factors may be
at work which shape the conditions in which conscious choice

is made. In considerable measure, the same factors which shape
the behavior of individuals in taking risk seem to apply to
the decisions of public agencies, but with somewhat different
weights and combinations.

Long-Term Adaptation

One of the difficult aspects of national response to hazard
is identification of those adaptations in daily use of resources which reflect much earlier recognition of the threat
of extreme events, or which represent the winnowing out of
successful and unsuccessful encounters with the events over a
long period of time. The choice of crops and crop varieties,
the decisions on time of planting and harvest, and numerous
other agricultural practices are linked with the concrete
experience of farmers in contending with threats of late and
early frost.

Usually, good reasons can be found for most of these practices. To understand how they have evolved is to probe deeply
into the evolution of the culture and to lay the groundwork
for estimating how they might be expected to change with new
inputs of knowledge or technology.

The kind of built-in adaptations involved in planning for
frost-susceptible crops applies in many other hazards. Similar factors are at work in decisions to plant crops that are
susceptible to hail. Farmers usually have assessed the danger
to them of cultivating flood plains subject to periodic overflow. Practices for construction of buildings often reflect
judgments that are not explicitly incorporated in the design
so far as earthquake and wind risk are concerned.

Some adaptations may reflect personality factors contributing to individual choice. These traits may not show in public
discussion or the decision of individual building contractors.

Some of those personality traits are reviewed in a later
section.

Individual Decision

There has been remarkably little investigation of how individuals who are affected by hazards decide what to do, and
what accounts for differences in their behavior. For example,
insurance against crop failure is available under the terms of
the Federal Crop Insurance Act. About 10% of all farms in the
United States take advantage of this insurance. Virtually all
of them are subject to threat of failure from drought, hail,
frost, flooding, wind, or the like. Why do some farmers
choose to insure and others to self-insure? If they do not
insure as part of a government or private offering, is it a
reflection of the inadequacy of the system of providing insurance, or an indication of the unsuitable terms for calculating premiums and providing indemnification? What are the
other factors that make it either undesirable or, if desirable, impracticable for the farmer to take advantage of this
opportunity? A more basic problem is whether the nation
gains or loses from that behavior.

The fact that there are no ready answers for these questions indicates that little attention has been paid to the
conditions in which people do or do not turn to insurance as
a means of coping with crop failure. The same observation
should be made with respect to many other aspects of individual behavior toward hazard. Behavior often is accepted
without question, as when it is assumed that people will continue to build on the flanks of an Hawaiian volcano. Or
behavior is explained with unfounded generalizations, as when
it is argued that people locate within the range of severe
hurricane winds because they are stupid. Neither of these

description turns out to be accurate. To accept them is to lay
the framework for public policy that is likely to be misleading
or counterproductive.

From comparative research on risk-taking behavior in a variety of cultures (Burton, Kates and White, 1975), it is known
that at least three major factors influence these individual
variations in choice.

One is the experience of the individual with hazard. Individuals with no experience of the hazard may be slow to accept
information about its probability. It is difficult for individuals who have not lived in an area where houses slip and
crack under landslide conditions to grasp the likelihood that
their own house may be subject to such destructive forces on an
outwardly placid hillside. At the other extreme, there is evidence that individuals subject to frequent hazard experience
may tend to minimize its impact, as in the case of residents
of cities with frequent heavy snowfalls.

In the intermediate range are individuals who are subject
to an extreme event from time to time, as in the case of flood
plain occupants who experience a flood every five or ten years.
They are likely to show a greater awareness of risk and keener
perception of the range of alternatives that are open to them.

To the extent that public action reduces the frequency of
occurrence of damaging events (as when protection is given
against intermediate size floods but not against the very large
and highly infrequent flood), awareness of the hazard is decreased, complacency generated, and susceptibility to disruption from the extreme event increases. Where the effect of
human activity is to increase the frequency of the occurrence,
(as when extensive building on a hillside will increase the
likelihood of landslides throughout the slope, or where more
intensive cultivation of cereal or vegetable crops will increase

the loss potential from the occasional hailstorm), the people
affected become more acutely aware of the risk and are more
disposed to take community action to cope with it.

A second important factor is the material wealth of the individual as it is reflected in available capital, in access to
information, and in security against crippling losses from an
unexpected change in the environment or from a miscalculation.
Poor residents of vulnerable areas are less able than upper-
income neighbors to make readjustments in their housing or
cropping to deal with a threatening extreme event. The owner
of a decrepit trailer home has more trouble finding the necessary $200 for anchoring his home than the wealthier resident
of a nearby mobile home park.

It is well known that commercial farmers who have large investment in machinery and land are more likely than their diversified neighbors to take risks with frost and other threats to
crop production. They are prone to do so when they have a segment of their land that is relatively free from damaging events,
as in the case of a farm where part of the crop land is protected from flooding by a levee and the other part is exposed
to flood losses. The small operator may stand to suffer much
more serious long-term losses if and when he loses a substantial part of his crop: he does not have the financial resources
with which to set aside reserves or to recoup, he has difficulty in obtaining credit, and he has less access to information
on ways of rehabilitating or of coping with the hazard.

A third factor is personality. The individual's sense of
efficacy in planning for the future or in guiding events
around him may be strongly associated with his response to
new information about environmental threats. One example
of this is in the case of differential response to tornado
warnings. Some of the evidence suggests that the extent to

which individuals feel they have the capacity to control their
environment and fate has important implications for the way in
which individuals act upon receiving a warning of a threatening tornado (Sims and Baumann, 1972). There is still a good
deal of uncertainty as to the way in which locus of control is
related to risk behavior in a variety of behaviors, including
job seeking, and it is recognized that the force of differences in personality traits is tempered by the type of
situation in which the individual is obliged to make decisions
(Higby, 1972; Higby and Lafferty, 1972).

Although there has been a considerable amount of research
on how people take gambles or choose among risky courses of
action, and how they order the options open to them, only a
small amount of this work has been applied directly to natural
hazards (Kogan and Wallach, 1967). A theory developed by
Pollatsek and Tversky (1970), after making assumptions about
the ordering of options with respect to risk, suggests that
risk can be expressed as a linear combination of expectation
and variance. This opens a way of arriving at precise quantitative measurements of risk, but has not been subject to
careful test in a variety of situations.

An alternative approach to the definition and measurement
of risk is within the framework of personality theory (Jackson,
Hourany and Vidmar, 1972). This attempts to find out whether
risk-taking disposition applies to a wide variety of risks.
Although many efforts have been made to measure "risk-taking
propensity", there has been meager success in establishing the
validity of such measures (Slovic, 1964). There does not
appear to be a general risk-taking disposition. If it exists,
it is found only among certain people.

If risk-taking is a multidimensional product, the actual
behavior can be explained only in terms of a combination of

factors. Those examined in a few instances involve monetary,
physical, ethical and social factors. It may well be that
other components are important, and that they combine in
quite different ways in different situations related to
degrees of risk, individual beliefs about the world, and
sense of efficacy in dealing with external situations. Other
aspects may be at work, such as the possibility that an individual's capacity to develop a vivid image of the future and
the need to avoid some futures may be directly related to
behavior (Nisan and Minkowich, 1973).

More investigation is needed on the way in which measures
proposed from laboratory or theoretical inquiries can be
applied. It is from a few such practical tests that the
emphasis on possible locus of control has emerged. These
promise understanding of basic processes at work in concrete
decisions which individuals make in the face of threatening
events in nature.

Somewhat more is known about how stress and individual
reaction is generated in a disaster, whether triggered by
natural or social cause. There is evidence that danger increases an individual's arousal level and results in increased efficiency up to some point, beyond which competence
decreases as danger and disruption mount. People who are
trained or experienced in disaster situations do not suffer
the same loss in efficiency, and apparently learn to adapt to
situations which create anxiety and incompetence in others.

Inasmuch as most people are not likely to be trained to
respond in an experienced professional matter, there is reason
to think that people can be taught to develop certain contingency responses. They may learn when to become concerned,
and how to identify danger signals which would indicate the
need to take some previously planned action, as in response to

a warning. As will be noted in Chapter 9, information is not
necessarily helpful. A few programs of public education to
acquaint people with how to recognize danger and to take
certain preconceived actions are underway, but more needs to
be known about the effects of the extreme stress on cognitive
and physical functioning, how it differs among people, and
how people can best be trained to choose wisely and live
with or ignore stress in disaster situations.

Public Decision

It was argued in the preceding chapter that public decision
with respect to natural hazards commonly is associated with
major disasters. The dramatic occurrence promotes new procedures or legislative policy.

The crisis usually finds the administrative and legislative agencies unprepared to submit precise proposals. As a
result, agencies sometimes are obliged to come forward with
positive measures. Often they are faced with public clamor for
immediate and positive action which they may regard as unsuitable, but for which they have no well-planned and defens-
ible substitute. Counterproductive measures, such as protection works which will induce further exposure to extreme
events, are adopted through default because more effective
measures had not been planned and subject to legislative
scrutiny.

As with individuals, many public agency reactions gather
strength with accumulated experience with a hazard, as in the
case of mounting concern over landslides in residential areas
of California. They also reflect the material status of the
governing agency: the wealthier the public body, the less
likely it is to accept severe dislocations from natural
events, including those suffered by its poorer components.

In a number of instances the sense of efficacy of a public agency in dealing with a hazard strongly affects its choice of corrective or preventive action. In dealing with drought experience during the early 1970s, there was a tendency for public bodies to regard cloud seeding as a promising adjustment in situations for which the long-term solutions clearly rested in readjustment of land cultivation practices and land tenure and management. Cloud seeding was not a solution for the long run, but it was accessible and helpful in some situations, and at the time it seemed highly manageable at low cost. It was easier for the Bureau of Reclamation to give attention to cloud seeding as a means of increasing water supply for irrigated lands in the Lower Colorado Basin than to canvass ways of readjusting land use in those irrigated areas in the face of prior overestimates of available water supply.

This tendency to turn to the readily available technological solution in preference to more complicated social solutions is to be expected, and in many instances may lead to what in the short run are cheaper and more effective modes of public action. When, however, concentration upon the technological solution excludes research on alternative measures, the danger of exacerbating the situation mounts rapidly. In the case of the Colorado River cloud seeding operations, the Bureau of Reclamation was prepared to put substantial amounts of money into studying modes of cloud seeding and its ecological effects, but meanwhile was reluctant to invest in studies of how water consumption and land use management in the downstream areas of the basin might be readjusted in response to the possibility of a long-term trend of decreasing streamflow from the basin.

National Forces Shaping the Choice

What appear to be the principal national forces--not directly

related to hazard policy--which might shape future adjustments
to geophysical hazards?

Population size and distribution are significant forces. If
current trends are continued, population will continue to increase, but will level off as the year 2000 approaches; internal regional migration routes will persist; and rural-to-urban
migration will continue, but at a much slackened pace. There
is no assurance that these movements will continue at the same
direction and rates. The speed of population growth slackened
significantly in recent years. The need for considering hazard
policy in relation to those broader changes is important, whatever the new directions.

Urbanization means concentration of population. Overall
vulnerability to extreme events within a specific state is not
necessarily increased thereby, but vulnerability to catastrophic losses is enlarged. The problem of promoting patterns of
urban growth which minimize the further build-up of catastrophic situations is acute.

Movement of population within the nation presently is in the
following directions.

1. West, where California has been the larger growth
leader, but is stabilizing. Arizona, Nevada and Colorado
are also exploding. In all these areas the proportion
of new urban sites subject to flood, earthquake or landslides is large.

2. South, where the pattern is uneven. Texas and Florida are the growth leaders, with Georgia somewhat in the
running. Other southern states do not show anything
spectacular. Along the South Atlantic coast the growth
rate in counties with shorelines subject to hurricane
storm surge is on the average three times as high as in
adjoining inland counties (see Figure 5-1).

3. Northeast, generally declining but there are three
spectacular exceptions: Delaware, Maryland and New Jer-
sey. Virginia is increasing to a lesser extent. All of
these are distinguished by rapid growth in the coastal
zone.

FIGURE 5–1
PERCENT CHANGE IN POPULATION: 1960–1970

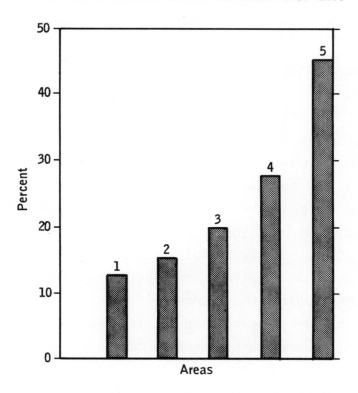

KEY

1   United States
    Atlantic and Gulf coasts:
2   Coastal States
3   Coastal Counties
4   Coastal County subdivisions
5   Coastal County subdivisions excluding
        any which extend more than
        one mile inland.

(U.S. Bureau of the Census, 1961; 1971)

Most of the growth leaders are the same states that are
above average in percent increase in urban population, 1960-
1970. Thus, the growth leader states are increasing in hazard
vulnerability generally due to total population increase, and
to catastrophic events specifically because of urbanization.

Overall, it would appear that the nation's population pattern is increasing in vulnerability to earthquake, tsunami,
hurricane, landslide, avalanche, volcano, coastal erosion, and
perhaps to urban drought. Vulnerability to snow, lightning,
tornado, and frost may be slightly decreasing.

The national trends in the establishment of *second homes*,
for people who are able to afford transportation from the cities and the cost of building a second residence for recreation,
are accompanied by marked changes in the pattern of land use
in rural areas. The newcomers generally make a different assessment of the hazard potential than the farmers and fishermen
who had their place in the area, and may be better able than
others to bear the losses. Second homes are built disproportionately in higher risk areas: along the coast (coastal erosion and storm surge), in mountainous areas (landslide, avalanche), and along rivers (flood).

One of the striking changes in the housing industry in the
United States since 1960 is the steady increase in number of
mobile home shipments in proportion to single unit housing
starts (see Figure 5-2). By 1971, 30% of all single family
unit starts were mobile homes, and 20% of total family housing
starts were mobile homes. It was estimated by one research
group that mobile homes accounted for 94% of single family home
sales under $15,000 (Institute for Local Self-Government,
1972). In 1973 the number of manufacturers' shipments of mobile homes exceeded 500,000.

The 1970 census indicated that of a sample of two million

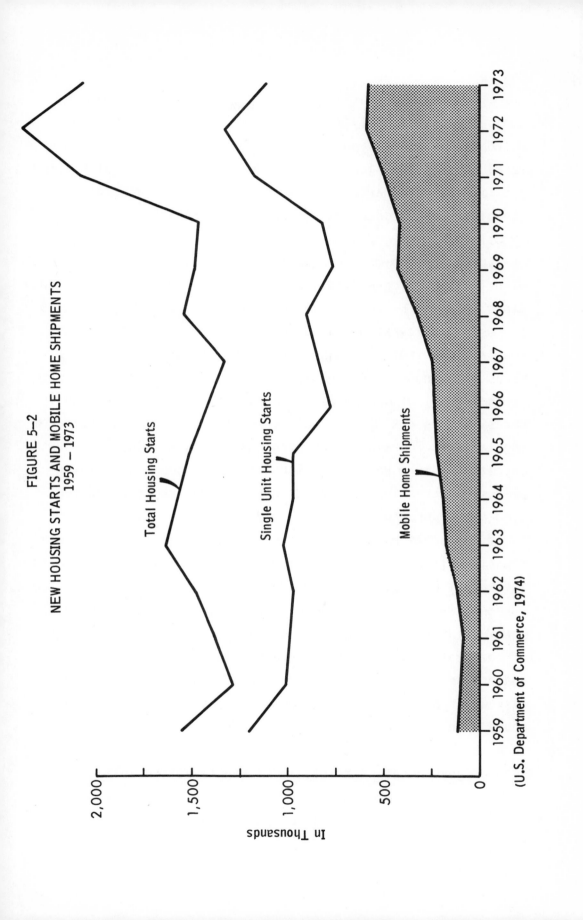

FIGURE 5-2

NEW HOUSING STARTS AND MOBILE HOME SHIPMENTS
1959 – 1973

(U.S. Department of Commerce, 1974)

mobile homes, slightly more than half were outside standard
metropolitan areas, and that about the same number were in
rural nonfarm locations. The larger single concentration, approximately one-quarter, was in the South Atlantic states and
the other large concentration was in the Pacific states, chiefly California.

Typically, the mobile home is more vulnerable to damage from
windstorm, hurricane wind, and tornado than houses with foundations. It may be located in an isolated place not subject to
the usual municipal building codes. In developed parks, the
requirements from the standpoint of safety are often less rigorous than in ordinary subdivisions.

The effect of *corporate organization and size* on hazard vulnerability is not clear. On the whole, corporations are becoming larger. There are more conglomerates with widely dispersed
investments in a variety of industrial and commercial enter-
prises. Increasingly, agricultural production is being managed by corporations.

If corporate bigness and diversification mean that proportionately larger financial reserves could be used to cope with
infrequent events, as in investment in hurricane-proofing, then
unnecessary losses from those occurrences could be reduced.
However, bigness and physical disperson makes the possibility
of corporate self-insurance more feasible. It could guard
against severe disruption, and it could encourage acceptance of
risk which a smaller company could not carry readily. Bigness
could also enlarge potentiality for catastrophe.

A major shift over the 1960s and early 1970s was the extension of government restriction of private action as far as
safety, consumer protection and environmental impacts are concerned. The philosophy behind "buyer beware" was seriously
challenged.

The demands of citizen's organizations about safety, consumer protection and environmental quality begin to have impact upon hazard vulnerability. The new Occupational Safety and Health Administration (OSHA) activities apparently will have three years in which to demonstrate how effective they can be in administering the workers' safety codes, and in extending or revising them.

OSHA has the theoretical capacity to designate any working place as being adequate or inadequate for working purposes, and it could, although it has not yet, specify that freedom from flood, wind, earthquake, or other natural hazards would be an essential condition for the design of such places. A program of information for architects and engineers is intended to warn them that future working places must be able to meet the OSHA standards. The attention to be given natural hazards, and the effects it will have in either increasing or decreasing vulnerability to property losses and public safety, remains to be determined in practice.

Under the Office of Consumer Affairs, initiatives on *consumer products safety* are made to require safe actions, e.g., testing of toys, and more adequate labeling. These could have an influence upon susceptibility of equipment to lightning, wind and earthquake stress. A decision to regard mobile homes as consumer products places Federal agencies in a position to specify the design and anchoring of such homes, and their location with regard to flood, wind, and earthquake.

These measures affecting occupational safety and consumer protection are in addition to the conventional devices of insurance underwriting requirements and municipal and county *building codes*. The codes are intended, in part, to assure minimum levels of public safety in design as well as in site requirements. They are subject to severe erosion in the form

of variances and ineffective administration, and it may be expected that they will be strengthened rather than weakened by
the expansion of the other measures.

Similarly, the requirement of *environmental impact statements* under the National Environmental Policy Act of 1970 is
requiring specification of locations in areas of hazard, thereby increasing the possibility of public debate over the wisdom
of the locational decision. The requirement that alternative
measures be identified, such as a nonstructural alternative to
a coastal-protection structure, strengthens that possiblity.

There seems to be increased concern in many quarters about
"safety" and about "consumer protection", but it is not clear
how far it may affect the natural hazards arena. There are two
known recent exceptions to that statement, both in California.
Following the 1971 San Fernando earthquake, legislation was
passed requiring significant alteration in the seismic resistance of hospitals. But an even more significant action was
also taken. Those parties responsible for dams and reservoirs
were required to prepare inundation maps that indicate where
flooding will occur in the event of rupture or collapse of a
dam or retaining wall. This information subsequently becomes
part of the legal description of the parcel of land. The private citizen who is alert, wishes to avoid such risk, and has
viable options now has a more adequate basis for such a decision.

This was accompanied at the national level in 1972 by a law
requiring the Corps of Engineers to inspect dams 25 feet or
over to determine danger to life and property. The *legal system* in the United States can work in at least three ways in
influencing or modifying the decisions that affect what is done
about natural hazards. Legal rights or obligations can be
changed by creating rights; by enforcing subsequent rights, as

for damages caused; by imposing taxes on certain activities;
and by granting tax benefits for other activities. This often
allows for a carefully articulated private suit.

The second way is to change legislative or administrative
standards in the form of directions to take or not to take certain actions, ranging from simple definition of performance
standards to modes of regulation by government agencies.

The third is to change the legal structure through the creation or alteration of organizations that have the responsibility for making appropriate decisions. This may also include
the creation of special interest lobbies to change the point
in the administrative structure at which decisions are made
about land use or property.

The Internal Revenue code provides that *tax deductions* may
be made for casualty losses occurring as a result of a declared
disaster, as well as for other types of losses. After a declaration, the Internal Revenue Service usually makes special
public announcements on what can be done to take advantage of
the several tax possibilities. A simplified brochure and a
more complicated publication (Internal Revenue Publication
#547) outline the procedures.

The deduction provision allows the individual to claim whatever portion of the loss is equal to the amount of taxes paid
on income which is offset by loss. In these circumstances the
deductions subsidy is available only to people who have taxable
income within a certain period of time after the loss occurs.
Its operation commonly excludes people who are elderly, ill,
or those with poor business performance.

There is also provision that individuals who are required
to relocate under the Uniform Relocation Assistance and Real
Property Acquisition Act of 1970 (Public Law 91-646) may not
be obliged to claim any such payments or assistance as taxable

income. This could be a further incentive to relocation to
less hazardous sites.

At present, tax incentives are not used to promote new practices with respect to mitigating natural disasters. There
would be two ways of using them: deducting losses from natural
disasters, which might turn out to encourage vulnerability to
such events; and deducting taxes for improvements that would
prevent later losses.

Communication patterns are in course of flux, and it is
argued in some quarters that slight alterations in the system
could have a profound influence upon disaster vulnerability
and response. Civil defense experts have been talking about
the Decision Information Dissemination System (DIDS) for a long
time. This envisages a few powerful transmitters capable of
activating radio or television within any selected area so as
to transmit information at any time. For the present, the "big
brother" component has stood in its way, but interest persists
in some way of reaching all households in an area simultaneously.

The NOAA Weather Radio Service which provides continuous
weather information and warnings is being expanded. More than
330 planned VHF/FM facilities will make broadcasts available
to over 90% of the population.

There may be some increased local TV programming forced by
the Federal Communications Commission, but that will not necessarily bring any change in the use of commercial TV for hazard
education or hazard warnings. A small slice of optimism may
be justified. Were home "mini computer terminals" for shopping
and other purposes to be installed, it would presumably be done
on an individual subscription basis, and capacity to receive
warnings could be an option.

Cable TV is slowly getting started. If opposing interests

do not weaken it by limiting programming to canned types, it
could be useful for hazard warning. Under private or quasi-
public control, the "big brother" fear might be lessened. Many
cable TV operations now have a weather channel, and a problem
in warning dissemination would be to induce viewers to switch
to the weather channel when important to do so. Cable TV would
seem to offer significant potential for "hazard education."
But educational programs have notoriously few viewers when compared to the exciting fare of commercially sponsored entertain-
ment on TV, and findings on the efficacy of long-term TV educational efforts are inconclusive.

A significant new communication mode is the satellite.
Their use has already increased the number of weather observations. NOAA and the National Aeronautics and Space Administration completed in 1974 a feasibility study on a disaster warning satellite system. There are now no scientific or technical
constraints to the use of satellites to activate hazard warning
devices at the local level. This possibility is especially
attractive under conditions where: 1. communities are small,
and therefore have no around-the-clock personnel authorized to
receive and act promptly on warning messages; 2. standard modes
of communication are interrupted as a result of the hazard; and
3. the usual modes of communication are overloaded and therefore undependable.

These factors--population, consumer safety, tax incentives,
communications and the like--are a selection of national forces
which may well change the conditions in which decisions are
made about natural hazards. They are reviewed in order to emphasize that a hazards policy which ignores them does so at
peril of going far wrong in anticipating what the next decade
will bring.

Studies to date suggest that the choice of adjustments is

affected by one set of factors influencing the conscious choice
made by both individuals and public agencies, as well as by
another set of factors that are external to the decision situation, but which profoundly shape the circumstances in which
individuals and public agencies may act. Neither set of factors has received extensive and searching attention over recent
years. Were they to receive such attention in future, it would
be easier and less risky to suggest points at which changes
could be made in order to bring about improvements at the local,
state, and Federal level in coping with hazards. This raises
the question of what constitutes or might constitute improvement in current response to hurricanes, floods and other extreme events.

Chapter 6

POSSIBLE IMPROVEMENTS

On what grounds may we expect a change in understanding of
natural hazards and the application of that information to
public and private decisions to foster improvement in the national situation? The answer requires definition of national
aims; with a defined set of aims, the probable effects of
a policy change can be anticipated. In addition to the customary comparisons of prospective benefits and costs, there are
ways of estimating the possible improvements by simulating
the interactions of the physical and social systems or by
creating scenarios of what the situation might be, or could
have been.

National Aims

As in all realms of public action, the United States has no
single goal in dealing with harmful geophysical events. In
many aspects of hazard management the nation displays an
ambiguous combination of goals with respect to one hazard
as contrasted with another. It would be relatively simple to
gauge all possible improvements in terms of a computation of
the net social benefits from a particular combination. This,
however, would assume a precision of national purpose that
does not prevail in the administrative, legislative, or
individual decision processes.

Wherever natural resources are managed, this same ambiguity
appears, and there have been a variety of ways in which national and state governments have tried to cope with it. The
most explicit effort on the part of the Federal government is
contained in the Water Resources Council standards which were
promulgated in the Federal Register, September 10, 1973.

These standards propose that there will be two aims considered
in the planning of water resources projects, such as flood
control and irrigation projects. They assert that the overall
purpose of water and land resource planning is to promote the
quality of life by reflecting society's preferences for attain-
ing the objectives defined below:

1. To enhance national economic development by increasing the value of the nation's output of goods and
services and improving national economic efficiency.

2. To enhance the quality of the environment by the
management, conservation, preservation, creation,
restoration, or improvement of the quality of certain natural and cultural resources and ecological
systems.

These standards and procedures differ markedly from those
proposed earlier by the Water Resources Council, and from
others employed in certain detailed studies such as the North
Atlantic cooperative water resources investigation. In the
latter there were four aims: national economic efficiency,
regional economic development, social well-being, and environmental quality.

At least five aims figure in one way or another in public
decisions about the choice of adjustments to natural hazards.
In some cases one or two of these offer a strong basis for
explanation of public judgment, as when prevention of loss of
life is the primary motivation for a flash flood warning system. In other cases certain aims plainly are irrelevant to
the particular hazard. The five aims which we identify as
significant in more than a few cases are:

1. national economic efficiency;

2. enhancement of human health;

3. avoidance of social surprise and disruption;

4. environmental protection or enhancement; and

5. equity in distribution of costs and benefits.

The customary mode of stating *national economic efficiency* is to estimate the combination of adjustments which yield the largest marginal returns. It deals with the nation as a whole, and probes the possible allocation of resources in relation to net benefits. By this criterion the optimal combination of hazard adjustments for the whole range of national resources would be that which, for the aggregate of all hazards and all other economic activities, yielded the largest marginal net returns from the investment in those activities. The efficiency criterion often is advanced as being the most likely to contribute to the national welfare. It is stated explicitly in the case of some Federal legislation dealing with natural hazards. The Flood Control Act of 1936 provides that funding may be authorized for "any projects in which the benefits exceed costs to whomsoever they may accrue." However, the more demanding marginal criterion is followed neither in letter nor in spirit in flood control. The emphasis is on a favorable benefit-cost ratio rather than on the maximizing of the incremental returns.

Enhancement of human health and, especially, the preservation of human life often are advanced as the single determining criterion of expenditures for adjustments, as was the case in carrying out the flood control plans in the Ohio Basin following the great floods of 1936 and 1937. Such criteria raise explicitly or implicitly the credibility of calculations of the value of human life. Engineering design may require quantitative assessment of what it is worth to the nation to prevent a death. Recent estimates by a committee of the American Society of Civil Engineers dealing with spillway safety factors figure $246,000-$365,000 per life for a housewife with two children. Awards by some courts go much higher. An accompanying problem is calculating the effects of casualties and of reduced productivity among workers during a disaster or periods of rehabilitation following the disaster.

It is equally difficult to assign precise figures to the effects of *avoiding social surprise and disruption* resulting from extreme natural events. Indeed, there is doubt whether in some instances the benefits of surprise may not exceed the costs. Inasmuch as a considerable number of changes in community structure seem to be linked with events which release social tension built up in less stressful times, it can be argued that the benefit of an extreme event may outweigh the costs. For example, the severe experiences of the great drought of the 1930s on the Great Plains induced drastic changes in the farming system in the area, thereby rendering it more efficient in the long run. It is doubtful that the readjustments in farm size and techniques would have been undertaken unless and until the tragic circumstances of the Dust Bowl drove home in the public arena the necessity of making these changes.

It would be desirable to include an estimate of the *net environmental effect* of any given adjustment in calculations of economic efficiency. This is not practicable because: 1. many of the environmental impacts, such as from cloud seeding, are difficult to identify; 2. even when identified, quantitative values are hard to calculate, as in judging the habitat degradation induced by stream channelization; and 3. some of the impacts are uncertain or probabilistic, as in the possible effects of a shift in land use upon wildlife habitat. In the first and third circumstances it becomes necessary for society to assign some kind of value to the preservation of environmental options. This is especially important where irreversible processes are at work, as when construction of permanent structures in a coastal zone makes

it impossible thereafter to recreate the original habitat of
the area.

Even though something approximating efficiency were to be
achieved in dealing with hazards in the national aggregate,
the *equity of the distribution of the net costs and benefits*
from a set of adjustments varies tremendously among affected
sectors of society. As already noted, the more common differences occur with regard to income, age, and geographical
location. The benefits may accrue primarily to one income
group, as in the case of Small Business Administration loans
which tend to go to people in the middle and upper income
brackets. They may be concentrated in particular age groups,
where the young and the old are more likely to suffer than
those in later youth and early adult years. Studies of public
works projects indicate that those who benefit most from a
particular measure, such as an irrigation project for the reduction of drought effects, are different from those who pay
for the project.

The often suggested criterion that those who benefit from
public expenditures on hazards should pay proportionately has
not been practiced. Rather, there has been a tendency to sub-
sidize one area at the cost of another. More common is the
attempt to benefit one age or income group at the cost of
others. Some efforts to cope with hazard may be viewed as
ways of counteracting otherwise inequitable distributions of
income, but they may lead to further degradation of the
recipients.

In all of these instances the individual and public process
is one of tradeoffs among two or more alternative goals.
Rarely is this an explicit consideration in the choice of
adjustments. More commonly, the aims go unspoken, or one aim
is stated explicitly while others are taken into account

implicitly. The National Environmental Policy Act stands
alone in requiring environmental considerations in designing
activities which have an express purpose of preserving human
life or optimizing national economic efficiency.

*The Assessment analysis does not attempt to choose among
the five enumerated aims. Nor does it calculate trade-offs
among them. It seeks to provide basic information on which
choices can be made among research needs, in relation to the
degree to which the suggested work shows promise of achieving
particular aims.* It is recognized that goals are mixed, and
that they will change in response to new information about
opportunities or the impacts of policies. For example, it
is likely that as new information is published on the ways in
which depressed poverty and ethnic groups are affected by
disaster relief and rehabilitation policies, there will be a
change in the emphasis placed upon enhancement of human health
and on equitable distribution of net social costs. Identification of the impacts can lead to a change in goals, and also
to well-intentioned but counter-productive remedies.

Simulating the Effects

In order to test judgments of the way in which new research
might affect national capacity to reach one or more of the
aforementioned aims, benefit-cost analysis was employed as
indicated in the following chapter. In addition, an effort
was made to estimate how potential losses would change if
specified policies and practices, such as improved building
codes, were adopted. This was done through computer simulation as well as by development of scenarios. Simulation and
scenarios were linked with less rigorous estimates of likely
effects.

Simulations of the interaction between natural event systems

and human systems was attempted with respect to hurricane,
flood, and earthquakes (see Friedman, 1975, for a detailed
description from which this is drawn). They were intended to
provide more precise information on the possible effects of
adopting different mixes of the adjustments, thereby adding
precision to the very incomplete kinds of estimates that were
available from statistical projections. They also explored
ways in which simulation might, in the future, identify the
relative significance of various types of research.

One method of estimating the effects of various adjustments
on the natural hazards is to isolate and, on the computer,
work with the three elements that interact to produce natural
hazard-caused losses in the United States:

1. Natural event generator, e.g., frequency and
severity of earthquakes and storms by geographical
area;

2. Population-at-risk in each area, expressed as a
density or geographic distribution (persons, buildings); and

3. Vulnerability of population-at-risk to loss for a
given severity of an event.

The natural event generator, as built into the computer program, produces an impulse (earthquake or storm) at irregular
times which affects the population-at-risk in a section of the
United States. Frequency and severity of the impulse is consistent with the climatology or seismology of the region. The
consequences of this geophysical event depends upon the vulnerability of the population-at-risk. The aggregated effect
of these interactions can be expressed as a loss-producing
potential.

The level of loss potential can vary from very low (when a
weak storm or earthquake occurs over a sparsely populated
area) to a very high (when a severe storm or earthquake occurs

near a densely settled region). In the latter case, many
losses can result over a wide geographical area from the same
geophysical event and lead to the creation of a major catastrophe.

A mathematical approximation of this loss-generating mechanism has been used to provide a means to estimate the effect
of various time-sequenced combinations of adjustments in reducing the loss-producing potential. There are difficulties
inherent in this approach which result from the set of assumptions that must be made and the lack of firm data in many
cases. Those who developed the simulations are painfully aware
of the deficiencies. However, Friedman (1975) found that this
approach in insurance applications can provide useful information and a somewhat different viewpoint from the traditional
methods of analysis, so long as the underlying assumptions
and data deficiencies are kept in mind when interpreting the
results.

Spatial correlation of natural hazard loss potential - Much
work has been done on developing techniques, such as engineering inspections, for estimating damage potential to properties
at a given site. Damage potential for a number of properties
located in various parts of a large geographical area can be
estimated on a site-by-site basis assuming independence between sites. Very few attempts have been made until recently
to incorporate the fact that a large percentage of the loss
from geophysical events does not occur independently and at
random times in various sections of a region, but occurs
simultaneously to properties spread over an area of many
hundreds of square miles (Steinbrugge, 1973; Taylors Digest,
1972; Friedman, 1972). This regularity can be incorporated
into a simulation model.

Natural event generator - The approach is to construct a mathematical model which produces a geographical pattern of intensities with properly spaced contours that are consistent with
the size, shape, and configuration of observed patterns.
Local conditions that may affect the degree of severity in a
particular locality are included. For the earthquake hazard,
an earthshock intensity pattern is generated which corresponds
with observed patterns resulting from an earthquake of given
magnitude, depth, geographical location, and local ground
conditions. For the hurricane hazard, the pattern of maximum
wind speeds associated with the passage of a hurricane is
generated, based upon input measures of storm intensity (central barometric pressure), size, speed, direction, and curva-
ture of path relative to the coastline (see Figure 6-1).
Effect of friction in causing winds to decrease as the storm
moves inland is included in the model. Local degree of exposure to high winds (urban, suburban, rural tree-covered) can
also be incorporated. The calculated and observed intensity
patterns are compared whenever possible. The calculated patterns were found to be good approximations of observed
patterns.

Population-at-risk - The geographical distribution of properties is obtained by using a grid system. Size of the grid
areas depends upon the application. For a study of the earthquake hazard in the San Francisco Bay area, a system of grid
areas of less than one-half of a square mile each was used.
For general studies of the natural hazards in various parts of
the United States, a system of grid areas of about 35 square
miles each is utilized. Approximately 85,000 grid areas are
needed to represent the land area of the contiguous 48 states.
Each of these areas is addressed on a computer disk so that

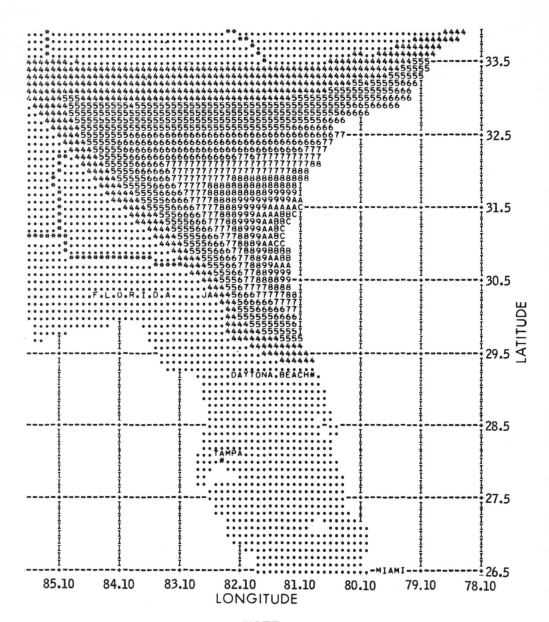

NOTE

Maximum wind speed during the storm's passage is denoted by a single digit at each affected grid point. For example, a "7" denotes a peak wind speed somewhere between 70 and 79 miles per hour. An "A" represents a maximum speed between 100 and 109 miles per hour. Damage potential is calculated at each affected grid point based upon the size and characteristics of the population—at—risk located within each of the 35 square mile areas and its vulnerability to loss at the computed wind speed.

FIGURE 6—1

COMPUTED PATTERN OF WIND SPEED SEVERITY ASSOCIATED WITH THE PASSAGE OF A HURRICANE ACROSS GEORGIA

property characteristics, such as number, type, value, exposure, and vulnerability, can be stored on the disk for each
grid area. Two measures of population-at-risk are used:
number of persons, and number and value of one-family dwellings.
Currently, updated information from the 1970 Census on these
items is being put into a computer system at The Travelers
Insurance Company. Population-at-risk of 203 million persons,
and property-at-risk of 47 million one-family dwellings are
being allocated to the 85,000 grid areas.

Vulnerability relationships - For dwellings, the degree of
vulnerability measured relative to wind speed or earthshock
severity, is determined from claim reports, engineering studies, and other available information. For other types of
buildings, the vulnerability relationships are different and
may require an individual on-site engineering inspection.
This engineering information also can be put into the computer's memory file. A simple two-stage relationship for
dwellings was found to be useful. The first stage determines
the expected percentage of exposed structures which would be
affected in a given grid area. Except for extremely severe
geophysical conditions, only a percentage of dwellings in a
given area will be damaged, due to differences in age, type,
quality of construction, and degree of exposure. The second
stage represents the expected amount of damage if the structure is one of those damaged. Casualty and social impact
curves are also as used as input to obtain estimates of effects on human health and on social disruption. The simulation run will depend upon national aims.

Hurricane wind hazard - To determine loss potential for the

population-at-risk extending from Texas to Maine, available
information relating to the physical characteristics of hurricanes that occurred in the past 100 years along the Gulf and
East coasts (such as path, storm size, storm speed, and storm
intensity) is being read into the computer in order to develop
individual geographical patterns of maximum wind speeds consistent with these interrelated physical measures (Figure
6-1) for each past hurricane. Future calculation could reflect
the use of more accurate input data as it becomes available.
For instance, there is some evidence to suggest that the landfall locations of "extreme hurricanes" are different from those
of less severe hurricanes (Friedman, 1971). The impact of
this possibility upon loss potential along the Gulf and
Atlantic coastlines can be examined through computer simulation techniques (Friedman, 1973).

A second phase of the study is an analysis of the interaction of wind speed patterns derived from "hurricane occurrences", based upon a simulation of storm path, size, speed,
and intensity. Sequences of these "hurricane occurrences"
in a series of, for instance, 25-year periods are calculated
and the effect upon the current geographical distribution of
properties estimated. Differential growth in the number,
value, and vulnerability of properties in the 25-year period
can also be incorporated.

It is convenient to pose "what if" questions about the
probable improvements in adjustment mix which can be answered
by holding one or more of the items in the computer model
constant and determining the effects upon the output. To
obtain an upper bound on the magnitude of the loss potential,
the "what if" question to be answered relates to the effect
of assuming that each of the 20,000 grid areas in the 300-

mile wide coastal strip contains the maximum possible number
of single-family dwellings that the size of the grid area
could accommodate, that is, a saturated array. This provides
a means of estimating the maximum level of loss potential
based solely upon physical characteristics of the hurricane,
such as storm intensity, size, speed, and path relative to the
coastline.

A second "what if" question deals with the effects upon the
level of loss potential of changes in hurricane landfall
location and changes over time in the number and value of
dwellings in the coastal strip. To answer this question, a hurricane with each of the five levels of intensity, in turn, was
simulated at the 31 landfall locations placed at equally
spaced intervals from Texas to Virginia. The initial series
of runs was based upon the 1960 Census data to give a property
array of number and value of dwellings. During the ten-year
period from 1960 to 1970, there was a notable growth in the
number and value of dwellings in seacoast counties. This
growth, of course, had a momentous impact upon the loss potential in various sections of the Gulf and Southeast coastlines.
The level of loss potential also is strongly affected by the
hurricane's landfall in relation to population density.

Coastal flooding - A computer simulation model was prepared
for the Department of Housing and Urban Development to estimate the magnitude of this hazard to dwellings during the
development of the joint Insurance Industry/Federal Government
National Flood Insurance Program (Kaplan, 1971-1972). A
refined version of the surge model is currently being constructed utilizing some of the work of Jelesnianski (1967; 1972),
Jelesnianski and Taylor (1973) and others (Nickerson, 1971;
Bodine, 1969, 1971; Harris, 1963). A realistic envelope of

maximum surge depths associated with the passage of a hurricane has been developed, based on the wind profile calculated in the hurricane wind model, and the local bathymetry conditions defined by Jelesnianski. Examples are given in the supporting monograph by Friedman (1975), and provide a base for evaluation of hurricane research in Chapter 11.

Inland flooding - A computer model for inland (riverine) flooding was also constructed for HUD in 1966 and was used in determining the magnitude of that hazard to urban dwelling properties in the United States during development of the National Flood Insurance Program (Friedman and Roy, 1966). A modified version of the same program was utilized in the Assessment as a basis for estimating in Chapter 11 the impact of various combinations of adjustments to the inland flood hazard. The factors which were incorporated in the modified model are shown in Figure 6-2. These may be varied to show the effects of improved warning services, new protection works, flood proofing, and land management measure on the level of damages, casualties, and social disruption. The model can be run for a randomized series of floods or for a flood of specified magnitude, such as one with a 500-year recurrence interval.

Earthquake hazard - An analysis of the earthquake hazard to the 4,700,000 single-family dwellings in California was conducted using an identical approach to that used for the hurricane wind hazard to dwelling properties along the Gulf and East coasts of the United States.

A mathematical model generates a geographical pattern of earthshock intensity based upon the assumed physical characteristics of the earthquake--Richter magnitude, depth,

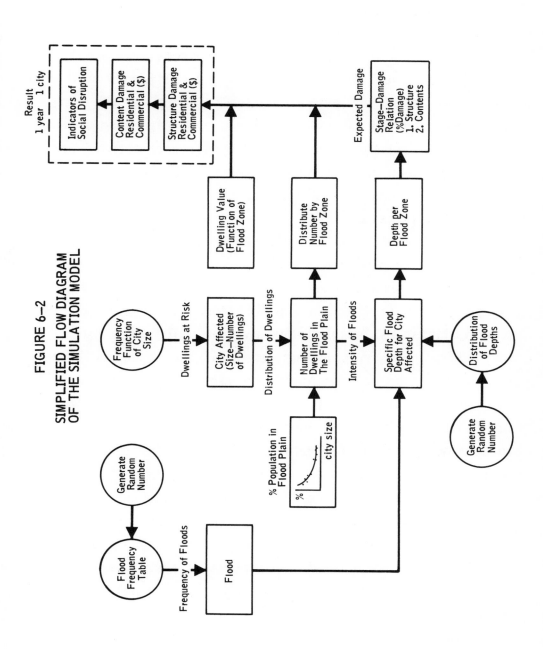

FIGURE 6–2
SIMPLIFIED FLOW DIAGRAM
OF THE SIMULATION MODEL

geographical location--which can be either input or internally
generated data. The resulting intensity pattern is expressed
on a continuous scale which parallels the Modified Mercalli
intensity scale (Figure 6-3). This earthshock severity pattern
reflects the effect of an index of representative "local
ground conditions" for each of the 4,400 California grid areas.
This index is stored in the computer's memory system. The
computer-generated intensity patterns provide a good approximation to actual Modified Mercali intensity patterns. Comparisons between actual and computed patterns are made whenever possible. An earthshock intensity pattern on "bedrock"
is also calculated.

The first step in examining the earthquake hazard loss
potential is to simulate a recurrence of earthquakes that
are reported to have occurred in the historical record of
the past 160 years in California (Friedman, 1969; 1975). As
more realistic estimates become available for input to the
computer program from various research studies currently being conducted by government and university research teams,
the representativeness of the output will increase. (Earthshock intensity will be expressed in terms of response
spectra acceleration for various wave lengths rather than in
Modified Mercalli units.)

An advantage of computer simulation is that the effect of
various sets of assumptions about future occurrences of earthquakes upon the estimate of loss potential can be examined by
posing a series of "what if" questions regarding earthquake
frequency. One set of assumptions that should be used is that
the probability of occurrences of large earthquakes along a
fault zone changes with time (Friedman, 1973a).

Other ways of characterizing the loss potential of the
earthquake hazard can be found by asking, "what if the

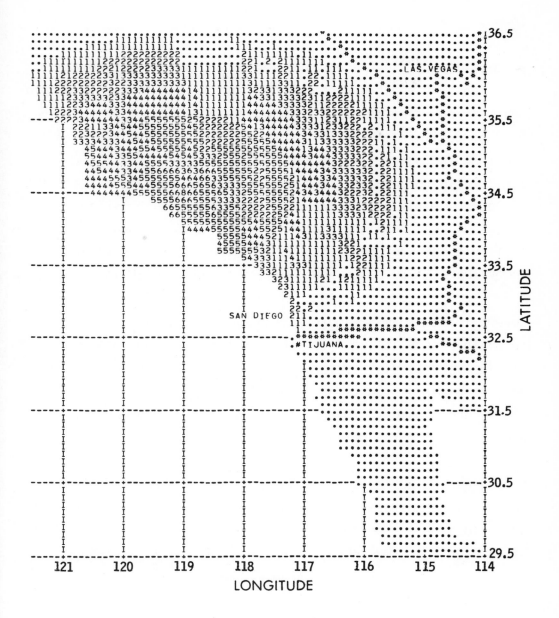

NOTE

The level of severity is denoted at each affected grid point by a single digit taken from a continuous scale that roughly parallels the Modified Mercalli intensity scale. Damage potential is calculated at each affected grid point based upon the population—at—risk within the grid area and its vulnerability to loss at the computed level of earthshock severity.

FIGURE 6—3

COMPUTED PATTERN OF EARTHSHOCK SEVERITY ASSOCIATED WITH AN EARTHQUAKE IN SOUTHERN CALIFORNIA

probability of occurrence of moderate and severe earthquakes
were constant throughout the length of the San Andreas and
Inyo-Garlock fault system? How would a measure of loss potential to California dwellings vary if these earthquakes were to
occur at various points on these major fault systems?" A
similar type of analysis was made for other populations-at-risk,
including multi-unit residences, nonresidential buildings, tall
buildings, and populated numbers. This used the meager amount of
available information on the number, geographical distribution,
and vulnerability of the populations to earthshock intensity.

Severe local storm hazard - A mathematical model is currently
being developed at The Travelers Insurance Company which,
hopefully, will yield severity patterns which are good approximations of actual patterns associated with the tornado, hailstorm, and thunderstorm-wind hazards. The 85,000 point grid
will be used as the measure of population-at-risk.

Strengths and weaknesses - This approach has been useful in
analyzing the natural hazards as related to planning insurance
operations. It also provides a means of estimating the effects
of various adjustments to the natural hazards in reducing
their future loss potential or other effects in relation to
specified national aims. For example, it is possible to incorporate:

    1. Weather modification which could affect the out-
    put of the *natural event generator;*

    2. Land use changes which might affect the geo-
    graphical distribution of *population-at-risk;*

    3. Building code changes which affect *vulnerability*
    (National Bureau of Standards, 1973); and

    4. Insurance which could affect the distribution
    of the output of the system--the *aggregated loss
    potential.*

The Assessment encountered a number of disadvantages in
using computer simulation as an analytical tool under the conditions noted above. They include: 1. the number and con-
straining effects of underlying assumptions that must be
made; 2. lack of pertinent input data on various populations-
at-risk and of information on interrelationships among physical variables; 3. the difficulty of obtaining an adequate
representation of the natural hazard loss-producing system
without making the mathematical and statistical models unduly
complicated and unyielding--how good is good enough?; and
4. uniqueness in some of the characteristics of each geophysical event which cannot be reproduced by a simple model.
Of broader importance, the simulation is not usually able to
take account of the unprecedented incidents that may change
the course of events in an area. Here, the scenario approach is useful.

Computer simulation has at least three advantages over
other approaches to estimating how the national situation
might improve if policy changes were adopted. It provides a
method of tying together information from a number of sources
so that implications are expressed in terms of the problem
at hand. A rough estimate can be made in response to many
"what ifs" regarding national policies and aims.

Long-term climatology of severe storms can be translated
into a measure of loss potential to a given population-at-
risk. For example, information implicitly contained in charts
of the paths of past hurricanes along the Gulf and East
Coast can be expressed in terms of loss potential to a specified population-at-risk array. This is done by utilizing
consistencies inherent in relationships between such things as
storm path and intensity which imply resultant size, shape and
gradient of the high-wind pattern produced as the hurricane

moves through an area. The same translation can be made for
the earthquake hazard by converting information contained in
long-term maps of epicenter location and intensity of past
earthquakes into measures of loss-producing potential to a
specified geographical array of exposed population-at-risk.

Natural hazard simulation occasionally creates a "natural
disaster" resulting from the occurrence of a moderate or severe
geophysical event near a populated area in a fashion similar to
that produced in nature. Natural hazard loss potential is expressed on a continuous scale ranging from zero to very high
(implying a natural disaster), which is comparable to that
actually observed, depending upon the interaction of the severity pattern of the geophysical event with the population-at-risk
and its vulnerability to loss.

A major opportunity associated with the use of simulation
techniques is that cross-hazard comparisons on a comparable
basis can be made of the loss potential of various natural
hazards, including the possible frequency and severity of
future "natural disasters." The impact of geophysical events
can be simulated in any section of the United States, and
measures of the relative riskiness due to the various natural
hazards can be approximated for those locations.

Scenarios of the Process

Identifying areas in the natural hazard system where it is
thought likely that investments in research will efficiently
reduce dollar losses, casualties, and social disruption requires judgments reflecting expectations about a future that
cannot be readily predicted. The systems are complex and
ever-changing. Land use in an earthquake zone almost certainly will change. Crop patterns can shift drastically. The
scenario approach offers one means to anticipate those possible
impacts and outcomes, and to help generate a desirable change.

It thereby supplements the approach of the simulation model
(see Ericksen [1975] for a detailed description from which
this is drawn).

The scenario method is an explication of possibilities. It
attempts to set up a logical sequence of events in order to
ask how, starting from a given condition, alternative futures
might evolve. As an exploration progresses along one possible path, a point of fundamental change in the system serves
as a new starting point from which new paths may be explored.
Scenarios provide one systematic way of asking, "What do we
expect the consequences of a given decision to be?"

Their usefulness lies in their ability to provide insights
into decisions needed for preventing, diverting, or encouraging the evolution of a social system at specific points in
time. They help improve understanding of present day emphases, major alternatives, and the consequential differences
between these alternatives. In that fashion, they serve as
tools in the kind of assessment of research priorities presented in Chapter 11.

To provide a degree of rigor and replicability, and to
treat all factors in an internally consistent fashion, a four-
part model is used. The relationships between the four parts
(base conditions, environing factors, progressions in a
scenario, and cross-sectional images in a scenario) in a
natural hazard context are illustrated in Figure 6-4.

Base conditions - The base conditions consist of an historical
review of a natural hazard in a particular place over a specified time, and of choices of adjustment to that hazard which
in fact were considered, rejected, or adopted. It is handled
as a system whose dynamic elements and their relationships
make up the essential characteristics of the scenario subject--

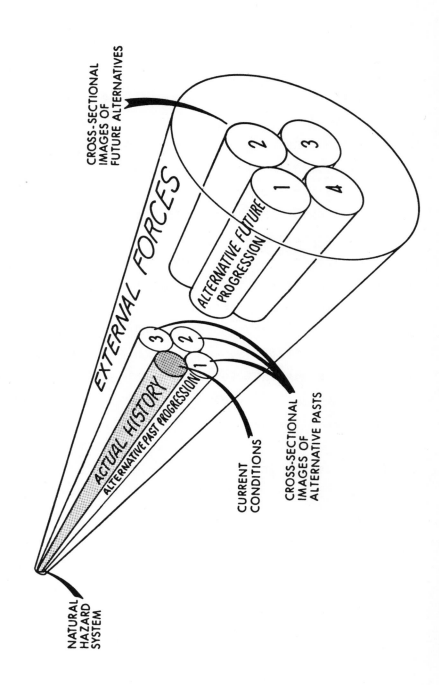

FIGURE 6-4
SCHEMATIC REPRESENTATION OF THE SCENARIO MODEL

a natural hazard. The historical review provides basic conditions against which scenarios of alternative pasts may be
generated. Used in this way, scenarios help demonstrate the
changes in loss-reduction possible if various types of adjustments (like levees or land use management) had been adopted by
a community at plausible points in historical time. The
common use of scenarios as a means of exploring alternative
futures is extended to a study of alternative pasts.

External forces - The natural hazard system is bound by environing factors, such as the national forces enumerated in
the preceding chapter, which should not be ignored, yet need
not be emphasized to the extent that they obscure the scenario
subject. For example, the new Federal revenue sharing policy
would not be examined in great detail, but the question would
be posed, "Given the new revenue sharing scheme, what impact
would it have on the natural hazard system in an urban community?"

For urban communities, environing factors may be thought
of as two basic kinds: those that affect the natural hazard
system from within the community, such as urban renewal,
transportation, or open space programs; and those that impinge
on the natural hazard system from outside the community,
including, for example, Federal cost-sharing in flood protection projects, national insurance schemes, or state enabling
land use management legislation. Assumptions regarding external forces can be changed during the progression of a
scenario and increase the scenario's complexity.

Progressions in a scenario - The progression or evolution of
the natural hazard system through time is derived from factors
identified in the base of current "real world" conditions,

and is controlled by the environing factors. Likely (or even unlikely) changes in key elements and their interrelationships can be specified.

One of the main objectives in writing progressions in a scenario is to illuminate the possible impacts of any one adjustment on other elements in the natural hazard system, including its influence on decisions to adopt other adjust- ments. For example, what effect would adopting levees have on flood plain encroachment and how would levees influence the search for alternative means of protection, such as land use management or a warning system? This inquiry must draw heavily upon whatever knowledge is available, as outlined in Chapter 3, on how adjustments interact.

A cross-sectional image in a scenario - Whereas progressions are concerned with long-term patterns of decision-making that take account of decision nodes and alternative paths, cross- sectional images focus on the short-term impact of the hazard event. It is here, in a thin cross-section of time, that the efficiency of the system's change is tested.

The time when the event occurs and the test made may be arbitrarily chosen. The effects on the system are in part dependent upon assumptions as to its magnitude and intensity (as suggested by the historical review), and in part upon changes to society indicated in the progression. As an image of what might have been (a past alternative) or could be (a future alternative), the cross-section provides a new repre- sentation of a possible situation. It is the consequential outcome of decisions assumed to hold true. It is also a hypothetical base from which a new progression of scenarios may be generated and, therefore, new sets of possible impacts and outcomes assessed.

Only a few efforts have been made to carry out careful scenario analysis of experience with natural hazards. Floods in Rapid City, South Dakota may be taken as an example (details are given in the supporting report on flood [White, 1975]). There, it was asked what would have happened in the course of events at Rapid City if information on technical and social approaches for individuals and public agencies concerned with floods on Rapid Creek had been applied at times when the devices were well-established and theoretically available.

Base conditions were stated, beginning with an historical review of experience with floods along Rapid Creek, and including reports on the earliest recorded major flood of August 15, 1890. The subsequent hydrologic events were traced. Environing factors included a series of flood plain studies beginning in 1930, the construction of partial protection works for multiple purposes upstream, plans for watershed protection, unsuccessful efforts to apply flood plain regulatory measures, and an urban open space project. The city had requested preparation of a flood plain information report in December, 1970, and in March, 1971 it made application for coverage under the new flood insurance program. The city was in process of seriously reconsidering its policy of flood plain encroachment when the disastrous flash flood of June 9, 1972 struck with a loss of 231 lives and damages estimated to exceed $18 million.

As shown in Figure 6-5, the adoption of a warning and preparedness program in the mid-1950s would have reduced total damages by about 10% but the trend would have continued the same. A protection program of the sort proposed as practicable in the 1940s would have thought about a drastic reduction in damage potential but the amount of property exposed to

1. Historical development assumes a 3 1/2% per year growth rate.

2. Hypothetical flood plain land use regulatory program assumes a 1/2% per year decay rate.

3. Hypothetical protection program assumes a 80% reduction in damage potential and a 5% per year growth rate.

4. As in 3, but assumes in addition a 10% reduction in damages with an effective 2 hour warning period and effective emergency system.

5. Hypothetical warning and preparedness program assumes a reduction in damage potential of 10% per year.

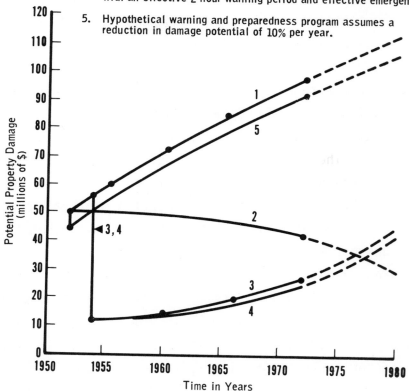

FIGURE 6—5

POTENTIAL PROPERTY DAMAGE OF ALTERNATIVE
ADJUSTMENTS BASED UPON THE JUNE 9,1972, FLOOD

damage would have then continued to mount. A land use regulatory program would have encouraged progressive reduction in
the amount of vulnerable property in the flood plain. With
the land management program, including urban development in
higher areas, by the 1980s the total potential property damage from a flood such as that on June 9, 1972 would have been
less than had the major flood control works been built in the
1950s.

Review of the historical record shows that critical turn-
ing points were the actions on proposed protection works, on
development of a warning system, and on the enactment of land
use management for the flood plain. While the enforcement of
national flood insurance regulations speeded up the consideration of more rigorous land use regulations, increases in
national recreational needs induced further buildings in the
Rapid City flood plain. The record suggests that short of
the kind of catastrophe that struck Rapid City in June 1972,
other similar communities would be slow to make any drastic
changes in flood plain use. The scenario focuses attention on
the importance of research which would facilitate early and
effective adoption of land use management in areas recognized
to be vulnerable to flood losses, and it points out the
serious obstacles lying in the way of moves to change the use
of hazardous areas.

The simulations of hazard effects and the scenario analysis
of past events and future possibilities help appraise the consequences which changes in policy toward a hazard would have
in achieving designated national aims. Neither approach may
be satisfactory taken alone. They were employed in the assessment for a selection of hazards and always supplemented by
other estimates of the degree to which a new policy or practice would improve the national situation. These estimates

always involve some assumption as to how research results,
once in hand, would be applied.

Chapter 7

APPLICATION OF RESEARCH

For persons unfamiliar with the research enterprise, it is
easy to conclude that good research will, in time, lead to
significant and useful application. For those doing research,
a problem is whether the findings will be used, by whom they
will be used, and to what end. Even when research meets initial expectations and is effectively completed, will the
results stimulate improvement as judged by national aims in
the specified problem area? What has the record been of
application of research findings to hazard problems? What
is known about the way in which findings have been used or
neglected? What is the influence of research procedure and
organization on the use of research for advancing public
policy?

The experience in recent decades shows that research on
hazards problems has a spotty record of application encompas-
sing prompt utilization, mixed effects, and virtually complete
neglect. It also shows that a few general observations seem
to describe ways in which research activity may work effectively to reduce hazards to life, health, property, and general
tranquility, and thereby achieve the kinds of improvements
described in the preceding chapter.

What the Record Shows

There is not even a partially adequate source to assist in
answering these questions. Some tentative answers are obtained by examining the history of adjustments to individual
hazards, and by reviewing the activities of persons or groups
who have conducted research on hazards and hazard mitigation
during recent decades. Inquiries were made of selected
researchers in the earth sciences, engineering, meteorology,

and the social sciences; from analysis of the replies, four
characteristics of research appear to have been especially
influential on application of research findings.

A few lines of hazard research demonstrate direct application to policy and practice. Much of the investigation of
earthquake movements and earthquake resistance by groups such
as those active at the California Institute of Technology,
University of Illinois, Massachusetts Institute of Technology,
and University of California, Berkeley, yields results which
find their way into new designs or public regulations. The
chief channels are to investigators who commonly serve as
consultants to private and public agencies, and who are active
in state advisory committees.

The classic series of disaster studies, initiated by the
National Opinion Research Center in 1950 and followed in 1952
by the National Research Council under its Disaster Study Committee, and then by the Disaster Research Group at the request
of Defense agencies, established disaster research as a scientific field. It trained a number of workers who were able
in their personal activities to influence the policy of
government agencies. It laid the conceptual groundwork for
the Disaster Research Center at the Ohio State University.
Many of the results were incorporated in specialized training
programs for state and local officials sponsored by the Office
of Civil Defense.

On the other hand, some of the disaster study findings have
gone unheeded; certain processes, such as convergence behavior,
which might be taken into account in every disaster plan, are
then neglected. Likewise, the suggestions for the establishment of a clearinghouse for disaster-related research
(Institute for Defense Analyses, 1971) were not translated
into action. There is no persuasive evidence that the studies

of community disasters by the National Opinion Research Center
in 1950-54 were influential in local communities, or that the
Institute for Defense Analyses series of "critical incident
studies" during 1962-68 were applied outside of military
circles.

Federal agencies maintain four institutional forms of
research related to hazards, and these differ greatly in the
application of their findings (see Figure 7-1). A relatively
small volume of research, chiefly in the Office of Water
Research and Technology, operates through grants to academic
institutions. The record of direct utilization is modest.
The National Institute of Mental Health has funded only a few
studies on disaster problems. A much larger body of activity
is by the agencies themselves for general dissemination. The
Geological Survey distributes its flood frequency studies to
any engineer, hydrologist, or land planner who wants them.

A third research mode is the program managed by an agency
which also carries design, operation, or construction responsibility. This is the case with the National Oceanic and
Atmospheric Administration's research on hurricanes, lightning
and severe storms; with the Department of Agriculture's
research services interest in soil and water processes; with
the Geological Survey's Hawaiian Volcano Observatory; and
with the Corps of Engineers' research center on coastal problems.

Fourth, the National Science Foundation supports the
National Center for Atmospheric Research with its concern
for climatic change, hail, hurricanes, and related phenomena.

One of the recent research efforts cutting across the
activities of Federal agencies is the disaster project of the
Council of State Governments. It drafted an "example state
disaster act" as an aid to state officials in considering

FIGURE 7–1
PRINCIPAL AGENCIES AND RESEARCH FIELDS

HAZARD	OWRT	DCPA	FDAA HUD	Co E	USGS	NOAA	USDA	OTHER*
Avalanche							◉	
Coastal Erosion				◉				
Drought	●		□			◉	◉	
Earthquake		□	◉		●			□
Flood	●	□	◉	◉	●	◉	◉	◉
Frost							◉	
Hail						◉	●	
Hurricane	●	□	◉	◉	●	◉		◉
Landslide			◉		●			□
Lightning						●		
Tornado		□	◉			◉		□
Tsunami		□	◉			◉		□
Urban Snow		□				●		□
Volcano			□		●			
Windstorm			□			●		□

□ = User   ● = Research

* Including National Aeronautics and Space Administration and National Institute of Mental Health

possible legislation. This was followed by four supplements
prepared in cooperation with the National Association of
Attorneys General and the Federal Disaster Assistance Administration. Prepared under an initial contract with the Office
of Emergency Preparedness, it provided interested state officials with a compendium of provisions which could be employed
or modified to suit their particular needs (Council of State
Governments, 1972).

The National League of Cities has not been able to carry
out similar activities at the municipal level, and at neither
the state nor municipal level have there been serious investigations of methods by which states might prevent rather than
merely react effectively to disasters from natural sources.

The state which probably has taken most elaborate steps in
this direction is California. In addition to its statewide
program for emergency action in the face of disaster,
California has mounted a series of studies dealing with problems raised by increasing threats of disruption from flood,
landslide, earthquake, coastal erosion, and other geophysical
hazards (California Division of Mines and Geology, 1973).

In most states the responsibility for reaction to disaster
is vested in the governor and usually delegated to the state
disaster agency. In disaster relief the states probably are
better centralized than the Federal agencies. The latter have
regional offices whose functions and responsibilities overlap
without strong central management. The duty of trying to
prevent disasters is widely dispersed among a variety of
agencies. As with the Federal government, there is no single
agency with this responsibility, nor is there in most instances
a coordinated plan for collaboration at the prevention stage
by the state organizations. In no state is there a program of
research aimed primarily at disaster prevention. The

administrative duties are dispersed, and the research
activities are absent for the most part.

In Colorado the state geologist has heavy responsibility
for the review of the suitability of new subdivision plans in
terms of vulnerability to natural hazards; in the Commonwealth
of Massachusetts, the Department of the Environment has general
oversight for collaboration with Federal agencies on matters
of flood protection. The same is true for Connecticut and
many other states.

Only one state, the state of Illinois, has long had a
scientific agency which carries on original investigations of
the applications of knowledge on climatological hazards for
the welfare of the farmers and other property owners of the
state. The Illinois State Water Survey's investigation of
floods, tornadoes, hail, and related meteorological disturbances was unique in the nation. Texas now has a similar
office, and other states are showing interest.

The available information shows that while no single group
of characteristics and relationships always leads to utilization of research output, there are sets of characteristics
which increase the likelihood of utilization.

A study of the reasons that seem to account for success or
failure of applied research sponsored by the National Institute
of Mental Health found success in projects that were directed
at the original objectives, resulted in a clear and cogent
report, and disseminated their findings adequately (Glaser
and Taylor, 1973). The more successful projects appeared to
have a high degree of communication and involvement with persons and groups within and without the immediate project
activity, and made special efforts to develop interest and
cooperation with potential users. They were commonly designed
by a principal investigator who devoted full time to it,

enjoyed solid contributions of help from the host agency, and
were aimed at needs shared by a substantial number of people.

Recent studies by the Batelle-Columbus Laboratory, on the
significant events relating to several technological innovations of high social impact, show how research and development
interact in leading to innovations (Batelle-Columbus, 1973).
They place heavy stress upon recognition of technical opportunity and need, and on the way in which internal management
unfolds. No single formula seems determinative; the findings
stress the major role of a technical entrepreneur and of early
recognition of the need. The innovations studied were generally of a more technical character than those that are called
for in much of the research on natural hazards, but they suggest the importance of definition of social need and of identification of major entrepreneurs.

From analysis of some of the major advances in social science
in this century, it appears that interdisciplinary work has been
a major source of contributions, particularly in recent years,
and that the major advances are applied to social practice at
about the same proportions as they are stimulated by it
(Deutsch, *et al.*, 1971).

The four sets of characteristics associated with effective
application of research findings center on the researcher and
research organization, the potential user and user organization, the researcher-user relationship, and the research
product.

Researcher and research organization - Individuals and institutions which are effective usually have extensive experience
and display breadth of view. They are willing to learn the
user's problem and the constraints involved in any significant
alteration of the status quo. They also are willing to carry

out long-term efforts to promote utilization.

They have ability to translate and present findings in a
way the user can understand, and their reports contain specific
recommendations and point out concrete implications. Much of
this assumes sufficient funding over time to allow for cumulative results and continuing dissemination.

Potential user and the user organization - Typically, the
research begins with approval of the effort by those top
officials who have power to see that results are utilized. It
takes operating shape when the decision-maker is convinced that
he is dealing with highly salient matters for which he has
inadequate solutions.

Researcher-user relationship - The successful research project
commonly is aimed at users who recognize the researcher as having relevant expertness and research skills. In turn, the
researcher sees user problems as interesting and worthy of
serious intellectual commitment beyond the theoretical implications for other scientists in the field. Their interaction
either continues over an extended period of time, or a highly
sensitive link is established between them. Direct personal
contact is the predominant mode.

Research products - It is less easy to specify the characteristics of a useful report. It sets forth applications which
are at least moderately feasible within ongoing social,
political, and economic constraints. It is directly relevant
to significant user problems. Here there is the problem of
making the cautious language so customary in academic research
fit the user's rhetoric.

Ordinarily the utility of a research program need not wait

until a final report is published. If the work is lively, it
will yield significant insights on the problems with which it
is dealing as it goes along, there will be interaction between
the research workers and the prospective users, and the new
ideas and techniques which are developed by the research will
begin to be communicated to the user groups. The first
investigation of experience with flood plain management which
was carried out at the University of Chicago in the late 1960's,
with support from the Corps of Engineers, involved detailed
discussions with state and local officials in Nebraska, as well
as with Federal officials during the course of the investigation. The ideas were tested with the responsible state
officers and some of them were translated into action before
the report was completed.

The possibility of developing such relationships between
research producers and users adds weight to the argument for
some kind of clearinghouse in which these groups could be
brought together periodically to discuss needs and findings
before formal reports are completed.

How Findings Are Applied or Ignored

It is important to remember that findings from hazards research
will have their greatest impact if top officials or organizations (Federal agencies responsible for hazards, insurance
companies) and communities (cities located on the Gulf Coast)
make decisions to utilize them. How do such decisions get
made?

Some understanding of the process may be secured by noting
findings growing out of research on the diffusion of innovations (see Rogers and Shoemaker, 1971). A conceptual framework that is often used is as follows:

Source ——⟶ Message ——⟶ Channel——⟶Receiver ——⟶Effects

The source is the researcher or the research unit. The message is the research findings and the accompanying recommendations. The channel refers to the mode of dissemination for the findings (journals, technical reports, conference presentations, face-to-face discussions). The receiver is whoever gets the message.

The most critical aspect from this perspective is the "effect." What happens after the findings are received? Do they produce at least a ripple of rethinking or are they discarded or filed for possible future consideration? If decisions are made by organization executives and community governmental officials to utilize hazard research findings, some or all of the following may be expected.

1. Subordinate individuals, groups, and organizations carry out the decisions providing the changes involved are not too threatening to their autonomy, security and prestige (Haas and Drabek, 1973). If the necessary changes are considered as significantly threatening there will be resistance and attempts to make the changes unworkable.

2. There is wider acceptance within an organization of proposed utilization of research findings if the ideas are first introduced at the highest levels.

3. Adoption and utilization of the research findings by leading and prestigious organizations increase the likelihood that other similar organizations will do likewise.

4. Short-term payoff from using research output will increase the likelihood of continued adoption of the research findings.

There are research findings which may be applied directly by individuals and families quite apart from any organizational involvement. It is probably not a distortion to say that 95% of all hazard-relevant research findings never reach the citizen (Mileti, Drabek and Haas, 1975). Many of them would have no direct application by the individual citizen, but others

would be useful, and there are few systematic efforts to see
that the valuable messages get to the potential users.

The Role of Organization and Agency Mission

Much research on hazards is carried out within agencies with
day-to-day hazard-related operational missions. In that case
the principal potential user is also the financial sponsor of
the research, and the likelihood is high that the research is
responsive to one or more of the needs perceived at the time
by the agency. The research arm of the agency is likely to
have continuing, stable funding for agreed-upon research,
although not necessarily at an adequate level. Those conducting the research may be expected to have a better understanding than outside researchers of the agency's problems, and later
are more readily available, if willing, to assist in the application of the research results.

At least two significant constraints operate in that setting. First, it is rare that a mission-oriented agency has
within its research arm all the research specialties required.
Consequently, there is a temptation to request only that
research which in-house research personnel can handle within
their specialties. This problem is acute with agencies responsible for physical or engineering research who recognize that
social aspects require attention. They tend to dismiss social
research as not within their competence. Second, there are
times when the demand for certain types of research is so
great that in-house researchers are asked to conduct research
for which they do not have adequate background. In either of
these circumstances the mission-oriented agency may get less
than is minimally adequate to meet its responsibilities.

For the organizations involved with hazards which farm out
a part of the research efforts they pay for, there are

advantages and disadvantages. The advantages include: 1. the
possible wide range of research specialists available for
research of almost any type needed; 2. the flexibility to fund
a large or small amount of research in any given year as need
and budget dictate; 3. more rapid feedback of research findings; and 4. the smaller likelihood that researchers will see
the research problem with tunnel vision.

The disadvantages are not insignificant: 1. the research
contractor is less likely to be thoroughly familiar with the
agency's problems and to respond to the agency's needs;
2. researchers are unlikely to be available to assist in
implementing the recommendations; and 3. the agency must bear
the expense of soliciting competent contractors and carefully
monitoring the research effort if there is to be adequate
performance.

In reality, most of the organizations with responsibilities
to deal with geophysical hazards cannot afford to sponsor
research of any kind. This is especially true of organizations
at the state and local levels. At present, none exercises the
function of providing basic funding or coordination of research
for the natural hazards field.

The Defense Civil Preparedness Agency is handicapped by its
defense orientation. The Department of Housing and Urban
Development through FDAA has been unwilling to exercise
vigorous leadership. The National Science Foundation (NSF)
may hold a critical key which determines how much and what kind
of research on natural hazards gets done. In one sense that
organization is the broker between the research organizations
with the competence to carry out hazards research and the
many organizations who could use the research products to
lower our nation's losses to hazards. It is not clear that
NSF understands that role. The Research Applied to National

Needs Directorate pays some attention to "utilization efforts",
but, except for this Assessment, it has not taken steps to
canvass all of the major potential users of hazards research
and to ascertain what their principal needs are. Recently
some modest efforts, largely based on the personal initiative
of a few NSF program managers, were made to encourage potential
user organizations to outline their research needs.

For the most part, researchers propose to NSF research
projects which *they* wish to carry out. They are required to
state in the proposal who the potential users are and how
dissemination of the research findings will take place. This
whole exercise, however, can be more shadow than substance.

Budget Constraints

To recommend new lines or emphases in research at a time of
severe Federal budget constraints may seem wholly impractical
and unrealistic. However, it is exactly the time at which
assiduous attention should be given to the grounds on which
choices are made in allocating scarce research funds to
activities dealing with natural hazards.

A strong case can be made for financing the recommended
research by two shifts in allocation of funds. First, construction funds or other expenditures for conventional adjustments to natural hazards could be reduced in order to carry
the recommended promising research activities over a period
of years. For example, the annual expenditures for flood control construction could be reduced in the amount necessary to
provide for expanded research. More directly, expenditures
for flood plain information studies, now in the range of $6
million a year, could be reduced by $1 million a year in order
to cover the costs of desirable studies on flood plain land
use and hazard delineation. However, the likely benefits from

the immediate studies on flood data and flood plain use are far
greater because of the dynamic effects than are benefits from
construction of individual projects.

Second, expenditures on more conventional forms of research
could be transferred to less conventional forms in order to
provide greater diversity in types of work and in findings.
For example, research on the enhancement of communication devices for warning purposes could be reduced in order to provide for broader types of studies on comprehensive warning
systems.

These considerations of researchers and users, of organizational mission, and of budget constraints have been in mind in
evaluating likely research results as outlined in the following chapters. They also have influenced the way in which
users were consulted in the course of the Assessment. Whenever practicable, the suggestions for new work were reviewed
in terms of the ways in which the proposed arrangements would
enhance use of the results, build on agency strength, and
recognize the realities of funding.

Chapter 8

METHODS OF ESTIMATING RESEARCH RESULTS

In estimating the likely results for the nation of research to
support desirable improvements in the national response to
hazards, several methods were applied to each of the 15
hazards. All of those methods have been in use in the United
States in recent years. The major recommendations for research in the field that have come from private or government
agencies were first reviewed, noting the methods employed and
their relevance to the findings from the assessment. Out of
these grew the relatively uniform procedure employed in this
report.

Review of Research Needs

More than 18 public and nongovernmental agencies contributed to
discussion of priorities for research affecting natural
hazards over the period 1962-1972. Some of these were the
product of interagency committees within the governmental
framework, others were organized by the National Academy of
Engineering, the National Research Council, or nongovernment
groups.

The only completely comprehensive recent venture was undertaken in 1971-1972 by the Office of Emergency Preparedness
(OEP) of the Executive Office of the President in response
to section 203(H) of Public Law 91-606. That report embraced
contributions from all interested Federal agencies and drew
heavily upon the experience and outlook of state and local
agencies and of scientific institutions and associations.

Its major findings dealt with vulnerability analysis, prediction and warning, public information, disaster legislation at the state level, disaster plans at the community and
Federal level, problems of emergency operations, the applica-

tion of science and technology, and disaster mitigation.

In addition to the OEP report, a more detailed examination
of opportunities for Federal collaboration in improving disaster warning and preparedness was undertaken by the Federal
Committee for Meteorological Service and supporting research
under the auspices of the Department of Commerce and was released in 1973. A Federal Plan for Natural Disaster Warning
and Preparedness (National Oceanic and Atmospheric Administration, 1973) dealt carefully and from a technological standpoint with the means by which detection of hazards and dissemination of warnings might be improved.

At the state level at about the same time, the California
Division of Mines and Geology, as noted in the preceding
chapter, examined a broad range of hazards in a relatively
consistent manner (1973). It reviewed possible benefits
from loss reduction programs, and recommended priorities
for work including desirable research initiatives.

A 1973 report from the Committee on Public Engineering
Policy of the National Academy of Engineering suggested
priorities for research that would qualify under the National
Science Foundation (NSF) program on Research Applied to National Needs (RANN). In addition to dealing with certain
common problems of such research--institutional functioning,
conservation and patterns of consumption, coordination and
balance, user orientation, international aspects, and lever-
age and risk taking--Priorities for Research Applicable to
National Needs made detailed recommendations on six separate
programs, of which natural hazards and disasters were one.
The recommendations suggested levels of funding in Fiscal
Year 1974 within the context of the approximate size of the
RANN program, and specified three categories of priority
for each funding recommendation.

Highest priority was given to various modes of optimizing
the nation's adjustments to natural hazards, including monitoring of economic losses, social impacts, needs, and hazard
vulnerability and history; dissemination of information between experts and potential users; and assessment of the effectiveness of various projects and study of improved technology for decision-making in that realm. Somewhat lower
priority was given to specific studies focused on flood-
control projects, interdisciplinary attacks on flood hazards,
the development of criteria and procedures for designing
flood control, regulations and insurance schemes, as well as
research on problems of fire and the modeling of fire processes. Earthquake resistance, prediction, and control received
support above the current level of research under NSF on
earthquake engineering, which includes more attention to
earthquake-resistant design codes, expanded knowledge of
earthquake phenomena, and modes of effectively transferring
new earthquake technology. Continuation of work on weather
hazard modification was recommended to include the continuation of the National Hail Research Experiment; research on
ice nuclei and on new concepts of models for weather modification; studies of the effects of pollution and urban growth
on local climate and weather; and social, economic, and ecological impacts of weather modification. Of doubtful priority
was a proposal for an experimental short-range weather warning service.

All of these proposals were within a general framework
which emphasized the importance of maintaining four basic
functions of monitoring, dissemination, effectiveness assessment, and improvement of decision-making.

A prospectus for the development of a national emergency

center was prepared by an advisory committee on emergency
planning at the National Research Council in 1968, and dealt
with assistance in disaster preparations, hazard monitoring,
and coordination of relief activities. It was envisaged that
an emergency center would be organized to coordinate and conduct research on disaster causation and effects, disaster
operations, and systems evaluation and planning. No positive
action was taken on that proposal.

Perhaps the field which has received the most consistent
attention over recent years in terms of definitions of research needs was earthquake engineering. The more recent
recommendations for investigations along these lines included
Earthquake Engineering Research, a report from the Committee
on Earthquake Engineering Research of the National Academy
of Sciences-National Research Council (1969), and the very
detailed set of reports of the Committee on the Alaska
Earthquake. The opportunities and problems of work on earthquake prediction had an early airing in the report of the Ad
Hoc Panel on Earthquake Prediction in 1965, Earthquake Prediction: Proposal for a 10-year Program of Research.

Earthquake engineering for new structures played an important part in the review of possibilities for improvement
in building design sponsored by the National Bureau of
Standards in 1972 (National Bureau of Standards, 1973).

In its report on the atmospheric sciences and man's needs
(National Academy of Sciences-National Research Council,
1971), the Committee on Atmospheric Sciences of the National
Research Council noted the problems associated with tornadoes,
severe thunderstorms and squall lines, hurricanes, and
pollution disasters, and recommended that a major objective
in the atmospheric sciences should be "to reduce substantially human casualties, economic loss, and social

dislocations caused by weather." To this end it recommended
collaboration in the conduct of the International Global
Atmospheric Research Program to explore ways of extending the
range of useful prediction into the one- to two-week period.

It also recommended determining the potential of short-
period extrapolations of local weather by maintaining pilot
local weather watches in selected urban areas as well as in a
selected rural area that would provide real-time visual
presentation of critical weather features.

The Atmosphere and Man's Needs: Priorities for the Future,
while based on social assessment of the needs for new information, emphasized how illuminating the understanding of
atmospheric processes would make possible better definition
of hazards, improved warning services, and strengthening the
capacity to modify weather.

A special review of atmospheric problems was carried out
by the National Advisory Committee on Oceans and Atmosphere,
which in 1972 undertook a rapid and wide appraisal of the
experience with the Agnes Floods of June, 1972. The Agnes
Floods (1972) put forward a series of suggestions on ways of
improving the forecasting system, but also included suggestions on ways in which community preparedness might be
stimulated through research and information activities and
on reconsideration of changes in public policy.

A broad assessment of selected problems in the environmental sciences was conducted by the National Science Board in
1969-71. Environmental Science: Challenge for the Seventies
(1971), is a selection of topics deserving special attention, but makes no effort to set priorities among programs,
or to estimate the justification for new activities.

Most reviews of Federal policy and practice in the water

resources field over recent years have carried recommendations
for research related to floods, hurricanes, drought, and
other water-caused disasters. _Water Policies for the Future_,
the report of the National Water Commission in 1973 included,
in addition to recommendations for changes in Federal policy,
indications of new emphasis that would either support or help
carry out such policies.

On a periodic basis, the Office of Water Research and
Technology reviews needs in the water resources field which
it and its advisers consider of value to scientists working
on water problems.

Types of Analysis

It is a rare scientific discipline or policy field which has
not been the subject of an evaluation of research needs.
These always require assumptions on public aims, although the
aims may not be specified. The reviews range from the hurried
to the deliberate, and reflect the composition and interaction
of the groups taking part. They may lay heavy stress on advancing a discipline, helping a particular user group, or
defining new problems; in stance they may be self-serving,
politically compromising, or highly objective.

The interim report by the Committee on Public Engineering
Policy (1972), illustrates one common type of analysis utilized in establishing appropriate funding levels for natural
hazards research. It utilizes an _informed consensus_ method
by which priorities and research expenditures are agreed
upon. Competent and experienced people are asked to share
their judgments. Figure 8-1 represents the process whereby
members of the committee each indicate their relative preferences (points a, b, c, d, e); the final decision is the

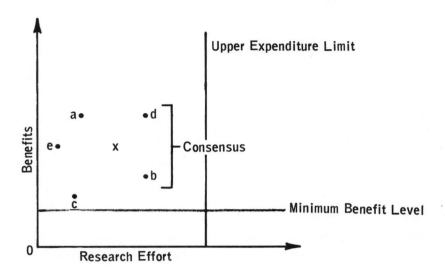

FIGURE 8–1
INFORMED CONSENSUS METHOD

mean of these (point x), with the mean often being affected by
the weight of influence exercised by each member as well as
by the composition of the committee and the ways in which they
form coalitions.

Agency review of research opportunities may include several
methods or ways of judging research payoffs or opportunities:
cost-benefit analysis; cost-effectiveness analysis; exploratory incrementalism; or a consensus of experts on the type of
research that should be afforded budgetary and authorization priorities. The National Science Foundation uses both
group and individual evaluation of research priorities during
its consideration of 14,000 research proposals in a year, and
other research funding organizations follow somewhat similar
methods of peer review. Such groups or individuals, in turn,
utilize cost-benefit, and other methods, sometimes made

explicit and sometimes implicit in a summary judgment.
Although more sophisticated procedures are used now, at one
time the Department of Agriculture periodically sent out a
questionnaire to all the land grant colleges and agricultural
schools asking what their research priorities were.

At the Federal level, the Congressional appropriation
process usually begins only after budgetary and legislative
clearance by the Office of Management and Budget. More quantitative methods of determining research priorities were enhanced by the adoption of a Program, Planning, Budgetary
System by the Federal government in 1966. Well-known to
every Federal administrator, this budgetary system specified
objectives and alternatives for achieving the objectives.
Within this framework, agency and Office of Management and
Budget (OMB) personnel ultimately determine the recommended
program which will be reviewed by Congress. Authorizations
may follow a different course, with the initiative coming
from the Congress. For example, Title V of the Disaster Relief
Act of 1974, providing for long-range economic development,
was strongly opposed by the Administration.

Congressional review usually is based on predetermined
priorities. Congress rarely initiates research priorities at
the present time, but it does approve or modify decisions
presented to it by the agency and OMB, i.e., the agency's
appropriations and the agency's authorization. Amounts of
appropriations may be increased or decreased, and research
direction can be changed during the authorization process.

Congressional concern with research ordinarily focuses
around three major questions: why the research is necessary;
how the agency arrived at its research priorities; and what
the research benefits are. The last question indicates a
concern on the part of Congressmen that research should have

one or several net benefits: an increase in basic science
knowledge, or a public or private use for the information.
The Congressional evaluation of research programs, in its
determination of whether Congress will approve and/or
increase or decrease appropriations or change authorization,
is based primarily on cost-effectiveness assumptions, i.e.,
assumptions that so much money can be spent in a research or
program area, and on a consensus of experts. In turn, the
ultimate decision of Congress is based on consensus at several
levels of subcommittees, committees, and houses, and the political weights placed upon the several national aims may differ from one program to another. An activity promising small
returns in reducing loss of life may claim more support than
one offering large gains in economic benefits.

Congressional approval may be forthcoming for a variety of
reasons. A public clientele desires the information, as in
the case of designers of earthquake-resistant structures or
state water engineers who need flood data. Research approval
may be viewed as a symbol that Congress is doing something
about natural hazards, as when special provisions are made
for relief immediately following a disaster. It also may be
a function of Congressional-agency communication, and the cultivation of those relationships by agency officials who explain the long-term goals.

Other common modes of analysis are represented in Figure
8-1. The *cost-effectiveness* approach either puts an upper
limit on expenditures, or determines a minimum level of benefits to be achieved at the lowest practicable cost. It begins with an agreed objective and examines the likely benefits of different actions. The cost-effectiveness approach
in government appears at times in the discussions between
OMB and individual agencies on how the agency fits into the

final budget of the United States. The President determines
an upper limit to the Federal budget; OMB officials are responsible for arranging upper limits among agencies in order
to stay within the President's budget priorities. Such methods of cost-efficiency analysis would be illustrated by the
appraisal of research and development programs with respect to
new energy technology in which the aim is to find those technologies which would offer new energy sources at the lowest
social costs (see Reubin *et al.*, 1974). It is applicable to
research where there is an agreed goal of reducing deaths
by a stated proportion, or of preventing a specified level of
social disruption.

Funds sometimes are allocated to spend a certain *percentage
of total expenditures* on research. Of the total cost of adjustments to a particular hazard--flood control works or
hurricane warning operations--a certain percentage could be
assigned to research and development activities. In both
private and public programs with sustained construction or
operational activity, this is a convenient means of dealing
with a complex choice. The highway research program provides
an interesting example of this approach in allocating proportions of expenditure to research. It has the weakness of
encouraging research to support adjustments, such as control
works or warning systems, that in some instances are less
likely to serve national goals than other activities which do
not require the same volume of expenditures.

When the basic problem is one of understanding the process
of natural or social systems, it may be impossible and impru-
dent to designate an expected benefit. The research must be
justified initially on those grounds without attempting to
anticipate applications.

Exploratory incrementalism is a means of determining future
research effort by reevaluating past results at frequent and
regular intervals. A somewhat arbitrary annual expenditure is
fixed at the outset, and the results are examined from time to
time to arrive at rough estimates of whether or not it is
worth continuing. The early days of weather modification research were of this character, and much of the activity continues to be supported on that basis. New technologies lend
themselves to that strategy, and in a number of the research
opportunities listed in Chapter 11 it is suggested an exploratory effort be initiated without commitment to continue after
a trial period.

While all of these approaches are utilized with varying
frequency in the natural hazards area, the most common is the
informed consensus method. Its outcome depends upon the political and administrative weights of those taking part.
Often lacking, however, is a comprehensive and systematic
analysis.

Limitations on data as well as on the adequacy of analytical methods make it undesirable to rely wholly upon any one
of these modes of analysis. No hazard has a sufficient base
of information about the full range of costs and of positive
benefits to the nation. The professional groups from which
judgment can be abstracted are strongly biased toward certain
modes of response in contrast to others, as is the case with
the heavy emphasis in dealing with earthquake problems by
either delimitation of seismic risk or engineering design
for high buildings. In these circumstances, it is neither
desirable nor practicable to rely on any one of the methods.
The Assessment analysis made use of bits of them as appropriate, frequently recognizing that deficiencies in data or in
professional judgment make the conclusions at best tentative.

The immediate goal was to develop a systematic approach which makes explicit the trade-offs existing within and among various adjustments to natural hazards.

Economic Efficiency, Trade-offs and Values

When considering only a single research project, net benefits would be maximized by equating marginal costs (MC) and marginal benefits (MB). Assuming diminishing returns from additional research effort, Figure 8-2 depicts the optimum level of research effort to be Q units. To the left of Q, MB is greater than MC, indicating that an additional unit of research will contribute more to benefits than to costs, while the converse situation exists to the right of Q.

The price of research which equates MB to MC is represented by P per unit. Hence, the total cost of Q units of research is P x Q or area OPAQ. The area OPAQ, however, does not represent the upper limit of justifiable expenditures to obtain Q units of research. The marginal benefit curve can be interpreted as a demand or willingness-to-pay curve for research. As such, it describes the maximum level of expenditure for each unit of research to be equal to the marginal benefit of that research unit; the area OBAQ represents the upper limit of expenditures which are justified to achieve Q units of research.

The above argument assumes continuity; and in the case of research, this assumption is rarely valid. It describes only one research alternative, and generally there are at least several alternatives.

A more important problem is that the conventional application of the economic efficiency criterion requires a common numeraire, and the one normally utilized is the dollar. The product of such an analysis is, then, the maximization of

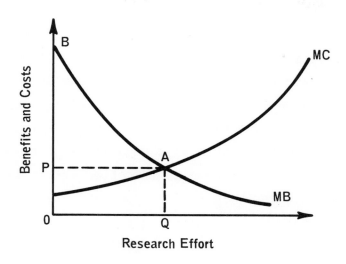

FIGURE 8—2

MARGINAL COST, MARGINAL BENEFIT CURVES

pecuniary net benefits. There is more to be considered than
the dollar values of benefits and costs. Other products of
further research may be fewer casualties, greater equality of
income distribution, less environmental destruction, or reduced social disruption.

Considering only the relationship between more research and
fewer fatalities, the reduction of deaths and the expansion
of pecuniary net benefits are complementary up to some point.
Further research over this range contributes positively to
both objectives. Beyond that point, however, the two objectives compete such that net benefits represent a trade-off
between fewer fatalities and more saved dollars. Application
of the efficiency criterion in strictly pecuniary terms may

dictate one point as the optimum solution. Social values,
however, may not correspond to this choice.

Appraisal of natural hazards thus involves dealing with
both multidimensional trade-offs and value functions. The
appropriate shape of the value function, such as how much
weight to place on saving lives, is a social decision and
belongs properly in the realm of politics. Specification of
the trade-off function, such as the possible gain in property
loss reduction from hurricane modification versus the risk
of irreversible changes in an ecosystem, is within the scope
of the Assessment.

Trade-offs exist both within and among the various adjustments to natural hazards. Not only may the avoidance of pecuniary losses and deaths eventually compete, but so will
environmental quality, social stability, and equity of income distribution. Differing levels of a particular adjustment, as in the range of possible resistance of a building
to seismic shock, may yield varying mixes of these considerations. Similarly, adoption of different sets of adjustments
will produce assorted combinations of the desired objectives.

Mathematical specification of the multidimensional trade-
off function, which exists for natural hazard adjustments,
would be a Herculean task. The Assessment seeks more real-
istically to specify a few points which define the practical
choices.

A significant component of any evaluation of research results deals with the pecuniary benefits and costs emanating
from each alternative adjustment. This is essentially a
conventional cost-benefit approach. However, other considerations limit the cost-benefit analysis to a necessary, though
not a sufficient ingredient of the evaluation.

The environment and social disruption are examples of the
intangible considerations. These have no quantitative measure,
though subjective evaluations are possible. Projects may be
compared in terms of their "poor", "average", "good", or
"fantastic" effect in preserving or enhancing natural amenities or social arrangements. Numbers can be used to mean the
same thing in a qualitative sense (1 = poor, 2 = average,
etc.).

The number of deaths averted by successful research in some
area is perhaps the most important incommensurable item. A
worker may earn $500,000 during his life, but it is absurd
to say that his life is worth this amount. The two things
cannot be compared. However, the number of lives saved by
alternative research products can be evaluated.

Uncertainty pervades the analysis. Not all research undertaken is successful; trade-offs exist between high-risk, high-
payoff projects and low-risk, low-payoff projects. If the
risk is known, the probability of success can be entered in
the matrix. If the problem is one of uncertainty, subjective
evaluations of the expected success ratio can be made.

Various adjustments will result in different income distributions. One national goal has been equity of income distribution, though the exact meaning and implementation of this
policy has generally been unclear. Various economic changes,
however, can be judged in terms of their effects on the relative *shares* of total income which different groups receive.

It will often be the case that nothing is known. When
this is the case, it is best to inform the decision-maker
of the fact, so that he may evaluate the consequences of this
hole in the trade-off estimates. A common fault of many
analyses is to hide the hole with erroneous or inconsequential
information.

The Evaluation Framework

These considerations enter into the design of an evaluation
framework used for each of the hazards. It is a rectangular
array listing research alternatives vertically and national
aims (described in Chapter 6) horizontally. Each element of
the matrix is a judgment of the effect of a particular
adjustment upon a certain national aim. The form of the
tableau is given in Table 8-1.

Evaluations down columns give the relative trade-off relationships with alternative adjustments. Cross-columns or
row evaluations are for trade-off relationships with alternative
adjustment schemes. For each cell a judgment is made as to the
probability that the research, if completed and applied, would
contribute to the specified national aim. Ratings of "high",
"medium", "low" and "negative" are used. Where there is
severe doubt this is shown by a "?". If the judgment is not
applicable, this is shown by "NA". In some instances there are
calculations, simulations, or scenarios to support the judgment.
In other instances it is the consensus of staff or consultants.

Under the aims of economic efficiency, enhancement of
human health, and avoidance of social disruption, a distinc-
tion is made between the effects on average net benefits and
potential for catastrophe, as outlined in Chapter 4.

Utilizing the concept of economic efficiency in its broad-
est sense, the decision-maker now may be better prepared to
evaluate the various alternatives. Given social values, the
decision-maker attempts to determine that order and combination of adjustments such that the last unit of cost (in terms
of dollars, lives) yields equal or equivalent units of benefits (defined in the same general terms as costs). The
equivalences of the various objectives are based purely upon
value judgments. By utilizing a framework enumerated in terms

TABLE 8-1
EVALUATION FRAMEWORK

Research Opportunity	National Aims								Research Findings	
	Economic Efficiency — Reduction of Net Losses Benefits–Costs		Enhancement of Human Health — Reduction of Casualties		Avoidance of Social Disruption		Environment — Protection or Enhancement	Equity — Distribution of Costs and Benefits	Expected Success of Research	Likelihood of Adoption
	Average	Cata-strophic	Average	Cata-strophic	Average	Cata-strophic				

Med = Medium Neg = Negative ? = In doubt NA = Not applicable

of a multiplicity of objectives and measures, the decision-maker has an explicit statement of trade-offs to which to apply the value judgments which remain his prerogative.

Wise and accurate application of the method requires data which often are lacking. If there is no valid information on damage from landslides, it is impossible to estimate how much could be gained from improving the means of preventing landslides. Were the cost of collecting and analyzing such data relatively small, a high priority would be to determine the damage dimension of the problem. Were it very high compared to other types of research, the question would arise whether that proposed expenditure were warranted. In numerous cases, the first reasonable step in investigation is to lay the groundwork for evaluation without making absurdly large outlays.

A basic criterion for selecting research is judgment of what is practicable. Often the administrator can define a problem which is eminently worth investigating in the sense that were it solved, the results would make important contributions to society, but which does not presently promise any reasonably useful results. If there were in sight a line of investigation which would promise a ready means of dissipating tornado vortexes before they formed, it would warrant priority over efforts at improving the forecasting and warning of tornadoes in vulnerable areas. So long as there is no promising line of attack on the problem, it must be noted as one which some day may be amenable to treatment but which may never lend itself to any kind of positive action.

A second criterion is the likelihood that research results may be translated into constructive action, as discussed in Chapter 7. The prospect of applying a new formula for design of a spillway in construction plans is generally brighter than

applying results of a land use study in a county zoning
regulation. Judgments of this sort are made at many points,
eliminating lines of work for which there might be abundant
payoff if results were to be produced or used, but for which
the opportunity for such products seems exceedingly small.
New techniques, or new understandings of natural or social
processes may shift a category of activity from the wholly
impracticable to the probable, and the responsible agencies
always need to be on the alert for the consequences of such
shifts. Judgments on the expected success and the likely
adoption of the research findings are given in the two columns
at the right of the table.

As one step in the direction of evaluations which could be
compared systematically, the reports on individual hazards
carry frameworks to provide some of the information specified
above. They also contain data on current funding levels, and
judgments on the likelihood that pertinent research efforts
could yield the expected returns within specified time hori-
zons and, if completed satisfactorily, could influence
changes in national response to extreme events. The tables
are presented for discussion purposes; most of the discussion
will hinge on the substantive evidence and judgments. Underlying that appraisal is the problem of how the framework can
be improved.

Common Assumptions

In most instances it is not possible to ascertain with even
modest precision the magnitude of the United States' investment in research on a particular hazard, or even on a particular set of adjustments (for example, forecasting and warning)
for a single hazard. Rather than make no estimates, the
available information on research expenditures is used to

designate order of magnitude expenditure levels. We show
estimated current yearly expenditures for various categories
as 0 to $10,000; $10,000 to $100,000; $100,000 to $1 million;
$1 million to $2 million; and $2 million to $4 million
annually.

Each of the individual hazard reports finds merit in at
least a few research efforts. These are grouped into what
are called "research opportunity sets". Those with no promising results are not listed. Some sets of doubtful value are
listed for discussion purposes. It is assumed that the returns will be interrelated, and that the work can be evaluated
in sets rather than in smaller, discrete projects.

Even though some of the efforts will need to continue for
longer periods, ten years seems a sufficient planning horizon
to accomplish the bulk of recommended research. Significant
changes are likely to occur within the next decade which
would make planning for research beyond that point fruitless.
At the same time, the research sets contain a number of small,
short-term projects that are plainly exploratory. It seems
probable that significant expenditures will be needed for a
long time on such problems as the adoption by local governments of land use regulations in hazard zones, but it appears
prudent to begin with shorter-term projects which would demonstrate the suitability of both method and personnel.

The evaluations generally assume that there are a sufficient number of competent researchers in the United States
to carry out much of the work which analysis shows is desirable. Many of them, however, are conducting research unre-
lated to natural hazards at the present time. Their interest
in switching from their current work to research on natural
hazards is largely unknown, and assurance of stable funding
over a five- to ten-year period might be a necessary incentive

to recruit them. While it is difficult to predict, it appears
that of all the specialties needed, capable and interested
social scientists may be in shortest supply.

These assumptions are made or in some instances altered
in the tables presented in Chapter 11. The framework for
evaluation is better understood if the assessment of research
on individual hazards is examined against the background of a
review of the themes they have in common and of an appraisal
of new strategies which would strengthen all of the suggested
work. The common themes are reviewed in Chapter 9, and the
new strategies are described in Chapter 10.

COMMON ADJUSTMENT RESEARCH THEMES

Each of the reviews of individual hazards touches on certain
problems that are common to other hazards. Five of these themes
run throughout the Assessment: warning systems, land use management, technological adjustments, disaster relief, and
insurance.

To the extent that research on one of these themes for one
hazard can be combined to advantage with work on another
hazard, cross-hazard studies should be encouraged. Some of the
problems cut across a large number of hazards from the outset.
The opportunities to pursue those common themes are reviewed
as a preface to the suggestion of new research strategies, and
to evaluation of research sets for each of the 15 hazards.
To the extent that the common themes are attacked, the need
for the more restricted studies outlined in Chapter 11 would
be reduced. Substantial savings would come from following
this approach as contrasted to research focused only on each
individual hazard.

Warning Systems
Research leading to new knowledge on hazard warning systems
may serve to lessen catastrophe potential, loss of life, and
social disruption (see Mileti [1975] for a detailed description
from which this section is drawn). Several unanswered questions retard benefits promised by the warning systems which
currently cost the nation in excess of $140 million annually
for direct operations exclusive of the expenses of people who
respond. Why do some people respond adaptively and in time to
disaster warnings while others do not? Why can some communities get good warnings to people in danger in time while a
large number of locales continue to be plagued by inadequate

warnings? What role can research and the application of existing and new knowledge play in upgrading all warning processes
to reduce loss from predictable hazards?

Warning systems must be assessed from an integrated perspective, including every stage of the total warning process
from the first detection and forecast of a hazard threat
through public response. Existing knowledge is not being put
to full use in warning preparedness. There are ways of using
research to help maximize the potential rewards.

Fields in which new inquiry promises useful results center
around 1. the social and psychological factors affecting public
warning response; 2. the organizational links in warning systems between the variety of groups and agencies which evaluate
threat information and disseminate public warnings; and 3.
means of encouraging integrated warning systems as part of
preparedness programs.

Relationship to research on specific hazards - Cross-hazard
warning research is closely related to the hazard-specific
warning research described in Chapter 11 in several ways.
Basic warning system process may be conceptually the same
across hazards. A conclusion that the study of a warning system for one hazard would not be worthwhile may not exclude its
utility in studying the basic components of warning systems.
Research on hailstorm warnings alone would not be justified,
but some aspects of possible hail warnings may be quite relevant to a more comprehensive inquiry on warning systems.

Integrated warning systems and dramatic events - Hazards possess
different physical characteristics which have direct implications for warning. The relationships of these factors, as well
as others such as preparedness and technology, to warning are

illustrated in Figure 9-1.

Hazards (flood, tornado, wind, tsunami, hurricane, and volcano) which pose a threat to life and property, and require
relatively quick response to avert catastrophe are those for
which warning systems can avert loss most dramatically. A
warning system is composed of more than the sending of a message. An integrated system actively incorporates three basic
processes: 1. *evaluation*, the detection, measurement, collation, and interpretation of threat data (typically referred to
as prediction and forecast); 2. *dissemination*, the decision to
warn, message formulation (when warning is not accomplished by
purely technical means such as sirens), and message convey-
ance; and 3. *response* by those who receive the warnings.

Evaluation begins when there is some indication of an impending impact of geophysical forces, dissemination is based
on evaluation, and response is the ultimate purpose of the
entire system. The relations among the various components of
a warning system are diagrammed in Figure 9-2.

Many hazards are weather-related (avalanches, drought, flood,
frost, hail, hurricane, lightning, tornado, urban snow, and
wind). Warning for each, despite variations in predictive
ability as well as in what might be considered appropriate
warning response, begins with similar agencies for environmental
monitoring, detection and forecasting. Weather observation
systems, interorganizational communication systems, forecasting centers, and public warning-dissemination systems for these
hazards vary in level of adequacy. Although all components
could be upgraded, public warning-dissemination systems currently are the least adequate.

The status of knowledge - Two types of knowledge are relevant
to any warning system: technical for forecasting, and

FIGURE 9—1

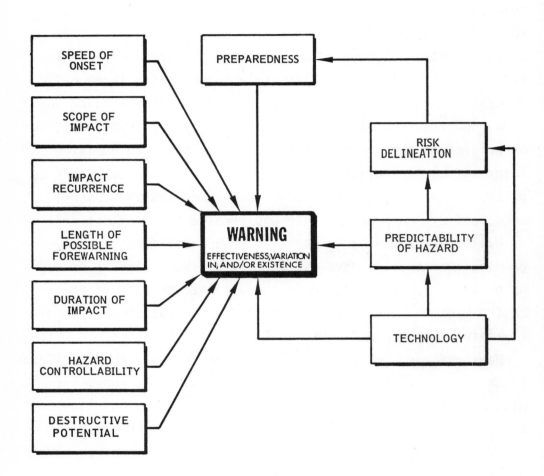

MAJOR VARIABLES AFFECTING WARNING

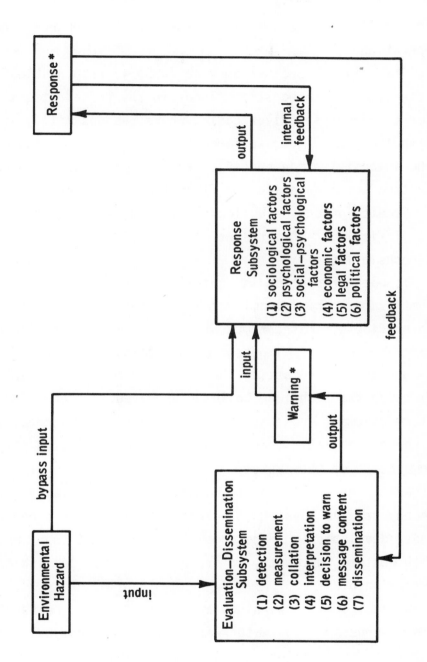

FIGURE 9-2
SYSTEMS MODEL OF A WARNING SYSTEM

* Major dependent variables in the system.

scientific for the system's structure, maintenance, and operation.

The National Weather Service (NWS) is responsible for the detection and forecast of floods in the United States except for the Tennessee River Basin, where responsibility is shared with the TVA. Accurate forecasting of precipitation quantities and intensities for specific areas is difficult, and current systems are inadequate for flash flood forecasting.

Prediction and detection for tornadoes and destructive wind is difficult at the present time. The NWS has the principal responsibility.

Tsunami prediction is inhibited by a lack of knowledge of the hazard. The Tsunami Warning System in the Pacific is able to provide estimated times of arrival; more specific forecast data are generally impossible to obtain.

Hurricane forecasting, based in the NWS, is possible, although the technique could be upgraded in prediction of storm movement and other factors. Hurricane watches, advisories, bulletins, and warnings are disseminated through components of the system.

Avalanche prediction is at best only a partially developed technique. An "avalanche hazard rating index" is currently under development. Once completed and used in conjunction with weather forecasts, an avalanche warning service can be established.

Coastal erosion warnings are extensions of the hurricane storm surge and high water warnings issued from NWS forecasting centers along the United States coasts.

Drought prediction is not now feasible. However, NOAA's Drought Index and the Palmer's Crop Moisture Index are used currently to assess accumulating drought conditions throughout the growing season.

Earthquake prediction and forecasting are still under development. No warning system currently exists, but recent research generates optimism that one could be put into operation by the U.S. Geological Survey (USGS) within a few years.

At present two specialized programs are operated by the NWS for frost forecasting. These are the Fruit-Frost Weather Service and the Agricultural Weather Service. The services do not exist for all portions of the country subject to the hazard; frost forecast is incorporated only into general weather forecast services in those areas.

The forecast of thunderstorms "probably with hail" can often be given as much as 24 hours in advance; however, such forecasts are for large geographical areas, and the actual hailstorm is of small areal extent. Individual hailswaths and hail intensities cannot be forecast presently with any demonstrable skill.

General landslide predictions based on seasonal considerations are possible in some areas of the country. More nearly precise forecasts are not possible at this time.

The NWS, at its Severe Local Storm Forecast Center at Kansas City, is capable of detecting potentially hazardous lightning storms. In conjunction with more general forecasts, the Forest Service can determine fire conditions, the principal danger posed by lightning.

Snowfall forecasts also are made by NWS, and there is disagreement on whether accuracy is improving. In terms of upgrading snow warning response, improvements in snow prediction are questionable.

The USGS prediction accuracy of volcanic eruption is variable. Many detection methods can be employed effectively only at a volcano which displays behavior favorable for their use.

Although such items as past experience, perceived negative public reaction, and perceived impact probability are known to affect how and if warnings are eventually disseminated to the public, little is known about the crucial link between this prediction and forecast agencies, and warning dissemination. Public response is the ultimate reason for having any warning system. The lack of serious attention given to it in warning system preparedness, and to research to assist in planning those systems is puzzling.

From past research efforts three important notions about how people respond to warnings have surfaced: 1. even though several persons may listen to the same warning message, there may be considerable variation in what they hear and believe; 2. people respond to warnings on the basis of how what they hear stimulates them to behave; and 3. people are stimulated differently depending on who they are, who they are with, and who and what they see. Figure 9-3 presents a summarized overview of the relationships between those factors which help in explaining how people respond.

Opportunities for research - Two important policy questions must be considered in estimating current research opportunities for warning systems: 1. how a system should be designed to serve economically and effectively; and 2. how to ensure its adoption and maintenance.

System design - The most decisive determinants of response in an integrated system of the type shown in Figure 9-2 are still conjectured. It is therefore difficult to make generalizations about how to improve warning content and dissemination procedures among the varied agencies and legal and social units in an integrated system.

Evidence suggests that many public education efforts to

FIGURE 9-3

MODEL OF RESPONSE TO PRE-IMPACT WARNINGS
SUGGESTED BY THE RESEARCH REVIEW

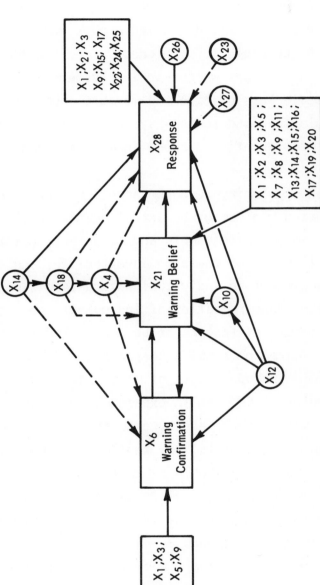

Where:——— = indirect relationship; ——— = direct relationship or no direction specified; X_1 = warning source
X_2 = warning content; X_3 = communication mode; X_4 = number of warnings received; X_5 = perceived warning certainty;
X_6 = warning confirmation; X_7 = interpretation of environmental cues; X_8 = observed action of others; X_9 = primary
group context; X_{10} = situational hazard perception; X_{11} = previous hazard perception; X_{12} = personal experience;
X_{13} = experience of others; X_{14} = geographical proximity to target area; X_{15} = socioeconomic status; X_{16} = organizational
membership; X_{17} = sex; X_{18} = age; X_{19} = urban/rural residence; X_{20} = race; X_{21} = warning belief; X_{22} = normative context;
X_{23} = perceived time to impact; X_{24} = role conflict; X_{25} = ethnicity; X_{26} = psychological locus of control; X_{27} = fear;
and X_{28} = response.

change warning response need improvement and that some portion
of a population fails to take appropriate protective action
regardless of warnings. Only with greater understanding of
the likely responses of individuals and groups under disaster
threat would it be possible to make precise and beneficial
refinements. In situations where warning systems can function
to avert large-scale loss of life and movable property, an
integrated sociological and social-psychological all-hazard
research project could refine present knowledge and expand upon
it.

An examination of warning-response across different hazards
would require that a minimum of 50 actual events be studied in
order to provide an adequate sample and to ensure that the findings are generalizable. It would be more fruitful and less
costly in the long run than individual hazard-specific studies.
It would allow for standardization of instruments of measurement, permit a variety of factors to be controlled for in each
hazard event, and make the results comparable.

The study should include events of major hazard types, in
which random samples of the public exposed to warnings in
each event are assessed for: exposure to the message, belief,
understanding and misinterpretation, knowledge of appropriate
action, and behavior. They should be examined in association
with response to different kinds of threat situations, circumstances, communities, and groups of people (for example,
the aged, the poor, the experienced, and the fearful).

Need also exists to determine how differences in the warning source, the message content, and the mode of communication affects psychological states in those who might respond.
A series of social-psychological laboratory experiments are
called for in which factors such as the number of warnings
issued, specificity in warning content, and the wording of

messages are related to psychological factors such as warning
belief, perception of danger, and fear.

These experiments should investigate both attitudinal and
behavioral effects of simulated warnings, and test the findings by field observations. The wisdom of carrying out a
rigorous field experiment, as contrasted to the laboratory, is
questionable, but the utility of findings could be assessed in
part by comparing disaster communities in which they had been
applied to those in which they were not.

Certain stipulations apply to the effectiveness of any
message from a warning system: 1. if the message or signal is
received at the local level without alteration, it must be
received promptly and contain clear, concise information which
can be easily and quickly understood by the local individual,
whether official or other resident (Anderson, 1970); 2. if the
local recipient successfully disseminates the information to
all relevant local persons, the message must be received promptly and must contain information necessary for residents to make
rapid, rational decisions about appropriate actions; and 3. if
the local resident interprets the message correctly, he must
know appropriate action to take and be motivated to act in
time. To be appropriate, action should prevent loss of life
and injury, minimize property damage, and be a "safe area" that
can be reached in time (Haas and Trainer, 1973, p. 9).

As demonstrated, there are many links in the effective warning chain; each link is of the same importance. Because
numerous groups and government agencies divide the responsibilities among themselves, it is difficult to assure the
functioning of the evaluation-dissemination sector.

A project designed to assess warning dissemination should
comprise a sample of events large enough to control for varied
factors such as community and hazard type. A minimum of 50

events in different communities would be necessary to assist in
generalizable policy recommendations. It should address the
manner in which warnings might best be disseminated, the means
for overcoming economic, legal, political, and social constraints which retard warning issuance, and what changes in
structure in responsible agencies would maximize good warning
dissemination. It should assess all aspects of the processes
preceding dissemination--detection, measurement, collation,
interpretation, the decision to warn, and formation of message
content--how those processes influence what is actually disseminated, and the feedback relationship from response to the
dissemination process (see Figure 9-2).

System adoption and maintenance - Warning systems cut across
a variety of legal boundaries, Federal detection agencies,
regional weather services, local jurisdictions and media networks. Once a particular mix of relations between these units
has been found desirable for an integrated system, those measures must be adopted at local levels if the nation is to benefit. Even when adopted, the functioning systems tend to decline over time. Knowledge is seriously deficient on what
affects adoption, and ensuing system maintenance at the community level.

System adoption as well as maintenance may result from a
combination of factors, among them hazard repetition, community officials' awareness, and legislated requirements at
the local level. Research into the adoption and maintenance
of warning systems would be least costly and most efficient
if integrated into one endeavor. Both components of the effort
are directly concerned with preparedness. Hazard-specific
research aimed at adoption or preparedness for existing systems
would also be beneficial. Studies of individual hazards which
are separate from each other might also be less comparable and

inhibit the potential benefit which could be realized in cross-hazard comparison. The latter offers the bonus of approximating an experimental design.

No significant benefit will be attained from research on any component of warning systems unless what is currently known and what is discovered is put to use in specific communities for preparing for specific events. Research which would enable the installation and maintenance of some such systems is urgently needed. It would not center on postaudits of warning systems. There has been no comparison of dormant systems in order to determine what explains adoption and preparedness. Such study, or even the more costly alternative of a series of studies, is central to reaping maximum benefits from warning systems, both in terms of average annual benefits or of catastrophe avoidance.

Table 9-1 evaluates the potential social, environmental, and economic benefits of these research opportunities, as well as their estimated potential for success and the political feasibility of the adoption of potential findings.

Land Use Management

A recurrent theme in dealing with all of the natural hazards is the potential of land use management to promote socially desirable uses of vulnerable areas in the United States (see Baker, *et al.*, 1975 for a detailed desciption from which this is drawn). The rapid encroachment in the hurricane zone of the South Atlantic coast, the progressive invasion of industrialized flood plains, the design of mobile home parks without shelters against tornado, and the continued building upon land fill in areas of high seismic risk illustrate the land use changes which are occurring and which call out for sober consideration of risk involved.

For each of the geophysical hazards it is apparent that

TABLE 9-1
RESEARCH OPPORTUNITIES—WARNING SYSTEMS

Research Opportunity	National Aims								Research Findings	
	Economic Efficiency — Reduction of Net Losses Benefits-Costs		Enhancement of Human Health — Reduction of Casualties		Avoidance of Social Disruption		Environment — Protection or Enhancement	Equity — Distribution of Costs and Benefits	Expected Success of Research	Likelihood of Adoption
	Average	Catastrophic	Average	Catastrophic	Average	Catastrophic				
Warning Response	Med-Low	Low	Med	High	Med	Med-Low	Low	Med	Med	High
Warning Dissemination	Med-Low	Low	Med	High	Med	Med-Low	Low	Med	Med	High
System Design, Adoption and Maintenance	Med-Low	Low	Med	High	Med	Med-Low	Low	Med	Med	High

Med = Medium   Neg = Negative   ? = In doubt   NA = Not applicable

attention should be given to ways in which land use planning
may contribute to effective use of the soil and water resources,
candidly examining the hard political considerations that shape
what a community finally does about exposing itself to risk.
In each case a needed study of land use problems is closely
linked with associated questions of control and protection
work, warning and emergency action, insurance, and relief and
rehabilitation.

Every instance in which the opportunity to affect land use
patterns arises poses a question of what uses are compatible
with the risk in view of the benefits to society which will
derive from using the resource. Evaluating what is suitable
management for any one area at one time calls for a wide set
of considerations. Aside from the scientific and technical
problem of delimiting and defining the quantitative importance
of any risk, there arise questions of estimating social effects,
legal restraints, political complications, environmental impacts, and the net economic benefits or losses.

Decisions about land use are made either by private property
owners or by public owners, of which the Federal government is
the major holder. Private decisions take place within the
context of local regulatory and planning activities as
guided by state law. The Federal role thus far has been one
of providing information, managing Federal properties, and
giving encouragement to state and local groups through a
variety of measures such as the Department of Housing and
Urban Development (HUD) planning grants, and the National
Oceanic and Atmospheric Administration (NOAA) Coastal Zone
Management Program of 1972. Although strengthened Federal
land use planning legislation was proposed in 1974, its enactment was delayed.

In any event, it would be a mistake to think that early

initiation of such aids to national land use planning would
have a major effect upon the occupation of hazardous areas
unless accompanied by research along four lines: 1. Methods
should be found to step up the pace of delimiting hazardous
areas; 2. The factors affecting successful local management
of hazard areas in terms of community goals need to be appraised; 3. The effects of those activities on the local
agencies and property owners have not been studied; and 4.
Ways of coordinating hazard considerations with other complex
aspects of local planning need improvement.

As indicated in Table 9-2, some of this work already is
receiving heavy emphasis. Other parts are deserving of higher
priority than they now receive when their possible influence
upon further occupation of hazard areas is considered. In all
cases where a high priority is assigned to the activity, it
also is believed that the feasibility of the research is high.
In some other cases, the need for the research is moderate,
but the feasibility of carrying it out is low.

The information which is needed most widely in the management of hazardous areas is scientific *delimitation of hazard
zones* and assignment of probability of occurrence to various
types of events. Research is needed on ways to speed up this
process as cheaply as possible. It should be accompanied by
careful attention to ways of transferring the resulting information into policy decisions.

Canvass has shown that a number of legal uncertainties will
dog the provisions of hazard delimitations unless they are
anticipated from the outset. These include the questions of
reasonable precision in delimitation of a hazard zone; suitable map scale (this is particularly important in considering
possible applications of remote sensing where legally de-
fensible resolution is not established); the credentials and

TABLE 9-2

FEASIBILITY, PRESENT LEVEL, AND PRIORITY OF RESEARCH BY HAZARD

EVALUATIVE CRITERIA	RESEARCH AREAS	Avalanche	Coastal Erosion	Earthquake	Drought	Flood	Frost	Hail	Hurricane Storm Surge	Hurricane Wind	Landslide	Lightning	Snow	Tornado	Tsunami	Volcano	Windstorm
FEASIBILITY	Delimitation	High	High	Low	High	Low	Low	High	Moderate	High	Low	Low	Low	High	High	Moderate	
	Adoption	Moderate	High	Low	High	Low	Low	High	Moderate	High	Low	Low	Moderate	Moderate	Low	Moderate	
	Effectiveness	Moderate	High	Low	High	Low	Low	High	Moderate	High	Low	Low	Moderate	Moderate	Low	Moderate	
	Coordination	Moderate	Moderate	Moderate	High	Low	Low	High	Moderate	High	Low	Low	Low	High	Moderate	Moderate	
PRESENT LEVEL OF RESEARCH	Delimitation	Moderate	High	Low	High	Low	Low	High	Moderate	High	Low	Low	Low	Low	Low	Low	
	Adoption	Low	Low	Low	Moderate	Low	Low	Moderate	Low	Low	Low	Low	Low	Low	Low	Low	
	Effectiveness	Low	Low	Moderate	High	Low	Low	Low	Low	Low	Low	Low	Low	Low	Low	Low	
	Coordination	Low	Low	Low	Moderate	Low	Low	Moderate	Low	Low	Low	Low	Low	Low	Low	Low	
PRIORITY	Delimitation	Moderate	High	Low	High	Low	Low	High	Moderate	High	Low	Low	Low	High	High	High	
	Adoption	High	High	Moderate	High	Moderate	Moderate	High	Moderate	High	Moderate	Moderate	Moderate	Moderate	Moderate	Moderate	
	Effectiveness	Moderate	High	Moderate	High	Moderate	Moderate	High	Moderate	High	Moderate	Moderate	Moderate	Moderate	Moderate	Moderate	
	Coordination	Moderate	High	High	High	Low	Low	High	Moderate	High	Low	Low	Low	High	High	Moderate	

SCALE*

● denotes High   ◑ denotes Moderate   ○ denotes Low

authority of the delimiting agency; and the reliability of the
judgments.

Thus far, little is known about how successful various local
groups have been in working out regulatory and management alternatives. Except for the experience of the grading regulations and application of engineering geology to reducing landslide damages in the Los Angeles area, only casual critical
analysis has been addressed to how land use management has
worked. Even in that instance there are a number of unanswered
questions about the economic effects and the *effectiveness* of
the actions of individual agencies. Some of the questions
apply to land management with respect to virtually all of the
hazards, whereas others, such as the question of subdivision
regulations or tornado shelter requirements, are limited to a
single hazard.

The rate of *adoption* of new land use regulations in hazardous areas has been greatly accelerated in hurricane and flood
zones, but there has been virtually no review of what actually
happened, or why some of the communities withdrew from participation in the Federal flood insurance program by failing
to enact required land use controls.

Much of the regulatory action that has affected hazardous
areas has come about through concerns with environmental
quality rather than from direct identification of areas
hazardous to human occupation. On the other hand, there are
notable examples, such as the Colorado state legislation affecting subdivision design, and Oregon state land use planning
which deals explicitly with hazard areas involved in new
development within the state.

What is needed is an integration of multiple use and
multiple means principles of management affecting hazard areas
to insure that the consideration of hazard is only one aspect

of a *coordinated* approach. In some instances hazard may turn
out to be the lead aspect, in others it may be incidental to
purposes such as open space preservation or wildlife management. Ways of accomplishing this integration are still understood only casually, and the need for achieving it is a
repetitive theme.

The opportunity for spurring research along all of the four
lines indicated above is not likely to be met by concentrating
the investigations in one agency or at one level of government.
A very large part of the responsibility for both activity and
research rests at the local level. Each of the Federal agencies
concerned with major adjustments to natural hazards should be
aware of the land use management components and should include
these as part of its research activities. This would include
the Corps of Engineers, NOAA, Department of Interior, HUD, and
the Department of Agriculture. It is to be expected that in
whatever form national support for land use planning emerges,
a significant sector of the new work to be stimulated by that
program will focus on ways of taking account of hazardous
characteristics of land as an element in integrated management.

The needed research on individual hazards summarized in
Table 9-2 would be strengthened by investigations cutting
across all hazards in five ways. In each case a broad study
would provide support for studies limited to a single hazard.

A closer examination should be made of *Federal land use
policies* as they may affect the decisions of private land-
owners or other units of government in dealing with hazards.
The possible influence of Federal action on use of adjacent
or nearby lands needs to be recognized more explicitly.

The relation of *Federal, state and local tax structures* to
decisions to locate or not locate in hazardous places should
be probed. The present incentives and disincentives, as in

the Internal Revenue Code, have powerful effects upon locational decisions.

Public finance policy needs evaluation from the standpoint of possible effects upon new development. States and local governments are not generally aware of the opportunities and complexities of this form of guidance to land use where the subsequent public costs for welfare or corrective works may be high.

The possible use of *housing policy and regulations,* including urban renewal, in affecting the vulnerability of settlements needs exploration. The potential savings for future relief and rehabilitation and in Veterans Administration and Federal Housing Administration loan foreclosures are large.

The effects of *relief and rehabilitation and insurance programs* upon land use also deserve examination. These could be combined with studies along those lines noted later in this chapter.

Technological Adjustments

Technology plays an influential role in the adjustments made to extreme events in five different ways. It may be used to 1. modify natural systems; 2. detect and disseminate information about the coming of a hazardous event; 3. protect against the event when it occurs; 4. design structures to mitigate the effects of the event; 5. assist in providing relief and rehabilitation following the disaster (Figure 9-4). Among the wide variety of activities encompassed by these five classes, two currently receive most concerted attention in new research proposals--weather modification and building design and construction. The first of these commands enthusiastic and loosely coordinated activity by Federal agencies. The second receives only meager support in relation to its possible

FIGURE 9–4

TECHNOLOGICAL INTERVENTIONS IN HAZARD SYSTEMS

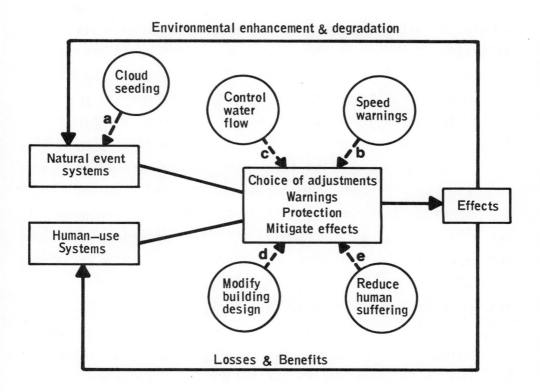

a — Modify natural systems
b — Detect and disseminate future event
c — Protect against event
d — Design structures to mitigate effects
e — Assist in providing relief and rehabilitation

influence upon the vulnerability of the nation to losses and
dislocations.

Analysis shows that any technological intervention in the
natural hazard system involves some kind of recognition of
basic physical systems, of the living part of the community
which is related to those systems, and of the constraints
imposed by materials and interactive processes upon the kinds
of action which may be taken. Figure 9-4 suggests some of
the relationships among these interlocking systems, and the
way in which particular technological adjustments span them.

For 15 years following the great floods and droughts of the
1930s, the prevelant technological mode of *modifying natural
hazard systems* was in land treatment for the purpose of reducing peak run-off from floods or of minimizing water and wind
erosion of soil. Those activities developed from research of
the Department of Agriculture in its field experiment stations
and experimental watersheds, and centered upon reducing movement of water or soil at critical times under the impact of
extreme conditions of precipitation, temperature, and wind
velocity. The work continues, and much of it reveals severe
limitations, as well as opportunities for improved cultivation practices to reduce vulnerability to wind and water. The
task of the experimental efforts remains large, but no major
shift in emphasis seems required beyond those changes made
over recent years.

Beginning in the early 1950s, intense interest centered
upon the possibility of modifying weather to deal with
hurricane, tornado, hail, fog, drought precipitation deficiencies, and forest fire vulnerability. Within a few years,
weather modification attracted research and development commitments from a number of Federal agencies. Aside from the
classified activities of the defense agencies, weather

modification became the subject of vigorous experimentation
by the Bureau of Reclamation in seeding clouds to increase the
water supply of the Colorado and other southwestern streams,
by NOAA in exploring modes of modifying the velocity and
course of tropical cyclones, by the National Center for Atmospheric Research (NCAR) and the National Science Foundation (NSF)
in canvassing the possibilities of controlling hail in the
northern Great Plains, and by the Department of Agriculture,
Forest Service in its experiments on the prevention of lightning and on precipitation enhancement as a means of observing
forest fires. All of this work proceeded under a loose kind
of scientific collaboration provided through NSF (National
Science Foundation, 1966; National Oceanic and Atmospheric
Administration, 1973b).

A third type of modification which claimed attention only
in recent years is that of altering distribution of fuel supplies in forest areas by prescribed burning in order to
influence the vulnerability of forest to fires induced by
lightning or human causes.

A small but important sector of technology developed with
regard to the *detection* of hazardous effects and the rapid
transmission of information on their timing and whereabouts.
Perhaps the most elaborate application of technology developed
with regard to the flood forecasting system of the National
Weather Service, but complementary activities were the tornado
identification service and the hurricane research center in
Miami. These required more sophisticated use of telemetering,
radar detection, remote sensing, automatic data processing,
and computerized analysis. A new and still untried technology looms in the detection of earthquakes through the
application of dilatancy and related theories in predicting
the place and occurrence of earthquakes.

The monumental types of *technological intervention* are
those designed to protect against great events when they occur.
Flood control structures are notable, including detention dams,
storage dams, channel improvements, levees, and flood walls.
The works for protection against coastal erosion and storm
surge on the Atlantic, Gulf and Pacific coasts are less extensive. Advances are being made in engineering of slopes to
restrain damaging landslides.

In some degree every *structural design* for residential,
commercial or public purposes contains provision to deal with
a certain magnitude of stress induced by earthquake, wind or
water. However, explicit investigation of the design and construction of structures in order to minimize such losses centers for the most part upon the engineering of large buildings
against earthquakes (National Academy of Sciences-National
Research Council, 1969). As indicated in Chapter 11, a heavy
investment is made in research on earthquake engineering,
including the development of shaking tables and other equipment for simulating major crustal movements. Much less attention is given to other aspects of design of buildings against
wind and water. The primary interest there has centered in
the National Bureau of Standards, but its facilities have been
small and it has not been able to take a major role in affecting either the application of new technology to building
design or in speeding up research in those directions.

A small amount of attention has been given to the enhancement of *relief and rehabilitation* measures following a disaster, such as in facilitating emergency air transport. This
has not been the responsibility of any one agency and has been
scattered, except as it has been focused in work relating to
the storage and transport of emergency supplies under the
Defense Civil Preparedness Administration. A special kind of

structural provision is involved in shelters from nuclear
attacks, which conceivably could have application in some
areas to shelter protection against tornadoes and high winds.
The Agency for International Development has been concerned
with improving the quality of its relief operations overseas.

For each class of technological activity, at least seven
types of opportunities present themselves. One is the application of general principles of technological analysis and
design to questions of safety, such as redundancy of load paths,
provision of shelters and exits, and refinement of analysis of
load-carrying systems.

Much basic information important for design is lacking.
This is the case with detailed studies of structural failures,
of the causes of human casualties and property damage, and of
the behavior of real-life units in controlled environments. A
wide variety of problems present themselves in detailed design of connections and fastenings, ceiling, insulation, and
load transfer devices.

Construction practices themselves deserve a more thorough
investigation in terms of the appropriateness of the construction methods in various hazardous environments. In large
works such as flood control dams, costs may be reduced by
design improvements. For scattered, small activities such as
single-family residential housing, it is desirable to provide
for efficient and cheap supervision during the construction
period.

Use and maintenance problems include ways of assuring user-
compatible design and continuing inspection. Attention needs
to be given to new means of repair as an alternative to abandonment and destruction and as a way of facilitating basic readjustments in the design of old buildings during the repair
process. Technological design needs to be closely integrated

with heightened understanding of the extreme events themselves, as well as with the social constraints that govern investment in, or operation of the changed technologies.

Reviewing the whole range of technological activities as reported under the separate hazards in Chapter 11, it appears technological research currently offers large promise in two main directions. One is in the field of weather modification, where experimentation with cloud seeding and related devices already receives attention, and where the coordination among the efforts is perhaps as effective as practicable in view of the diversity of agencies involved. It is notable that the basic technology, as well as the definition of associated social problems, have not changed significantly over the past 15 years. A field that was expected by many enthusiasts to unfold in the early 1960s with massive import for national response to natural hazards, thus far fails to satisfy those high hopes.

The field of design and construction of buildings to mitigate damage from extreme events has proceeded in a less rapid and more lopsided fashion. A major part of the activity focuses upon improvement of engineering for high buildings. As noted in Chapter 11, this has made it possible to advance design for certain classes of new buildings, but it has not touched upon the large problems of redesign and repair of old buildings that are posed by the large proportion of buildings currently in use which were built under the old standards.

The San Francisco situation reveals the magnitude of the problem (Figure 9-5). Two-thirds of the floor space in the central building district was constructed before the Riley Act began earthquake regulations. Those were subsequently strengthened by successively higher standards. The chart does not show the extent to which existing buildings fail to conform to

FIGURE 9–5

Decade of construction of present buildings (1974)
in central district (ground floor space)

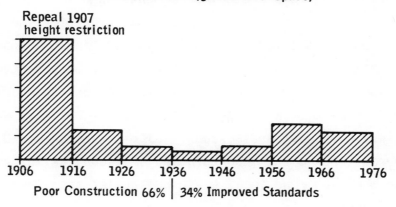

Repeal 1907
height restriction

1906   1916   1926   1936   1946   1956   1966   1976

Poor Construction 66% | 34% Improved Standards

Chronology of San Francisco building standard changes
affecting earthquake hazard

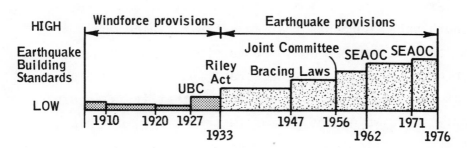

HIGH   Windforce provisions   Earthquake provisions

Earthquake
Building   Joint Committee SEAOC SEAOC
Standards   Riley   Bracing Laws
                        Act
                UBC
LOW

1910   1920 1927   1947   1956   1971
                1933   1962   1976

(Bowden and Kates, 1974)

prescribed standards.

Except for the activities of the National Bureau of Standards (National Bureau of Standards, 1973) there is no widespread movement to promote improvements in building design for flood-proofing, wind-proofing, and reduction of vulnerability to tornado. The effort is handicapped by lack of vigorous leadership from HUD. That department might be expected to be the principal agent through which improved designs for residential properties are widely disseminated. Similar opportunities in the commercial and industrial sector could be furthered through the incorporation of technical information in the municipal and local planning studies sponsored by HUD. HUD's investment in research has been notably low in relation to its total expenditures for mortgage insurance, housing construction, flood insurance, and urban planning.

Review of the situation with respect to floods, hurricanes, and earthquakes suggests that an activity which would offer early positive returns would be to step up research on the design of more resilient structures, and to assure dissemination of existing or new information so that it is incorporated promptly in building design and construction. NSF has taken a first step in this during 1974 through its announcement of a pilot grant program, but the work deserves expansion, particularly in close association with the basic research facilities of the NBS, and the wide-ranging potential influence of HUD.

Disaster Relief

Research on disaster relief and rehabilitation in the United States may have a great influence upon the national disaster scene at a time when nation, state, and local policies, both public and private, are in a state of flux. (See Mileti

[1975a] for a detailed description from which this is drawn).
Since 1953, the President has declared over 440 major disasters.
In contrast to a total of 141 declarations by the President in
the first decade (1953-62), there were 222 such declarations
in the next ten years (1963-72). During 1972 and 1973, almost
23% (94) of all declarations made since 1953 were issued in
just two years. This trend continued during the first half
of 1974, during which 38 declarations were made by August 30th.
Three general trends are apparent: 1. an increasing number of
major disasters to which the Federal government will respond;
2. increasing kinds of aid which the Federal government will
make available; and 3. increasing Federal expenditures for
involvement. Federal involvement in relief continues to
escalate, and an ever-widening gap continues between bene-
factor and beneficiary.

Relief and rehabilitation is performed by numerous groups,
agencies and individuals, and is composed of varied activities
cutting across national, state, and local boundaries. Several
important processes in the adjustment are understood--its
typical course of events, how people are helped, and who
usually helps--but equally important facets remain in doubt:
how the adjustment affects other adjustments and future vulnerability; how to best coordinate all the varied short- and
long-term services which the adjustment includes; what those
services should be in terms of their immediate and long-run
consequences; and how to prepare for use of the adjustment.

Relief and rehabilitation is not a one-dimensional adjustment to natural disasters; it is a series of linked activities.
These consist of three unique facets which are all related,
may overlap in time, and may exist for different lengths of
time depending upon the disaster event.

The emergency or *relief* period encompasses the first few

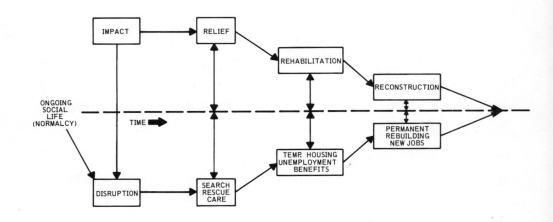

FIGURE 9—6
RESTORATION OF "NORMALCY" THROUGH TIME

---

hours or days after disruption and damaging impact, during
which efforts are made to provide care for all inhabitants
(food, water, clothing, shelter, medical care), and to stop
continued loss and disruption directly related to the hazard
agent.

The restoration or *rehabilitation* period is composed of the
subsequent few weeks or months, during which actions are taken
to put things and people together in such a way that they can
function temporarily. For example, temporary housing may be
offered subsequent to mass shelter, and the injured may be
transported to regular hospitals after field hospitals are
closed down.

Reconstruction is the third and final period; it is com-
prised of efforts to put things together and possibly to
improve on the past. Changes are then seen as permanent.
Figure 9-6 illustrates these interconnected sets of activities
as they occur after disaster.

In the last ten years the costs of relief and rehabilitation
efforts to the Federal Disaster Assistance Administration were
in excess of $1540 million; Small Business Administration Dis-
aster loans exceeded $3000 million, with over $800 million
canceled; and Farmer's Home Administration emergency loans exceeded $1375 million, with over $450 million canceled. Other
Federal, state, local, and private agencies are also involved
in relief and rehabilitation, increasing greatly the costs of
the adjustment. Policy is in flux on the character of what
and how Federal aid is offered. Public Law 93-288 shows intent
to provide for more planning in the reconstruction of a community than ever before, and a shift of responsibility to states,
including the authorization of new regional development agencies to assist in reconstruction. The nation has an opportunity to provide significant direction to the relief effort
through research which will bear on new policy formation and
preparedness.

Research opportunities - There are four central categories of
research opportunities on relief and rehabilitation: 1. what
services should be made available; 2. how they should be delivered; 3. how to be sure that they will be delivered when
they are needed; and 4. what are suitable research methods.
Services - Research is needed to determine the extent, if any,
to which specified relief and rehabilitation policies influence
other components of community vulnerability, preparedness, and
adjustments such as land use planning and enforcement, building codes and their enforcement, and the purchase of insurance.
It is urgent because of the increasing trend for relief and
rehabilitation policy to direct the use of other adjustments;
for example, Public Law 93-234 attempts to influence insurance,
and Public Law 93-288 to control land use.

The feasible policy alternatives should be assessed in light
of their primary effects; secondary effects; and long- and
short-run effects vis à vis future vulnerability through links
to the initiation and level of adoption of other adjustments.
Disaster situations, with all of the attention they receive
from public and voluntary agencies, can be catalytic in bringing to bear engineering, urban renewal, and social welfare
activities for fresh and integrated approaches at reducing
vulnerability in local communities.

This effort will require sophisticated analyses of political
processes at local, state, and, to a limited extent, the
Federal level. It will also require an examination of the
working of pressure groups, as well as the economic and social
interests of significant influentials in a community. It
would best be conducted by an interdisciplinary team.

In a cross-hazard design, a variety of disaster-prone communities should be studied in concert to achieve comparability
through standardized measures. These should be communities affected in the past, or potentially in the future, in which a
variety of alternative relief and rehabilitation policies were
or will be in operation. To permit generalization to the
alternative policy issues, it should cover varied types of
events, community policies, and areas. A sample of about 70
affected communities should be assessed.

An investigation of the effect of alternative policies on
local economies might produce significant results after five
years. Standardized indicators of aspects of the local
economy such as unemployment, underemployment, tax bases, and
trade should be developed. A series of disaster-stricken communities should be matched on relevant policy issues, community size, function, and other appropriate factors in the
recovery of a local economy. Some 40 communities would be

required.

The most direct and obvious indications of social disruption
can be seen in changes in family functioning following disaster,
and for an extended time period thereafter. A primary aim
should be to find how to anticipate which communities, families,
and individuals are most likely to suffer from a particular
geophysical hazard. For slow-rising floods, the answer may
not be too difficult, at least in certain years. For hurricane
and drought, however, sampling becomes much more difficult.

The monitoring of families and individuals should cover an
extended period of time and would be expected to be more
intense in the immediate aftermath of disaster. Selection of
samples should be from a variety of disasters, representing
the spectrum of geophysical hazards.

Service delivery - Searching studies need to be made of the
methods for providing assistance. Two such studies commend
themselves as promising information on the consequences of
the various possible assistance policies.

Most voluntary and public agencies involved in relief and
rehabilitation are striving to reach those they might serve;
however, the evidence is that certain groups are under-repre-
sented when it comes to the dispersal of opportunities and
benefits. Among these are the aged, the poorly educated,
members of the lower socioeconomic classes, persons whose background has instilled a negative value for anything perceived
as "charity", and a variety of other segments of the population.

Research on this issue would have three aims, each one contingent upon the findings of the latter: to what extent services are inequitably distributed; why this is so; and what
policy changes can be made to ameliorate the problem. It
might best achieve its ends by assessing the equity issue in a

variety of disaster situations such as Presidential, SBA, and
FHA declarations, and by reviewing the full range of degree
of disaster impact. For a four-year period an assessment could
be made of the dispersal of services in all three phases of the
adjustment in 30-35 disasters.

The coordination of all postimpact activity becomes more
tenuous as new agencies are formed, old ones are discontinued,
some reorganize, and shifts in personnel occur. Under Public
Law 93-288, increased efforts are made to upgrade efforts at
coordination and to build action for long-term recovery. However, if more and more responsibility for efforts moves to
state and local organizations, as current trends suggest,
agencies without much experience will find themselves faced
with a series of new events with which to cope. Although
problems of coordination do exist in the emergency and early
rehabilitation phases, the most serious problems of coordination are in later restoration and reconstruction, or in coordinating earlier relief and restoration efforts with long-term
reconstruction.

A cross-hazard study is needed which would examine the
ways of coordinating response both *within* restoration and reconstruction, and *between* relief, restoration, and reconstruction. For example, little is known about what temporary housing in restoration may mean to subsequent reconstruction. The
research effort should view relief, restoration and reconstruction as a total system and should include analyses of all units
within the system, and the role of personality traits and
individual experience in shaping personal needs.

A variety of hazard types and degrees of impact should be
assessed in terms of program effectiveness. It should make
some 20-30 case studies, and follow them through for several
years after the initial disaster through a good portion of

reconstruction.

Timing of service delivery - The adoption and maintenance of preparedness is the result of a combination of factors, some of which are known to be how often a hazard repeats itself in a locality, community hazard awareness, and legislated requirements for preparedness. However, other factors are not known.

Because preparedness adoption and maintenance are conceptually the same regardless of hazard, the research should address itself to all natural hazards, and may well include man-made hazards in its purview. It would have several goals: 1. to identify what factors account for varying levels of preparedness; 2. to identify the factors affecting the intensity with which preparedness is maintained; 3. to determine what level of before-the-event preparedness is needed to achieve adequate postimpact performance; and 4. the transformation of the knowledge into practical action through such agencies and groups as DCPA, FDAA, and the University of Southern California, and through the establishment of action groups in other universities and state governments.

Study of "before" measures of preparedness, of factors explaining different levels of preparedness, and of "after" measures of postimpact performance would require more than 100 communities because most communities in any such sample will not be subjected to serious events. There would be a small number of "experimental" communities (those suffering impact), and perhaps two types of control communities; communities which do not experience disaster during the course of the study (in addition to those which do), could nevertheless serve as sources of data for the studies of preparedness adoption and maintenance.

The study may well need to be continued for an extended period of time. Results may be expected on adoption and

maintenance within three to four years. However, results pertinent to how preparedness relates to adequate postimpact performance might not be realized for one to two decades.

Research methodology - Work is needed to develop and test the
validity and reliability of methods for monitoring the short-
and long-term effectiveness of all the efforts which comprise
relief and rehabilitation. The aim would be to develop monitoring procedures which are socially acceptable and accurate in
determining the primary and secondary consequences of efforts
during the emergency, restoration, and reconstruction periods.
It would require extensive pretesting, and later extensive
field testing, with a design which covers varied types of
events, regions of the country, and rural and urban communities. A minimum of some 60 to 80 different disaster and
relief and rehabilitation efforts would need to be assessed.
Once developed, the methodology would assist in carrying out
most other research on relief and rehabilitation.

Central research center - Many alternative relief and rehabilitation policies exist in an atmosphere of continuous changes.
However, improvements in policy and subsequent action generally
come only when adequate data are available on their consequences. A program may have a desired outcome during the
emergency and early restoration periods, but have a strong
negative effect recognizable only during the later reconstruction period. An alternative program may work well in
one part of the country, but poorly in remaining areas. Parts
of certain programs may produce highly desired outcomes when
used with lower social class clients, but not with persons of
other socioeconomic levels, producing a high level of inequity.
The true consequences of new or altered programs are often
unknown for many years. The hearings of the Senate Committee
on Public Works in 1973-74 were the first major attempt to sift

out the experience.

Improvements are not likely to occur when government policies are inconsistent and often in conflict, when the long-run effects of different programs are unknown, and when constraints to effectiveness are unknown. Although such knowledge is no guarantee for achieving improvements, it certainly is a prerequisite.

It should be the purpose of a central coordinating research center to initiate and coordinate research on relief and rehabilitation among interested researchers throughout the country, and to serve as a center through which findings could be made available to those responsible for practical action. A center could be established within an academic institution or some nongovernmental association. However, it should be formally linked to Federal and state agencies to facilitate the implementation of research findings.

Insurance

As in the case of land use planning and management, insurance figures as a possible adjustment for each of the hazards. It is involved in any investigation of practicable means of adopting one or more of the other adjustments. Insurance plays two major roles, as indicated in Chapter 3. First, it is a means of distributing losses without resorting to the devices of bankruptcy, reconstruction loans, and relief and welfare payments. Second, in the course of distributing those losses, with or without public subsidy, it has a capacity to exercise guidance over the extent to which people expose themselves to risk from natural causes.

Even if insurance were no more effective than a public welfare system in redistributing losses promptly from a natural disaster to prevent severe hardship to disaster victims, it

offers other benefits which would commend it to private and
public consideration. On the private side, it might provide
more direct and less cumbersome means of indemnifying losses
with greater dignity on the part of the recipient. On the
public side, it might guide future exposure to hazards in a
fashion that would reduce the net public losses from future
events.

It is abundantly plain that insurance, if provided on a
wholly subsidized basis, or on a basis that does not distinguish degrees of risk, would exacerbate rather than reduce
the nation's difficulties with natural hazards. An insurance
plan with uniform premiums which took no account of differences in risk would encourage continued or greater occupation
of hazardous areas. A system which would be so heavily subsidized that the individual policy owner regards the premiums
as insignificant would also have the effect of enlarging the
property and population subject to hazard if premiums were
substantially below subjective expected losses.

For each of the hazards the question has been raised on the
extent to which a well-designed insurance plan might affect
adoption of other adjustments. For example, it could be a
means of encouraging property owners to install devices or
rearrange their buildings in a way which would reduce losses.
As in the case of flood insurance, it could be contingent upon
enactment of suitable local land use regulations or building
ordinances.

This generates a set of subsidiary questions, some of which
are common across hazards and others of which are distinctive
to them. The traditional homeowners policy commonly covers
hazards from wind, lightning and tornado, without discrimina-
tion on local differences in exposure. Rates do differ re-
gionally. Insurance of flood and earthquake damages is never

carried in the same policy, but has a great deal in common
with processes involved on the part of property owners in
deciding whether or not to purchase a policy. It is important
to find out more about the reasons people buy or reject
insurance offerings, and in what circumstances they would
purchase additional or fewer amounts of insurance, were it
to be made available on different terms. The investigation
which was launched on flood and earthquake insurance at the
University of Pennsylvania in 1973 may be expected to point
the way to other detailed investigations.

Beyond the problem of understanding conditions affecting
insurance purchase for specified hazards, lies the question of
whether or not any radical changes should be made in the offerings of insurance, including all-risk insurance and systems of
mandatory or partly mandatory coverage.

A policy of mortgage institutions requiring insurance
against all or some segment of natural hazards, with the
premiums adjusted to the degree of hazard, might have a profound effect upon future changes in property at risk. The
beginnings of such a policy, so far as Federal agencies are
concerned, gets under way in 1975. Enlarged coverage insti-
gated by mortgage agencies would, however, heighten the need
by smaller insurance companies for a system of reinsurance to
protect them against catastrophic losses and possible bankruptcy.

The effect of mandatory insurance without proper safeguards
needs to be explored. It is potentially highly disastrous for
the nation, but the determination of suitable guidelines requires more investigation. The insurance industry is composed
of highly diverse units and groups with quite different methods
of operation. Any new investigations should deal carefully
with ways of building on, and cooperating with the immensely

complex organization of private insurance activity which carries
so much potential for influencing exposure to risk.

Analysis of individual hazards emphasizes the importance
of coordinated investigations into the reasons for adoption or
rejection of insurance, and into its consequences for individual
property owners. It also points the need for broader reviews
of the present offerings of the insurance industry and of ways
in which extension of coverage, with and without public support,
might affect the economy and its vulnerability to extreme
events.

Common Themes and Individual Hazards

Detailed estimates of cost for all of the research outlined
above are provided in the supporting reports cited in the
text.

Insofar as these new investigations of warnings, land
management, building design and construction, relief and
rehabilitation, and insurance are initiated, it would not
be necessary to carry out a number of the studies of
individual hazards described in Chapter 11. Those could be
scaled down in proportion to the depth of the research on
common themes. Contrariwise, launching all of the individual
hazard studies would make the work described in this chapter
less urgent, but at the cost of partially duplicating expenses
and less coordinated activity.

A principal obstacle to organizing research on these
common themes is the lack of a single Federal agency to take
the lead. In the absence of initiative from the Department
of Housing and Urban Development, the one agency with capacity
to initiate and guide such work is the National Science Foundation. Annual expenditures of the order of 50-100 person years
would be involved. Either agency or some combination of them

must take responsibility if the possible gains from work on common themes are to be reaped. Such efforts should proceed in tandem with practice of new research strategies.

CHAPTER 10

NEW RESEARCH STRATEGIES

Examination of individual hazards and of common research themes reveals the need for five new strategies in advancing investigations on major problems in this field. Three of these relate to modes of research. Two bear on how research results are applied and disseminated. All have very broad application to hazard research, and cut across common sectors of adjustment activity.

The three types of research dealing with new approaches to hazard studies are those related to postaudit, longitudinal observations, and a clearinghouse service. In the interest of translating research findings into prompt action, these should be supplemented by two quite different types of initiatives at the state and Congressional levels.

Taking all of these into account, along with the suggestions on individual hazards and research themes, it seems desirable to designate a few lines of work that deserve early initiation in the face of severe budget constraints.

Postaudits

Although for many years it has been common for Federal and private research groups to make hurried investigation of disaster situations following the occurrence of the event, no systematic provision is made for comprehensive and incisive postaudits of disaster situations. The common procedure is for an agency such as the National Oceanic and Atmospheric Administration (NOAA) to initiate a rapid review of the experience with a given disaster such as Tropical Storm Agnes. Agency personnel associated with forecasting or emergency measures are drawn into the appraisal, attention is concentrated upon lessons having immediate administrative and operational implications, and the results generally are used within the agency concerned.

In the case of Tropical Storm Agnes, the agency review was supplemented with a study by a panel appointed by the National Advisory Committee on Oceans and Atmosphere (1972). That form of outside appraisal is rare.

A variation of administrative review is sponsored by the Committee on Natural Disasters of the National Research Council which, with support from the National Science Foundation, provides small grants, generally in amounts of less than $5,000, to investigators to look into the circumstances and effects of an earthquake immediately after its occurrence. This provides a modest degree of flexibility and speed in making prompt response to a disaster. The reports commonly are from individual investigators or small teams of investigators on problems which they found to be of significance when they entered the disaster area.

Occasionally, a special report goes deeply into the effects of a localized disaster as in the case of the Lubbock tornado of 1970 (Thompson, *et al.*, 1970). A few appraisals have been made of public programs, such as the 1957 study of what was happening in use of the urban flood plains (White, *et al.*, 1958). None of these attempted to cover all aspects of the hazard.

Perhaps the most systematic set of sociological investigations was that initiated by the Disaster Research Center at the Ohio State University which, over the years, concentrated on the character of organizational response to disaster from the period of receipt of the first warning until the longer-term rehabilitation and reconstruction activities begin.

A recent effort by the Earthquake Engineering Research Institute (1975) shows promise. Under a grant from the National Science Foundation, the Institute developed a set of guidelines to be used in collecting geophysical, engineering, and social data after an earthquake. Support for the data gathering remains a problem.

The time is ripe to provide for thorough and imaginative investigation of all relevant aspects of a hazard situation from the time the disaster begins until a significant portion of the reconstruction period has elapsed. There is no precedent for such a comprehensive postaudit, but by putting together segments of types noted above, it is possible to outline what it would be desirable to do, and to estimate the funds, personnel, and administrative flexibility required to carry out the work.

At a minimum, the postaudit would state: 1. basic information about physical characteristics of the hazard in the study area; 2. characteristics of land use in the hazard area and adjoining areas; 3. types of adjustments which had been adopted in the area; 4. types of adjustments which had been proposed but rejected at some earlier time; 5. the extent to which the adjustments functioned during the extreme event in reducing losses of property, life, and social cohesion; 6. the way in which local, state, and Federal agencies responded to the disaster as related to their plans for preparedness and their legal missions; and 7. how changes in operating procedures or legislative and administrative policies of the agencies might have led to a more effective response to the disaster, as with the scenario approach described in Chapter 6. Other items might be included but this would be the essential set of points to be canvassed. These inquiries would cover many of the common themes noted in the preceding chapter. If completed, they would reduce the need for a number of specific data collection projects proposed in Chapter 11. Such studies nevertheless are listed in Chapter 11 to emphasize their importance in dealing with individual hazards.

The work should be organized so that a general plan of investigation is defined by those agencies which might be expected to participate. The plan would not be put into effect until a disaster occurred, but then it should be commenced on very short notice, marshalling whatever facilities would be brought together from the Federal agencies. A university group should be available on a standby basis to bring in personnel who had been trained for the purpose but have other employment. Personnel from the interested Federal and private agencies should be involved, but they should not be permitted to dominate the operation.

There should be a continuing interplay between individuals associated with agencies having direct administrative responsibility and those playing a more critical observer's role.

The study of the great Alaska Earthquake of 1964 was undertaken with ponderous negotiations, without any prior preparation, and with extreme difficulty in gathering either the funds or the scientific personnel to participate on such short notice (Krauskopf, 1973). The investigation and publication of findings stretched out over a period of eight years: work having to do with reconstruction activities properly should have taken that length of time, but other parts were unduly delayed because of administrative and physical difficulties. A project of that magnitude is not contemplated for each postaudit, but it is believed that from the experience with the Alaska studies and with short-term investigations after other earthquakes, it should be possible to put together a program in which three studies could be initiated in a year. The program would cost approximately 16 person years annually. The total cost allocated for a postaudit should be extended over the period required to follow up the activities during the reconstruction period.

The only precedent for a thoroughly independent postaudit
of this sort is in studies by the General Accounting Office.
The GAO's investigation of execution of responsibilities under
the Flood Insurance Act and under the President's Executive
Order of 1967 demonstrates the desirability of such review of
the operation of Federal programs. It would be important,
however, for the studies to be designed to take account of
the full range of responses, as well as the exercise of specified Federal authority. Research on the functioning of state
and local agencies should go on simultaneously.

The responsibility for the postaudits might come properly
either under a designated research arm of the Executive Branch
or under the General Accounting Office. In either event it
would be important to provide for participation by a standby
research facility in a university or several universities, as
well as for collaboration with the state and local agencies
involved.

It would be desirable to limit the number of investigations
initiated in any one year to two or three, and to maintain a
minimum of one such investigation each year. Even at a relatively small scale, at least one postaudit would flex the administrative muscles of the agencies and research institutions
involved and gradually build up a store of experience which
could be compared and applied more widely.

Longitudinal Observations

A number of the promising research efforts require repeated
data collection over time. This is especially true of
research aimed at better understanding of the impact that
one adjustment (such as increase in the proportion of homeowners buying insurance) has on the adoption of other

adjustments (municipal land use management, for instance).
When investigating such interactive consequences, it may be
necessary to gather data periodically over a period of years
within a sample of communities.

The longitudinal approach stands in contrast to the cross-
sectional or static approach where observations are made at
only one point in time. The cross-sectional approach is con-
siderably less expensive, but it does not provide the basis
for measuring and understanding change. A longitudinal design
may do that, but has its pitfalls. Most basic questions about
the effectiveness of flood hazard adjustments must be answered
by examining time series data not from a single flood, but
from several floods within the same community over time. To
assess the long-term effectiveness of a campaign to sell
hurricane insurance to homeowners, evidence must be obtained
on not only the proportion purchasing the insurance for the
first time, but also the proportion failing to renew their
policies.

The nation should learn what type of community preparedness
planning leads to adequate response when disaster threatens.
As stated in Chapter 9, a basic problem is how to maintain an
adequate level of preparedness in communities where direct
impact or "near miss" disaster events are widely spaced in time.
What are suitable measures of preparedness? What is a measure
of adequacy of response when the disaster occurs? To obtain adequa
answers to these questions, longitudinal research will have
to be funded even though it is expensive and does not promise
early results.

When initiated, longitudinal studies require stable support.
Experience with them in the social sciences has been mixed; in
some fields large volumes of data have been collected without
providing major new insights into the processes at work.

Longitudinal research on hazards adjustment has rarely been
done (Mileti, Drabek and Haas, 1975; Drabek, *et al.*, 1973;
Haas, 1973-75).   Sometimes, as in the case of Drabek's study
of the Topeka tornado aftermath, it was by accident.   Project
design should proceed with care, and it probably would be desirable to divide the responsibility among two or more institutions so that there would be opportunity for imagination and
experimentation in setting up the study programs.

Because it is impossible to predict areas in which the
extreme events will occur over the next ten years, ingenuity
is required in design (Baker and Chapman, 1962).   A program
might provide for base observations for a large number of
communities supplemented by intensive studies in those where
events occur.   As indicated above, it is just as important to
understand what happens in communities which go long periods
of time without a disaster as it is to pursue the disaster
trail.   Moreover, much insight into the reasons for the growing susceptibility to catastrophes can be gained from examining the communities where dramatic events have not spurred
action on the part of public authorities.

A funding level of approximately 150 person years over a
period of ten years would seem to be in order.   The funds
should be assured so far as practicable for the entire period
of observation, and they could be divided among two or more
institutions for purposes of comparative design and observation.   A firm commitment to long-term data collection and
analysis is needed.   That commitment can be secured only with
firm assurances of stable funding.

Clearinghouse Service

At least two dozen traditional academic disciplines contribute
insights and method to the reduction of losses and disruption

from natural hazards. Workers in one discipline proceed with
only a limited knowledge of the perspectives and findings flow-
ing from the others. No single approach to the study of hazards
is adequate and no single adjustment will suffice.

It has been demonstrated that almost all of the disciplines
within the physical sciences, social sciences, engineering and
a few within the biological sciences are needed. The professionals, such as seismologists, hydrologists and city planners,
tend to associate with each other and to read almost exclusively from the publications within their own discipline or
trade. For those who are interested, it is difficult to find
out what hazards research is being carried out by workers in
other disciplines.

There is now no central location, within or outside government where a scientist can go for basic information on who is
engaged in research on hazards or who could use the findings.
Few gatherings attract workers from more than a limited number
of disciplines. Workshops provide a ready opportunity to exchange detailed information and to argue the merits of various
perspectives, but they need to be attended by professionals
from the full range of disciplines and by policy makers from
the various levels of government.

If the tempo of studies on hazard problems is to be quickened, there is need for a service which:

1. can secure relevant information covering current
research efforts, programs, and publications and conferences dealing with geophysical hazards;

2. will disseminate that information including
access to data banks and simulation programs, to
potential users; and

3. can spot emerging trends and special needs and
initiate conferences, symposia, and meetings at
appropriate intervals among scientists and representatives of user groups.

A further function of a clearinghouse would be to facilitate
systematic exchange of experience and information with other
industrialized countries carrying on research and action programs related to natural hazards. There already is such a
clearinghouse activity in Japan. The United Nations family
provides several agencies, including the United Nations
Disaster Relief and Preparedness Office, the World Meteorological Organization, the United Nations Educational, Scientific and Cultural Organization, and the United Nations
Economic and Social Council, through which bits of information
on disaster work may be exchanged. There is, however, no one
point in the United States at which the diverse stream of
natural hazard research converges for communication purposes.
The nearest approach is the Ohio State program centering on
organized response to disaster impact.

A clearinghouse service would provide constructive links
between those who develop information, knowledge, and perspectives on geophysical hazards and those who need those
products. It probably can be carried out best outside of a
single governmental agency, although there is strong legislative authority for the Department of Housing and Urban Development to move in that direction. It would require management
with broad perspective and wide contacts, since most of the
data collected will have to flow from voluntary cooperation.
An initial budget of three person years annually would be
required.

Comprehensive State Studies

The Disaster Relief Act of 1974, (Public Law 93-288) authorized Federal grants of up to $250,000 within one year to each
state for the preparation of plans to deal with prevention
and preparedness of natural disasters. The pertinent

language follows:

SEC. 201. (a) The President is authorized to establish a program of disaster preparedness that utilizes services of all appropriate agencies (including the Defense Civil Preparedness Agency) and includes--

(1) preparation of disaster preparedness plans for mitigation, warning, emergency operations, rehabilitation, and recovery;

(2) training and exercises;

(3) postdisaster critiques and evaluations;

(4) annual review of programs;

(5) coordination of Federal, State, and local preparedness programs;

(6) application of science and technology;

(7) research.

(b) The President shall provide technical assistance to the States in developing comprehensive plans and practicable programs for preparation against disasters, including hazard reduction, avoidance, and mitigation; for assistance to individuals, businesses, and State and local governments following such disasters; and for recovery of damaged or destroyed public and private facilities.

(c) Upon application by a State, the President is authorized to make grants, not to exceed in the aggregate to such State $250,000, for the development of plans, programs, and capabilities for disaster preparedness and prevention. Such grants shall be applied for within one year from the date of enactment of this Act. Any State desiring financial assistance under this section shall designate or create an agency to plan and administer such a disaster preparedness program, and shall, through such agency, submit a State plan to the President, which shall--

(1) set forth a comprehensive and detailed State program for preparation against and assistance following emergencies and major disasters, including provisions for assistance to individuals, businesses, and local governments; and

(2) include provisions for appointment and training of appropriate staffs, formulation of necessary regulations and procedures, and conduct of required exercises.

(d) The President is authorized to make grants not to exceed 50 per centum of the cost of improving, maintaining and updating State disaster assistance

plans, except that no such grant shall exceed $25,000
per annum to any State.

It is significant that under the earlier version of the
act the states were authorized to receive funds on a match-
ing basis and that only a few states made the necessary
commitments and applications. This reflects previous lack of
interest or understanding of the possible significance of
such work.

There probably will be more alacrity in claiming the new
funds. The crucial question at this stage is how far the
funds will go in laying the groundwork for genuinely comprehensive plans that incorporate prevention activities. If
that aim is to be attained, the states need help with the ways
in which the funds could be appropriately expended and the
kinds of results that might be expected within the low level
of expenditures authorized. The Federal Disaster Assistance
Administration (FDAA) has organized a few workshops, but
there is no positive effort to use the Section 201 funds to
stimulate a continuing research and planning program in each
state.

The Council of State Governments may be of special use in
applying the results of its study of natural disasters. Personnel of the Council's Disaster Assistance Project work
closely with FDAA's regional offices in an endeavor to improve
state legislation and planning. It will be essential to share
the experience of states such as California which are far advanced in planning to prevent natural disasters.

This Assessment suggests a few lines of fruitful action for
the states that have not yet moved vigorously: 1. identifying
those areas in the state which are particularly vulnerable to
natural hazards; 2. specifying the range of choice that is open
to public agencies in dealing with preparedness for or prevention
of disasters in such areas; 3. drafting preparedness plans for

those vulnerable areas; and 4. instigation of actions
at the local and state level which would reduce the
vulnerability of the areas to disaster.

The study should draw heavily upon information already available in the hands of Federal and state agencies, and should
work closely with whatever clearinghouse may be established.
More difficult would be the allocation of responsibility among
state agencies, local agencies, academic institutions, and consulting and nonprofit organizations in each state. The
number of qualified people in this field at the national level
is small, and the pool of experience is small.

A Federal agency should be designated to take the lead
either directly or through the Council of State Governments in
arranging for conferences, bibliographic services, and consulting assistance in organizing these state studies over the
next two years. An expenditure of approximately ten person
years would be in order for this purpose.

Congressional Overview

In view of the large number of Federal agencies that share
responsibility in one fashion or another for hazards research
and of the urgency of relating this research to the practical
daily problems that are encountered at the local, state and
Federal levels, it would be desirable to provide for some kind
of periodic overview by a Congressional committee of the whole
range of activities in the field. The need is sharpened by
the lack of a single Federal agency that is prepared to exercise leadership in coordinating and stimulating research on
hazards. Although HUD-FDAA has large legal authority in the
field, it has been unwilling to take a lead role. In these
circumstances an overview would seek to take account of the
current status of Federal response to hazards, identify those

points at which the need for new research or the obligation of
existing research findings are most urgent, and ask how the
status of activities with respect to one hazard such as earthquakes compares with those with respect to other hazards such
as landslides.

It is not clear under the reorganization of Congressional
committees where such a responsibility might best lodge, but
it seems likely that the exercise can be carried out at very
low cost, that it could be correlated with the budget reviews
which are carried out by the Office of Management and Budget,
and that it might help in providing perspective for work in
individual fields or sectors of the field, as well as in
suggesting desirable reallocations of research funding from
year to year. Unless there were clear agreement among the
Congressional committees having some authority for the Federal
activities that a single overview would be helpful, the exercise could create fruitless trouble for the agencies.

A number of problems which deserve attention cut across
agency lines. The natural hazard activities should be related
to broader policies in disaster relief. The Federal government should determine whether or not, and to what extent, it
will encourage the development of a model or set of models
that would make it possible to simulate the occurrence of
various extreme events in the United States economy. The
type of work outlined in Chapter 6 suggests what might be done
in this direction if an appropriate data bank were built up.
There would be no point in initiating the project unless there
were continuing interest in using the facility on the part of
Federal agencies or research groups supported by Federal
agencies, and unless it were judged that the returns from such
simulations would warrant continuing expenditures for the maintenance of the model and data base. This is only one of the

issues meriting consideration in the absence of strong executive leadership.

There would be merit in making such a review once each ses-
sion of Congress, and in publishing the resulting hearings with
a staff summary as a framework for more detailed hearings on
substantive authorizations and appropriations which would apply
to individual agency programs and appropriate committees.

What To Do First

Considering these strategies and the specific needs for work
on individual hazards presented in the concluding chapter, a
few of the suggested new activities warrant early attention,
even in the face of budget restrictions. These are activities
that either promise very substantial and early returns, or
that would be likely to influence the course of other research
programs bearing on natural hazards.

As may be seen in Chapter 11, the priorities given to each of
the sets of research opportunities would depend upon what combination of national aims is in view. However, some of the
proposed efforts have such broad implications that they commend themselves for early action as consonant with most of the
national aims. The following are selected as especially
influential:

1. Support and extension of state emergency planning
for disaster prevention and preparedness under Section
201 of the Disaster Relief Act of 1974 (see pp. 231-234).

2. Formulation and dissemination among municipal
officials, architects, engineers and housing agency
financial officers on proved and improved methods to
design buildings so as to resist damage from earthquake, flood, tornado and windstorm (see pp. 206-208).

3. Refinement and extension of ways of introducing
considerations of hazard vulnerability into land use
planning at local and state levels (see pp. 193-200).

4. Studies and experimentation intended to develop a warning service associated with NWS forecasts to enhance thorough dissemination to, and response by people affected (see pp. 188-193).

5. A clearinghouse for information on current research and new research findings of use to municipal, state, and Federal officials and private consultants (see pp. 229-231).

HAZARDS AND THEIR DISTINCTIVE OPPORTUNITIES

Each of the 15 geophysical hazards has its own physical characteristics and social effects. Likewise, each offers distinctive opportunities to improve the national welfare through new
research.

The common themes which cut across desirable studies of the
various hazards, as reviewed in Chapter 9, embrace the four
clusters of work which would benefit from being carried on by
groups of interdisciplinary investigators. They would be
advanced best by employing the five strategies outlined in the
preceding chapter. Large benefit is to be gained from attack-
ing the problems of natural hazards by strengthening those
methods.

Whether or not new studies are organized around the common
themes employing the suggested strategies, distinctive combinations of investigation are required for each hazard. These
sets of research opportunities are described in this chapter.

Certain of the work recommended could be undertaken either
in pursuit of a common theme or independently. For example,
the warning studies in flood hazard areas could be launched
separately from studies of hurricane warning systems or they
could be joined in a larger effort. As a practical matter, in
view of the organizational structure and funding arrangements
of the National Oceanic and Atmospheric Administration (NOAA),
it might prove easier to let the flood and hurricane warning
studies go their own ways, providing only for coordination,
rather than forcing them into a single mold. Whichever way
the research is organized, the urgent need is to get on with
studies of warning systems to balance the present emphasis
upon forecasting methods.

The procedure used in assessing these sets of research

opportunities, as outlined in Chapter 8, pursued the questions
in Figure 1-1. These included the following steps. The available information on the hazard, its cost and benefits, and the
present public policies for dealing with it were examined.

Estimates were made of the ways in which likely changes in
understanding or techniques would lead to alterations in individual or public policy, and thereby affect national aims with
respect to:

1. reduction in net losses to property;
2. reduction of casualties;
3. avoidance of social disruption;
4. protection and enhancement of natural environment; and
5. more equitable distribution of costs and benefits.

In some instances these estimates were developed through
simulation of the systems involved, and in a few instances
they were checked by reference to scenarios of events in a
selected area.

The descriptions of present conditions and likely effects
of a change in adjustments were reviewed by individual consultants, by special workshops, and by participants in a national
conference.

In the light of those reviews, the statements were again
revised and an effort was made to assign weights to the probable impacts of new research upon each of the national aims.
The economic, health and social stability aims were considered
in terms of the likely effect for 1. average conditions over
time, and 2. the nation's vulnerability to catastrophic dislocation.

In addition, judgment was made on the expected success of
the research, if undertaken, and on the likelihood that those
results would be translated into action affecting individual
and public policy.

Upon the basis of those judgments, the possible lines of research either were eliminated as promising no significant benefits, or were arranged in evaluation tables and in lists of recommended studies.

This assessment procedure involves a large number of judgments in which the weighting factors are difficult to identify or quantify. It nevertheless provides a systematic framework within which to compare the numerous opportunities in terms of their likelihood of advancing specified national goals. The grounds for selecting a particular set of research activities thereby are made explicit. For example, if reduction in casualties is the primary national goal, research opportunity sets for tornado warning systems offer greater promise than research on tornado insurance. Any of the judgments is subject to challenge, and all may be expected to change as new evidence becomes available, even if the national aims remain stable.

Research costs are estimated in terms of person years rather than dollars in order to suggest the number of professional personnel involved, and to avoid variance due to changes in costs and to the requirements of different types of research. The average figure at 1974 prices assumed for one person year is $60,000. This includes the salary of a full-time professional worker and clerical, computational and secretarial support. Where the research is wholly a review of available data, this average dollar cost may be high, but where it involves new data collection or the development of new equipment or observational devices it may be much too low.

The estimates of cost in person years will be regarded by many research administrators as too low to provide confidence that the results will be obtained. The estimates have been kept on the low side out of a concern to avoid the rather extravagant estimates of cost that attach to so many pleas for new research, and also out of conviction that if new work is begun in a modest fashion and then demonstrates effective results, its continuation and expansion can be justified more readily.

The assessments which follow are drawn from detailed reports and are colored by judgments of individual authors and workshop participants. A detailed list of supporting documents is given in the Bibliography. They provide a basis for evaluating a wide variety of research opportunities according to the stated criteria.

Hurricane

A hurricane is a severe tropical cyclone that produces winds with sustained velocities of 74 miles per hour or higher. Such storms are called hurricanes when they occur over the North Atlantic Ocean, the Caribbean Sea, the Gulf of Mexico, or the Pacific Ocean off the west coast of Mexico. They are known by other names in other parts of the world.

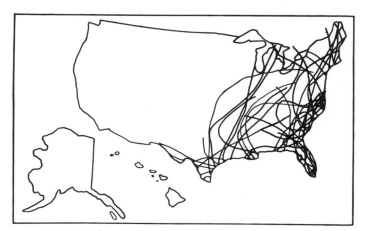

Tracks of Devastating Hurricanes 1938-1973

In the United States, most hurricane damage occurs in a narrow zone along the coastlines of the Atlantic Ocean and the Gulf of Mexico. Hurricanes, more than any other natural hazard affecting the United States, have been characterized in

recent years by decreasing loss of human life but rapidly
increasing property damage. These trends have two main causes
in that major improvements in hurricane warning services have
occurred concurrently with accelerating residential and commercial development along the Atlantic and Gulf Coasts. During
the last decade, the rate of capital development in these vulnerable areas was three times that for the United States as a
whole. Research directed toward developing new management
policies is needed to ensure that increasing development will
not result in growing losses to the nation.

The hurricanes that strike the United States are born as
tropical weather disturbances over the Atlantic Ocean north of
the equator. Many tropical disturbances develop during each
hurricane season, but meteorologists are not able to predict
which ones will grow into hurricanes of the magnitude shown in
the sketch map and which ones will not.

The structure of the hurricane is usually characterized by
spiraling bands of clouds separated by lanes of relatively
clear air. The bands spiral inward toward the hurricane's
"eye"--a comparatively calm circular area at the center of the
storm. As the air spirals in a counterclockwise direction
toward the hurricane's low-pressure center, it picks up great
amounts of heat and moisture from the warm ocean. In the wall
around the eye, the warm air rises, producing clouds and heavy
rain and releasing heat energy which enhances the upward
motion and accelerates the velocity of the inward-spiraling
winds. Driven by the enormous energy of the tropical ocean,
the hurricane may continue to grow in size as well as intensity as it approaches the United States coast. By the time it
moves across the coastline, it may have a diameter of 300
miles, with an eye 30 to 40 miles across. In spite of the
high wind velocities within the hurricane, the storm itself

travels fairly slowly; hurricanes usually pick up speed as they drift northward from the tropical easterlies into the midlatitude westerlies.

Radar and aircraft penetrations have yielded substantial information about the structure of hurricanes, but not much is known about the mechanisms that govern their development and movement. Of the six hurricanes that develop in the North Atlantic in an average year, two may be expected to strike the coast of the United States. Figure 11-1, which shows estimates of the probability of a hurricane affecting 50-mile segments of the United States coastline in any one year, reveals that all parts of the United States coastline are not equally vulnerable.

A large proportion of the damage is caused by the storm surge, an influx of high water driven by the hurricane. Other components of the hurricane hazard are high velocity winds, flooding of streams induced by the heavy rainfall, and accelerated erosion by coastlines. Occasionally a hurricane is accompanied by tornadoes. The major property damage and loss of life come from a combination of storm surge and wind.

More than six million people currently are exposed to the storm surge hazard. About 40% of them live in zones where hurricanes may be expected with a return interval of 1-25 years, and more than half of that population is located along the Gulf Coast.

As noted in Chapter 10, a dramatic increase in population, several times the average for the United States, has taken place in the most hazardous zones. Typically, this population has a larger proportion of people in the over-64 age group, particularly in the coastal counties of Florida; is highly urbanized; and relies increasingly upon the use of mobile homes. The value of capital in manufacturing activities in

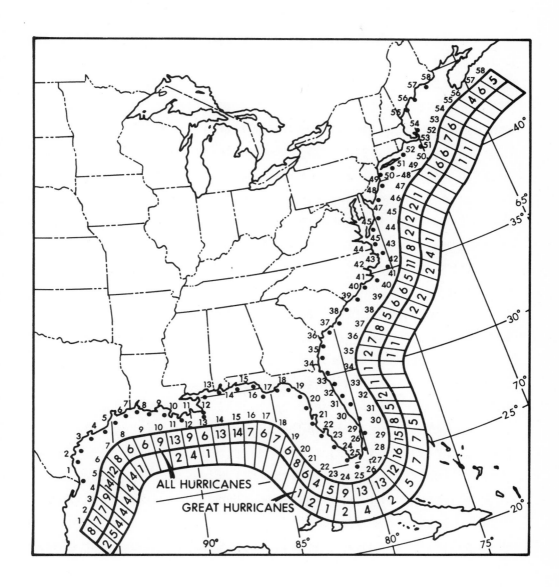

FIGURE 11–1

PROBABILITY (PERCENTAGE) THAT A HURRICANE (WINDS EXCEEDING 73 MPH 33 m s⁻¹) OR GREAT HURRICANE (WINDS IN EXCESS OF 125 MPH 56 m s⁻¹) WILL OCCUR IN ANY ONE YEAR IN A 50 MILE (80 km) SEGMENT OF THE COASTLINE (after Simpson and Lawrence, 1971).

the coastal areas almost doubled over the period 1959-1969.

Figure 11-2 shows the dollar damage per hurricane from 1934 through 1970. Note that the vertical scale is logarithmic, and that the volume of losses in the upper brackets is very high. Average annual damages from hurricanes in the United States during the period 1951-1960 were about $250 million, in constant (1957-1959) dollars, and increased to about $400 million in the next decade. Loss of life, chiefly by drowning, tended to decrease, but there is now some suggestion that the trend of decreasing fatalities may be reversed as a result of increasing urbanization, inadequacy of evacuation routes, insufficient places of refuge, and failure to enforce codes of building safety.

Reduction in losses from hurricanes may be achieved in a number of ways. The first full-scale hurricane modification experiment was conducted in 1961. It has been difficult to interpret the results of such experiments because of the large natural variability of hurricanes and the very few suitable opportunities to experiment with mature storms. Marginal reductions in wind velocity produced by cloud seeding could reduce property damages substantially.

Protective structures against storm surge have been authorized for construction by the Corps of Engineers in more than 30 localities at costs ranging from $100-$400 per foot of shore protected. As much as 70% of the cost of a project on non-Federal public land is met by the Federal government, but about 68% of the hurricane coast is privately owned, and is therefore ineligible for Federal financial aid under existing legislation. An important problem regarding the protection offered by such structures is the fact that earlier estimated probabilities of hurricane occurrence and storm surge height are being revised rapidly as better data become available. In addition,

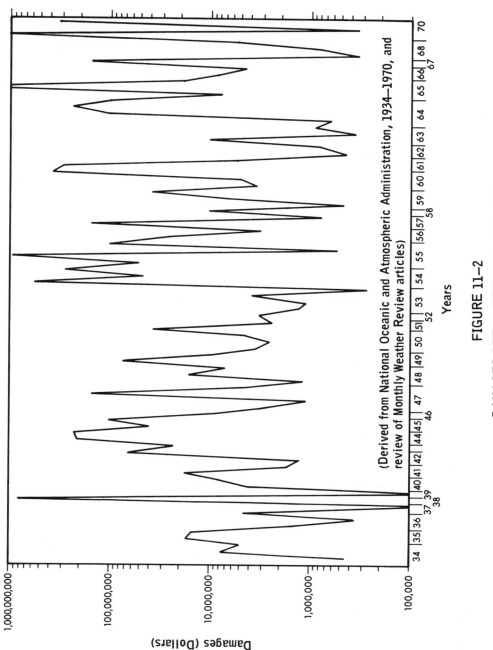

FIGURE 11–2

DAMAGES PER HURRICANE, 1934–1970

especially along the Texas coast, heavy withdrawal of petroleum
and other fluids from beneath the ground has caused the level
of the surface to drop as much as five feet.

In sparsely populated areas or recreational seashores,
defense systems of sand dune construction and stabilization
are used. Present cost-sharing arrangements indirectly encourage coastal communities to use such locally funded and relatively cheap techniques.

In some areas, with the encouragement of building codes,
structures are built to withstand certain specified intensities
of wave action and wind. Buildings can be constructed that
will withstand hurricane-force winds, but building to withstand
the heaviest wave action is impractical. Problems in enforcing
building codes are acute, and economic incentives as well as
governmental direction are necessary to apply available information effectively. The results of current research on the
effects of wind and water are not adequately communicated to
those responsible for implementing land use regulations.

Among the opportunities for reducing damage are the enforcement of mobile home tiedown anchorage requirements, and the
installation of shutters and other protective devices on buildings.

The hurricane warning system includes forecasts of velocity
and landfall which have increased in reliability over recent
years: the error in predicting the distance to be covered by
a hurricane in 24 hours has been reduced from 182 to 122 miles
over the past 10-15 years. Improved numerical hurricane
models, satellite observations, and better reconnaissance have
all contributed to better forecasting. However, it is believed
that a plateau in forecasting methods may have been reached.
In the years immediately ahead, only modest reduction in forecasting error will come from more precise application of

methods already in use, including refined observational techniques and improved computer calculations of storm surge. Public responses to the hurricane watches and warnings are variable, and the National Hurricane Center warning offices face the
problem of "overwarning." A few examples illustrate the varying response: 97% of the residents of Cameron Parish, Louisiana, evacuated before Hurricane Carla, whereas only 65% of
Chambers County, Texas, responded to the same type of warning.
The hurricane warning system is estimated to save about $25
million during an average season.

Chiefly as a result of the National Flood Insurance Act of
1968, the number of local governments adopting land use controls for the hurricane zone has increased rapidly. Major problems include the exact delimitation of contours of equal vulnerability and the calculation of probability of storm surge
levels. Local government leaders are often reluctant to impose
land use restrictions because of the potential economic repercussions.

In summary, research on hurricanes is concerned primarily
with physical studies designed to improve prediction and test
the feasibility of hurricane modification. Future efforts must
also focus on understanding the social ramifications of the hurricane hazard and encouraging more adaptive human responses.
This shift poses the problem of the institutional responsibility for new research. The National Oceanic and Atmospheric
Administration's past emphasis has been on meteorological research, whereas the new questions that arise are concerned with
social responses and economic implications, particularly in the
light of rapid changes in the economy. Research in five major
areas is needed to ameliorate the effects of hurricanes: 1.
hurricane modification, 2. land use management, 3. insurance,
4. relief and rehabilitation, and 5. warning systems.

TABLE 11-1
RESEARCH OPPORTUNITIES-HURRICANE

Research Opportunity	National Aims								Research Findings	
	Economic Efficiency — Reduction of Net Losses Benefits-Costs		Enhancement of Human Health — Reduction of Casualties		Avoidance of Social Disruption		Environment — Protection or Enhancement	Equity — Distribution of Costs and Benefits	Expected Success of Research	Likelihood of Adoption
	Average	Cata-strophic	Average	Cata-strophic	Average	Cata-strophic				
Hurricane Modification: Hurricane dynamics Technology Socioeconomic effects	High	Low-Neg	High	Low-Neg	High	Low-Neg	?	Low	Low	Med
Warning Systems Evacuation methods Dissemination and response	Low	Low	High	High	Med	Med	NA	Med	High	Med
Land Use Management Hazard mapping method Adoption of management Socioeconomic effects Hurricane-proofing technology adoption	High	High	High	High	High	High	High	Low	High	Low
Insurance Policy formulation Adoption of insurance	Med	Low	Low	Low	Low	Med	Low	Med	Med	High
Relief and rehabilitation Trends, policy, socioeconomic effects	Low-Neg	Low-Neg	Low	Low	High	High	NA	High	Med	Med

Med = Medium   Neg = Negative   ? = In doubt   NA = Not applicable

Hurricane modification - Continued research on hurricane dynamics should provide a better basis for assessing hurricane modification techniques. Studies should be conducted on the economic, political, social, and psychological impacts of modification in order to determine more accurately under what conditions and at what risk a hurricane should be seeded. These impact studies will require new funding for 15 person years of effort over a three-year period.

Land use management - Rapid changes in land use continue to expose more people and buildings to the storm surge from hurricanes, and to concentrate people in areas where evacuation and rescue operations are difficult. Land use management to assure that development is adjusted effectively to the hurricane hazard requires determining the productive use of coastal land, considering the market for land and buildings, and estimating the potential risk of hurricane damage and the possibility of mass deaths of people stranded by hurricanes. Such estimates for individual communities are difficult to make, as well as to explain to interested citizen groups. Uniform zoning regulations, building codes, and subdivision regulations will not solve the problem. These measures need to be adjusted to local conditions and closely coordinated with other measures of land acquisition and overall urban planning if they are to receive serious consideration by communities.

Obstacles to the adoption of new land use plans and regulations must be recognized. They include not only opposition from real estate interests, but also psychological and social difficulties in dealing with extreme stress. Studies should also develop new measures or combinations of measures that would suit the particular needs of specific communities such as Augusta, Georgia, and Miami, Florida.

Research on hurricane-proofing should play an integral part in the decision to locate activities in hazard zones. It would involve development of flood- and wind-proofing technology, together with studies of how technology is adopted by individuals and public agencies. One hundred fifty-five person years of effort are needed over a ten-year period.

Insurance - A careful examination of the conditions in which flood insurance is adopted in areas with flooding problems from rivers is already underway. It should be extended to hurricane areas. Wind hazard is covered in the standard homeowners package. Investigation should be made of the special insurance requirements which distinguish the hurricane hazard from flood or wind, and the relation to other public policies, including tax deductions, concerned with distributing the losses. Means should be found for accelerating and improving the accuracy of mapping of hazard zones. Finally, the complex determinants of an individual's decision to purchase or not to purchase insurance need to be identified. The work should be done over a four-year period and will require about 19 person years of effort.

Relief and rehabilitation - Knowledge of the efficiency and equity of current relief and rehabilitation measures in dealing with hurricanes is meager. Moreover, very little attention has been given to effects of relief and rehabilitation activities on the national or regional social systems in contrast to alternative adjustments which might be adopted. It is important to identify the obstacles that hinder communities from organizing community preparedness programs and to study the effectiveness of rehabilitation programs. Specifically, there is need to probe the efforts and goals for dealing with family

disruption. Such studies should also consider public expectations of relief and rehabilitation, in contrast to the realities of operating programs. Thirty person years of effort over
a five-year period will be required to carry out the research.

Warning systems - An effective hurricane warning system is the
best immediate line of defense against massive loss of life
along the increasingly crowded coastal areas. More effective
observations from aircraft and satellites, combined with dynamic modelling offer the possibility of reducing landfall estimate errors to as little as 100 miles within a decade. Given
the prospective level of detection and forecasting skill and
assuming that meteorological research at present levels will
continue to advance that skill, improvements in warning dissemination and response can come from three research foci.

    First, the modes of delivering the forecasts and the charac-
ter of the message content should be examined. This would
include ascertaining what messages people receive in addition
to the official messages produced by the National Weather Service; how the various messages are interpreted; whether the
credibility of a message varies by medium (radio, television,
newspaper, neighbor); to what extent messages are outdated when
received; and what type of message content tends to produce the
desired response most consistently. This research thrust will
allow us to spot ways to improve current dissemination practices.

    The second research focus should be on individual and family
response to hurricane-threat information. Examination should
be made of what kinds of individuals and families have contingency plans for taking prompt protective actions; the extent to
which property owners take simple, relatively inexpensive steps
to reduce potential damage; certain key events in many

communities which may trigger prompt action among the majority
of the threatened population (police cruisers with loudspeakers
going block-to-block); the extent to which people are aware of
the limited evacuation routes from densely populated, low-lying
areas such as in southern Miami; and what impact, if any, various types of public education efforts have on response behavior.
The research should consider effective ways to help residents
new to coastal areas learn quickly about the hurricane threat
and the protective actions they should take. Hurricane watches
and warnings are valuable only to the extent that citizen response to the information reduces casualties and property loss.
We need to know how to reduce casualties further and how to
keep property losses from soaring.

Finally, research should be aimed at ways of improving evacuation to safe areas. As population density increases in many
coastal areas, it may cease to be practical to rely on evacuation by a few routes. It may be necessary to evacuate vertically as well as horizontally by using well-constructed high-
rise buildings as evacuation centers. Although this technique
has been considered by a few cities, the legal, political,
logistical and structural considerations need to be carefully
examined. Among these considerations are how many owners of
highrise buildings will permit their halls and rooms to be
occupied by evacuees; who is liable for any damage or personal
injuries that might occur; and how city officials and others
involved in planning for vertical evacuation can anticipate
how many persons will come to highrise buildings rather than
evacuating to other areas. Where vertical evacuation is used,
its impact on all other aspects of warning response needs to
be examined.

These three research foci complement each other, and the
work should be conducted concurrently, preferably by a single

research group. It will require the close cooperation of the
National Weather Service, Federal Disaster Assistance Administration, Defense Civil Preparedness Administration and state
and local officials. Seventy-four person years of effort over
a ten-year period will be required to complete all three components.

Flood

Floods are the most widespread geophysical hazard in the United
States. Nearly every community in the nation has some kind of
flood problem, chiefly resulting from inadequate drainage systems for runoff water produced by heavy rainfall from storms.
Overflowing rivers and streams cause significant flooding in
about half of the communities and over at least 7% of the total
land area of the United States (see Figure 11-3). The time of
year when floods are likely to occur varies widely for different regions.

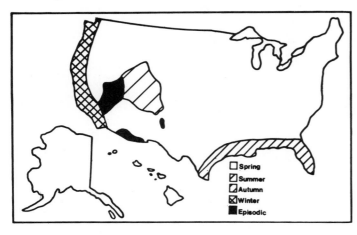

Seasons of
Flooding

□ Spring
◪ Summer
◩ Autumn
⊠ Winter
■ Episodic

Floods account for larger average annual property losses
than any other single geophysical hazard. In recent decades,
total property losses from floods increased, although the per
capita loss remained fairly constant. There is no solid evidence as to whether or not the benefits increased

FIGURE 11–3

LOSSES IN UNITED STATES FLOODS 1905–1972

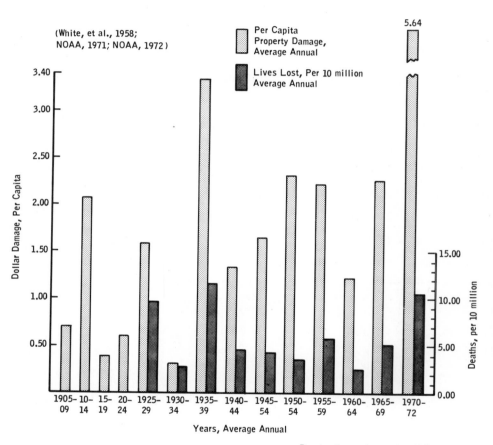

proportionately. The number of deaths caused by floods has decreased, but a series of catastrophic events such as the floods that occurred at Rapid City, South Dakota, and in the wake of Tropical Storm Agnes in 1972, could result in an increasing death toll from floods.

Now, more than any time since 1936, new research could lead to great benefits in reducing deaths and property damage from floods. This research should be designed to gain new knowledge, or to identify new applications of existing knowledge, in the management of lands that are subject to flooding.

The nation's capacity to deal with flood problems can be greatly enhanced without increasing the total level of Federal expenditures by reallocating funds from conventional flood-control construction and survey operations to research efforts designed to develop innovative and powerful new methods for dealing with flood problems.

Although dams on the mainstreams and tributaries of major rivers throughout the nation stand as massive monuments to flood-control policies established in 1936-1938, those policies have been seriously questioned in recent years. Their emphasis on mainstream dams and a combination of smaller dams and land treatment along tributaries has proved to be highly effective from an engineering point of view, but other complementary approaches that are being developed and tested show considerable promise, and the present situation is remarkably flexible.

Federal flood insurance became an operating reality through the Flood Insurance Act of 1969, and in the next five years policies covering more than $8 billion in property damages were written in 4,339 communities. Land use management policies suggested by a national flood task force in 1966 are beginning to operate at the working level as the result of a Federal Executive Order and new administrative procedures. The Federal

Disaster Assistance Act of 1974 incorporated new Federal assistance and cost-sharing policies that are being tested. The
Flood Insurance Act provided Federal incentives that have resulted in increasing land use regulation by local agencies, and
state agencies have been given additional authority to deal
with flood problems. Flood plain information reports have been
produced for about 1,000 communities. Insurance, flood-
proofing, and land use management are taking an increasing
share of the mix of adjustments to flood hazards.

The pace of this activity was quickened by record-breaking
flood disasters of recent years, which showed that existing
flood-control measures fell far short of providing adequate
protection against such catastrophes.

Most publicly supported research on floods has been concerned with the behavior of the flood waters themselves--the
hydrology and the hydraulics of flood flows. Most of the few
studies of the social impacts of floods that have been done have
sought solutions to specific flood-related problems or have
examined the responses of communities to particular flood disasters.

If the nation's capacity to deal with floods is to be enhanced, it is important to move rapidly along different lines
of research. A review of the Rapid City experience and of
potential effects of changes in the mix of adjustments to the
flood hazard suggests that new research could reveal changes
that would greatly reduce the costs that result from present
uses of flood plain lands. Five major lines of new research
are indicated: 1. improving control and protection; 2. warnings and flood-proofing; 3. land management; 4. insurance,
relief and rehabilitation; and 5. basic data and methods.

<u>Improving control and protection</u> - The principal limitation on

new construction of works for control and protection such as
levees, channels and dams is the availability of sites with
acceptable construction and environmental costs. Among all the
available measures, protection works can be undertaken with the
greatest confidence of success. However, the indirect results
have been shown to include additional encroachment on flood
plains by commercial and residential development. It should be
possible to reduce annual losses by at least 20% if the economically feasible works could be built rapidly and cheaply enough.
In addition, there is the possibility of reducing construction
costs by as much as 10% through changes in construction design.

There is little likelihood, at present levels of technology,
that capabilities or construction costs of the larger works
will change to permit a different range of social choice among
possible adjustments to floods. Design and construction characteristics of dams, levees, and channelization have not
changed substantially over the last quarter century. Less refinement and uniformity prevail in design methods and components for urban storm drainage.

There is an urgent need to improve storm drainage design in
close correlation with larger flood control works and with
highway design. The hydrologic basis for estimating flood size
and frequency also requires refinement. Greater attention
should be given to basic models of interrelations among precipitation, temperature, vegetation, soil, slope and groundwater
conditions. These models are particularly needed for areas
subject to urbanization which produces changes in runoff and
channel characteristics.

Special opportunities lie in improving the design of urban
highway, sewer, and storm drainage systems to reduce property
damage and social disruption, as well as to minimize environmental impacts of new works. Channel hydraulics should be

studied to permit designing new channels for maximum stability
with minimum environmental costs. Both lines of research may
be expected to develop slowly, and call for an effort of about
150 person years over a ten-year period.

Warnings and flood-proofing - More effective flood warnings
would promote a significant reduction in loss of life, as well
as in social disruption and damage to structures and their contents. Known techniques should be applied immediately to improve flood warnings, working with the whole network from the
forecast to response by individuals. Present flood warning
systems can be made more effective by improving responses to
warnings, including measures such as temporary evacuation and
rescheduling of activities or application of protective cover-
ings.

Forecasting methods and equipment should be improved by providing less expensive, more effective means of extending the
data base, partly through improved equipment for making observations or processing data and preparing forecasts. This
effort should build on the current research on numerical forecasts and on the data base for mesoscale phenomena, at a level
of about 100 person years over ten years.

Effective response to flood warnings at the local level
could significantly reduce losses of life and property. The
gap between actual and possible performance of a warning system
is large in most communities. Some causes of this discrepancy
are ignorance of emergency procedures, ignorance of the hazard
and the loss reductions that are possible, individual or group
preferences for other types of action, lack of forecasting system credibility, and institutional inertia. Changes in forecasting methods and equipment will not yield significant social
results unless they are accompanied by changes in the complete

warning system so that the forecast is heeded in a beneficial
manner.

New investigations are needed on how to get optimum response
to flood warnings by people in the areas that are threatened.
The special investigations which are often made on an ad hoc
basis after a major disaster should be evaluated. Conspicuous
examples of effective and ineffective response in communities
threatened by floods should be compared. A continuing review
should be made of the experience of specific communities with
the adoption of warning programs and of their operations over
a period of the next decade, comparing city types and physical
and administrative links between NOAA and the community. A
continuing examination of performance should be developed,
using a stratified example of communities subject to floods.

This research should be initiated by NOAA, using contractors
or grantees as suitable, and should be done in conjunction with
an operating system under another branch of the agency. An
effort of 60 person years over a period of ten years is appropriate.

Improvements in flood-proofing technology should be applied
as rapidly as new building or major renovation takes place in
flood plains. Much of it can be adopted at little or no cost
if included in the design of construction or repair operations.
Although there have been a few areas, such as the Golden Tri-
angle of Pittsburgh, in which flood-proofing has been developed,
and the experience summarized in a Corps of Engineers technical
report, no systematic research effort has been undertaken.
Work should be done to improve water-resistant materials,
water-tight joints, strength of walls against hydrostatic pressure, impervious sealants in various forms, and water-tight
closures for doors, windows and other openings.

Both laboratory tests and postdisaster field observations

should be involved. The work in materials test laboratories, including hydrostatic pressure test tanks, should be supplemented by studies of more effective emergency or warning-contingency actions. Accurate data are needed on stage-damage relationships of various types of flood-proofing, as applied to different kinds, sizes, and ages of structures. Any innovations would be tested and practical instructions prepared for use by architects and engineers. The activity would require collaboration among the Corps of Engineers, U. S. Department of Housing and Urban Development (HUD), and the National Bureau of Standards (NBS). Expenditures of at least 40 person years over ten years are needed.

While permanent flood-proofing has been utilized extensively in a few flood plains, it has not been generally adopted.

In that connection, it is desirable to trace out the effects new flood-proofing has on warning response and willingness to support land management and flood-protection programs. A careful inquiry would require about five person years over a five-year period. It is important to investigate the unanticipated consequences of flood-proofing and the conditions under which its adoption or rejection takes place. Social aspects of the choice among the new or available technologies, including economic and political obstacles, should be studied. An exploratory study of these questions would require about ten person years over five years.

Land use management - In the long run, flood plain land use management may be the single adjustment most likely to reduce national flood losses, although it is not certain that it would yield the largest net benefits to the nation. In the short run, the amount of damage reduction will be relatively low because of complications in removing existing properties from the path of flood waters. Nevertheless, structural measures, flood warnings, and flood-proofing will be of little value if the reduction in damages that they accomplish is more than offset by new damage potential resulting from additional development in flood plains.

The present rate of urban expansion into the flood plains of the nation, much of it gaining no special benefits from flood plain location, lies between 1.5% and 2.5% per annum. Land use management would need to prevent 80-90% of the uneconomic part of such expansion to be effective in damage reduction. It is likely to work better in keeping new development out of flood plains than in encouraging the transformation of uneconomic use. A highly optimistic rate of removal from flood plains would be 3% per annum, but methods for doing this and the possible influence of subsidies or tax incentives remain to be determined.

Although the rate of adoption of flood plain land use management programs by communities was glacially slow until recently, many communities now have flood plain information and regulations, guides and model ordinances are available, and the availability of flood insurance is contingent on the adoption of adequate land use plans and management. A study of the adoption or rejection of land use management affecting flood plains could point to ways in which the spread of this innovation might be accelerated. To promote sound local measures, adoption processes must be appraised and evaluated. This investigation could be done by small university groups examining the adoption process in neighboring flood plains. One institution, working closely with interested Federal agencies, the Council of State Governments, Council of State Planning Agencies, the National Institute of Municipal Law Officers, and the National League of Cities, could give direction and encourage exchange of findings. A continuing study costing 30 person years over a ten-year period would provide a basic foundation for detailed local investigations.

There is widespread doubt of how well the brave efforts at insurance and regulation are working. It is notable that direct experience of the Federal government with enforcement of Executive Order No. 11296 has not been analyzed in a broad fashion, although evidence that it is not being enforced accumulates.

Examination of the social effects of land management measures is a continuing task, but there would be merit in a relatively short-term investigation of the experience of a few communities. Emphasis would be on methods of estimating impacts on unemployment, social amenities, and the welfare of individual property owners. The results would provide information essential to Federal and state efforts to stimulate solid community activity. The methods would help local appraisal of experience elsewhere. A pilot investigation would cost a minimum of eight person years over five years.

The question of how flood plain management is coordinated with other measures of local, state, and Federal agencies should be investigated in parallel. This should consider shifting policies of public agencies, impacts of the social forces that shape the consequences of those policies, and administrative obstacles to changes in standards and methods. The work should be based in a nongovernment group which is less directly subject to the friction of contending agencies. It would require about 30 person years over ten years.

Insurance, relief and rehabilitation - The effects of various policies on insurance, relief and rehabilitation on flood plains has not been analyzed with care, and it is important to examine the effects along six separate lines.

The effort to determine the factors affecting the decision to buy or refuse insurance, now under way at the University of Pennsylvania, should be supported and extended.

The precise and concrete ways in which insurance and relief activities can be associated with land management, as well as with flood-proofing and flood protection measures, deserve exploration and appraisal. This work should be done cooperatively by the Corps of Engineers and university groups.

There is much discussion of developing a comprehensive and compulsory flood insurance program. This recurrent idea should be subjected to careful assessment of opportunities and pitfalls, as related to all-risk insurance. An exploratory study of five person years covering five years would be in order.

Measures such as requiring rebuilding in less vulnerable locations, providing relocation plans in advance of disaster, or requiring flood insurance as a prerequisite for a loan should be examined within the framework of the Disaster Relief Act of 1974 to determine to what extent they could assist in promoting more socially effective use of flood plains. The actions of private property owners and public officials under these various policies should be observed in different land use and flood situations. Expenditures of ten person years over a five-year exploratory period are warranted.

The full range of costs and benefits, including social dislocation and social and psychological damages to individuals, should be carefully analyzed for a few sample communities over a period of time with an eye to reducing such costs. This type of analysis should be tried for ten person years over an experimental period of three years to see whether or not it yields results directly helpful to Federal and state administrators.

Studies should be made of the provision of public assistance to flood victims. A series of case studies over a five-year period should assess community and individual response, including coordination of public activities and long-run recovery measures, in the interest of assuring sensitive response to the needs of disaster victims. A selection of 10-20 communities per year would probably be sufficient to offer useful findings to local, state and Federal agencies. Fifty person years of effort are needed.

Basic data and methods - Additional knowledge of floods, the losses they cause, and the ways in which public choice can be facilitated is needed as a basis for all of the research described above. Such basic knowledge can be increased through studies of flood frequency, hazard mapping methods, damage variables, public participation in project choice, and methods of estimating an optimal mix of adjustments.

Flood frequency estimation methods should be improved, with special attention to estimating flood flows and conditions of changing rural and urban land use, and to the factors affecting the return intervals of extreme events. An expenditure of about 100 person years over ten years would improve application of current data and analysis in engineering design, and would improve on conventional techniques for frequency estimates for current projects.

The pace of work carried out by the Corps of Engineers in its flood plain information studies, and by the U. S. Geological Survey (USGS) and HUD in delineating flood hazard areas is slow in comparison to the rate at which growth is taking place. Research at a cost of 25 person years over five years should be designed to find quicker and more economical means of collecting and presenting flood plain information in a form that would serve administrators and be admissible in court.

More precise knowledge of the nature of flood damage as it
is related to differences in stage, flood onset, duration,
velocity, and sediment load would make it possible to evaluate
more precisely the effects of various management measures and
to take account of catastrophic events. The research in this
field which was recommended by the Task Force in 1966 still has
not been carried out. This research should be supplemented by
laboratory experiments, careful observations of field experience, and systematic surveys and the incidence of damage in
selected stream reaches. It should be done over a ten-year
period at a total cost of about 100 person years.

Because new concern with environmental quality has increased
the weight placed on environmental values, the methods employed
by local government and citizen groups in evaluating flood-
protection schemes require critical appraisal and improvement.
The reasons for these changes, as well as the means by which
public participation in project review can be increased, deserve thorough investigation. An expenditure level of 100 person years over ten years seems appropriate.

In facilitating community choice, simplified methods are
needed for optimizing the combination of adjustments for a
given flood plain, taking environmental effects into account.
Local governments need concrete help along these lines if they
are to react responsibly to Federal plans, and studies now
underway in universities should be expanded and intensified for
a period of five years at a total cost of 60 person years.

Budgets and institutions - Figure 11-4 suggests that the nation
has arrived at a certain level of tolerance for catastrophe in
the range between elimination of disaster and building of a
catastrophe of national proportions. This is shown on the
vertical axis. The nation also has attained a position where

TRENDS AND LIMITS OF ADJUSTMENTS TO FLOODS

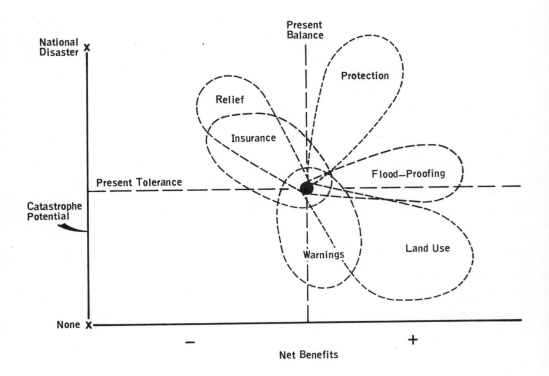

FIGURE 11-4

it still suffers large average annual losses from occupying its
flood plains, pays heavy adjustment costs, but reaps net benefits. Any change in flood plain use would either increase or
decrease those net benefits. These are shown on the horizontal
axis. (Similar diagrams were prepared for other hazards but
are not reproduced in this volume.)

The potential effects of changing adjustments as a result of
applying new research can be shown as either increasing or
decreasing catastrophe potential, and as either increasing or
decreasing the net benefits of flood plain occupation. Protection tends to increase catastrophe potential from property loss
although not from fatalities. Flood-proofing alone is beneficial without increasing catastrophe potential, but it may promote increased and more casual use of the flood plain. Warnings alone can reduce the catastrophe with a slight increase in
annual benefits. Relief would bring net social losses while
increasing catastrophe. Depending upon its character, insurance would foster moves in any direction. Land management
would reduce catastrophe while increasing net benefits. It
seems possible that as much as 25-35% of mean annual losses
could be reduced over a period of 20 years by a combination of
measures other than construction of protection works.

The several research sets that have been outlined here are
evaluated in Table 11-2 to indicate the extent to which they
would be likely to contribute to reductions in property losses,
fatalities, social dislocation, and environmental degradation,
as well as to changes in income distribution in society. They
also are rated as to the probability of achieving the expected
returns, and of those returns being translated into practical
action.

Present research expenditures favor research on hydrology
and drainage as applied to the design of new construction

TABLE 11-2
RESEARCH OPPORTUNITIES—FLOOD

Research Opportunity	National Aims								Research Findings	
	Economic Efficiency — Reduction of Net Losses Benefits-Costs		Enhancement of Human Health — Reduction of Casualties		Avoidance of Social Disruption		Environment — Protection or Enhancement	Equity — Distribution of Costs and Benefits	Expected Success of Research	Likelihood of Adoption
	Average	Cata-strophic	Average	Cata-strophic	Average	Cata-strophic				
Control and protection Urban sewer and storm drainage Channel hydraulics	High	Low	Low	Low	Med	Low-Neg	Low-Neg	Low-Neg	Med	High
Warning Systems and Flood-Proofing Forecasting methods Improved warnings Flood-proofing technology Aspects of proofing Feedback effects of flood-proofing	Med	Med, Low or Neg	Med	High	Med	Med	Low	Med	Med	Med
Land Use Management Adoption processes Social effectiveness Coordination of land measures	Med	Med	Low	Med	Low	Med	High	High	Med	Low

-continued

TABLE 11-2 continued

Research Opportunity	Economic Efficiency Reduction of Net Losses Benefits-Costs Average	Cata-strophic	Enhancement of Human Health Reduction of Casualties Average	Cata-strophic	Avoidance of Social Disruption Average	Cata-strophic	Environment Protection or Enhancement	Equity Distribution of Costs and Benefits	Research Findings Expected Success of Research	Likelihood of Adoption
Insurance Hazard awareness and policy purchase Linkage with land use Compulsory insurance Influence on flood loss potential	Med	Low	Low	Low	Med	Med	Low	High	Med	Med
Relief and Rehabilitation Impacts Methods of providing relief	Low-Neg	Low Neg	Low	Low	Med	Med	Low	High	Med	Med
Basic Data and Methods Flood frequency estimation Hazard mapping Flood damage variables Public participation in choice Optional mix of adjustments	High	Med	Low	Low	Med	High	High	Low	High	NA

Med = Medium   Neg = Negative   ? = In doubt   NA = Not applicable

projects. However, the combination of activities likely to
spur and strengthen the greatest flexibility in the development
of fruitful use of flood plains includes studies of land use
management, warnings and flood-proofing, and insurance.

Stubborn institutional blocks stand in the way of reorient-
ing research efforts. The Corps of Engineers has been reluctant to sponsor social and behavioral research. The Tennessee
Valley Authority has largely withdrawn from the field. HUD
has avoided commitment to numerous lines of investigation
relating to disaster preparedness and prevention. On the
other hand, both NOAA and USGS are demonstrating greater flexibility in taking on new problems. Reduction in the institutional obstacles presented by the other agencies does not
appear to rest primarily on provisions in legislative authority. Administrative adjustments are required.

Although all of the suggested research should proceed
rapidly, several areas have special urgency. Improvements in
estimating flood loss, methods of comparing alternatives,
and methods of flood-hazard mapping would strengthen the basis
for other investigations. The longer they are delayed, the
more slowly advances will come in applying available technology and social organization. At the same time, the studies
directed toward improving community warning and reaction
systems, insurance schemes, and the application of known
flood-proofing and land use regulation techniques should be
advanced. They promise substantial benefits for many communities, and they are not dependent upon technological innovations.

The present state of flux in national flood policy, and
the growing concern of local and state agencies with floods
sets the scene for major changes in the way the United States
manages its flood plains. Research along the five lines

outlined above could have significant influence on the nature
and direction of those changes.

Thunderstorm Hazards: Lightning, Tornado and Hail

The thunderstorm is a severe local storm produced by a cumulonimbus cloud, or thunderhead, a towering mass that can be six
miles or more across and six miles high, containing one-half
million tons of water and enormous amounts of energy that often
are released in the form of high winds and three violently
destructive natural events--lightning, tornadoes, and hail.

The thunderstorm results from a strong upward movement of
air produced by atmospheric instability created by heating at
the ground, or by the movement of a mass of cold air that
forces warm air upward along a line known as a cold front.

In the United States, thunderstorms are most common over the
Florida peninsula, where they occur on an average of 80 to 100
days per year in the southern part of the state. Another center of high thunderstorm frequency is over the Colorado and
Wyoming Rockies, where thunderstorms occur on an average of 70
days per year. West of the Rockies, thunderstorm frequency
decreases to a minimum of five days or less per year along the
Pacific Coast. Over the eastern two-thirds of the United
States, thunderstorm frequency generally decreases from south
to north.

Tornado - Of the three hazards associated with thunderstorms,
the tornado is the most violently destructive. Known colloqui-
ally as a "twister", the tornado nearly always forms a funnel--
a rapidly rotating column of air extending downward from a
cumulonimbus cloud. This phenomenon is usually called a funnel
cloud if it does not reach the ground, and a tornado if it
does. Maximum wind velocities in the funnel probably range

from 175 to 200 miles per hour, and the air pressure inside the
tornado may be 10%-20% below that of the surrounding atmosphere.
The physical capacity for damage depends on the violence of its
winds and the length and width of its path, as well as on the
pressure differential. Although tornadoes with tracks more
than 200 miles in length have been reported, the typical tornado track is about 16 miles long.

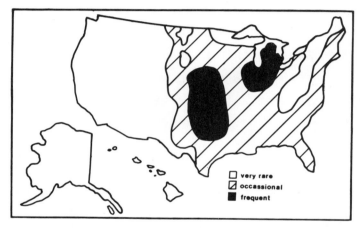

**Frequency of
Tornadoes**

☐ very rare
▨ occassional
■ frequent

   Tornadoes and lightning are the biggest killers among
weather hazards. During the last half-century, tornadoes
killed 9000 people, compared to 5000 deaths from floods and
4000 from hurricanes (Figure 11-5). Although the tornado death
rate has been declining, a family of tornadoes or a single
tornado with a long track can kill more people in a single day
than the long-term annual average number of tornado deaths.
   The 1925 Tri-State Tornado killed nearly 700 people as it
cut a path of destruction 219 miles long and up to a mile wide
across Missouri, Illinois, and Indiana. On Palm Sunday in
1965, 37 tornadoes killed 266 people in six Midwestern states;
the more than 125 tornadoes that occurred on April 3 and 4,
1974, killed more than 300 people in ten states. During the
1960-1970 decade, property damage from tornadoes exceeded $50
million in each of six years, but the average annual property

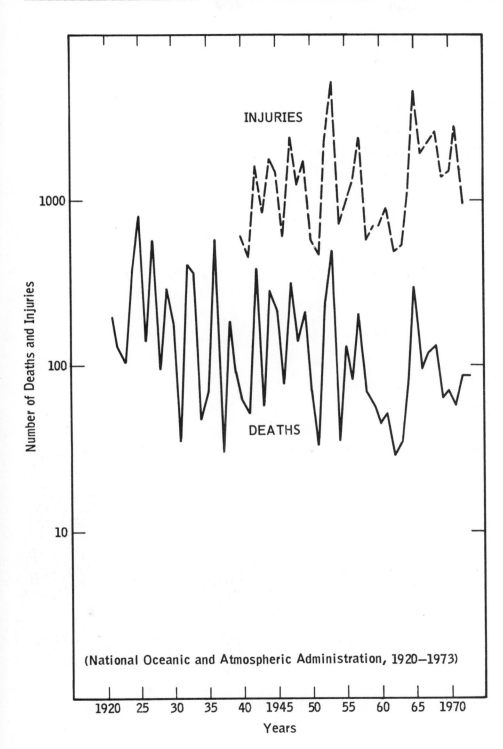

FIGURE 11–5

TORNADO DEATHS AND INJURIES,
1920–1973

damage from tornadoes is relatively low by comparison with
flood and hurricane damage.

Tornadoes have been reported throughout the United States;
they are most common in the Midwest and Southern Great Plains,
and occur only rarely west of the Rockies. Figure 11-6 shows
the tracks of tornadoes recorded in the United States between
1953 and 1958. The region of high tornado frequency known as
"Tornado Alley", extending from northern Texas through Oklahoma
into Kansas, is clearly discernible on this map as well as the
sketch map.

Several paradoxes are apparent in the pattern of tornado
losses in the United States. First, although the increase in
tornado damage to property over the years appears to be propor-
tional to the general economic growth, deaths from tornadoes
declined. Second, although the potential for human injury and
death from tornadoes appears to be greatest in the Midwest and
southern Great Plains, such casualties occur most frequently
in the South. Third, although the establishment of the National Severe Weather Warning System in 1953 undoubtedly influenced
the declining rate of tornado casualties, this decline had
already begun before 1953. Factors that may influence these
anomolies in loss patterns are differences in the frequency and
severity of tornadoes, urbanization, building construction
practices, community preparedness, hospital facilities, warning
systems, and distinctive behavior characteristics of individuals.

Modification of tornadoes by cloud seeding has been proposed
from time to time, but not enough is known about the physics
and climatology of tornadoes to judge whether or not such
efforts might be physically possible or economically feasible.
Even if cloud seeding should prove effective in modifying tornadoes, their short lifetime would make it difficult to reach

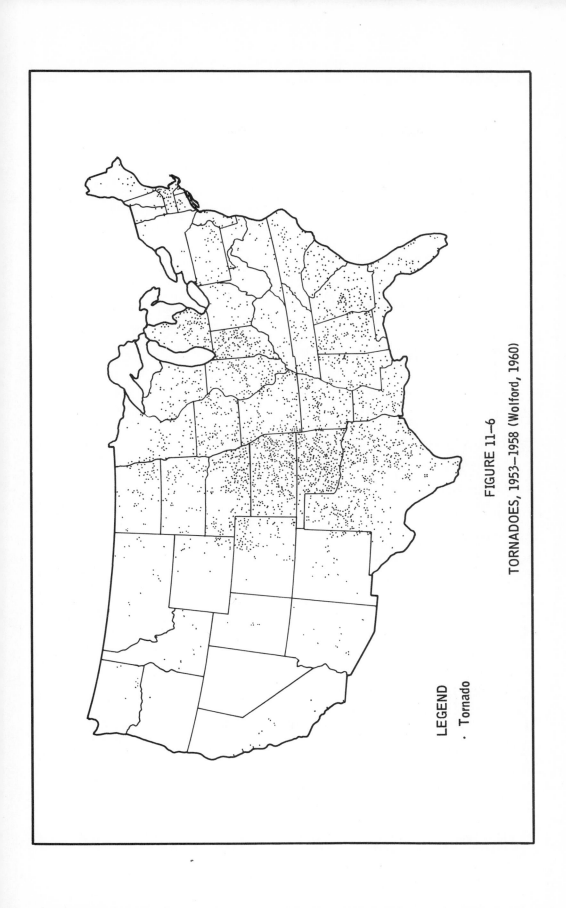

LEGEND

· Tornado

FIGURE 11–6

TORNADOES, 1953–1958 (Wolford, 1960)

TABLE 11-3

TORNADO INCIDENCE AND DEMOGRAPHIC DATA FOR TEN TORNADO-PRONE STATES

State	Ranking	Tornadoes per 10,000 square miles	Number of tornadoes[1] 1953-1970	Population[2]		
				1960	1970	1990[3]
Oklahoma	1	8.7	1092	2.368	2.559	3.173
Kansas	2	6.2	905	2.179	2.249	2.635
Indiana	3	6.1	396	4.662	5.193	7.037
Massachusetts	4	5.1	79	5.149	5.689	7.710
Florida	5	4.6	481	4.952	6.789	9.913
Iowa	6	4.5	450	2.757	2.825	3.317
Missouri	7	4.3	533	4.320	4.677	6.245
Nebraska	8	4.2	585	1.411	1.483	1.737
Illinois	9	3.9	388	10.081	11.113	14.278
Texas	10	3.9	1879	9.580	11.196	14,960
Total			6788	47.459	53.773	71.005
United States			11556	179.334	203.185	269.759
%			58.7%	26.4%	26.4%	26.3%

[1]Data from OEP, 1972, Volume 1, p. 38
[2]In Millions
[3]OBERS projections (U. S. Water Resources Council, 1972)

the storm and seed it quickly enough to avert damage to communities in its path. No research aimed specifically at tornado modification is being conducted now; most research efforts are aimed at understanding the dynamic processes and at developing more effective detection and warning systems.

The warning system is the single most important factor influencing human response to the tornado hazard. Forecasting is difficult because of the suddenness of the onset and the relatively short duration of tornadoes, the extreme variability of the typical tornado striking any particular area, the limited knowledge of the dynamics of tornadoes, and the limited extent of the weather observing system. The National Severe Storm Forecast Center has the responsibility for monitoring areas that may have severe local storms.

It appears that people sometimes become "immune" to tornado watches because the watches occur so frequently in a particular area without being followed by a tornado strike or funnel cloud. This topic points to a more basic problem that should be examined carefully: with current tornado forecasting skills, what *modes of delivering* the messages and what type of message content are most effective for the majority of the threatened population? Radio may be quite effective during commuting hours and television in the evening, but the hours from 11:00 p.m. to 4:00 a.m. are also vital ones. Information is needed regarding protective actions which the listener should take, but the specificity is unknown. Effective alerting for large numbers of persons who are in shopping centers, theaters, and other places of public congregation is an important area of investigation. It is in such situations that catastrophes are made.

Most students of the subject agree that improved structural changes in buildings would greatly reduce the death toll and property loss. However, an improved understanding of tornado characteristics is necessary before some of the required structural adjustments can be specified. The problem is compounded by the very rapid increase in the number of mobile homes. While mobile homes can be tied down for $200 to $500, the unit itself may not stay intact in high winds accompanying a tornado. Another approach to tornado-resistant structures is the tornado-safe room in residences and public buildings. In mobile home parks and neighborhoods where most of the homes do not have basements, provision could be made for a shelter as part of a multipurpose building. The success of this structural approach to loss reduction depends chiefly on upgrading and enforcing zoning regulations and building codes.

Tornado insurance is included as part of comprehensive home-owners policies, but the insurance policy does not require the owner to take any steps to reduce potential loss. It is not known what proportion of all buildings are insured against wind damage.

⌈Past research on the tornado hazard was concerned primarily with physical studies aimed at understanding the mechanisms of tornadoes and predicting their occurrence. To obtain the maximum possible benefits from research on tornadoes, future efforts must also focus on understanding the social ramifications of the tornado hazard and encouraging more adaptive human response.⌉ This shift in emphasis poses an immediate problem--identifying the appropriate institutional context for the proposed new directions in research. Inasmuch as NOAA's past emphasis was primarily on meteorological research, that agency is not well prepared to undertake research on social dimensions. The question arises on whether a separate social science research group should be established within NOAA or elsewhere in the Federal establishment, or whether the recommended research should be

accomplished through government grants to universities and
research institutes already staffed with appropriate personnel.
Answers to these questions are imperative to the success of the
recommended research efforts (see Table 11-4). The more promising research activities lie in improved building codes and in
improved warning systems.

Building codes - Research into improved design of tornado-
resistant structures and mobile homes, coupled with research
into the problems involved in stimulating *adoption* of such
improved technology, should have high priority. This should be
accompanied by exploration of the storm cellar or equivalent
requirements as part of the building code for houses without
basements in areas of high tornado frequency. All of these
efforts should take into account building costs, effectiveness
of materials, impact on construction and sale of new units, and
the response of local officials, contractors, enforcement personnel as well as the public to whatever new techniques become
available. It is suggested that research on structural considerations for the development of standards will require
approximately 80 person years of effort over four years.
Direct practical measures could be undertaken with stimulation
and guidance of the NBS, and could have a powerful effect upon
the vulnerability of new structures erected in tornado hazard
areas. Studies of how to achieve widespread adoption of the
new standards are equally critical. Those efforts should be
combined with a careful examination of the socioeconomic
effects of adopting new standards. These two efforts will
require about 20 person years over a three- or four-year period.

Warning systems - The warning system must be improved by research along three lines: detection, dissemination, and response. The development of more sophisticated technology for
prompt, positive identification of a tornado would build on the

TABLE 11-4
RESEARCH OPPORTUNITIES-TORNADO

Research Opportunity	National Aims									Research Findings	
	Economic Efficiency — Reduction of Net Losses Benefits-Costs		Enhancement of Human Health — Reduction of Casualties		Avoidance of Social Disruption		Environment — Protection or Enhancement	Equity — Distribution of Costs and Benefits	Expected Success of Research	Likelihood of Adoption
	Average	Cata-strophic	Average	Cata-strophic	Average	Cata-strophic				
Tornado Modification: Tornado dynamics Technology Socioeconomic effects	Low	Low	High	Low-Neg	High	Low-Neg	?	Low	Low	Low
Warning Systems Detection Dissemination Response	Low	Low	High	High	Med	Med	?	Low	High	Med
Building Design and Codes Design and code improvement Adoption of improved codes	Low	Low	High	High	Med	Med	Low	Low	High	Med
Insurance Influence on Building Design	Low-Neg	Low-Neg	Low	Low	Med	Med	NA	High	High	Med
Relief and Rehabilitation Trends, policy, socioeconomic effects	Low	Low	Low	Low	Med	High	NA	High	High	Med

Med = Medium   Neg = Negative   ? = In doubt   NA = Not applicable

present activities of NOAA, but would require heavy investment
in equipment to apply advanced Doppler radar techniques. This
work would be on the order of 100 person years over ten years.

To supplement current warning dissemination systems, a model
of the optimal dissemination system should be developed. Effective warning sources should be identified, specifying public
medium, visual or auditory characteristics, and format of bulletins, as well as obstacles to efficient operation of the
current dissemination system. Special attention should be
directed to effective ways of disseminating messages to locations where many people are concentrated, such as shopping centers. Expenditures on the order of 25 person years over five
years are warranted.

A related set of research activities should focus on individual actions to be taken when a tornado watch and warning are
received. It is important to determine which potential protective actions are most likely to reduce death and injury to the
person who is warned. Once those actions are identified, research on effective public education should be done. These two
efforts must be built upon a careful review of the social,
psychological, and situational factors that are related to
variability in human response to tornado warnings. Research
related to individual response could be carried out usefully at
a cost of approximately 30 person years.

Insurance - The present system of providing insurance should be
examined with a view to finding out how the availability and
cost of insurance could be used to influence the adoption of
building codes, including standards for mobile home tiedown and
storm cellars. This research will require five person years of
support over two years.

Lightning - Lightning probably kills as many people in the

United States in an average year as tornadoes, but this high
death rate is not apparent to the general public because most
lightning deaths are single events that do not receive widespread publicity.

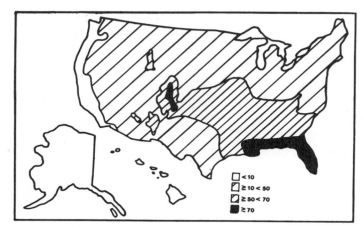

**Mean Annual Days
With Thunderstorms**

The internal physical processes of a thunderstorm tend to
concentrate a positive electric charge in the upper part of the
cumulonimbus cloud and a negative charge in the lower part.
When the difference in electric charge between two charge
centers--the base of the cloud and the ground, two clouds, or
two locations within a cloud--grows high enough to overcome the
resistance of the intervening air, a sudden and violent dis-
charge occurs in the form of a lightning stroke. In millionths
of a second, the temperature in the lightning stroke channel
rises to 50,000°F, producing a bright flash of light and a loud
clap of thunder caused by the sudden expansion of air.

Beyond this general description, not much is known about the
initiation of lightning in the cloud or its propagation to the
ground. A good deal of knowledge of lightning behavior has
come from a ten-year study of lightning strikes at the Empire
State Building and an investigation conducted since 1942 on
Mount San Salvatore near Lugano, Switzerland. However, a
detailed understanding and a mathematical description of

lightning behavior are still lacking.

Lightning damage results from four effects of the lightning stroke: electrocution of humans and animals; vaporization of materials along the path of the stroke; fire caused by the high temperature produced by the stroke; and a sudden power surge that can damage electrical and electronic equipment.

Although no exact figures on lightning fatalities are available, most estimates of the annual average number of lightning-caused deaths range between 100 and 200 (Figure 11-7). Most human deaths from lightning are single events. A notable exception in the United States occurred in 1963 when lightning struck a jet airliner over Elkton, Maryland. Three fuel tanks exploded and all 80 passengers were killed. Whereas a typical commercial airliner is probably struck by lightning about once a year, the electrical current usually flows through the metal skin of the aircraft without doing any serious damage. However, the lightning hazard for commercial aircraft appears to be mounting. The increasing use of larger aircraft and solid-state electronic circuitry, which is vulnerable to damage from power surge, has increased the potential loss of life from lightning striking a commercial aircraft.

Lightning-caused forest fires traditionally were regarded as unmitigated catastrophes. Large uncontrolled lightning-caused fires are still a serious threat to timberland, but now fire is recognized as a necessary element in the natural dynamics of some forest ecosystems. Lightning-caused fires in national parks are sometimes allowed to burn themselves out rather than being extinguished as promptly as possible.

Property losses from lightning include damage to buildings, livestock, electric power systems, the commercial aviation industry, and forests. Lightning-caused building fires claim at least $40 million annually, but there is some indication

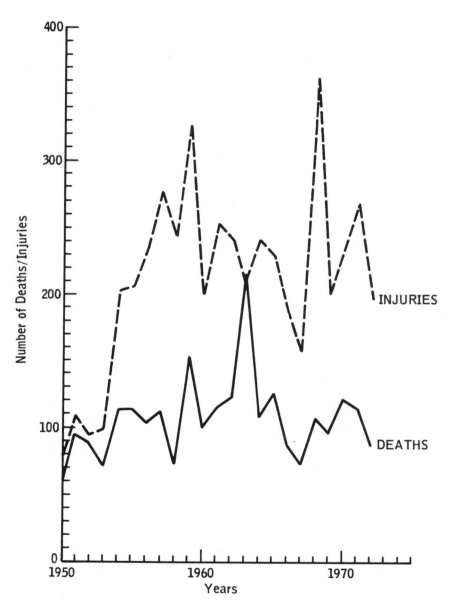

FIGURE 11–7

DEATHS AND INJURIES FROM LIGHTNING IN THE UNITED STATES

(based on Taylor (cited in Uman, 1971); Cobb, 1971; National
Oceanic and Atmospheric Administration, 1970–1972)

that such losses are decreasing. About 65% of the urban lightning strikes in a sample area in the Middle West affected nonresidential property; about 75% of rural strikes affected barns.
Rural fires tend to be more destructive than urban fires because of isolation, lack of fire-fighting equipment, and less
rigid building standards. Livestock losses, most often near an
isolated tree or wire fence, average about 500 annually.

On about half of the days during a two-month summer period
in 1968, lightning caused power failures or interruption of
telephone services somewhere across the country, and resulted
in the closure of several industrial plants, as well as in
severe damage to power stations by knocking out electrical
power in the areas affected for many hours.

The roughly 10,000 forest fires caused annually by lightning
are responsible for about one-third of the total number of
acres of forest and grassland burned in the United States, and
account for losses in excess of $50 million annually. Most
lightning-caused forest fires occur in the western states.

An expanding problem for the commercial aviation industry
results from the growing use of semiconductors and airborne
computers, which are vulnerable to transient voltages and current surges caused by lightning strikes.

Losses from lightning may be reduced by lightning modification, lightning rods and other protective measures. The loss
impact may be reduced by insurance and adequate relief and
rehabilitation.

Three different methods of lightning suppression currently
are under study: silver iodide seeding, chaff seeding, and
triggered lightning.

The protection of structures by the traditional lightning
rod may be augmented by use of fire-resistant structural
materials. A special field of technology has developed in the

protection of electric power systems and electronic and aircraft systems.

Warning systems for thunderstorms may be of high importance
in forest fire detection and readiness to carry out suppression
activities, but have relatively little significance for individual homeowners.

The U. S. Forest Service and the National Park Service currently are experimenting with different approaches for dealing
with forest and grass fires, including prescribed burning.

Insurance coverage is widely available for all of the important losses and is generally included in comprehensive homeowners policies.

Except for forest fire disasters, relief and rehabilitation
is rarely available for lightning-caused losses.

Different types of losses require different types of adjustments. Successful lightning modification might be beneficial
in forest fire management, but has little potential for reducing building fires or human casualties. The range of possible
adjustments applicable to a particular lightning-caused loss
is small, with the exception of forest fires, which have gone
through two major stages in adjustment and are entering a
third. Up to the end of the last century people adjusted to
forest fires by fleeing or protecting limited areas. Large-
scale fire control programs to combat lightning-caused fires
and education programs to prevent man-made fires were then
instituted. The Forest Service now is moving from a policy of
fire control to a policy of managed fire in which technology
still is used, but not to the exclusion of other approaches.

There are five sets of research activities which together
promise significant results in terms of reduction in the losses
resulting from lightning (Table 11-5).
Forest fire management - Forest fire management involves basic

TABLE 11-5
RESEARCH OPPORTUNITIES—LIGHTNING

Research Opportunity	Economic Efficiency — Reduction of Net Losses Benefits-Costs		Enhancement of Human Health — Reduction of Casualties		Avoidance of Social Disruption		Environment — Protection or Enhancement	Equity — Distribution of Costs and Benefits	Expected Success of Research	Likelihood of Adoption
	Average	Cata-strophic	Average	Cata-strophic	Average	Cata-strophic				
Protection of Structures Hazard mapping Socioeconomic effects Adoption of technology	Med	High	Low	High	Low	High	NA	Low	High	Low
Forest Fire Management Fire ecology Forest fire management program Technology Adoption of improved methods	Med	High	Low	Med	Low	Med	High	Low	Med	Med
Electrical and Electronic Systems Atmospheric electricity Protection technology Adoption of improvements Aerospace	High	High	Med	High	High	High	NA	Low	Med	Med
			Low	High						

Med = Medium   Neg = Negative   ? = In doubt   NA = Not applicable

research into the fire ecology of forest stands, more detailed
investigations of possible improvements in fire management
programming and technology, and inquiry into ways of developing public understanding and support for the new and ecologi-
cally sound forest fire management programs. It is important
that rather than concentrating upon one tool--lightning and
modification--the whole kit of tools receive balanced attention.

Protection of structures - High priority should be given to
the protection of structures by improving methods of mapping
lightning hazard, analyzing the socioeconomic effects of lightning strokes, and exploring the factors which would limit or
encourage the adoption of proven technologies for protection
of structures.

Individual measures - There presently is no indication of the
extent to which popular information literature, such as that
issued by the government agencies, is in fact utilized in later
emergency actions or how warnings and informational advice
affects the actions of people operating under dangerous conditions. If individuals are to be aided in taking effective
action, the experience with these measures needs to be appraised so that they may be made more useful.

Electrical systems - The development of methods for improved
protection of electrical and electronic systems would benefit
from heightened activity on the basic physics of atmospheric
electricity combined with steps to lessen the vulnerability of
equipment to lightning strokes.

Aerospace - More must be known about the physical processes
involved in atmospheric electricity and lightning in order to
improve the present technology, particularly to cope with the
more complicated electronic equipment used on the ground and
in aircraft. In both cases there is need for evaluation of

ways of gaining acceptance of technologies that are both technically and economically feasible.

The total additional research which is warranted in pursuing
these five questions is 85 person years over ten years.

Hail - Hail damage reverses the pattern of tornado damage--
hailstorms rarely cause human death or injury, but their economic impact is severe. Hail damage to crops and property in
the United States is estimated at more than $700 million annu-
ally (see Table 11-6).

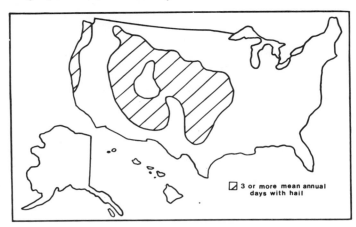

Hail Vulnerability

☑ 3 or more mean annual
days with hail

Hailstones are balls or irregular lumps of ice that may be
smaller than a pea or as large as a grapefruit. Hail damage is
usually considered a function of hailstone size, but the total
damage from a hailstorm often results from high winds and torrential rains, as well as from the physical impact of the hail
itself.

Although the factors that distinguish a hailstorm from a
similar thunderstorm without hail have not been clearly identified, two conditions appear to be prerequisites for hail formation. Updraft velocities in the storm must be strong and
persistent enough to support the hailstones as they grow in
size, and the upper parts of the storm must contain an ample

TABLE 11-6
MAJOR ANNUAL AVERAGE HAIL LOSSES BY CROP TYPE AND AREA (based on Boone, 1974)

	% LOSS (of total crop)		$ LOSS (millions)	
U.S.	Plums	7.3	Wheat	102
	Dry Beans	5.1	Corn	73
	Rye	4.7	Soybeans	54
West North Central	Dry Beans	17.9	Wheat	56
	Apples	11.2	Corn	55
	Barley	9.4	Soybeans	37
Mountain	Apples	13.1	Wheat	22
	Fresh Tomatoes	12.7	Barley	4
	Rye	10.8	Cotton	4
West South Central	Apples	13.7	Cotton	22
	Peaches	10.2	Sorghum Grain	10
	Rye	8.8	Cotton (seed)	4
Utah	Apples	20.4		
New Mexico	Apples	16.4		
Texas	Peaches	18.7		
Nebraska	Dry Beans	17.9		
Texas			Cotton	25
Kansas			Wheat	21
Iowa			Corn	18
Iowa			Soybeans	18

supply of super-cooled water--drops that are still liquid while
their temperature is colder than the nominal freezing point of
water.

Hail tends to fall in swaths that range from 20-150 miles in
length and 5-30 miles in width. A hailswath may consist of a
series of hail streaks produced by storms traversing the same
general area, with each streak typically about one-half mile
wide and five miles long. It is not known how the storms become organized, what the differing conditions are that lead to
the formation of either many small storms or a few large ones,
and what causes storms to align themselves in rows or to form
clusters.

Estimates of the distribution of hail storms are based in
part on observations at established stations, and in part derived from evidence about crop damage. The maximum number of
days with hail occurs in southeastern Wyoming, but hail damage
to crop property is largest in the Great Plains and in the
upper Middle West. A decline in harvested acreage in recent
years, accompanied by increased production of both wheat and
corn because of improved farming techniques and weather conditions, tended to reduce the area of vulnerability to the hail
hazard for wheat and corn. However, this trend is reversing
as increasing acreage is put back into cultivation. Concentration of crops on smaller acreages increases the potential for
crop destruction by individual hailstorms. Soybeans, the third
major crop susceptible to hail loss, increased in both harvested acreage and yield over the past three decades.

There is no fully comprehensive or detailed study of crop
and property losses due to hailstorms. In terms of total
dollar value lost, wheat, corn, and soybeans are the most important crops, but the highest percentage of crop value loss
occurs in plums, dry beans, and rye. About 2% of the national

crop production is lost annually through the hail hazard.   The
annual crop loss to hail in the United States is estimated at
$685 million, and the annual property loss may be about $76
million; the net economic impact on the nation is large.

Numerous attempts to suppress hail by cloud seeding have
been conducted.   The state of South Dakota, for instance, has
a statewide program of weather modification that attempts to
increase rainfall and decrease hail.   The results of such
efforts to suppress hail are regarded as inconclusive by many
atmospheric scientists.   The National Hail Research Experiment,
supported by the National Science Foundation and managed by the
National Center for Atmospheric Research, has underway a field
program to increase understanding of hailstorm dynamics and
microphysics and develop a practicable method for suppressing
damaging hail.

To cope with hail losses, farmers can adopt cropping patterns that are less vulnerable to hail damage, employ noncon-
tiguous land holdings to spread their possible losses, and
participate in crop-hail insurance which is available both from
commercial stock and mutual companies and from the Federal Crop
Insurance Corporation.

Total national insurance liability represents less than 20%
of the national crop value; something less than 25% of the
average annual crop losses due to hail is covered by insurance.
Crop hail insurance tends to rise after a period of heavy loss
years and fall after a period of light losses.   Because of the
farm surpluses of recent years it has not been clear that agriculture suffered sufficiently from hail to invest any large
amount in research aimed at reducing losses.   However, the
situation is now drastically changing.   With increasing world
populaton and demand for food and a decline in world food
reserves, accompanied by recent years of widespread crop

failures, hail losses become more important.

While the average annual losses are high, the opportunities
to reduce them with net benefits to the nation are relatively
slim.

Hail suppression - Probably the most promising direction of
research is in the set of studies centering on hail suppression
(Table 11-7), despite the influence on cost-benefit ratios of
expensive field equipment. Studies dealing with economic and
social consequences are an essential part of the effort. The
National Science Foundation should continue support of hail
suppression experiments and proof-of-concept projects. This
would call for additional research on hail dynamics at the
level of about 100 person years over a ten-year period, and
about one-half that amount for related studies.

Insurance and land use - Modest beginnings should be made in
the study of the insurance and land use aspects of the problem.
These studies would lend themselves to application by small
groups of investigators well versed in farm management and
insurance practices. The long-term effect of such studies on
national losses is not known, but the potential gains warrant
a more systematic effort. They could lead to a readjustment in
the mode of organizing land holdings and choice of crops.

Land use studies should be closely linked to an expansion of
the insurance system, with accompanying reduction in the impact
of catastrophic hailstorms in areas of intense agriculture, and
with enlarged educational and informational activity for farmers growing vulnerable crops. Studies on insurance would warrant about ten person years over five years and studies on
modes of changing land use management would involve about 15
person years over five years. The results of such studies
obviously would not lead to any change in the frequency of
hailstorms, but might reduce by a significant amount, perhaps

TABLE 11-7
RESEARCH OPPORTUNITIES-HAIL

Research Opportunity	Economic Efficiency				Enhancement of Human Health	Avoidance of Social Disruption		Environment — Protection or Enhancement	Equity — Distribution of Costs and Benefits	Research Findings	
	Reduction of Crop Losses Benefits-Costs		Reduction of Property Losses		Reduction of Casualties					Expected Success of Research	Likelihood of Adoption
	Average	Cata-strophic	Average	Cata-strophic	Average or Catastrophic	Average	Cata-strophic				
Hail Suppression: Storm dynamics, Technology, Socioeconomic effects, Environmental effects, Legal implications	High	Low	Med	Low	NA	High	Low	Low	Low	Med	Med
Warning Systems: Detection, dissemination	Low	Low	Low	Low	NA	Low	Low	NA	Low	High	Med
Land Use Management	Low	Low	NA	NA	NA	Low	Low	Low	Low	Med	Low
Insurance: Policy formulation, Adoption	NA	NA	NA	NA	NA	High	High	NA	High	High	Med

Med = Medium   Neg = Negative   ? = In doubt   NA = Not applicable

as much as 10%, the annual toll of losses from hail, a savings
which would be at least ten times that of the cost of the research over a short period of time.

Windstorm

The wind hazard associated with hurricanes and tornadoes has
already been discussed. Severe windstorms also occur with
thunderstorms, certain weather patterns along the lee slopes of
mountain ranges, and extratropical cyclones--the large-scale
weather systems that march across the central United States to
bring the familiar pattern of alternating fair and stormy
weather.

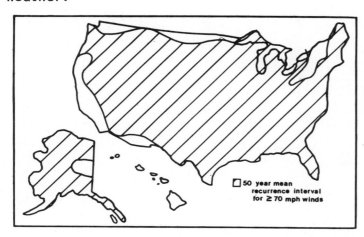

**Frequency of
High Winds**

□ 50 year mean
recurrence interval
for ≥ 70 mph winds

About 30% of the extreme wind situations that are not associated with hurricanes or tornadoes are caused by thunderstorms, but high winds from extratropical cyclones cause more
widespread damage in the United States (see Figure 11-8).
Downslope windstorms occur in mountainous areas of southern
California and along the eastern slope of the Rocky Mountains.
Although they can be violent, these windstorms usually last
only a few hours and affect a narrow area along the foot of the
mountains.

From analysis of wind speed-damage relationships, it seems

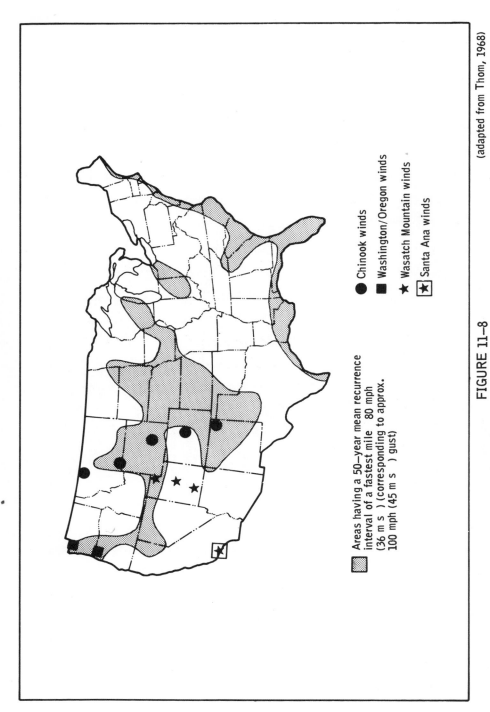

(adapted from Thom, 1968)

FIGURE 11–8
WINDSTORM HAZARD AREAS

likely that minor damage such as loss of a TV antenna or shingles can be expected at wind speeds of about 50 miles per hour; intermediate damage to windows and some structures begins at 80 miles per hour; and major structural damage can be expected when velocities exceed about 100 miles per hour. Besides damage to structures, high winds frequently cause overturning and destruction of mobile homes, airplanes, cars, and storage sheds, and the collapse of buildings under construction. Damage from flying debris can be at least as serious as damage due to wind pressure.

In an average year, the United States is threatened by about 800 severe local windstorms and perhaps a dozen East Coast winter storms. Most of these cause relatively little damage. About 33 storms annually are responsible for losses exceeding $500,000; and two or three cause damages in excess of $5 million. The largest single disaster in recent years was the Pacific Coast Storm of October 11-13, 1962, which caused about $250 million in damages in the coastal areas of California, Oregon, and Washington. Several thousand homes were damaged, California's wine grapes and walnuts suffered severely, and at the height of the storm, 70,000 telephones were out of operation. Downed trees accounted for losses of about 5 billion board feet of timber.

Average annual property losses over the past decade are estimated at $30-$300 million, and there are indications that damage and the number of damaging storms has increased. Insured losses from windstorms have run between $13 and $60 million annually over the past 20 years. In 1972, of the $13 million losses from pure windstorms, almost half were accounted for by mobile homes. Average annual losses to crops may be $5-$50 million.

Both deaths and injuries from windstorms are small by

comparison with tornadoes, but the trend has been upward over
the past decade (see Figure 11-9). Clustering of urban population leads to larger vulnerability to major losses, and the
increasing proportion of new family homes accounted for by
mobile dwellings means that such houses, wherever they are
located, are more liable to damage.

There are no serious attempts to modify windstorms other
than hurricanes, but there are ways of modifying the physical
event by planting trees as a protection for both structures and
crops.

The loss potential can also be modified by land use planning
and management and, principally, by the enforcement of adequate
building codes, tiedown anchorage requirements, and restriction
on flying debris, particularly during building construction.
Although many of the modifications that would make a structure
more wind-resistant are not expensive, some of them could add
a substantial fraction to the cost of the building, amounting
to as much as 6% of the price of a one-story dwelling. Tiedown
costs for mobile homes are relatively small, adding not more
than 3%-4% to the cost of a three-bedroom home.

Available wind data are sufficient to map windstorm hazard
on a national scale and to establish minimum wind pressures for
model building codes. A good deal of basic information on mean
velocity profiles and turbulence has been gathered, but it is
not readily available in the open literature, and practicing
engineers have difficulty locating information regarding design
for wind. There is also widespread opposition from homeowners'
associations and developers to stricter regulations. The adequacy of code enforcement is measured only by local agencies.

Model codes are of little value unless they are adopted and
enforced; there has been little or no study of the factors that
influence the adoption of codes. After construction is

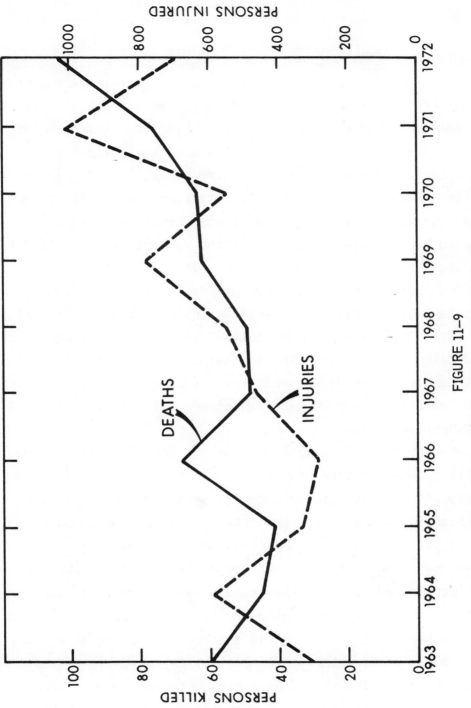

FIGURE 11–9

DEATHS AND INJURIES CAUSED BY WINDSTORMS, 1963–1972

completed, individual homeowners can reduce potential wind damage through the protection of windows by shutters, and, where a warning service is available, emergency action can be taken to anchor debris and reduce unnecessary traffic. Extended insurance coverage for dwelling structures is currently not tied directly to mitigation of the hazard except for some restrictions on mobile homes along the hurricane coast. At present, the insurance system requires coverage only for dwellings financed by a mortgage agency. Of the damages in the 1962 Pacific Coast Storm, only about 33% were insured.

A major assessment of wind engineering research is underway by the National Academy of Engineering Committee on Natural Disasters. This will give special attention to meteorological and climatological aspects, including air dynamics, air-sea interactions, stochastic methods, structural dynamics analysis, and the application of wind tunnel and full-scale studies of engineering design.

On the basis of current analysis of the windstorm hazard, it appears that opportunities to improve the situation lie along three lines: land use management, extended insurance, and forecasting and warning services (see Table 11-8). Work in the first two research areas seems to be more promising.

Land use management - The most significant opportunity lies in collecting and disseminating data on windstorms and their effects in critical high-wind areas. A sophisticated program of poststorm inspection should analyze both physical aspects and social costs rather than relying, as currently is the practice, on whatever bits of data happen to have been collected. This should be linked with continuing research into building response and construction technology in relation to changes in building design and material, but more emphasis needs to be put on details of such construction. A critical appraisal of the

Hazards and Their Distinctive Opportunities   303

TABLE 11-8
RESEARCH OPPORTUNITIES—WINDSTORM

Research Opportunity	Economic Efficiency — Reduction of Net Losses Benefits-Costs		Enhancement of Human Health — Reduction of Casualties		Avoidance of Social Disruption		Environment — Protection or Enhancement	Equity — Distribution of Costs and Benefits	Expected Success of Research	Likelihood of Adoption
	Average	Cata-strophic	Average	Cata-strophic	Average	Cata-strophic				
Forecast and Warning Storm dynamics Dissemination and response	Low	Low	High	High	Low	Low	NA	NA	Med	Med
Land Use Management Data collection and dissemination Building technology for wind resistance Adoption of improved techniques Socioeconomic effects of management	High	Med	Med	Low	High	Med	Low	Med	High	Med
Insurance Current trends Policy formulation Adoption of coverage	Low	Low	Low	Low	High	Med	NA	High	High	Low
Relief and Rehabilitation	Low	Low	Med	Low	Med	Low	NA	High	High	Low

Med = Medium Neg = Negative ? = In doubt NA = Not applicable

various national building codes is required, and with this should go investigation of effective ways of helping local communities in initiating, modifying, and enforcing suitable codes, taking into account the effects of codes on building cost.

Research on data collection and on building technology could run on the order of 40 person years over ten years. These should be supplemented by new research on the adoption of land use regulations and their socioeconomic effects. Such work would call for about 15 person years over five years.

Insurance - Studies of the limitations and consequences of insurance in this field are now almost completely lacking, and work is needed to evaluate the utilization of current insurance offerings, to study alternative schemes, and the social response to new policy offerings. This research would include an exploration of the possible effects of wider use of mandatory insurance and community response to it. Expenditures on the order of seven person years for five years would be warranted to determine what is happening in this sector of the insurance field.

Frost and Freezing

The frost and freezing hazard is generally considered to be an agricultural problem, with the most severe losses being incurred by individual farmers and agricultural communities. But the significance of the hazard is more widespread, as the effects of frost and freezing losses extend through the entire economy in the form of food shortages and higher prices.

While voluminous statistics exist for practically all aspects of agriculture in the United States, there is a severe lack of data on the socioeconomic effects of natural hazards affecting crops. This is particularly true for losses caused by frost and freezing.

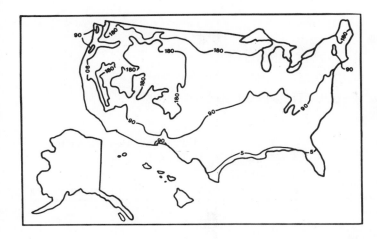

**Mean Annual Days
Below Freezing**

The Office of Emergency Preparedness (1972) estimates annual losses attributable to frost and freezing to be approximately $1.1 billion. The largest losses occur for orchard crops, which account for approximately half of the total losses (see Figure 11-10).

Although available data are not precise, the pattern of losses does not appear to have changed significantly over the past 10-20 years. Crop losses continue to represent roughly the same proportion of total crop value, indicating that frost and freezing adjustments have been ineffective in reducing losses.

It is possible that changes in climate are in progress, increasing the frequency of early fall and late spring frosts and freezing temperatures. If the climate, including patterns of variability, is fairly constant, the persistence of crop losses indicates that past adjustments have merely stabilized losses. If the trend is toward colder weather, increasing losses may be expected unless new mixes of adjustments are adopted.

Effective weather modification techniques have not been developed to reduce the severity of freezing events, and protection methods for crops have not improved significantly

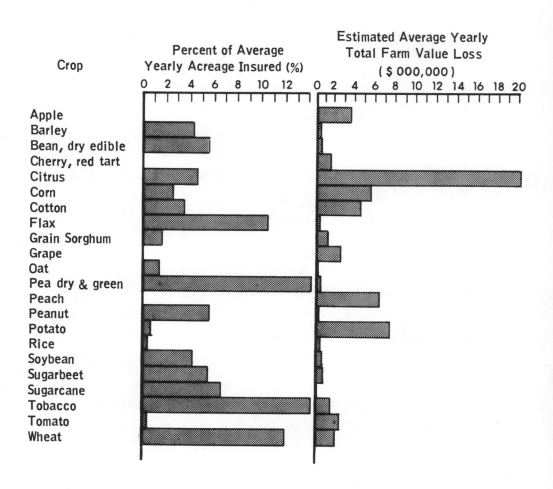

FIGURE 11–10
PERCENTAGE OF ACREAGE INSURED
AND PRODUCTION LOSS DUE TO FROST

(U.S. Department of Agriculture, 1972)

since the 1920's. Only in a third area of adjustments--modify-
ing the loss potential--has recent work yielded significant
results.

Frost and freezing protection measures can be classified as
either active or passive. Active methods are carried out immediately before or during the occurrence of the frost or freeze
to try to prevent damage to crops. Passive methods require
earlier planning so that they are in effect before the threat
of the freeze. Active freeze protection methods require weather forecasts, but passive methods rely on climatological information.

The most popular active protection devices are heaters, wind
machines, and surface or overhead irrigation. In general,
these devices are used mainly for orchards, where the crop is
relatively concentrated and the potential economic loss is high.
Other methods include artificial clouds or fog, foams, and
cover by glass or plastic. Field crops are usually protected
by passive methods, since the value of the crops does not jus-
tify large expenditures for protection measures.

Passive methods of protection include such activities as the
selection of a site, choice of growing season, choice of crop,
and cultivation techniques. These methods require advanced
planning and implementation.

In addition to attempting to prevent or avoid losses due to
frost and freezing, another method of adjusting to the hazard
is to ameliorate the impact of losses when they occur. Crop
insurance, relief, credit and replanting are methods of spread-
ing the risk and losses so that the individual farmer does not
bear the full burden, but shares it with others.

Weather phenomena are not the only factors influencing agricultural decisions, which may indeed be affected more heavily
by nonweather factors. Many elements of agricultural

decision-making change in ways that make extrapolation of current trends a weak base for projecting future dimensions of the hazard.

A growing world population means an increasing demand for agricultural products. As a result, it becomes more profitable to cultivate land that is marginal in terms of weather and other factors of productivity. Moreover, production has been increased through multiple-crop plantings during one season, with earlier plantings and later harvests. Both the use of marginal land and the extension of the growing season have contributed to current frost and freezing loss trends and, at least partially, have offset advances in protection measures.

A growing population also means urbanization and the use of more land for nonagricultural purposes. Major urbanization of the Atlantic and Pacific coastal zones of the United States has drastically reduced the availability of agricultural sites with a low risk of frost and freezing damage to crops. Spatial distributions of population will probably continue to change even if the population size remains constant, and urbanization in temperate climates will probably continue to reduce the availability of agricultural land with a low risk of frost and freezing damage to crops.

Five major fields of research needs are identified as: 1. crop insurance; 2. prediction and forecasting; 3. protection methods; 4. adjustment selection; and 5. data collection methods. These five fields of research are so interrelated that achieving benefits from any one of them depends upon success in one or more of the other fields. Furthermore, realization of benefits from each field of investigation is constrained by the political feasibility of adopting results (see Table 11-9).

A primary requirement is some means of speeding up the systematic and detailed collection of data on actual crop losses

due to frost and freezing. A crucial use of such data is to
correlate losses with the mode of adjustment. The availability
of such data would strengthen the basis for making intelligent
suggestions for research and policy directed towards ameliorat-
ing the effects of this hazard.

Continuing research in weather processes is required since
all physical adjustments to frost and freezing depend upon
accurate weather predictions. Particularly in the area of
long-range forecasts--which allow growers to alter planting
and harvesting schedules--further development is needed. The
prospects for improved long-range forecasts depend on advances
in numerical prediction through atmospheric modeling.

Research on protection measures includes the development of
improved physical methods of reducing frost and freezing
losses. At present, not even a complete inventory of research
in this area exists, let alone a definition of new techniques
needed. Therefore, two components of this area of research
are the delineation and the fulfillment of physical adjustment
needs.

Even though new mechanical devices for protecting crops are
available, losses continue to be significantly large. Among
the reasons that current physical adjustments are not utilized
fully are their unsuitability to actual farm practice and the
growers' perception of the hazard. Behavioral research is
required to determine the impact and possible remedy for failures to recognize or apply new techniques.

The process by which farmers select established or new
adjustments requires investigation. Even where reasonably
adequate weather information and effective adjustment techniques are available to many growers, losses often appear to
remain constant or even increase. Investigation of the decision process should provide a better understanding of the

possible role of nonphysical types of adjustments, the reasons
for failure of crop insurance programs, the extent to which
growers absorb frost and freezing losses as normal production
costs, and the mode of selection of physical protection methods.

Unlike hazards such as flooding or hurricanes, the frost and
freezing hazard does not represent a major threat to human life.
It does, however, result in heavy economic losses, and sometimes causes social disruption, primarily in agricultural communities. Adjustments to frost and freezing may also affect
the enhancement or degradation of the natural environment.
Therefore, it is appropriate to evaluate potential research in
terms of economic (net dollar benefits), social disruption and
environmental criteria.

Table 11-9 summarizes an evaluation of these research opportunities. Different research priorities emerge depending upon
which objectives are selected. Placing heaviest weight on economic benefits, research on crop insurance probably would yield
the highest payoffs, and research on protection measures would
yield the lowest payoffs.

If only 10% of the estimated $1.1 billion annual frost and
freezing losses could be avoided through the application of
research findings, then even with a 12% discount rate, the
present value of these savings would be approximately $913
million over a 50-year period. Others (OEP, 1972, Volume 1)
would estimate much larger potential savings.

At least 140 person years are warranted for additional expenditures over a ten-year period for research on frost and
freezing in terms of reduction in economic losses to the nation.
This sum should be allocated among the five sets of research
opportunities shown in Table 11-9, with data collection given
first priority, followed by crop insurance and adjustment selection.

TABLE 11-9
RESEARCH OPPORTUNITIES—FROST

Research Opportunity	National Aims								Research Findings	
	Economic Efficiency — Reduction of Net Losses Benefits-Costs		Enhancement of Human Health — Reduction of Casualties		Avoidance of Social Disruption		Environment — Protection or Enhancement	Equity — Distribution of Costs and Benefits	Expected Success of Research	Likelihood of Adoption
	Average	Cata-strophic	Average	Cata-strophic	Average	Cata-strophic				
Protection Methods	Med	?	NA	NA	Med	?	Low	Low	Low	High
Forecast and Warning	Med	?	NA	NA	Low	?	NA	Low	Low	Med
Crop Insurance Operations and effects	Low	?	NA	NA	Med	?	NA	High	Med	Med
Aids to Selection of Adjustments	High	?	NA	NA	Med	?	Med	NA	Med	Med
Improved Loss Data	High	?	NA	NA	Low	?	NA	NA	High	NA

Med = Medium Neg = Negative ? = In doubt NA = Not applicable

The net effect of such a shift in research activities would
be to launch new initiatives on methods of data collection and
on the process by which farmers select adjustments to frost and
freezing. While research would continue on improved forecasting and prediction, more attention would be paid to development
of protection methods and the problem of crop insurance.

Urban Snow

Snow is similar to other urban hazards in its potential to
cause social disruption and because technological adjustments
are relied on almost exclusively. However, the snow hazard is
an anomaly in that adjustment to it is financed almost entirely
by the local community and individuals; the Federal government
bears little of the burden. Furthermore, little is known of
the type and magnitude of damages from the disruption caused
by infrequent very heavy snowstorms.

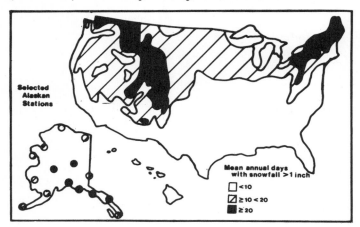

The extent of social disruption from the urban snow hazard
depends on three meteorological factors, snowfall, temperature,
and wind, as well as on the level of adjustments practiced by
a community and the city size and industrial mix. Unexpected
occurrence of a relatively large amount of snow in a very short
period of time overwhelms urban snow-removal operations and

curtails movement. Effects of different management policies
have been examined in simulations of sample communities, using
a simplified model of the social impacts (see Figure 11-11).
This suggests how the forecast accuracy in a given climate may
be related to the prevailing levels of long-run and short-run
adjustment to set the ways in which a city responds to snowstorms.

Approximately 60 million persons in the United States live
in urban areas of the northern states which have the highest
climatic risk of snow. Many of these people live in the heavily urbanized area of the northeast where heavy snowfalls have
proved to be highly disruptive in the past. The medium-risk
region consists largely of rural states with relatively low
urban populations and a resulting lower impact from snow. The
lowest-risk states (of the middle south) have only 28% of the
total population, but have proportionately more persons living
in urban areas. Snow in these regions is rare and the impact
of infrequent storms is great.

The research expenditure directly associated with snow hazard is probably not greater than $1 million per year--much less
than 1% of the cost of the hazard, and probably the lowest of
any of the 15 hazards under investigation. It is concentrated
on technological adjustments, including snow-removal equipment
and weather modification. Recent energy shortages which have
resulted in a shift in emphasis toward mass transit may produce
a redistribution of expenditures for snow-related research.

Research should follow several lines: 1. analysis of local
government finances and management related to snow removal; 2.
study of society's willingness to forego mobility and tolerate
disruption, and of the performance of various mixes of snow-
fighting equipment; 3. research on the dissemination and content of warning messages; 4. study of the feasibility of

FIGURE 11–11

MODEL IN SYMBOLIC FORM

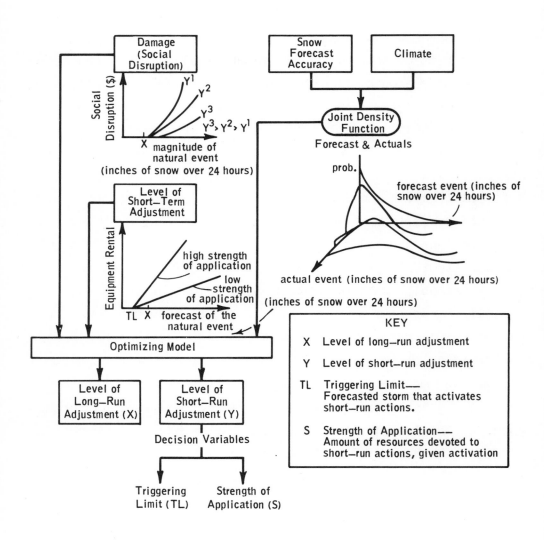

"snowfests"; and 5. studies to improve the range of insurance available for catastrophic urban snow events (see Table II-10).

Analysis of local government finances and management - There is a wide range of possible ways for a city to cope with snow hazard. The divergence between optimum and actual levels of preparedness can be explained by reference to the financial structure of the communities. Capital investments and operational expenditures for snow removal equipment are financed wholly by the local government. While new Federal revenue sharing programs may provide additional municipal funds, most funds are collected and allocated at the local level.

The municipal government generally receives most of its revenue from the property tax and the sales tax, although some cities levy either a gas or utility tax to help pay for snow removal. While additional revenue can be generated through sale of bonds, these must eventually be paid off, utilizing either the income from the financed activity or the city's tax revenues. Since snow adjustment measures tend not to be revenue-generating, their final source of funding must be taxes.

Since increasing urbanization tends to cause land values to rise, the net result of a growing urban population is usually a more-than-proportionate increase in property tax revenues. This apparent relationship has contributed to the commitment of many cities to the fallacy that urban growth produces fiscal solvency.

The other side of the fiscal balance issue is the cost involved. In the case of urban snow, the costs involved are those of servicing more miles of city streets as urban growth occurs. These costs appear to increase exponentially with city size. While increased efficiency accompanied by increased

TABLE 11-10
RESEARCH OPPORTUNITIES--URBAN SNOW

Research Opportunity	National Aims								Research Findings	
	Economic Efficiency — Reduction of Net Losses Benefits-Costs		Enhancement of Human Health — Reduction of Casualties		Avoidance of Social Disruption		Environment — Protection or Enhancement	Equity — Distribution of Costs and Benefits	Expected Success of Research	Likelihood of Adoption
	Average	Cata-strophic	Average	Cata-strophic	Average	Cata-strophic				
Methods of Optimizing Protection	Med	Low	Low	Med	High	Low	High	Low	High	High
Forecast Social mobility indicator Equipment performance Forecast accuracy	High	High	Med	High	High	High	NA	High	High	High
Warning Dissemination	High	High	Med	High	Med-Low	High	NA	High	Med	Med
Disruption Insurance	Low	Low	NA	NA	Med	Low	NA	Med	Low	Low
Snowfest Experiment	Med	Med	Low	High	High	Med	NA	Med	Med	Low

Note: all opportunities for Warning Dissemination are contingent upon improvement in forecast accuracy.

Med = Medium   Neg = Negative   ? = In doubt   NA = Not applicable

expenditures may take place over some initial range of growth, further increases in city size may be accompanied by more-than-proportionate cost increases.

Street mileage usually increases at least proportionately with population; however, traffic congestion increases exponentially. A four-lane one-mile strip of road is effectively twice as long as a two-lane one-mile road with respect to snow removal.

The higher density of development associated with urban growth requires increasingly elaborate adjustments. For instance, streets in downtown areas not only require snowplowing, but also snowhauling to open spaces. The cumulative effect of these costs is a more-than-proportionate rise in snow adjustment costs with population size.

Local government finances and management practices should be analyzed as they relate to snow removal, and compared with other forms of financing, e.g., categorical grants from state and Federal governments. Such a study need not cover a large number of cities, but could involve a selection of cities chosen for size and for variety in the character of its adjustments. Funding of about two person years over two years would be required for this research.

Snow forecasting - A false warning of heavy snowfall may lead city officials to instigate costly mobilization activities. When that happens with sufficient frequency, the forecasts tend to be ignored. Snow forecasting accuracy does not appear to have improved in the last decade. If forecasting improvements are not forthcoming, an effective warning system may have only limited value to communities.

It is recommended that research related to utilization of snow warnings be postponed until two pilot studies can be performed.   The purpose of these studies would be to develop more rigorous estimates of damages incurred and costs of adjusting to the snow hazard.

A study requiring about three person years should be conducted to develop an indicator of society's willingness to forego mobility and tolerate disruption. This study should be limited to problems caused by rapid snow, would involve examination of both individual and corporate response to stress situations, and would call for a combination of psychological, sociological and geographical analysis.

A study requiring two person years should be done to determine the effectiveness of various mixes of snow-fighting equipment for urban areas of varying sizes. Findings should be used to determine whether additional research directed at assisting resource managers in the use of warnings is justified.

The present accuracy of forecasts should be reviewed along with a projection of likely improvements. Not more than three person years would be required. If improvements in snowstorm forecasts are found to be worthwhile, additional research on dissemination of snowfall predictions should be initiated. Such study should focus on distribution and content of warning messages in the flow from a forecasting organization to decision-makers at all levels. Research requiring approximately two person years is warranted.

Snowfest - In rare instances, major employers, school administrators and public officials in a city will agree in advance that if the snowfall exceeds a certain depth everyone will take a holiday or snowfest. Little is known about the social benefits and costs of using the snowfest as an adjustment to the snow hazard.

Cities that have adopted the snowfest should be studied to

determine how their size, population density, and types of economic and social activities influence their decision to adopt
and continue that policy. Research on the snowfest and constraints on its adoption will require one person year of effort.

Insurance against disrupted activities - Research should focus
first on a design for disruption insurance, including such
topics as level of deductible amounts and whether property
damage must precede disrupted activities for the loss to be
insurable. A second aspect is financial feasibility of such a
program for insurance companies. A third topic concerns the
demographic characteristics of those who will benefit from the
program. Finally, the relationships between insurance and
other adjustments, such as snowfest adoption, should be investigated. Two person years are required for this research.

Earthquake and Tsunami

The popular conception of the earthquake hazard in the United
States often limits it to the Pacific Coast, especially California, and to such well-known disasters as San Francisco
(1906), Long Beach (1933), the Alaskan coast (1964), and San
Fernando (1971). But major earthquakes have occurred in the
interior of the country and on the eastern seaboard: in the
St. Lawrence River region on several occasions; in the vicinity
of Boston (1755); at New Madrid, Missouri, in the central
Mississippi Valley (1811 and 1812); at Charleston, South Carolina (1886); and at Hebgen Lake, Montana (1959). Most of the
nation displays some risk of seismic disturbance.

Tsunamis are sea waves generated by submarine disturbances.
Often associated with earthquakes, they are sometimes referred
to as seismic sea waves. They also may be caused by volcanic
eruptions. They are scarcely noticeable to a ship at sea, but

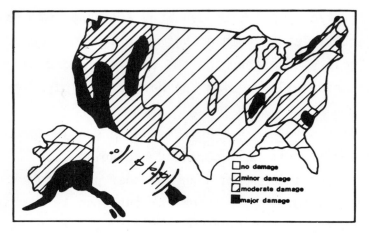

Seismic Risk

as they approach the shore their crests may build up to great
heights, depending on the amount of energy stored in the waves
and on the shape of the coastline.

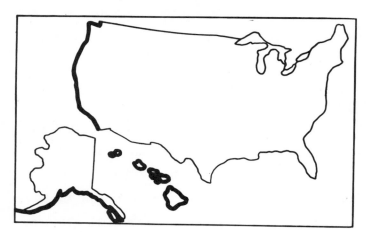

**Major Coasts
Vulnerable to
Tsunamis**

Tsunamis are limited in destructive effect to areas immediately adjacent to the coastline; they destroy by the impact of
water and by inundation. The destructive energy of earthquakes, except for surface faulting, is transmitted through
the vibration of the ground. The effects of tsunamis and
earthquakes on a community may closely coincide in time and
place, as in Alaska in 1964; or they may be widely separated
as in the tsunami at Hilo, Hawaii, in 1960, which was generated by an earthquake off the coast of Chile and took

many hours to reach Hilo. The Pacific coastlines are regarded
as most vulnerable, but the Atlantic coast is not entirely free
from a rare sea wave.

Earthquakes sometimes result in compound disasters, in which
the major event triggers a secondary associated event. The
secondary event may be natural, may result from the failure of
some man-made system, or may be a combination of both. In some
cases, the secondary event may overshadow the major triggering
event in casualties and damage (see Figure 11-12).

Fire is the greatest secondary hazard. More than 80% of the
total damage in San Francisco during the disaster of 1906 has
been attributed to fire, and the Managua disaster in 1972 also
involved devastating fires. The greatest disaster in this century due to the compounding of earthquake and fire was undoubtedly that at Tokyo in 1923, in which some 100,000 lives were
lost.

The compound disaster of an earthquake and a resulting
tsunami has been rare on this continent, but the event in
Alaska in 1964 indicates that it can occur in the United States.

A flash flood may result from an earthquake-caused dam failure. Flooding was narrowly averted in the partial failure of
earth dams at the Van Norman Lakes during the San Fernando
earthquake of 1971. A massive slope failure occurred in the
lower dam, and the fact that the reservoir behind it was only
about one-half full probably prevented a disastrous flash
flood. The potential for disaster resulted in the evacuation
of an estimated 80,000 people.

Other associated hazards which are often triggered by
earthquakes are landslides and avalanches, as was the case at
Hebgen Lake, and in Alaska in 1964. The most recent major
disaster of this sort which occurred in Peru in 1970, resulted
in about 70,000 fatalities. It is conceivable that disasters

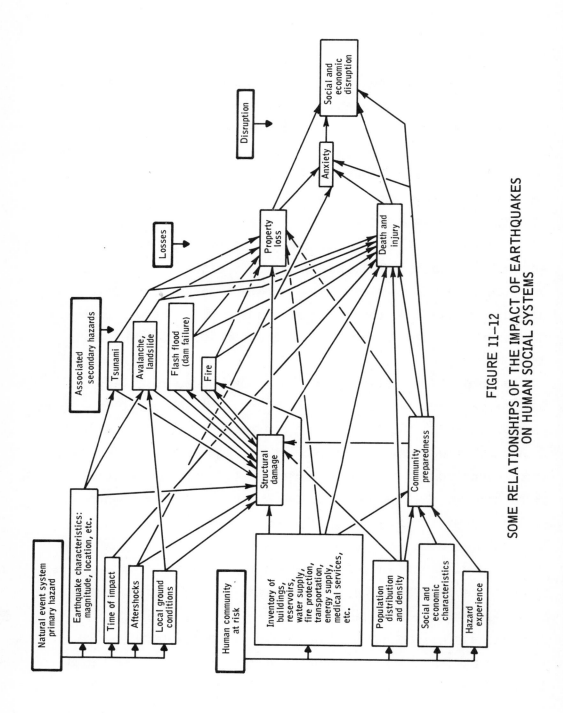

FIGURE 11-12

SOME RELATIONSHIPS OF THE IMPACT OF EARTHQUAKES
ON HUMAN SOCIAL SYSTEMS

combining earthquakes and landslides could occur in localized areas of overdevelopment on the coast of California.

More than 70 million inhabitants of the United States live in the two highest (of four) seismic risk zones. Earthquake damage has been on the increase in the United States. Dollar loss per capita shows an upward trend in recent years. Perhaps more than any other geophysical hazard, major earthquakes are likely to produce almost complete social disruption in modern urban areas. All life-supporting technologies of a city both above and below the ground may be shattered, and quick repair of below-ground life lines is almost impossible. Individuals may suffer physical deprivation, psychological trauma, pain, and death. Family life patterns may be altered for days, weeks, or even months as the economic loss and physical dislocation take their toll on the social web into which each family was embedded.

Some business organizations may profit from an earthquake or tsunami-produced disaster, but many more businesses would suffer economic loss. Many other organizations would be seriously disrupted. Loss and disruption at the family and organization level take their toll on the community as a total system. Needs for most governmental services would increase drastically while the tax base would be decimated. Many of the usual concerns and activities that make a community a humane place would have to be set aside during the emergency and early restoration periods.

Mechanisms used in the United States to cope with the consequences of earthquakes and tsunamis include: 1. attempts at reduction/prevention of earthquakes per se; 2. earthquake and tsunami-resistant construction; 3. land use management; 4. attempts to forecast and disseminate earthquake and tsunami warnings; 5. insuring structures against earthquake and tsunami damage; 6. efforts to prevent or minimize associated hazards such as fire and landslide; and 7. efforts to prepare the community to respond promptly and adequately when disaster does strike.

Public investment in research related to earthquakes and tsunamis has been focused primarily on geophysical, seismological, and engineering research. Only nominal amounts have been invested in research on insurance and community preparedness.

An analysis of significant research needs suggests that the emphasis should be shifted if economic loss and social disruption are to be reduced.

Land use management - Of all the potential mechanisms to cope with earthquakes, the simplest and most direct would be the avoidance of high-risk areas wherever economically practicable. However, San Francisco cannot be relocated, and undeveloped high-risk areas may be potentially very valuable, (as in some parts of the San Francisco Bay Area). The degree of risk is not always obvious. Several courses of action are indicated: 1. risk zoning of critical parts of the already developed areas to turn them into park land or other nonhazardous use as opportunity arises; 2. risk zoning of high-risk undeveloped areas to prevent future hazardous development; and 3. development of systematic techniques for collection and evaluation of data for use in microzoning (zoning of comparatively small areas), and the establishment of criteria for microzone levels of risk.

Research should be done on microzoning procedures with some detailed case studies, collection of local seismicity data and local fault mapping as needed, and the identification of especially hazardous areas, including potential landslides and soil liquefaction. Expenditures to support 200 person years of effort over ten years are required.

A research effort designed to point out ways in which restriction of building in fault zones might be encouraged and
adopted would have considerable payoff. This restriction of
building could begin in actual fault zones and other areas of
high hazard such as those in which the soil is known to be subject to liquefaction, and could be extended to other areas as
microrisk zones are assessed.

The study would analyze the question of how such zoning
could be adopted, especially for structures and facilities of
vital importance. Social, political, and economic constraints
to land use management would be assessed, as well as its consequences. The study of zoning adoption for the earthquake hazard may be similar to such studies for other hazards such as
flood plain management.

Research on zoning and subdivision regulation could be combined, in certain instances at least, with experimental research on building code adoption. Undeveloped areas subject
to high seismic activity could be used for certain economically
feasible purposes if improved building codes were first adopted
and used as a basis for seismic-resistant design.

An adequate investigation would run for a period of five
years at a cost of 40 person years.

Similar studies on a much smaller scale are needed for
coastlines where tsunami hazard is large or where invasion by
urban development is rapid. Two person years should be spent
on problems of local provision for tsunamis in land use management, and ten person years should be given to risk zoning.

Earthquake-proofing - Few structures can be made completely
earthquake-proof, especially against the shaking produced by
giant earthquakes. Figure 11-13 provides an estimation of
physical damage to buildings located in the Los Angeles area

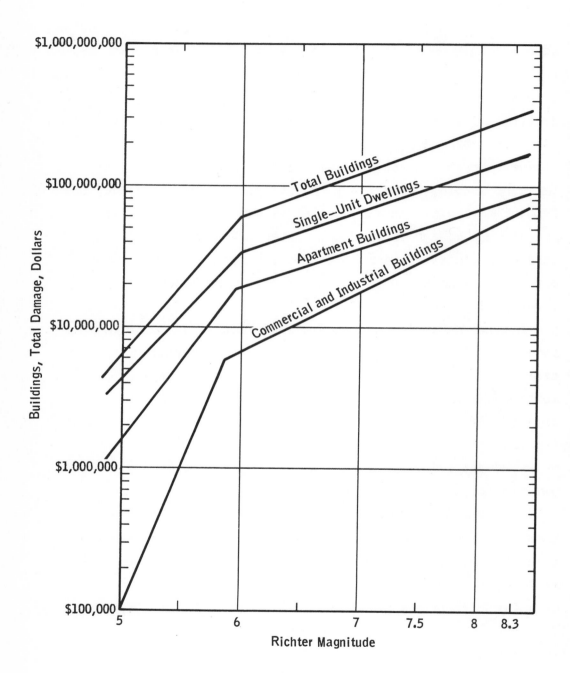

FIGURE 11–13

TOTAL DAMAGE TO BUILDINGS IN LOS ANGELES, 1970, FROM
SIMULATED HISTORICAL EARTHQUAKES

in 1970 if potentially damaging earthquakes of which there was
record after 1769 were to recur. This is based on a simulation
which estimates earthquake characteristics, the building inventory, and building design and construction. Public structures
were not included. The damage suffered by single-family dwellings is the largest category.

Most buildings could be designed and constructed to resist
significant structural damage, the possibility of total collapse. Loss of life and injury could be greatly reduced.

Most of the research attention to date, the largest single
program in the natural hazards field, has been applied to the
more spectacular and analytically interesting types of structures, for example, many-storied buildings, large dams, nuclear
power plants, and storage tanks. Relatively little attention
has been paid to lesser structures, including the ordinary
single-family dwelling. While this approach has produced positive results, it has neglected several important problems: 1.
potential weaknesses in certain methods (lift-slab construction, prefabricated construction, and other methods which may
result in lack of adequate structural continuity) have not been
investigated sufficiently; 2. low structures, with the exception of school buildings in California, generally have not been
given attention commensurate with their property value and the
human risks involved; 3. many-storied buildings that have been
adequately designed and constructed to withstand the motion of
major earthquakes without serious structural damage are not
necessarily safe for human occupancy if the elevator system
fails or if fire breaks out; and 4. a dam and the valley below
it, which seemed safe at the time of construction of the dam,
may later prove to be unsafe due to increased density of human
population in the valley, deterioration of the dam and its foundation, or the occurrence of a greater-than-expected earthquake.

Engineering research is needed on: 1. development of continuity in structural systems; 2. earthquake resistance of low buildings; 3. overall safety of multistoried buildings, including structural integrity, safe evacuation routes, and fire resistance; and 4. overall safety of dams and the valley below, and restrictions on land use in areas subject to flooding. Research is also needed for greater understanding of foundation conditions.

Additional funding of about 200 person years over the next ten years would be appropriate. The movement toward improving earthquake-resistant construction has been generally successful, with some exceptions, and needs further support.

The upgrading of building codes should be studied in light of the fact that estimates of increased costs to *new* construction rarely exceed 6% of the total cost of the structure. Building codes for all classes and structures and the political, social, and economic constraints to their adoption and enforcement should be considered.

Some high-risk cities appear to be significantly more progressive in the upgrading of building codes than other cities. If this is true, a series of comparative case studies would provide answers on how this upgrading takes place, and what the secondary consequences are. Experimental efforts should be made to provide incentives to the local powers who could influence building code upgrading. For example, communities could be identified where the mortgage lenders are somewhat progressive. A small team of professionals (economists, structural engineers) could carry out a careful effort to demonstrate to the lenders why supporting an improved building code would be in their own best interest. Other approaches could be tried in other cities to see which approach was most effective in producing the desired change. It is suggested that

such a study should run for a period of five years at a cost of
25 person years.

Old buildings probably present the most difficult problem of
all. They may be lucrative rental property or tax write-offs
for the owners, homes and community foci for a great number of
persons who cannot or will not live anywhere else, and may also
be potential death traps due to the danger of collapse or fire.
The two general classes of problems concern the physical condition of the structures and the social and economic constraints
on doing anything about the conditions.

Research into ways of strengthening old buildings could
scarcely be expected to lead to general procedures because of
the great differences in construction and conditions. However,
it might be possible to arrive at suggested procedures for particular classes of buildings.

Both types of research--survey and evaluation, and procedures for strengthening--might well be carried out in connection with programs of demolition for urban renewal and community conservation or other purposes if arrangements can be made
well in advance of the start of demolition. Funding of about
100 person years over ten years would support a useful program
of investigation.

Research is needed which will contribute to quicker adoption
of policies that will sharply reduce the risk from old buildings. Economic constraints to the phasing out of dangerous
structures include not only costs to the individual owner,
community, state, or Federal subsidies, but also shifts in the
tax base. Social costs include the disruption of established
neighborhoods, a possible rise in social instability associated with urban renewal, and the problems inherent in the
relocation of families and businesses. Long Beach, California,
has undertaken a program designed to specify the seismic risk

for each structure and the social costs and benefits of
regulating future use or rehabilitation of each structure.   Such
a program could provide the basis for a valuable case study
carried on by an interdisciplinary team.

It is difficult to estimate how dangerous a threat older
buildings pose to lives and property.   Study is needed to determine the risk they present, as well as how this risk might
be lessened.   Such work might start by determining how many old
buildings exist in hazardous areas, as well as their conditions
and use patterns.   Of those that are dwelling units, knowledge
of their inhabitant density would clarify the degree of risk
they present.   Research could be designed to determine how the
risk might be reduced.   Determination of their natural rate of
abandonment could be followed by an investigation of how that
rate might be affected and what would be the cost of remodeling
appropriate structures to some level of acceptable safety.   All
alternatives should be examined.   In addition to alternatives
for reducing the risk, the research should address the social,
economic, and political constraints to the adoption of each
alternative.

The research would vary in time and cost with the size and
density of the areas selected for analysis.   However, a study
costing on the order of 30 person years over five years should
provide a good basis for action.

In addition, the analysis of tsunami-resistant structures
with a view to improving design and code provisions should be
undertaken.   Costs of seven person years are warranted.

Earthquake prediction and warning - Specific forecasts of
damaging earthquakes may be available in less than a decade,
and possibly next year, but it is not clear whether the forecasts will be more of a blessing or a curse.   Empirically

based research on the social, economic, political, and legal consequences of earthquake forecasts and warnings must be given a high priority, and it currently is under review by a panel of the National Research Council.

Specific forecasts of damaging earthquakes will have lead times on the order of a few months to ten years, and will be relatively specific as to location and magnitude. Such forecasts are qualitatively different from those used in other hazard warning systems.

A reliable method of reasonably precise prediction, with a low false alarm rate, could significantly reduce earthquake casualties and might reduce property losses. It seems very likely that earthquake prediction will have additional and perhaps large-scale impacts, some of which will probably be positive and others negative.

There may be two types of forecasts and therefore the possibility of two types of "false alarms." The first is a forecast that an earthquake *will* take place, the second is a forecast that an earthquake will *not* occur. Furthermore, the very existence of an earthquake prediction and warning system may to some extent generate a false sense of security and a tendency on the part of the public to infer that *no* warning means that *no* damaging earthquakes will occur.

The public's response to earthquake prediction is exceedingly difficult to estimate. There are no good parallels to use as a basis for estimating the response. If, in advance of credible forecasts for damaging earthquakes, responsible public agencies and private interest groups develop plans and policies which are based on realistic assumptions about the actions of other organizations and people, the whole situation will be less volatile and less likely to produce adverse economic effects, unnecessary social disruption, or political upheaval.

There are no existing social mechanisms to assist responsible officials and organizations in arriving at plausible and realistic estimates of responses to the forecasts. If the results of careful research on the probable response of organizations and the public are reported to all responsible officials, they will have adequate, realistic knowledge upon which to develop their plans.

Negative consequences could also be enormous during the extended period following forecast of a damaging earthquake. Insurance companies might decide to stop selling or renewing earthquake insurance coverage. As a result, investment agencies might drastically reduce their commitments to construction and development in the area, an action which could trigger an extended slowdown in the local economy. Many people might move away from the area. Others might converge on it.

Because of the potential for very large-scale negative consequences, it is imperative to learn how to cope with earthquake prediction as early as possible. Support for at least 50 person years over five years is required.

The Pacific-wide Tsunami Warning System detects tsunamis rapidly and effectively. Where lead time is sufficient, dissemination of relevant information to the threatened communities is generally adequate. The actual forecast is handicapped by difficulties in estimating the flood depth or "run up", and in calculating the generation of waves from seismic data. Preparedness at the local level to disseminate needed information for prompt evacuation appears to be lacking in most cases. This may be due in part to the rarity of a tsunami warning in any given community. It is not known what incentives are required to insure that vulnerable communities maintain adequate local warning-response capability. Information on that question could be gathered by a research effort on the order of

ten person years over a six-year period. Ideally such an effort would be part of a more comprehensive study of warning
response described in chapter 10.

The tsunami warning problems are more like those for flash
floods and tornadoes than for earthquakes. The current studies
of their geophysical and engineering aspects should be supplemented by ten person years on ways of improving the response
and the socioeconomic consequences.

Insurance - While insurance against earthquake damage is generally available, relatively few property owners have taken out
such policies. In California less than 5% of the property
insured against fire is also insured against earthquakes, and
the percentage is even smaller in Alaska.

The reasons for this low rate of adoption should be analyzed.
Insurance companies are concerned about the possibility of
severe losses. The industry now is handicapped by lack of a
sound reinsurance program. The low rate of adoption may also
result from insufficient awareness of the earthquake hazard,
or misinformation on the availability of coverage and the rates.
The factors affecting decisions to buy or refuse insurance, as
well as those affecting how it is made available, are being
examined at the University of Pennsylvania. So long as the
insurance adoption rate remains below a socially desirable
rate, these issues will require probing. It seems likely that
current studies should be extended by at least ten person years
over a period of five years.

Investigation is needed to assess the opportunities and pitfalls in providing earthquake coverage in all-risk insurance.
A study of the feasibility and possible design of an all-risk
insurance program would cost 20 person years over a period of
five years.

The difficulties encountered with tsunami insurance are of
a different character. Because of the very long recurrence
interval for tsunamis and the short history of damages, it is
suggested that a review of historical evidence be joined with
review of insurance use and limitations.

Community preparedness, relief and rehabilitation - Risk in an
area is a function not only of the geological and topographical
features, but more importantly of the types and density of
human use to which the area is subject. Detailed community-
specific vulnerability studies which define risk in terms of
special physical problems such as buildings and gas and water
lines, and community function problems such as transportation
and health, are needed to complete risk definition and subsequent preparedness. Such studies should also take into account
the compound hazards associated with earthquakes. These studies might be modeled after those for the San Francisco Bay area
and the Los Angeles area conducted by NOAA (1972a, 1973a). The
cost would depend on the size and density of the community
analyzed. It is estimated that a total of 30 person years
would be required for such research.

At least three person years also should go into pilot studies of a similar character in tsunami areas.

Community preparedness for earthquake disasters is vital for
adequate community response, especially since secondary hazards
such as fire require immediate attention after an earthquake.
In most communities, however, present levels of preparedness
fail to provide for all the eventualities of an earthquake
disaster. A study should be conducted on how emergency planning and levels of preparedness could be improved. The study
might be incorporated into ongoing preparedness programs at a
level of 25 person years over a period of five years.

Research should be conducted on the long-range social costs of relief and rehabilitation programs in which costs are defined more broadly than those involving administrative organizations. It would examine the extent to which present loan and grant practices are successful in aiding individual recovery and which aid programs retard the adoption of other adjustments, thereby possibly increasing the hazard potential in an area. It should be possible to restructure present programs to improve the character of the services offered. In selected communities relief efforts should be assessed for their consequences in rehabilitation, which in turn could be assessed for long-term social and economic costs and interaction with the adoption of other adjustments. The study would also determine the major policy issues involved in implementing the adjustment and their effects on economic costs, social disruption, and the speed of recovery. Such a study would cost about 25 person years over five years.

More specific case studies of earthquake impact could contribute needed baseline data that would be relevant to many of the adjustments to earthquakes, as well as to other lines of hazard research. The most efficient and fruitful way to perform the studies is through the organization of interdisciplinary postdisaster field teams. Such a comprehensive effort should also: 1. develop a methodology for estimating earthquake loss (social, economic, and political); 2. document comprehensive interdisciplinary field observations; 3. maximize information flow to responsible officials; and 4. develop comprehensive field research techniques. A start in this direction has already been initiated by the Earthquake Engineering Research Institute.

Earthquake reduction - The general aim of earthquake reduction is to release by physical means the energy in relatively small steps to bring about many small earthquakes, rather than one or a few major earthquakes. There are unevaluated risks in attempting to reorder the forces of nature; there is no certainty that attempts to trigger small earthquakes will not release a large one, nor is it known to what extent the results of experiments conducted in one geological area can be applied to another.

Earthquake reduction is an ongoing field of geophysical and engineering research which may have potential long-term benefits, but its ultimate success cannot be predicted at this time. Such research should be done with provision for an interdisciplinary research program, including investigation of the social and economic consequences of earthquake reduction. If and when techniques for earthquake reduction become feasible, knowledge will be needed on how those techniques might be implemented. If many small earthquakes cost less socially and economically than one or a few large ones, questions of implementation become paramount.

Research should focus on the constraints operating to thwart implementation, and the means by which these may be overcome. The economic consequences should be addressed. If an area were to shut down temporarily in order to accommodate a series of artificially triggered, small earthquakes, what would the costs and effects be? It would be desirable to analyze how conflict between special interest groups might be resolved, the amount and cost of any resultant social disruption, and the level and structure of necessary community preparedness. The political implications of implementation and liability for damages should also be addressed. It should also look into the means for implementation, to indicate who would decide when such an event would occur. At such time as reduction techniques seem

TABLE 11-11
RESEARCH OPPORTUNITIES-EARTHQUAKE

Research Opportunity	National Aims								Research Findings	
	Economic Efficiency — Reduction of Net Losses Benefits-Costs		Enhancement of Human Health — Reduction of Casualties		Avoidance of Social Disruption		Environment — Protection or Enhancement	Equity — Distribution of Costs and Benefits	Expected Success of Research	Likelihood of Adoption
	Average	Cata-strophic	Average	Cata-strophic	Average	Cata-strophic				
Earthquake Reduction — Geophysical and engineering — Adoption of techniques	Med	Low-Neg	Med	Low-Neg	Low	Low-Neg	NA	NA	Low	Low
Earthquake-Resistant Construction — Analysis, design of building codes — Code implementation and adoption — Old building treatment	High	High	High	High	High	High	NA	Low	High	Med
Forecast and Warning — Geophysical aspects — Detection, dissemination and response	Low	Med-High	High	High	Low-High	Low-High	NA	Neg-Low	Med	High
Land Use Management — Seismic risk zoning studies — Zoning adoption	Med-High	Med-High	Med	Med	Med	Med	Med	NA	Med	Low
Insurance — Adoption processes — All-risk insurance	Low-Med	Med-High	Low	Low	Med	Low	NA	Med	Med	Med
Relief and Rehabilitation — Micro-studies of vulnerability — Community preparedness studies — Relief processes and socioeconomic effects	Low	Low	Med	Med	Med	Low	NA	High	High	Med

Med = Medium   Neg = Negative   ? = In doubt   NA = Not applicable

TABLE 11-12
RESEARCH OPPORTUNITIES- TSUNAMI

Research Opportunity	Economic Efficiency — Reduction of Net Losses Benefits-Costs		Enhancement of Human Health — Reduction of Casualties		Avoidance of Social Disruption		Environment — Protection or Enhancement	Equity — Distribution of Costs and Benefits	Expected Success of Research	Likelihood of Adoption
	Average	Catastrophic	Average	Catastrophic	Average	Catastrophic				
Protection Works / Engineering / Socioeconomic effects	Low-Neg	Low-Neg	Low	Low-Neg	Low	Low-Neg	Low-Neg	NA	Low-Med	Low
Tsunami-Resistant Construction / Analysis, design, building codes / Adoption processes	Low-Neg	Med	Med	Med	Med	Med	NA	NA	High	Low
Forecast and Warning / Geophysical aspects / Detection, dissemination and response	Low	Low	High	High	High	High	NA	Low	Med	Med
Land Use Management / Risk zoning studies / Zoning adoption	Low	Med	Med	Med	Med	Med	High	Low	High	Low
Insurance / Socioeconomic effects / Adoption processes	Med	Low	Low	Low	Med	Med	NA	Med	Med	Low
Relief and Rehabilitation / Community preparedness / Vulnerability studies	Low	Low	Low	Low	Med	Med	NA	High	High	Med

National Aims / *Research Findings*

Med = Medium   Neg = Negative   ? = In doubt   NA = Not applicable

promising, the research might run for a period of five years at
a cost of 25 person years.

The opportunities for earthquake research are evaluated in
Table 11-11, the recommendations for tsunami in Table 11-12.

Landslide

Past landslide research has had an extremely narrow focus, em-
phasizing the application of engineering protection works,
without a firm grasp of the physical processes. This situation
developed because relatively small losses, distributed over
large regions, led to a situation in which the nation largely
ignored landslide risk.

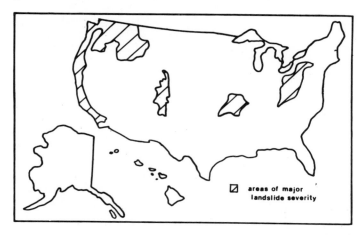

**Major Landslide
Severity**

However, losses from this hazard appear to be rising. As
residential growth expands into more marginal lands, the rate
of loss can be expected to increase further. Currently, landslides cause damages estimated at hundreds of millions of dol-
ars annually. It is predicted that landslide losses from
1970-2000 will total nearly $10 billion in the state of Cali-
fornia if present management policies continue. Figure 11-14
shows the distribution of landslide costs in typical areas,
indicating the heavy commitment to maintaining protection
works.

FIGURE 11–14

DISTRIBUTION OF AVERAGE LANDSLIDE COSTS
IN THE UNITED STATES

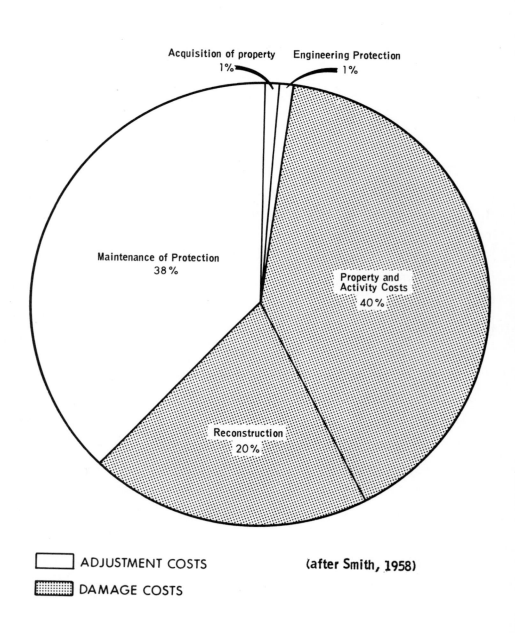

The scope of adjustment to the landslide hazard has been limited chiefly to stopping the landslide after it has been released. Since damaged parties were forced to bear the loss when these attempts failed, a reliance developed on technological means to avoid damages. Subsequently, broader social measures to prevent rather than correct the situation were perceived as adjustments. The full set of theoretical adjustments, some widely adopted, others rarely, are summarized in Figure 11-15.

The past emphasis on protection used short-term, specific predictions. Damage resulting from disastrous events was variously distributed through Federal and state relief and rehabilitation programs but most were borne by property owners. Growing environmental concern, coupled with increased losses throughout the 1960's, generated interest in regional predictions, land use management, and subsidized insurance. It is expected that the Disaster Relief Act of 1974 will accelerate this trend in future by its inclusion of mudflows.

Landslide research followed the same trends. Before the recent trends in adjustment can become effective in preventing or reducing losses, seven new avenues of research need to be followed: 1. refined protection and engineering techniques; 2. improved landslide prediction methods; 3. land use management techniques; 4. disaster preparedness programs; 5. relief and rehabilitation; 6. extensions of hazard insurance; and 7. information dissemination.

Protection - Engineered structures such as restraining walls and drainage systems are the primary techniques now used for protection against landslides, and significant changes in design concepts do not seem likely in the near future. Furthermore, adequate analysis of soil conditions is often absent,

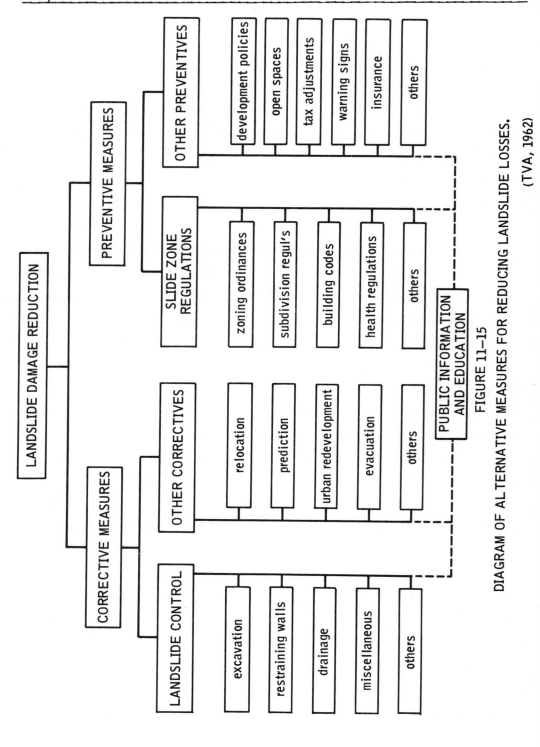

FIGURE 11-15

DIAGRAM OF ALTERNATIVE MEASURES FOR REDUCING LANDSLIDE LOSSES.

(TVA, 1962)

and the actual risk of landslide in specific areas is not even
known to developers and builders. Engineered protective works
are therefore not installed. But even where the landslide hazard is known and protective works are considered, there are
drawbacks because huge walls violate the aesthetic preferences
of many citizens.

Large expenditures in the design of protection structures
seem unwarranted. Current research on design probably does not
exceed $50,000 annually, a figure which should be maintained,
although with a different set of priorities and goals. Research should be focused upon more economically efficient protection structures, and upon designs which would minimize adverse environmental effects. These studies will require refinement of existing techniques rather than major new design solutions, and would be strengthened by a review of the state of
the art.

Research should be conducted into existing protection methods, their condition of application, and degree of success and
failure. A study on the order of at least two person years
would be required for this project.

Prediction - This assessment suggests that landslide hazard
prediction is the key element in an integrated loss-reducing
program. Prediction must be based upon sound data on soil
characteristics, geology, and related natural processes if
engineering protection, land use management, and an expanded
insurance program are to be used effectively.

While much has been learned about the causal mechanisms of
landslides, much more knowledge is required for design and
planning purposes. Given the great range and variety of conditions that exist within and among the seven major landslide
regions, an increased program of research on causes of

landslides could be expected to lead to large loss reductions. Currently, the annual expenditure on soil mechanics aspects is probably no more than $50,000. Intensified research is recommended in the field of prediction.

The most immediate priority lies in identification of the landslide hazard on a nationwide basis. Initially, this effort would involve no more than the synthesis of existing geological and related information and its correlation with human occupance of the hazard zone. It would represent an evaluation of the hazard in terms permitted by current knowledge and techniques. The project should be completed within one year at an expenditure of two person years.

It is recommended that relatively small areas be selected as representative of major landslide hazard regions for studies to identify the distribution and type of existing landslides and their causal mechanisms. Studies to increase understanding of the causes and mechanics of landslides will also require improvements in the means of analysis. The case studies and methodological improvements could be carried on within one program which should take two to three years to reach full level of research activity, and then should be sustained at a cost of at least 40 person years over a period of ten years.

Finally, there is need for research aimed at developing more reliable means of predicting the time, type, rate, and amount of landslide movement in a specific place. Research has already led to a method for predicting slope failures in areas of California during periods of intense rainfall. These efforts should be extended to other areas and types of landslide. Although this work is of lower priority and of longer term than the other predictive research suggested, an expenditure of ten person years should be made over the first five years, increasing to 25 person years over the next five years.

Land use management - If landslide risk zones can be adequately identified, land use regulations could assure that development is commensurate with the level of risk. However, at this point little is known about the development, adoption, and effectiveness of land use regulations on community, regional, or national scales. The following research, which could be integrated successfully into a larger comprehensive study with other hazards, is recommended.

The immediate priority is for a thorough examination of regulations pertaining to landslide hazards in the United States to provide a basis for developing Federal and state activities to promote sound management.

There is a range of regulatory measures for reducing landslide loss at both local and state levels, but no evaluation of that information is available. High priority is accorded research that would evaluate regulations at the state level and at selected local authorities within those states. The evaluation should include not only an account of present conditions, but also of the way in which they have developed historically. This would provide an analysis of the rate of adoption of measures, and of the factors accounting for differences. The findings are highly relevant to the establishment of model codes.

Communities need guidance in facing the problem of developing codes and regulations in terms of the fiscal, land use and political consequences. Research should begin with a sample of communities that have already developed and adopted landslide regulatory measures (for example, Los Angeles). It would attempt to evaluate how effective such measures have been in reducing losses and fostering beneficial community development, the extent to which they have deviated from the original intent, and the extent to which they were coordinated with other

elements of community planning. The investigation of the status, development and effectiveness of landslide regulations
would require funding of 15 person years over a five-year period.

Insurance - Insurance, especially if mandatory, not only forces
an awareness of hazard upon the primary users of landslide-
prone land, but internalizes the costs of adjustments and damages among them. Those living in hazardous areas bear the full
cost of that location in terms of hazard damage and adjustment.

The National Flood Insurance Program provides a partial
cover for landslides in terms of mudslide, but in areas of
flooding only. It has been suggested that coverage be extended
to all landslides regardless of causal mechanism.

A total expenditure of one person year should be sufficient
for investigation of the extent that mudslide provisions of the
National Flood Insurance Act (1968) have resulted in adoption
of the National Flood Insurance Program (NFIP) by local communities. Questions should be asked such as, are landslides
being zoned in areas coming under the NFIP, to what extent, and
at what level of efficiency.

There also is need for research into the costs and benefits
of extending the existing NFIP to include all landslide types
regardless of origin. Research on complete landslide insurance would need to consider relations with other adjustments,
especially predictive risk mapping and land use management
practices. Complete investigation would require perhaps three
person years over two years, and would call for collaboration
of the Federal Insurance Administration and the U. S. Geological Survey.

Landslide information - Perhaps the most basic need is the

establishment of a landslide information program for long-term
data storage and retrieval. This would plan for the dissemination of pertinent information on landslide hazard to governmental, public, and professional agencies in a form that could be
utilized effectively in the evaluation of risk and development,
and in the implementation of land use plans and engineering
technology. The best of research on adjustments will be of
little use unless it is properly communicated to the appropriate user. The extablishment of a center for this information
priority is seen as a high-priority short-term need. Its establishment and maintenance would probably cost 50 person years
over ten years.

In Table 11-13, average net benefits appear promising for all
research except relief and rehabilitation. In the extreme situation, net benefits are large only for land use management, prediction and disaster preparedness. Land use management and disaster preparedness are probably associated with the reduction
of fatalities in both average and catastrophe situations.

There appear to be few political or institutional constraints for most of the research. Protection is an outgrowth
of the "technological fix" which historically has been predominant in resource management. Prediction is currently the largest research field in the U.S.G.S. Landslide Hazard Reduction
Program. On the other hand, a reorientation to research
stressing land use in relation to urban planning responsibilities of HUD will be more difficult to achieve. This is exem-
plified by problems in implementing state and local land use
regulations.

With annual damages in the range of the hundred millions,
implementation of the research recommended seems worthwhile.
If successful, it is believed a reduction of damages by 30% to
40% could be achieved in the next two decades.

TABLE 11-13
RESEARCH OPPORTUNITIES-LANDSLIDE

Research Opportunity	National Aims									Research Findings	
	Economic Efficiency — Reduction of Net Losses Benefits-Costs		Enhancement of Human Health — Reduction of Casualties		Avoidance of Social Disruption		Environment — Protection or Enhancement	Equity — Distribution of Costs and Benefits		Expected Success of Research	Likelihood of Adoption
	Average	Catastrophic	Average	Catastrophic	Average	Catastrophic					
Protection Works Design Usage	Med	Low	High	Low	Med	Low	Low	Low		Med	High
Prediction Hazard region delimitation Case studies and regional methods Site-specific predictions	High	High	High	Med	High	Low	Med	Low		High	High
Land Use Management Model codes Code adoption	High	High	High	High	High	High	High	Low		High	Low
Insurance Expansion of NFIP Adoption processes	Med	Low	Low	Low	High	Med	Low	High		High	Med
Relief and Rehabilitation Methods	Low	Low	Low	Low	High	High	Low	High		Med	High
Disaster Preparedness	Med	High	High	Med	Med	Med	Low	Low		Low	Med
Information Program	High	NA	Med	NA	Med	NA	Low	NA		High	Med

Med = Medium   Neg = Negative   ? = In doubt   NA = Not applicable

Snow Avalanche

In recent years research to find effective ways of dealing with
the avalanche hazard has intensified. In spite of these efforts, the risk to population and property continues to increase
in harmony with the movement of population to mountain recreation areas of the western United States. With greater risk
should come increasing support to research which is aimed at
alleviating the hazard to people and property.

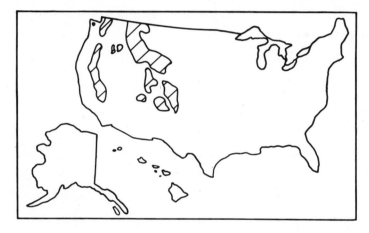

**Areas of
Avalanche Hazard**

Snow avalanches have brought natural disasters as long as
man has dwelt in the mountains. They are common features of
mountainous terrain throughout the temperate and arctic regions
of the earth, and they may occur wherever snow is deposited on
slopes steeper than about 20°. Small avalanches, or sluffs,
run in uncounted numbers each winter; larger avalanches, which
may encompass slopes a mile or more wide and millions of tons
of snow, run infrequently but inflict most of the destruction.

The hazard of snow avalanches to life and property enlarges
yearly. This is brought about by the general rise in population, which places more communities and structures in the hazardous areas; by the growing popularity of winter-related
recreational activities such as skiing and snowmobiling, which
attract thousands of persons each year to snowy mountainsides;

and by the expanding networks of communications--highways,
pipelines, power lines, electronic relay systems--with mountain
crossings that must be protected.

Snow avalanches occur most often in the western United
States and Alaska. The avalanche forecasting areas, Figure
11-16, represent locations of risk in the continental United
States. These areas are supplemented by the very hazardous
south and southeastern Alaskan regions.

A comprehensive avalanche reporting network has existed in
the United States only since 1971. Average annual death loss
is surprisingly low at seven a year, in spite of the 6800 avalanche runs per year. Property losses are estimated at an
average of $500,000 per year.

Current population growth projections for avalanche-prone
regions promise expanding potential for catastrophic avalanche
events. In other regions of the world where population density
is higher than in United States avalanche regions, extreme
events have occurred which presage the potential for catastrophe in later years in the United States. In 1962, the Huascaran
avalanche in the Santa Valley of Peru traveled 9.9 miles and
caused severe damage or destruction of nine towns and 4,000
persons. In World War I an estimated 10,000 soldiers were
killed by avalanches during a 24-hour period in the Alps. At
least 40,000 persons died as the result of avalanches in the
Alps during the period from 1915 to 1918.

To date, the highest death toll from an avalanche disaster
in the United States occurred in 1910 in the Cascade Range in
Washington where 118 persons were killed. Some urban areas,
such as Juneau, are highly vulnerable and carry the threat of
impending disaster (see Figure 11-17).

Avalanches often run in the same paths year after year, the
danger zones being well known in normal circumstances. However,

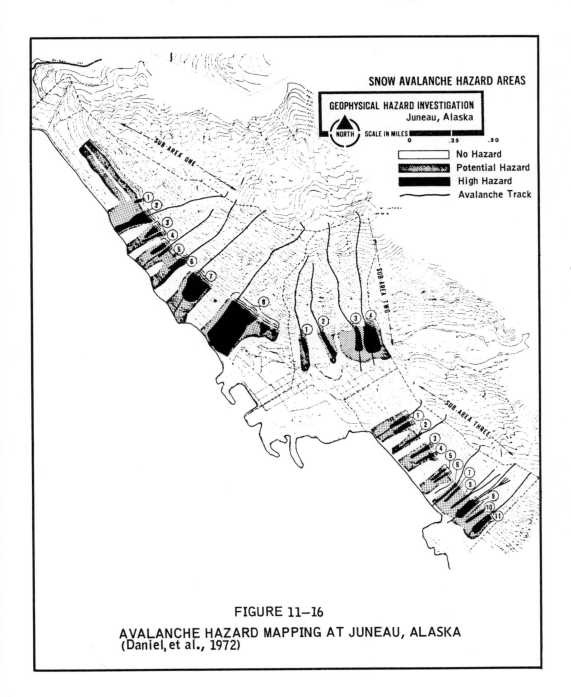

FIGURE 11–16

AVALANCHE HAZARD MAPPING AT JUNEAU, ALASKA
(Daniel, et al., 1972)

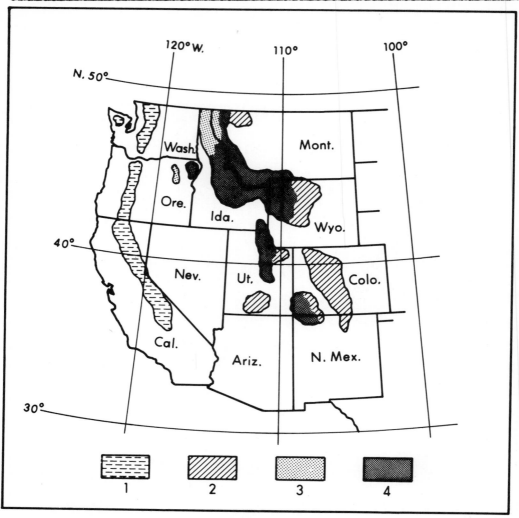

FIGURE 11–17
AVALANCHE FORECASTING AREAS

1) Generally deep and stable snow covers; extensive surface avalanching
2) Often stable snow covers ; extensive surface avalanching
3) Shallow, unstable snow covers with depth hoar formation common; climax,
   hard slab avalanches frequent
4) Snow covers in which conditions 2) and 3) overlap, with one or the
   other usually predominating in a given winter

(LaChapelle, 1966)

exceptional weather at intervals of many years may produce avalanches which overrun their normal paths, and even break new
ones where none existed for centuries. Unwise timber removal
in alpine terrain can cause avalanches where none have occurred
before. Under unusual snow conditions, even short slopes such
as the walls of a ravine can become dangerous. Snow avalanches
may run wherever enough snow is deposited under the right circumstances on an inclined surface.

These circumstances sometimes consist of abnormally large
snowfalls, but not always. Avalanches find their genesis in
snow cover structural weaknesses which are often induced by
internal changes. A large overburden of snow alone may not
result in avalanching if it is anchored to a solid underlayer.
On the other hand, even a shallow snow layer can slide from
the mountainside if it is poorly bonded to the snow or ground
surface beneath. The snow avalanche is a complex problem in
mechanical stability which can only be understood by thorough
investigation of the physical processes taking place in the
changeable winter snow.

Several useful techniques for controlling the hazard are
operational, while other methods are under study. Fundamen-
tally there are two different ways to prevent or control avalanches: modification of the terrain, and modification of the
snow, which includes deliberate release of the slide when and
where it will do little or no harm. Within the first category
the intent is either to anchor the snow on the slope in order
to prevent the initiation of an avalanche or to divert the flow
of the moving avalanche away from threatened areas. Retention
or diversion structures required for this method are expensive
and require continued maintenance, but are reasonably permanent
and offer maximum protection. Modification of the terrain is
usually chosen when the problem is to protect a large area or

fixed installations. This method is used more in Europe than
in North America.

The second category includes one of the oldest and simplest
strategies, that of artificially triggering small avalanches
before the potential for a large one develops. Properly applied artificial release can bring down piecemeal the snow load
deposited along a path where avalanches are likely to occur.
In addition, the deliberate release of snow at chosen times
makes it possible to give adequate warning and see that the
danger zone is cleared. The artificial release of avalanches
is usually achieved by detonating explosives in the zone of
potential avalanche release. Generally this is done either by
placing explosives in the snow by hand or by firing artillery
at the slope. Stabilization of the snow cover by mechanical
compaction and chemical means has also been tried. Techniques
involving the modification of the snow are most commonly applied in situations where smaller areas such as highways and
ski slopes require protection.

The most elementary defense against avalanches is to attempt
to forecast their occurrence so that people can be warned to
stay clear. Although physical studies and experience have
provided numerous clues, avalanche forecasting is still generally considered an art rather than a science. The variables
that determine when conditions are ripe for the triggering of
an avalanche are numerous and complex. It is difficult to measure the mechanical properties of snow samples with any precision, whether in the laboratory or in the field, because the
characteristics of the sample change rapidly while it is being
handled.

The other problem related to effective warning systems is
the dissemination of the forecast to people in a way that will
stimulate appropriate response. The increasing use of back

country areas by snowmobilers and cross country skiers is of
urgent concern.

Another method of avoiding avalanche hazard is the use of
regulations ranging from minor construction modifications to
absolute denial of human use. Alaska, California, Colorado,
Utah and Washington appear to be likely foci for the initiation
of land planning measures as an adjustment to the avalanche
hazard in the United States. Avalanche zoning is virtually
nonexistent in the United States for private lands, with only
Alta, Utah, and San Juan County, Colorado, having adopted avalanche zoning measures. On public lands these constraints are
more widely used in the evaluation of construction activities;
e.g., highways and powerlines. Accurate mapping of avalanche
zones is essential to the development of effective management
of land in hazardous areas. Since avalanches have specific
locations of occurrence, extensive mapping and surveys are
technically feasible. However, the costs of producing detailed
maps for planning uses are high.

Notwithstanding recent strengthening of avalanche research
in the United States, public awareness and local, state and
Federal policies remain at a rudimentary level compared with
more sophisticated strategies for dealing with other natural
hazards.

The U. S. Forest Service has been extensively involved in
avalanche research for over ten years. Universities and highway departments have contributed more recently to the research
endeavor. Current research efforts include investigation of:

Basic physical and mechanical properties of snow

The avalanche release mechanism

Avalanche occurrence forecasting

Mountain weather forecasting

Methods for the artificial release of avalanches

Avalanche defense structures

Reforestation of avalanche slopes

The destructive force of avalanches

Structural requirements for buildings exposed to avalanches

Avalanche zone mapping and the implementation of avalanche zoning ordinances

Research opportunities of greatest benefit are control and protection, prediction and warning, and land use.

Control and protection - Construction of control works is limited by the availability of suitable sites and by environmental costs. Among the various adjustments, control and protection can be undertaken with the greatest confidence that the anticipated reduction in risk will be achieved, either by more reliable techniques or by more efficient application.

Concern for environmental values may well lead to restriction rather than expansion of the use of such techniques, especially where control structures are highly visible. New research should be aimed at developing effective control methods with the highest aesthetic compatibility for an environmentally sensitive population. Nonstructural controls, such as artillery, have much lower environmental consequences. Extensive experimentation with structural controls has occurred in Europe, but a similar high level of investment seems unlikely in the United States, except in limited areas such as highways where risk reduction is of primary concern.

Risk and liability are politically sensitive issues; any methodology which is environmentally acceptable and reduces either risk or liability will notably be welcomed and may be readily adopted. Adequate research personnel and facilities are already devoted to this research. Priority should be given to environmental aspects of developing methodologies.

The design of better avalanche-resistant construction techniques requires more research. Development of materials and design would directly reduce both fatality risk and social disruption so long as reliance on such techniques does not increase the catastrophe potential.

Prediction and warning - More reliable avalanche warning would have the obvious benefits of reduced risk and loss, especially in the case of short-term warnings of potential occurrences along highways and in ski areas. Two general areas of research are required for the improvement of avalanche warning systems. Basic investigations of snow mechanics would produce data that would then be applied to studies of forecasting techniques.

Snow mechanics research involves the physical properties of snow, and the relationship of these properties to avalanche occurrence. Opportunities for research lie in finding key indicators of potential avalanches which can be economically sampled in the field. Research should emphasize snow characteristics of the particular preavalanche period in which forecasting reliability can be improved. Emphasis should also be placed on improvement of sampling techniques in that period. Avalanche forecasting includes the ability to predict both the location and the time of an event. Adjustments would be improved by research that could lengthen the time between the reliable forecast and the occurrence, improve the level of reliability, reduce the costs of implementation, make the information more understandable, and expand forecast application. Research in forecasting methodology should be aimed at one or more of these goals. One promising area is the use of acoustics as an indicator of avalanche. This is tied closely to snow mechanics and must utilize related research in that area.

Statistical techniques of probability forecasting based on past records of occurrences are severely limited by the dearth of available accurate records, except in a few areas. As records are developed, research should be undertaken to analyze the reliability of the statistical approach. A major advantage to probability forecasting is the low costs involved and minor structural installation.

Land use management - If avalanche risk zones can be adequately identified, land use regulations can be created which will require that development be commensurate with the level of risk. Such regulations should lead to substantial loss reduction, in the long run.

The first research priority is for a program that would thoroughly examine the nature of land use regulations pertaining to avalanches in the United States. Such a review would provide the basis for developing Federal and state model codes and regulations for avalanche hazard. High priority is accorded to identifying and evaluating regulations at the state level and at selected local authorities within those states.

Table 11-14 depicts a generalized assessment of these three research fields with respect to national aims. It points to some of the tradeoffs, in relation to personnel, fiscal, and political considerations, which need to be considered when research priorities have to be set. Each of these fields requires continued funding. All would be enhanced by an increase in expenditures to develop cheaper, more rapid mapping techniques. Continuing development of forecasting techniques at an increased level of funding is also warranted. The total warranted increase in research is on the order of 100 person years over a ten-year period.

With these recommended activities, it is strongly suggested

TABLE 11-14
RESEARCH OPPORTUNITIES—SNOW AVALANCHE

Research Opportunity	Economic Efficiency — Reduction of Net Losses Benefits-Costs		Enhancement of Human Health — Reduction of Casualties		Avoidance of Social Disruption		Environment — Protection or Enhancement	Equity — Distribution of Costs and Benefits	Research Findings — Expected Success of Research	Research Findings — Likelihood of Adoption
	Average	Catastrophic	Average	Catastrophic	Average	Catastrophic				
Control and Protection — Design, Usage	Med	Low	High	Low	Med	Low	Low	Low	Med	High
Forecast and Warning — Geophysical aspects, Hazard region delimitation, Site-specific predictions, Detection, dissemination and response	High	High	High	Med	High	Low	Med	Low	High	High
Land Use Management — Model codes, Code adoption	High	High	High	High	High	High	High	Low	High	Low
Information Program	High	?	Med	?	Med	?	Low	?	High	Med

Med = Medium   Neg = Negative   ? = In doubt   NA = Not applicable

that an avalanche resource center be established to collect
data on avalanche occurrence, provide technical assistance to
avalanche-prone communities, and act as the coordinating link
in the research and dissemination process. The center would
likely be most easily established in conjunction with the Rocky
Mountain Forest and Range Experiment Station under the auspices
of the U. S. Forest Service (USFS).

One of the major concerns of avalanche researchers is that
the USFS considers reduction in its commitment to avalanche
research at a time when population shifts require that it be
strengthened.

Coastal Erosion

Research on coastal erosion has traditionally been centered on
control and protection works designed to eliminate erosion
causes or to reduce direct damages. Since 1970, Federal initiatives have prompted the development of new adjustment options
which hold the promise of diversifying attempts to cope with
the hazard. This has set the stage for research which would
enable the nation to make more effective use of new developments in coastal erosion management.

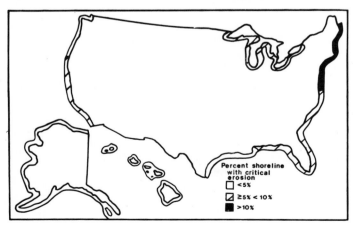

Coastal Erosion

Approximately one quarter of the national shorefront is

significantly affected by erosion. Critical erosion occurs
along 2700 miles of coastline, chiefly on the heavily populated
Atlantic and Great Lake coasts. Problems are caused when ero-
sional processes and human activities conflict. Average shoreline recessions of less than one foot per year on densely settled coasts may produce heavy damages, while elsewhere, in
sparsely populated coastal areas, annual recessions of more
than 20 feet may pose no significant hazard (see Figure 11-18).
Both erosion and accumulation are influenced by man-induced,
as well as natural processes.

Current average annual losses from coastal erosion, primarily to private property and protection structures, are nearly
$300 million, perhaps a conservative figure. Although deaths
from this hazard are extremely rare, losses have been rising
steadily in the past several decades. With no changes in management policies, this trend will accelerate, primarily because
of increasing human occupance of the shorefront.

Present erosion control policies are in a state of flux.
Federal responsibility for research on shore problems rests
with the Coastal Engineering Research Center, a branch of the
Corps of Engineers. With a few exceptions, this agency is
authorized to build protective devices only for public lands
and can offer only engineering and technical advice to private
property owners.

Since the Federal government first became active in erosion
control work, the Corps of Engineers has gradually expanded the
range of adjustment options to which it gives attention. Sea-
walls, bulkheads, and similar protective structures dominated
the limited program of Federal responses to erosion during the
1930's and 1940's. Although dune stabilization and beach
nourishment were used to a small extent under the Work Projects
Administration during the 1930's, it took extensive research

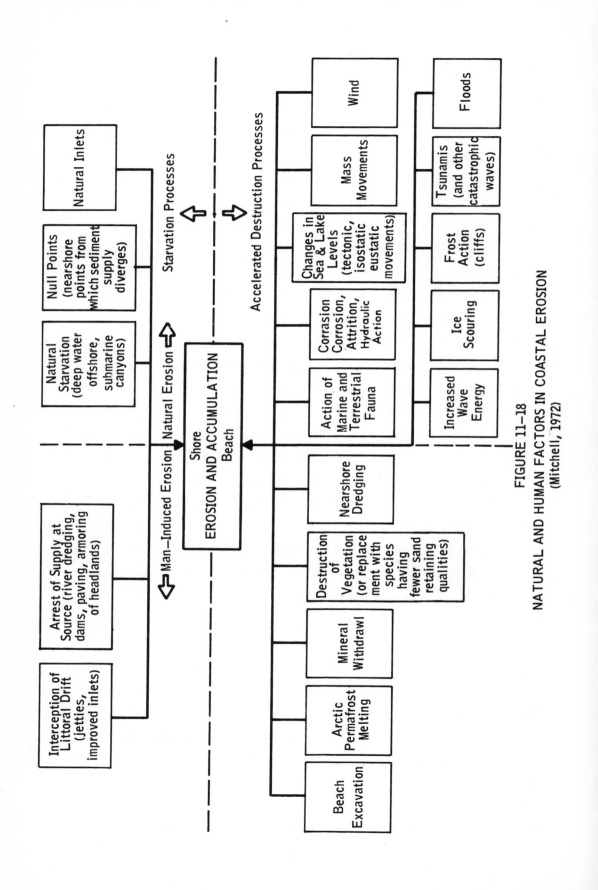

FIGURE 11–18

NATURAL AND HUMAN FACTORS IN COASTAL EROSION
(Mitchell, 1972)

before they were added to the general repertoire of adjustments
in the late 1950's. Beach nourishment has become the most
widely preferred Federal erosion control technique. Sand by-
passing was also adopted as a specialized adjustment in the
early 1960's. Otherwise, no significant changes in strategy
occurred until 1971.

Following completion of the National Shoreline Study, an
extensive program of land use management controls was advocated
by the Corps of Engineers. Together with recent attempts to
provide technical advice on protection methods to private property owners, the shore management guidelines indicate a potentially far-reaching shift in basic erosion control strategy at
the Federal level. The present broad range of adjustments
available to combat losses from coastal erosion is summarized
in Table 11-15.

Research on coastal erosion is indicated along four major
lines: 1. control and protection works, 2. land use management,
3. warnings and forecasting, and 4. relief, rehabilitation, and
insurance. The emphasis reflects shifts in management policies
in the past few years which may allow significant reductions in
erosion damages if the necessary technology and knowledge becomes available (see Table 11-16).

Control and protection - The past research emphasis in this
adjustment class was given primarily to designing improved
engineering works. However, continued effort in this direction
is unlikely to produce significant reductions in the problems
created by this hazard. Instead, five types of investigation
offer promising prospects for research payoffs.

At present, information on shore morphology is collected on
an intermittent basis by a variety of investigators in an
uncoordinated manner. These include the Corps of Engineers,

TABLE 11-15

ADJUSTMENTS TO THE HAZARD OF COASTAL EROSION

Adjustments to Loss	Modifications of Loss Potential	Modifications of Erosion Hazard	Adjustments Affecting Hazard Cause
<u>Major</u>	<u>Major</u>	<u>Major</u>	<u>Major</u>
Loss bearing	Coastal zoning	Dune stabilization	Prohibition of beach excavation and harbor dredging
Insurance	Building Codes	Groynes	Sand bypassing
	Public purchase of eroding land	Bulkheads, seawalls and revetments	
	Land fill	Beach nourishment and "perched" beaches	
		Breakwaters	
<u>Minor</u>	<u>Minor</u>	<u>Minor</u>	<u>Minor</u>
Emergency public assistance	Moving endangered structures	Regulations against destruction of dune vegetation	Removal of river dams
	Installing deep pilings	Phraetophyte removal	Biological control of marine fauna
	Storm warning and forecasting systems	Artificial seaweed, bubble breakwaters	Reduction in soil conservation activities
		Emergency filling and grading	Storm track modification
		Grading slopes	

(After Mitchell, 1972)

TABLE 11-16
RESEARCH OPPORTUNITIES—COASTAL EROSION

Research Opportunity	National Aims								Research Findings	
	Economic Efficiency — Reduction of Net Losses — Benefits-Costs		Enhancement of Human Health — Reduction of Casualties		Avoidance of Social Disruption		Environment — Protection or Enhancement	Equity — Distribution of Costs and Benefits	Expected Success of Research	Likelihood of Adoption
	Average	Cata-strophic	Average	Cata-strophic	Average	Cata-strophic				
Control and Protection										
Data collection	High	NA	NA	NA	NA	NA	NA	NA	High	High
Loss evaluation procedures	High	NA	NA	NA	Med	NA	Med	NA	Med	High
Sand resources evaluation	Low	NA	NA	NA	NA	NA	High	NA	Low	Med
Environmental aspects / Effects of controls on littoral processes	High	NA	NA	NA	Med	NA	Low	High	High	Med
Broadening range of adjustments	High	NA	NA	NA		NA				
Forecast and Warning										
Long-range forecast	?	NA	NA	NA	High	NA	High	Low	Low	Med
Land Use Management Delineation of risk zones / Adoption of codes	High	NA	NA	NA	High	NA	High	Med	Med	Low
Comprehensive Coastal Hazard Insurance	Low	NA	NA	NA	Med	NA	Low	High	Med	High

Med = Medium   Neg = Negative   ? = In doubt   NA = Not applicable

units of NOAA, the U. S. Department of Agriculture (USDA),
agencies of state and local government, academic researchers,
engineering consultants, and private individuals. Data are
subsequently recorded in a large number of places. Because
systematic data acquisition and analysis is a basic requirement
for a refined understanding of coastal processes and the development of erosion forecasts, the establishment of a central
agency to coordinate this activity is greatly needed. Two person years will be an appropriate expenditure.

Acquisition and dissemination of data on short-term oceanographic and marine meteorological changes are presently organized through NOAA's Marine Environmental Prediction program
(MAREP). This program provides limited information on beach
erosion trends to military sectors of the Defense Department
and the Coastal Engineering Research Center, but its potential
for civilian use is unexploited.

Supporting activities necessary for the operation of a central data system should include the establishment of procedures
for continuous monitoring of sediment budgets and coastal energy regimes in a network of locations with critical erosion
problems, and a regular and inexpensive national program for
surveying sample shore profiles. One possible approach is
through remote sensing of shore changes, perhaps as part of the
ERTS (Earth Resources Technology Satellite) program. Forty
person years over ten years are necessary for these activities.

Effective responses to emergency and long-term erosion problems are hampered by lack of accurate information on the nature
of erosion losses. Estimates are frequently derived by using
rough rules of thumb. Even more than in the case of flood
damage data, there is need for guidelines outlining categories
of loss to be evaluated and procedures for making such assessments. Sand losses, and socioeconomic losses would be

included at a cost of five person years over two years.

Methods of reducing the costs of nourishment programs and offsetting any undesirable environmental impacts are high priority. The Coastal Engineering Research Center is already engaged in locating new sources of sand fill and studying the ecological effects of offshore dredging. These projects should be accelerated and extended to include a comprehensive maritime sand resources mapping program and a feasibility analysis of the use of novel types of nourishment material. Twenty person years of effort over ten years are recommended.

If significant negative environmental affects of offshore dredging are revealed by current research, exploratory investigations of measures to reduce their impact are warranted. Attention should also be directed toward overcoming present cost and operational constraints on pumping and delivery systems for nourishment materials. The use of significantly cheaper nourishment sources is likely to bring about a rapid expansion in the numbers and scope of shore protection projects. This can be investigated at a cost of five person years over two years.

Although the consequences of human interference with maritime ecosystems are known only in vague outline, improperly designed or constructed shore protection devices clearly are an important cause of erosion. In Florida, lee-side starvation near improved inlets, jetties, and groynes accounts for a significant amount of the state's critical erosion problems. Accelerating shoreline recessions in some parts of New England have been attributed to the construction of revetments at eroding headlands which formerly supplied sand to adjacent beaches. Recent legislation makes the Corps of Engineers responsible for redressing losses caused by its navigation structures, and destruction caused by inadequately engineered protective works is considerable. Attention must therefore be

given to identifying and analyzing the effects of man-made
structures on maritime systems. Expenditures of 20 person
years over ten years are warranted.

The Coastal Engineering Research Center's current studies
of groyne systems can provide a starting point for examining
the effects of a broad range of coastal structures on sedimen-
tation rates, shoreline morphology, submarine contours, and
associated landform characteristics. Similar field tests of
other experimental structures should be attempted at a number
of demonstration sites around the nation's shorelines. Research
on remedial measures to counteract the detrimental effects of
structures is also required. All research should be pursued
for a ten-year period with an investment of 40 person years.

Federal and state aid for coastal protection projects does
not apply to most eroding shores because they are privately
owned. Studies designed to upgrade and expand the range of
protection methods which could be used by private resource managers are likely to produce the most important benefits of any
of the five research avenues. The Shoreline Erosion Control
Demonstration Act of 1974 is an initial step in broadening aid
to private adjustments. However, more work is needed.

Improved knowledge of existing private erosion control practices is a prerequisite for further research. Inventories of
existing private adjustments are desirable, together with
analyses of the influence of public schemes on their adoption.
Subsequent research should evaluate the effectiveness of erosion information, technical protection services, subsidies and
tax concessions, or other fiscal devices, as methods of encouraging improved private protection strategies. Ten person years
of effort over ten years will be adequate investment.

Land use management - Since returns from land use management

research programs are likely to be slow, and the pace of encroachment in the coastal zone is rapid, much of the research
will come too late to prevent large expansion of vulnerable
property unless it is given high priority. Three areas of inquiry appear fruitful in land use management policy analysis,
and are properly the concern of NOAA's Coastal Zone Management
program and the many agencies with which it works.

Efforts to develop land use management programs for eroding
sections of the United States coast should be viewed against a
background of sustained population and investment growth in
shore areas and of intense competition among resource uses.
Research on the effectiveness of various tools for restricting,
channeling, or promoting human occupancy in different coastal
settings is likely to reduce expensive errors and would speed
up the application of successful measures. Study should include identification of reasons for adoption of successful
types of land use management in some communities, and their
rejection in others. Analysis of public response to measures
currently practiced by coastal communities, and investigation
of methods which have potential value but are not widely used
at present (regional economic development programs designed to
divert demand for water-based outdoor recreation from the
coast) should be included. Methods of reducing interagency and
intergovernmental barriers to cooperative purchase of shore
frontages and common adoption, administration, and enforcement
of land use regulations also merit exploratory investigation.
Twenty-six person years over ten years would be appropriate
expenditure.

Delineation of erosion risk zones can be pursued concurrently with the creation of a coastal data system, and the establishment of rate scales for coastal hazard insurance discussed
below. In addition to delineation of risk zones, guidelines

on legal definition of property lines should be established.
This remains a difficult problem because the dynamics of beach
processes result in changing shorelines. These two areas of
research should be pursued at a total cost of 40 person years
over ten years.

Given the potential for public opposition to some aspects of
land use management programs, attempts should be made to devise
suitable procedures for soliciting the views of all affected
citizens and for integrating this information into the decision
process at an early stage. Methods of stimulating and sustain-
ing ongoing citizen participation throughout the complete planning process should also be reviewed. Ten person years of effort over ten years will be appropriate.

Warnings and forecasting systems - Even with a warning there is
little a homeowner can do, on short notice, to prevent loss of
beach sands, dunes, or structures. In any event, many people
who maintain oceanfront vacation homes are absent during seasons when severe erosion occurs. Consequently, they do not
receive or cannot utilize erosion warnings issued by local mass
media services. Given the cost and difficulty of emergency
measures and the relatively small number of structures affected
by a short period of accelerated erosion, it may be desirable
to focus attention on forecasting long-term coastal changes.

The development, at a cost of 15 person years over ten years,
of dynamic models of coastal change represents one possible way
of achieving this end. These models should be geared towards
the eventual prediction of monthly to ten-year shoreline fluctuations under varying natural conditions and differing shore
management programs. The improved data gathering and analysis
procedures recommended above under control and protection works
should greatly aid this task.

Relief, rehabilitation and insurance - Given the temporary nature of much coastal occupance, the relative absence of provisions for relief and rehabilitation for persons affected by erosion seems partly justified. Yet this policy leaves permanent residents inadequately protected against financial reverses incurred as a result of the destruction of their homes by shoreline recessions.

In situations such as these, insurance can offer a means of protecting vulnerable segments of society without subsidizing the activities of other citizens. However, failure of previous attempts to market erosion insurance bodes ill for future schemes. Since the coast is an area of many hazards, a more logical approach might involve assessment of the need for a comprehensive coastal hazard insurance program. This effort will cost five person years over five years.

Priorities and costs - It is not yet possible to estimate with confidence the degree to which alternatives to presently practiced erosion adjustments will succeed in reducing losses. At least in the United States, few nonstructural adjustments have been tried on a scale sufficient to permit assessment of their relative merits. In this context, knowledge of experience with coastal protection in other nations would be helpful and should be collected in a systematic fashion.

There is reason to believe that Federal investment in long-range erosion forecasting, community adoption of land use controls, the use of hazard insurance, and more sophisticated control technology by private property owners would go far to redressing the present scale of loss. Although massive engineering works might be successful in reducing erosion losses in some areas, heavy economic costs and presently unknown side effects may ensue.

Further investments in public works projects, improved
short-term warning systems, and relief and rehabilitation
services are likely to bring less significant loss reductions.

With Federal research on control and maritime erosion hazards averaging at least $3.5 million annually, and estimated
national erosion losses exceeding $300 million each year, a
minimum research budget of 238 person years, over and above
current Coastal Engineering Research Center activities, seems
justified over the next decade.

Substantial reduction in losses is possible, providing
this research is formulated and carried out by qualified personnel.

Drought

Drought is a creeping phenomenon, unlike flood and most other
geophysical hazards which have a relatively quick onset and
short duration. It is defined in terms of its impact rather
than its genesis; precisely when a drought begins and when it
ends is often difficult to say. The question of whether or
not an extended dry spell has in fact become a drought causes
considerable debate at times among meteorologists, farmers and
public officials.

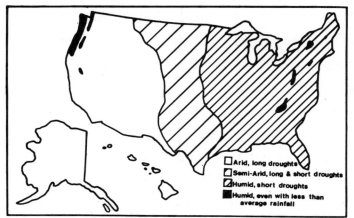

Drought Vulnerability

Agricultural drought - A practical, if imprecise, definition of agricultural drought characterizes it as a period when water is deficient enough for long enough to cause serious crop damage over a sizable area. The degree of hazard from agricultural drought depends on the extent to which demands of agriculture are overextended in terms of a highly variable resource, precipitation.

Although previous droughts in the United States have had serious adverse impacts on individuals, regions, and the nation as a whole, a major agricultural drought in this country during the next few years could result in greater economic, social, and political repercussions than any drought in history. The converging trends of increasing world population and decreasing world food reserves create a situation in which the survival of large numbers of people depends on the availability of agricultural exports from the United States. A drought serious enough to reduce those exports substantially could upset the stability of many domestic and international institutions and relations.

The changes in the nature and extent of the potential consequences of agricultural drought that have occurred over the last few decades call for a broader and more balanced approach to adjustment to this hazard. Research designed to provide new knowledge, or new applications for existing knowledge, may support measures to deal more effectively with the social impacts of agricultural drought.

There is general disagreement on the primary causes of meteorological drought. Theories involving sunspots, volcanic dust, terrestrial alterations, ocean currents, and atmospheric pollutants from human sources have been put forth. Some claims for drought cycles are made, but are discounted by many on the grounds of lack of statistical evidence. Development of

prediction or forecast capabilities is hindered by the inadequate understanding of causal processes.

The most vulnerable regions of the United States are the
arid Southwest and the semiarid Midcontinent, particularly the
Great Plains. Humid areas are subject to shorter periods of
deficiency. The Great Plains region is characterized by periodic, wide climatic shifts in precipitation amounts which, historically, were misleading to early agriculturists who established agricultural patterns better suited to a more consistently humid or subhumid environment. During the last hundred
years, major sustained droughts have occurred in this region
roughly once every 20 years. The worst was that of the 1930s--
the Dust Bowl years. The last was in the early 1950s. Drought
conditions in the summer of 1974 seriously damaged crops in the
Midwest and the high plains.

Many of the social effects of agricultural drought are difficult to quantify. Estimates of the average annual dollar
losses in the Great Plains states, derived roughly from tabu-
lated sources of production and crop losses, range from $200
million to $1200 million; a figure of $700 million annually
can be considered reasonable. Other serious effects of drought
include financial hardship, bankruptcy and geographic dislocation for the farmer; regional economic disruption and migration; massive government relief and rehabilitation, food shortage, rising prices and health effects at the national level;
and severe health effects, disruption of social systems, international conflicts, and starvation and famine at the international level.

The 1930s drought struck hard at the farmer and the Great
Plains region as a whole, and elicited massive aid from state
and Federal sources. Maladjusted farming techniques, poor
market prices, and a depressed economy lay at the heart of the

problem. Drought prompted the conscious adoption of new
drought adjustments, stimulated the creation of governmental
agencies to promote agricultural and regional adjustment, and
accelerated trends already underway. Thereafter, conservation
practices spread; irrigation increased; operations became more
flexible with larger farm sizes, diversification, and improved
management practices; a Federal crop insurance program was established, and credit institutions liberalized; and the regional economy was diversified.

During this period, impressive drought-related research was
carried out by the U. S. Department of Agriculture (USDA),
State Agricultural Experiment Station System, and agricultural
colleges and universities. Notable accomplishments were technologies for soil erosion control, soil moisture conservation,
higher yielding grain varieties, improved fertilizers, and
better farm management.

When drought struck again in the early 1950s, the impact was
much less severe. The widespread financial distress, interstate migration, and regional disruption characteristic of the
Dust Bowl era were largely absent. Though comparable in meteorological severity (even if not spatially uniform) the impact
was moderated by the trends in adjustment, as well as by improved farm prices and a healthy economy (see Figure 11-19).
In addition to the types of adjustments emphasized a decade
earlier, strong emphasis was placed on weather modification
research, weather prediction and control, groundwater recharge,
irrigation and river basin development, increasing runoff,
evaporation control, desalination, phreatophyte control, and
irrigation canal lining. An added concern of the 1950s was
water augmentation and water conservation.

A number of factors emerging during the sixties and early
seventies appear to have altered the nature of drought hazard

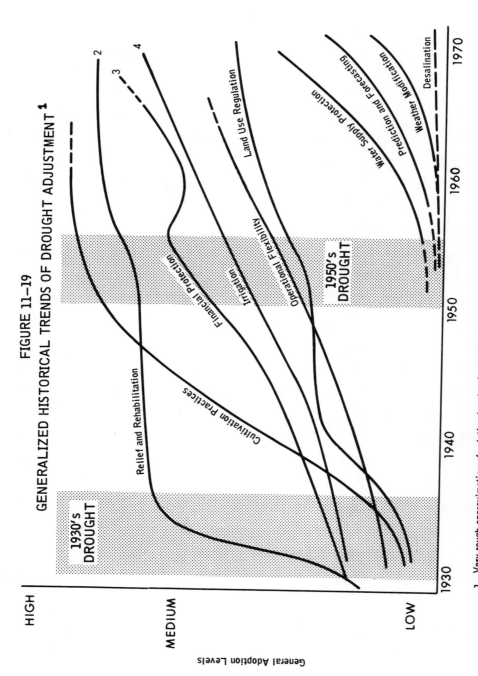

FIGURE 11-19

GENERALIZED HISTORICAL TRENDS OF DROUGHT ADJUSTMENT [1]

1. Very rough approximation of relative levels of adoption.
2. Institutional arrangements for R&R — not payments.
3. Shape of curve generalized from number of acres insured and amounts of loans in the United States (dip in 1950's reflects lower adoption of insurance at that time)
4. Based on total irrigated acres in the United States.

vulnerability in the United States. The world moved from food
surplus (surpluses existed in the 1930s as well as the 1950s)
to food shortage, and to relative scarcities of fertilizer and
energy vital for maximum food production. Interdependencies
between nations grew stronger, with the United States being the
major exporter of food in the world, and in turn relying more
heavily on other nations for resource imports. When the next
major drought reduces crop production, many of the social consequences of the hazard event may be manifested at higher social system levels, as depicted in Figure 11-20.

In light of the probable social consequences of future
droughts, the trends of adjustments to drought, and the past
and present emphases and achievements in drought-related research, recommendations for research are indicated along eight
major lines: 1. increased efficiency of irrigation and water
supply conservation; 2. technology and evaluation of weather
modification; 3. defining the role of land use regulation; 4.
developing effective prediction and forecast capability; 5. increasing operational flexibility and improving cultivation
practice adoption; 6. improving financial protection (crop
insurance) strategies and adoption rates; 7. studying long-term
effects of relief and rehabilitation policies; and 8. developing food supply management alternatives in relation to drought
hazard (Table 11-17).

Irrigation and water supply conservation - Use of surface and
groundwater for irrigation in the United States has risen
dramatically during this century. About 10% of all farms now
practice irrigation, and these farms produce 20% of the value
of all farm crops. The prairie and plains regions witnessed a
sixfold increase in irrigation since the 1930s.

Gross problems of efficiency are inherent in irrigation.
Evaporation loss is sizable in the Western United States, where

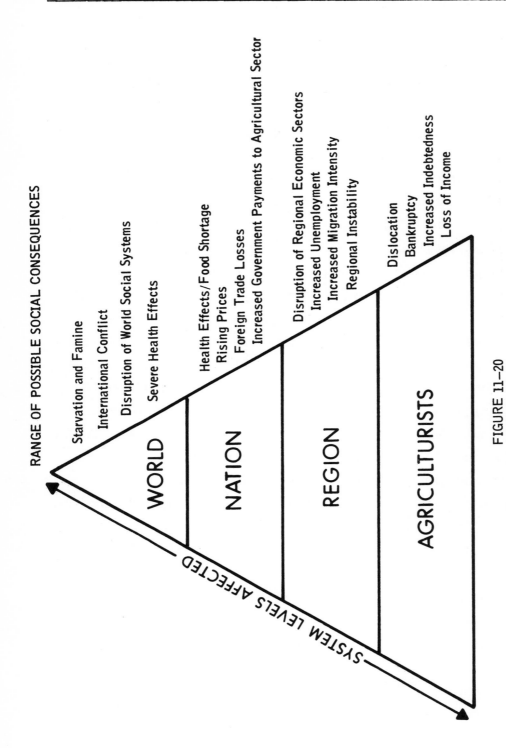

FIGURE 11–20

RANGE OF SOCIAL CONSEQUENCES OF DROUGHT VIS À VIS SOCIAL SYSTEM LEVELS

TABLE 11-17
RESEARCH OPPORTUNITIES—DROUGHT (RURAL)

Research Opportunity	National Aims									Research Findings	
	Economic Efficiency — Reduction of Net Losses — Benefits-Costs		Enhancement of Human Health — Reduction of Casualties		Avoidance of Social Disruption		Environment — Protection or Enhancement	Equity — Distribution of Costs and Benefits		Expected Success of Research	Likelihood of Adoption
	Average	Cata-strophic	Average	Cata-strophic	Average	Cata-strophic					
Control-Weather Modification Technology Legal and social aspects	Med	Neg	NA	Low	Med	Low	Low	Low		Med	Med
Protection-Irrigation and Water Supply Technology of water supply protection User efficiency Water laws and institutions	Med	Low	NA	Low	High	Med	Med	Low		Med	Low
Forecast Climatic models Drought probability studies Response to information	High	High	NA	High	High	High	Low	Low		Med	High
Land Use Management Long-term use alternatives Drought impact on land use legislation	Med	Med	NA	Med	Med	Med	High	Low		High	Med

-continued

TABLE 11-17 continued

| Research Opportunity | National Aims | | | | | | | | Research Findings | |
| | Economic Efficiency — Reduction of Net Losses Benefits-Costs | | Enhancement of Human Health — Reduction of Casualties | | Avoidance of Social Disruption | | Environment — Protection or Enhancement | Equity — Distribution of Costs and Benefits | Expected Success of Research | Likelihood of Adoption |
	Average	Cata-strophic	Average	Cata-strophic	Average	Cata-strophic				
Insurance Adoption Alternative policies	Low	Low	NA	Low	Med	Med	Low	High	Med	Med
Relief and Rehabilitation Long-term socioeconomic effects	Low	Low	NA	Low	Low	Med	NA	High	Low	Low
Operational Flexibility and Cultivation Practices Drought-resistant, high-yield crops Normative models for decision-making	Med	Low	NA	Low	Med	Low	Low	Low	Med	Med
Food Supply Management Drought contingency plans Alternative agricultural patterns	Low	Med	NA	High	Low	High	High	Med	Med	Low

Med = Medium   Neg = Negative   ? = In doubt   NA = Not applicable

it has been estimated that four to eight acre feet are lost
yearly from each acre of water surface. Seepage losses from
unlined canals and ditches may amount to as much as 25%. Transpiration losses from phreatophytes--plants that draw water
from the water table--especially saltcedar, may be as much as
20-25 million acre feet annually in the 17 western states.
Overpumping in new irrigation projects can have serious consequences for groundwater supplies. On-farm irrigation efficiency, according to one estimate, is only about 50%. Attempts to
improve irrigation water use are frustrated by inconsistent
water laws, regulations, and policies administered within
Federal, state, and local institutions. These problems suggest
the following lines of research.

Additional research on the technical aspects of water supply
conservation appears promising. A modest increase in efficiency of water storage or transfer should have significant benefits in water savings, particularly in terms of estimated withdrawal demands in the future. Three sections of this research
field appear important:

First, although canal lining is an effective means of reducing seepage, the major constraint at the present level of technology to the widespread adoption of this adjustment is cost--
especially for existing unlined canals and ditches. Additional
research on the technological aspects of reducing the cost of
canal lining and increasing the rate of adoption should offer
moderate benefits.

Second, evaporation control (monomolecular films) is far
from effective at present and costs remain high. Additional
research in this direction seems to be warranted.

Third, although loss of water from phreatophytes in the
western states is enormous, control of these plants has been
limited to a few techniques, primarily chemical control. Two

complementary efforts are worthy of attention: 1. examination
of full consequences of chemical treatment to the natural and
social systems--the widespread use of chemicals to eliminate
phreatophytes may produce unexpected costs in the form of negative secondary effects in the environment, and therefore reduce
benefits of its use in the long run; and 2. alternative means
of dealing with transpiration losses could provide for greater
flexibility and reduce costs of adjustment.

Each of these activities is a part of current programs of
the Department of the Interior and the Department of Agriculture and the land grant research institutions. They should be
encouraged with the knowledge that increased capacity to respond to drought may be one of the outcomes.

Research leading to increased user efficiency would be highly desirable, at an annual funding level of about 25 person
years over five years. Specifically, basic data on such things
as relationships between crop yield and water requirements
would be helpful, along with technical research on more efficient water application systems. Although the development of
managerial models for promoting greater efficiency in water
application has been given considerable attention in recent
years, additional research seems warranted. More important is
the need for research directed toward gaining a fuller understanding of the factors influencing the adoption of such water
conservation techniques.

Research is needed to define more clearly the nature of the
deficiencies in water laws and institutions, and to develop
alternative models of water supply management to overcome them.
This requires an interdisciplinary approach rather than a narrowly legalistic one. Expenditure of 20 person years over
five years would probably assure successful completion of the
research. Given the existing laws, institutions, and policies,

a low confidence has to be attached to the likelihood of widespread adoption of the research results.

Technology and evaluation of weather modification - Since the
1950s, a large amount of research has been devoted under NSF,
NOAA and Bureau of Reclamation auspices to weather modification. Although operational cloud seeding programs to augment
rainfall have been instituted in some states, the relative
effectiveness of cloud seeding in various climatic locations
under differing weather conditions is quite uncertain. Several
aspects of the research which would have special significance
in coping with drought are noted here.

Continuing research on cloud seeding technology evaluation
is necessary if the technology is ever going to be utilized on
a widespread basis with a high degree of certainty of the outcomes of its application.

Mitigation of continuing drought by summertime cloud seeding
may prove to be possible, but its feasibility has not been established. If it proves feasible, the semiarid regions of the
Great Plains could probably best be served by increasing soil
moisture through continuous seeding every season, except in
unusually wet years. However, this might increase the impact
of droughts by encouraging expansion of agriculture in marginal
areas, so that the damage is greater when a major drought does
occur. Knowledge of cloud seeding technology for precipitation
enhancement in the arid Southwest is even less certain, and
much more research is needed before operational programs become practical.

One of the most serious concerns among the public, it appears, is the possibility of unintentional weather modification
outside the target area. Uncertainty and controversy over this
subject must be resolved.

Detailed studies of how storm processes differ among

regions, in conjunction with more satisfactory physical evaluation techniques, would go far in clarifying numerous uncertainties surrounding the effectiveness of cloud seeding. There is critical need to assess accurately the effects of different types of seeding agents, rates of seeding, and methods of delivery under differing meteorological conditions and regional situations.

A second field of research lies in the methods of social evaluation of short-term and long-term costs and benefits of cloud seeding. It is important to consider not only the obvious short-run benefits (as, for example, the dollar value of increased crop yield during the seeded years), but also the more long-term effects on the system as a whole, including potential effects on natural systems and alterations of agricultural patterns. Weather modification has many links to the adoption of alternative adjustments; research to define more clearly what those interactions are likely to do in the adjustment process may prove valuable at early stages of weather modification adoption.

In the areas of legal and social aspects of adoption of cloud seeding, knowledge lags far behind. If cloud seeding is to be adopted and effectively utilized as an adjustment to drought, the public must be informed about the scientific findings, the particular projects planned, who is responsible, what the limits of that responsibility are, and how any one project fits into a larger regional water management plan.

Land use regulation - The Federal government began direct purchase and retirement of marginal lands during the 1930s, as well as regulation of government land leased to agriculture. Most states passed enabling legislation authorizing land use regulation or zoning by soil conservation districts; however, actual adoption or enforcement is relatively uncommon.

Indirectly through Conservation Reserve and price support programs the Federal government has had a profound influence on
guiding land use.

While the national trend seems to be a more favorable attitude toward land use regulation with the increased attention
given to environmental protection in recent years, the rising
demand for food has encouraged abandonment of marginal land
reserves and certain conservation practices. By 1975, much
land which was once intentionally withheld from production is
back in full production.

Studies of appropriate long-term land use alternatives with
respect to drought hazard would be valuable, taking into consideration regional population growth and distribution trends
and the implications of various land use relationships. Basic
to such analysis is determination of the maximum demand which
should be placed on available water or soil moisture in light
of periodic precipitation deficiencies. The alternatives for
choice need to be clarified in terms of the effects of recurrence of major drought. Past droughts have not provoked heavy
long-term depressions in farm income (see Figure 11-21), but
the prospect is changing. A total of 100 person years over
ten years would be well spent for a detailed study of this sort.

Emerging national, state, and regional land use planning
legislation should take into consideration the risk of drought.
In states where the mention of land use regulation would have
been unthinkable a few years earlier, land use bills are receiving widespread support; Colorado and Oregon are examples.
As the momentum builds within this movement, there is uncertainty about how drought hazards should be handled. At this
formative stage, it would be useful to explore how drought hazard could be integrated into these land use efforts. A total
expenditure of 40 person years over five years would be in order.

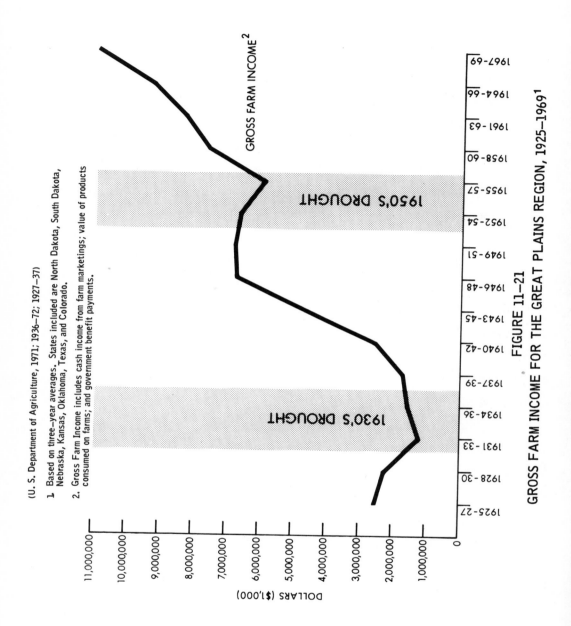

FIGURE 11-21

GROSS FARM INCOME FOR THE GREAT PLAINS REGION, 1925–1969[1]

(U. S. Department of Agriculture, 1971; 1936–72; 1927–37)

1. Based on three-year averages. States included are North Dakota, South Dakota, Nebraska, Kansas, Oklahoma, Texas, and Colorado.

2. Gross Farm Income includes cash income from farm marketings; value of products consumed on farms; and government benefit payments.

Prediction and forecast capability - The major constraint to
the development of long-range prediction and forecast capability is the lack of an adequate model of atmospheric circulation
processes.

Work on climatic modeling should be supported and a sound
theory of climatic change should be developed and incorporated
into a predictive model. A precise understanding of climatic
change and a predictive capability are becoming more and more
critical with decreasing food reserves. Even a modest decline
in production can create a dangerous situation unless it is
expected and prepared for. It would be extremely beneficial
to know the likelihood of persistence of a meager rainfall year
like 1974, or the combination of factors foretelling the occurrence of drought in North America.

A second, complementary field of research is on the use of
prediction and forecast information. There is only meager
understanding of how credible prediction and forecast information could be utilized, and what effect this would have on
social and economic activities and structures. Three needs
emerge: 1. how the agricultural or urban manager would use
the information, if available; 2. the development of operational management models which integrate the new information; and
3. the impact of prediction and forecast information on higher
order social and economic systems.

A third field is drought probability study. In order to
get a clearer understanding of the probabilities of drought
events--the duration, intensity, periodicity--more adequate
long-term data on occurrence is necessary. Promising methods
include tree-ring analysis and varve analysis, in addition to
historical data. Although the value of such additional information to the individual farmer is questionable, the information may prove valuable in land use planning.

Most investigators agree that climatic events in one part of
the world are tied, to varying degrees, to events elsewhere;
for example, the 1972 drought in the Soviet Union and the failure of the monsoons in India. A greater understanding of these
relationships between regions becomes increasingly urgent.
What can be said about the chances of major drought occurring
simultaneously in two or more major food-producing regions of
the world?

These three research opportunities related to prediction and
forecast are an integral part of the efforts of meteorologists,
in the universities, in NOAA, and in NCAR, to model global
atmospheric circulation. No suggestions are made as to desirable level of funding. The whole activity deserves continuing
support.

Operational flexibility and cultivation practices - Two fields
of research emerge as being especially important to increasing
operational flexibility and cultivation practices: drought-
resistant, high-yield crop varieties, and normative decision
models.

Although much research related to drought-resistant, high-
yield varieties has been conducted within the field of plant
genetics, its importance in terms of drought and world food
supply warrants continued and bolstered attention. Many of
the revolutionary high-yield varieties are dependent on
greater--not smaller--amounts of water and fertilizer, which may
lead to decreased stability of the system and greater susceptibility to major climatic variation. Combining high yield
with drought resistance would appear to be a crucial goal.

Research in the area of plant genetics is carried out at a
number of geographically dispersed centers; for example, Department of Agriculture research installations, the International Maize and Wheat Improvement Center (CIMMYT) in Mexico,

the International Rice Research Institute (IRRI) in the Philippines, and other international and private research institutions. Funding has come from the Department of Agriculture, the Rockefeller Foundation, the Ford Foundation, the U. S. Agency for International Development, along with the FAO, the World Bank, and other agencies. The level of funding has been in the tens of millions of dollars annually, though it is difficult to say what proportion of this could be regarded specifically as drought-related research. Continuation of these programs is of paramount importance, with possible boosting of the funding levels.

Research directed toward the development of normative models of decision-making to aid agricultural managers in their choice of drought adjustment strategy may have large benefits. Currently, for example, computer models are in use to help facilitate efficient water applications among irrigators. The large range of alternatives, even though they may combine to reduce the drought hazard, is often overwhelming to the individual decision-maker. In past years, decisions were less complicated but the farmer today is faced with choosing an optimum strategy out of many alternatives, complicated by government policy, market conditions, and farm technologies. Decisions about drought risk often are made in a probabilistic context, complicating the picture for the farmer even further. It has been estimated that the effective use of management skills by leading farmers results in as much as 50% higher yields on major crops when compared to average producers. Research on decision-making models, using careful systems analyses and possibly simulation techniques, might prove helpful in efforts to narrow this gap in dealing specifically with drought risk. An expenditure of 40 person years over five years may provide large benefits.

Crop insurance - Crop insurance has been available through the
Federal government since 1938. Although all-risk crop insurance covers a wide range of hazards, drought accounts for the
largest proportions of endemnities paid. The number of acres
insured doubled between 1948 and 1974, and reached a peak during the drought of 1953. Approximately 10% of all farms are
insured each year.

Research on decisions to adopt crop insurance would seek to
find out, first, if less-than-desirable use is made of insurance as an adjustment to drought, and, second, if so, why. A
total expenditure of 20 person years spread over ten years may
go far in providing a fuller understanding of crop insurance
adoption where drought is a frequent hazard and thus hopefully
lead to socially desirable adoption levels.

Studies of alternative insurance policies may provide insights on how to help shape a more effective, overall pattern
of adjustment to drought. What would be the effect of a policy
which created stronger, additional links to other adjustments,
as, for example, by making eligibility contingent upon adoption
of certain conservation practices? Or, what would be the overall effect on drought vulnerability of changes in eligibility
requirements, premium rate schedules, or government subsidy?
A three-year study at a funding level of 12 person years would
be in order.

Relief and rehabilitation policies - Federal relief and rehabilitation programs in drought areas are well established.
However, the decision to make the Presidential declaration
that makes the benefits of those programs available is funda-
mentally a political one, and presidents such as Johnson and
Nixon differed in their readiness to recognize droughts as
disasters. Certainly, for the short run these programs have
gone far in relieving financial stress and reducing drought

impact. However, it is felt that a closer examination of the
long-term system effects of relief and rehabilitation policies
is warranted. It may be that relief and rehabilitation is
perpetuating the existence of marginal, drought-susceptible
practices, or discouraging the purchase of insurance or the
maintenance of reserves. An analysis of the effects of relief
and rehabilitation on drought management decisions is clearly
needed. An expenditure of 20 person years over five years
would be desirable.

Food supply management alternatives - The shift of the social
consequences of drought in the United States to include potentially severe effects at international levels also suggests two
research opportunities related to food supply management.

Development of comprehensive drought contingency plans is
sorely needed. Instead of continuing to assume favorable food
production, the occurrence of a major drought in the United
States should be the subject of a systematic plan. This would
require a good deal of information on how the world system
would behave under the drought impact, information which in
part could be provided through the development of food-climate
models, and what sorts of measures could be instituted to lessen the adverse effects. This is a large undertaking, and one
requiring careful interdisciplinary, systems-oriented analysis.
Given the potential catastrophic impact of United States
drought, its importance cannot be overstated.

Ways of altering agricultural patterns to make them more
stable, flexible, and responsive to domestic and world demands
in the long run need exploration. From a long-term perspective, a more heterogeneous pattern of United States agriculture might better withstand natural and man-made variability
in the system--a reversal of past trends toward homogeneity.
Considerations of waste recycling and energy conservation

methods are important in this regard.

The United States should examine alternatives in agricultural patterns not only for its own agriculture but also for other countries where the United States intentionally, or unintentionally, shapes the development of agricultural systems. The implications go far beyond drought into questions of comparative advantage, trade balance, and monetary policy, but the point of departure is instability in the face of future droughts. An exploratory effort is needed to examine a variety of new approaches. For each research opportunity noted above, 100 person years over a period of five to ten years is a minimum expenditure.

Research evaluation - The prospective effects of changing adjustments as a result of new research can be shown as either increasing or decreasing the catastrophe potential, and as either increasing or decreasing the net benefits of agricultural activities. Land use regulation, and prediction and forecast have the potential for reducing catastrophe potential while at the same time increasing the net benefits to be derived from agricultural land use. Food supply management could also decrease the potential for catastrophe, but probably with only slight increase in net benefits. Conservation cultivation practices/operational flexibility could decrease catastrophe potential but only slightly. Though in the long run the net benefits from these adjustments are on the plus side, major droughts can still be expected to take a large toll. Through augmentation of existing moisture, weather modification might increase net benefits after adjustment costs are considered, but the prospect for cloud seeding to affect major drought occurrence is doubtful. It may even encourage drought-susceptible activities and practices, thereby raising the catastrophe potential. Drought relief has negative net benefits, and may in fact help sustain unfavorable agricultural practices in the face of drought risk. Major irrigation projects are extremely costly, and from a national viewpoint the total agricultural benefits rarely exceed the costs. New projects may or may not decrease catastrophe potential, depending on local circumstances. Water supply conservation measures would reduce catastrophe to some extent, but whether or not net positive benefits are realized depends on particular adjustment costs and water supply characteristics. It is very uncertain which direction the nation as a whole would move for financial protection.

Estimated average losses from drought in the most drought-prone region of the United States may amount to about $700 million annually. Successful application of findings from the research opportunities presented here might result eventually in a 20% reduction in these losses. New expenditures amounting to 5% of that amount, or about $14 million annually represents a minimum level, as the full social consequences, including health effects and social disruption, have not been considered. If all drought effects were to be quantified and aggregated, surely a doubling or tripling of this minimum expenditure level would be entirely justified.

The drought research outlined here generally suggests a somewhat innovative approach. Emphasis is placed on use of existing or forthcoming research findings. There is strong emphasis on careful evaluation of prospective adjustments such as weather modification or land use planning, in the social context.

The nation now has an opportunity to respond to the risk of drought *before* it occurs, and to creatively push ahead with drought research and readjustment *in the absence of disaster*. It is difficult to conjure an image of the coming event. The

old hazard may have a new face. The sets of research opportunities presented herein represent a more balanced approach than
current efforts, and might lead to reduced impact when the next
big drought gathers.

Urban drought - Much of the research for agricultural drought
is of direct benefit for urban drought also, particularly water
supply protection, weather modification, land use regulation,
and prediction and forecast research. These need not be repeated, but research activities specific to urban drought
should be added (see Table 11-18).

Desalination and water recycling - Efforts relating to desalting and recycling of water call for technological studies to
refine the processes so as to make desalted or recycled water
economically competitive with other sources of supply. Current
wastewater recycling projects are underway at a small scale,
and it appears that cost-efficient techniques for large-scale
potable supplies in urban areas may become available in 10-20
years. Less expensive recycled water suitable for extensive
agricultural and industrial uses may become available much
sooner. The grounds on which community decision-makers may
accept or reject recycled wastewater now are becoming clearer.

Probably less than $10 million is being spent annually on
water recycling research, but a comparable sum is going into
methods of advanced waste treatment before stream dilution,
and this produces benefits to recycling technology. Similarly,
findings in desalination research bear on recycling problems
and vice-versa. Desalination research expenditures are difficult to estimate because they are often related to operating
desalination facilities. A fair figure would probably be
$10-20 million per year, a reduction from previous years.

The large expenditures on desalting have brought relatively

TABLE 11-18
RESEARCH OPPORTUNITIES—DROUGHT (URBAN)

Research Opportunity	Economic Efficiency — Reduction of Net Losses Benefits-Costs		Enhancement of Human Health — Reduction of Casualties		Avoidance of Social Disruption		Environment — Protection or Enhancement	Equity — Distribution of Costs and Benefits	Research Findings — Expected Success of Research	Research Findings — Likelihood of Adoption
	Average	Cata-strophic	Average	Cata-strophic	Average	Cata-strophic				
Desalination and Recycling Technology improvement	Low	Low	NA	Low	Med	Med	Med	Low	Med	Med
Improving Conventional Water Supply Systems Probability studies Institutional potential for furthering regional cooperation	Med	Med	NA	Med	Low	Med	Low	Low	High	Med-Low
Altering Water Demand Technologies of water-saving devices at user level	High	Med	NA	Low	Med	Med	High	Low	High	Med-Low
Mix of Adjustments Evaluative methods and criteria	High	Low	NA	Low	High	Low	Low	Low	Med	Med

Med = Medium   Neg = Negative   ? = In doubt   NA = Not applicable

few benefits, and have diverted attention from other alternatives to urban water problems. Perhaps a slight boost in
recycling-related research is warranted. Although these figures seem disproportionately large compared to research recommendations on other drought adjustments, it is important to
reiterate that these systems relate only partially to drought,
because drought is but a part of water supply considerations.
The systems would therefore produce benefits far in excess of
drought loss aversion. It does appear, however, that a larger
portion of total expenditures on these projects could be directed toward short-term implementation and emergency provisions. A reasonable time frame for expected payoffs is ten
years.

Conventional water supply systems - More accurate information
from refined probability studies on water availability could
improve design and management of urban water supply significantly. Research of this nature can be included under the
appropriate research recommendation on agricultural drought.

At present, relatively little advantage is taken of the
possibilities of regional cooperation among municipalities in
developing water resources. Research into ways of furthering
regional cooperation could be of benefit in helping delimit the
alternatives available, and their respective costs, benefits,
and constraints to adoption. A study of this sort could go far
in opening up an awareness of new water supply options. A
pilot research investigation, funded at a level of about 20
person years over two years, is warranted.

Altering water demand - The usual response to the threat of
urban water shortage has been to increase supply, however costly, instead of seeking innovative means to reduce demand, especially during average conditions. Research to date suggests
that there is much more flexibility in water demand than

commonly thought, and that great savings in water could result
from technological modifications, often minor, at the user
level. Research into the technologies of water-saving devices
at the user level should seek to discover new conservation
means, or refine existing ones; to delimit the alternatives in
a comparable fashion, thus broadening the perceived options
for the urban water manager; and, finally, to define the
constraints--as well as the possible incentives--to their adoption. A three to five year study funded at about 30 person
years is reasonable for this endeavor.

Mix of adjustments - A number of studies have shown that urban
water managers often contemplate only a narrow range of alternatives in the face of water shortage. Although this is partly
as a result of their past experience, their assumptions of public preferences, and other institutional and political considerations, it also reflects a lack of methods for judging the
relative economic merits of the alternative adjustments available to them--including means of altering demand. Research on
evaluation methods and criteria would help to pave the way for
greater consideration of a broad range of adjustments. The
research should aim at providing a means of assessing the value
of various combinations of adjustments, in addition to comparisons of individual adjustments. A two-year research effort
funded at a level of 20 person years would prove valuable.

During the last two decades, research emphasis rested heavily upon the technical aspects of increasing water supply.
Vast amounts of money were poured into making a reality out of
the belief that desalination could turn the deserts into agricultural fields and end urban water supply problems forever.
Technology to modify weather likewise received considerable
attention. These two programs accounted for a major portion
of all Federal funding for water resources research. Together

they represented the first massive Federal investment in research as a tool in water resource management. To a much lesser degree, research funds were invested in the technology of
advanced wastewater treatment, even though the conditions of
water use in the nation suggested that this research might have
proven more productive than desalination or weather modification.

The failure of those technological remedies to solve the
problems of drought-related water shortages is not a blanket
condemnation of such research; eventually, they may bear fruit.
Rather, they reflect a lopsided approach to a broad resource
problem. The relative neglect of research on alternative means
of reducing demand, guiding land use, encouraging institutional
modifications of water use and distribution, developing water-
saving devices, and other social, economic, and legal mechanisms, meant that full advantage was not taken of the role that
scientific research can play in solving the problem of urban
drought in the United States. The above set of research opportunities convey a broader perspective which could lead to a
more flexible mode of adjustment to urban drought problems.

Volcano

An examination of the volcano hazard in the United States shows
that the nation faces a low probability event of possible catastrophic proportions. The United States could go a long time
without a devastating volcanic eruption. It is also entirely
possible that a major eruption could cause severe damages to
an ill-prepared nation. Furthermore, there is some evidence
of expanding human occupance of volcanic hazard zones, a trend
which may be increasing the possibility for catastrophic loss
in the future.

The threat of volcanoes stems from a large range of specific

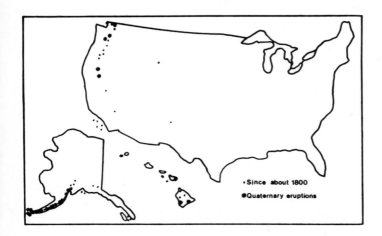

Active Volcanoes

volcanic phenomena, with an even more diverse range of effects
on man and his activities. These specific hazards include lava
flows, pyroclastic flows, ash falls, volcanic mudflows and
floods, as well as a number of volcanically generated events
such as tsunamis, forest fires, lightning, and debris avalanches and landslides. Although some general types of volcanoes can be recognized and associated with particular kinds
of activity, each individual volcano or volcanic area is apt
to possess its own particular set of specific eruptive characteristics and therefore must be examined and evaluated ac-
cordingly.

Volcano hazard is significant in three major areas of the
United States: Hawaii, the Cascade Range of the Pacific Northwest, and Alaska (see Figure 11-22).

Hawaii generally experiences frequent eruptions of a quiet,
effusive lava-producing nature. Population and area-at-risk
is relatively small. Losses will undoubtedly continue to
occur as in the past--proportionally small for each occurrence--
although loss potential promises to increase as population and
development crowd closer into the vulnerable zones.

Volcanoes of the Cascades are dormant, but have the potential to become violently active. The Cascades have experienced

FIGURE 11–22
VOLCANOES OF THE UNITED STATES

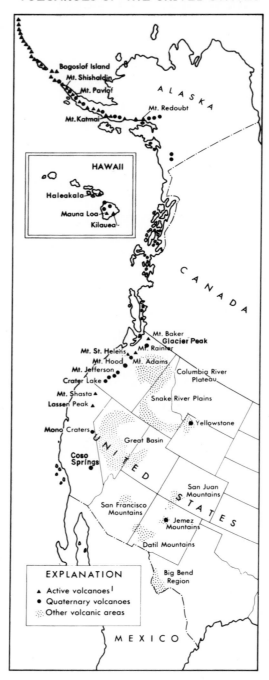

1. Certain or probable records of eruption since around 1800

Note: Slightly Modified by Authors
(U.S. Geological Survey, 1966)

fewer and less frequent eruptions when compared to either
Hawaii or Alaska. However, for the area as a whole, the
population-at-risk is greater than either of the other two
areas. The whole range of volcanic hazard phenomena could be
expected. Losses in the future, if they occur, could be of
catastrophic proportion. It is not fanciful to consider the
areas which would be affected by an eruption of Mt. Rainier
(see Figure 11-23).

Volcanic activity in Alaska is similar to the Cascades, that
is, characteristically violent pyroclastic eruptions, but
Alaska has experienced greater and more frequent eruptions in
historic times. Eruptions are likely to occur more often, on
the average, in Alaska than in the Cascades, but less often
than in Hawaii. Because of the extreme events associated with
volcanic activity in Alaska, the hazard potential is high in
the event of any large increase in population and development.

The potential for loss in terms of property damage, injury
and loss of life, and social disruption, appears to be increasing in light of significant population growth and urbanization
in all three major hazard areas. The development of energy
resources in Alaska and the Pacific Northwest is magnifying
the loss potential.

The types of adjustments that may be taken to mitigate the
threat of volcanic eruptions are 1. prediction and warning,
2. community preparedness and emergency evacuation, 3. protective measures, 4. land use management, 5. insurance, and 6.
relief and rehabilitation. The adoption of adjustments or
combinations of adjustments has been negligible, being limited
largely to Hawaii where volcanic eruptions and lava flows are
a relatively frequent occurrence. One major constraint to
deciding what to do is the lack of basic data on the physical
nature and social consequences of large volcanic eruptions.

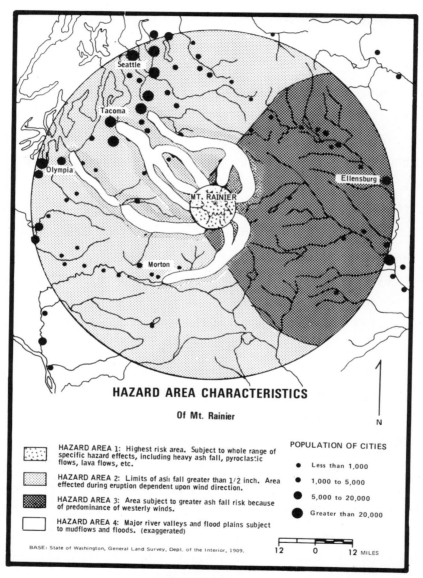

HAZARD AREA CHARACTERISTICS

Of Mt. Rainier

HAZARD AREA 1: Highest risk area. Subject to whole range of specific hazard effects, including heavy ash fall, pyroclastic flows, lava flows, etc.

HAZARD AREA 2: Limits of ash fall greater than 1/2 inch. Area effected during eruption dependent upon wind direction.

HAZARD AREA 3: Area subject to greater ash fall risk because of predominance of westerly winds.

HAZARD AREA 4: Major river valleys and flood plains subject to mudflows and floods. (exaggerated)

POPULATION OF CITIES

• Less than 1,000

● 1,000 to 5,000

● 5,000 to 20,000

● Greater than 20,000

BASE: State of Washington, General Land Survey, Dept. of the Interior, 1909.

12   0   12 MILES

FIGURE 11-23

HAZARD AREA CHARACTERISTICS
Of Mt. Rainier

Research is recommended along several major lines, corre-
sponding largely to the modes of adjustment noted above (see
Table 11-19).

Prediction and warning - The most advanced techniques for volcanic eruption prediction presently are applied for the less-
violent type volcanoes of Hawaii, where the Hawaiian Volcano
Observatory (HVO) has made significant gains in prediction
research. In comparison, predictive capability for the explo-
sive volcanoes of the Cascades and Alaska is minimal. The number of volcanoes, and their infrequent eruptive nature, are
constraints to the establishment of intensive HVO-like operations in these two areas. Yet, the highly dangerous and diverse specific hazards (like pyroclastic flows, volcanic mudflows and floods, and widespread ashfalls), make prediction
highly desirable. The large areal extent and population vulnerable to the characteristically pyroclastic-type eruptions
add further support, as do the projections for population
growth and urbanization.

To facilitate the development of effective prediction and
warning, four research efforts, integrally tied to each other,
stand out as necessary steps.

Monitoring and surveillance of individual volcanoes is crucial, since they would give some chance of early detection of
an eruption. An accumulation of valuable data on the characteristics of the volcanoes and their activity would also result. The National Aeronautics and Space Administration, the
U. S. Geological Survey, the University of Oregon, the University of Alaska, and others, have been involved in the effort.
This research needs expansion, with additional expenditures of
about 80 person years over ten years as a beginning.

There is strong need for geological and geophysical field

TABLE 11-19
RESEARCH OPPORTUNITIES-VOLCANO

Research Opportunity	Economic Efficiency Reduction of Net Losses Benefits-Costs		Enhancement of Human Health — Reduction of Casualties		Avoidance of Social Disruption		Environment — Protection or Enhancement	Equity — Distribution of Costs and Benefits	Research Findings Expected Success of Research	Likelihood of Adoption
	Average	Cata-strophic	Average	Cata-strophic	Average	Cata-strophic				
Prediction and Warning Surveillance and monitoring Geologic, geophysical and hydrologic	NA	Low	NA	High	NA	High	Low	Low	Med	High
Disaster Preparedness and Emergency Evacuation Social responses Warning response and capabilities	NA	Low	NA	High	NA	High	Low	Low	Med	Med-Low
Protection Measures Lava diversion barriers Reservoir vulnerability	NA	Med	NA	Med	NA	Low	Low	Low	High	Med-Low
Land Use Management Human adjustment Social evaluation of land use management	NA	Med-High	NA	Med	NA	Med	Med	Low	High	Low
Insurance	NA	Low	NA	Low	NA	Low	Low	High	High	Med
Relief and Rehabilitation	NA	Low	NA	Low	NA	Med	Low	Med	Low	Low
Individuals' Adjustments	NA	Med	NA	Med	NA	Low	Low	Low	Med	Low

Med = Medium   Neg = Negative   ? = In doubt   NA = Not applicable

investigations of individual volcanoes in the Cascades and
Alaska, the purpose being to get some notion of the probabilities, magnitudes, frequencies, areal extent, and nature of
eruptions. This would involve field studies of the geologic
history of the volcano, as well as its physical characteristics
and eruptive mechanisms. Hydrologic studies would be valuable
where mudflows and floods are potential dangers. Specific information of this type becomes extremely valuable to prediction
and warning because it not only helps to refine the judgment as
to when an eruption will occur, but also what to expect and
where. An expenditure of about 100 person years over a period
of ten years appears justified. This figure includes hazard
risk mapping--an opportunity to be discussed below--and may
seem very large by comparison with levels of expenditures for
more frequent events such as floods. It seems warranted by the
lack of attention given in the past to volcano hazard, and the
judgment that as an aid to long-term regional development,
these risks should be delimited promptly.

Geophysical research on volcanoes in foreign countries where
eruptions of volcanoes similar to those of the Cascades are
more frequent, may lead to the identification of important
predictive characteristics generally applicable to volcanoes
in the United States. With the possibility of integrating a
research program into some of the ongoing research in foreign
countries, an expenditure of around 40 person years over ten
years seems reasonable.

Inseparable from the two research opportunities just noted,
is the need for development and refinement of predictive methods, including new instrumentation applicable to Cascade and
Alaskan volcanoes. This is implied in the two previous research efforts, but not stated explicitly. Evaluating the
extent to which present predictive methods can be applied to

these volcanoes will point out the gaps that need to be filled by new research. Each volcano is apt to possess its own particular set of characteristics, necessitating careful examination of each individual volcano and the potential for its being predicted by existing or newly developed methods. The timing and cost of the research is largely indeterminable, since a great deal would be subsumed under the other efforts.

A fifth thrust of research important to prediction and warning is concerned with the dissemination of warning messages once they become available. It is particularly important for the more violent types of eruptions, where the lead time is commonly shorter in comparison to lava flow eruptions. An evaluation of existing warning systems and their applicability to the volcano hazard as outlined in Chapter 9 would clarify the need for new systems. Such an appraisal would not be costly and would take about ten person years over a three-year period. Some benefits possibly could be reaped almost immediately if an interim system specific to volcano hazard were to be organized.

Disaster preparedness and emergency evacuation - Disaster preparedness and emergency evacuation are strongly related to the effectiveness of warning. The results of research aimed at emergency evacuation and disaster preparedness would be useful in all three volcanic hazard areas of the United States, although the nature of the research needs varies slightly in Hawaii as compared to the Cascades or Alaska. The inhabitants of Hawaii have experienced many lava flows, and have developed disaster preparedness plans which take direct account of lava flow eruptions. The general public there is fairly well informed on what action to take. However, the volcano hazard situation in Alaska and, especially, the Cascades, is quite

different in this regard. The large range and magnitude of
effects which can be expected from a major eruption, the apparent lack of any volcano-specific disaster preparedness plans,
and the lack of awareness of the volcanic hazard and its consequences, suggest that research opportunities in this field may
have relatively high payoff.

Large-scale risk mapping of hazard areas is fundamental. It
is of primary concern to know what areas are most likely to be
affected by what hazard: which areas are subject to mudflows
and floods, what transportation routes are apt to be knocked
out, and which areas would most likely be least affected by
the eruption. This type of information is essential for the
formulation of effective plans for evacuation and preparedness.
Until recently, no work of this sort has been done. The time
required to complete an adequate site mapping would vary, depending to a large degree on how quickly and easily the necessary data from geologic and geophysical field investigations
could be made available. Large-scale risk mapping is tied
integrally to the geological and geophysical research opportunity noted earlier.

There is an important need for a thorough examination of
the full social consequences of a major volcanic eruption and
all its effects. It is clear that we really do not have a complete understanding of the possible outcomes of major eruptions,
especially if one were to occur in a relatively populated region of the Cascades. Research of this sort would require much
imaginative extrapolation, perhaps from some of the observed
effects on populations in other parts of the world. The cost
would be on the order of 40 person years over a ten-year period; it would be less initially, but increase as more basic data
become available. Until some understanding of the full social
consequences of volcano hazard effects comes, we will continue

to have a very limited basis for public policy decision-making on choice of adjustment to the hazard.

A third area of research relevant to disaster preparedness and evacuation would be the examination of the behavioral response of individuals to a volcanic eruption, or to the warning of impending volcanic disaster. The rationale for such research becomes clear in light of the experience of human behavior in other hazard situations. Even with elaborate means of evacuation and detailed preparedness, we are very uncertain of how individuals are going to react, especially when they have had no hazard experience. It is estimated that research of this nature would cost about six person years over three years.

Although the chances for successful completion of this research are fairly good, the lack of public experience with volcanic events and the overall low level of awareness of the hazard may pose serious constraints to the practical application of the results, particularly in the Pacific Northwest.

Protection - The opportunities for protective measures against the volcano hazard are limited. The enormity of the event makes the prospects of preventing volcanic eruptions unlikely. There are, however, two situations in which *control* of the specific volcanic hazard might be practicable--lava flows, and volcanic mudflows and floods. Specific research opportunities appear feasible for each of these cases.

An evaluation of the effectiveness, costs, benefits, and legal implications of lava diversion barriers may prove useful in preventing lava damage in Hawaii, especially in high risk areas where large amounts of damageable property already exist, or where building is likely to occur. At present, the effectiveness of such barriers is still a subject of controversy. The cost of research could be kept low, around two person years.

In the Pacific Northwest, mudflows and floods associated with volcanic activity are a real threat. The many dams and reservoirs constructed in the steep valleys of the Cascade Range may either compound the consequences of such an event by rupturing, or serve as protective barriers in retaining the onslaught. At present, no one is certain which effect would happen.

Studies designed to assess the effects of a volcanic hazard on existing dams and reservoirs in the Cascades are sorely needed. Although some exploratory work in this area has been initiated, a number of vital questions remain unanswered: how large a volcanic mudflow could each of the structures withstand; how much advance warning would be needed to accomplish drawdown of water levels; what would be the downstream effects if each were ruptured; and what structural or operational modifications could be imposed to enhance the protective qualities of the dams. Given the advanced state of engineering knowledge on such matters, the prospects for answering such questions are very good, with a cost of around ten person years over three to five years. However, successful completion of the research would depend in large part on basic data acquired from the geologic and hydrologic field investigations (described above).

Land use management - In all three hazard areas, the increase in population during the last ten years has been markedly rapid, with no effective attempts to regulate undesirable growth because of volcanic hazards. Although the population increase on the "big island" of Hawaii is not unusually rapid, there is a trend in some known high-hazard areas of change from agricultural land use to residential subdivisions and increased urbanization. Alaska has experienced recent volcanic activity, and although it is sparsely populated at present, there could be a

serious threat to future habitation, especially in light of the
recent attention being given to Alaska's energy resources.

There is a major research need for a social evaluation of
land use management as an adjustment to volcanic hazards, en-
compassing, at this stage, a broad overview of the economic,
political, legal, and institutional characteristics involved.
This type of preliminary research would investigate such subjects as the particular tools of land use management best
suited to specific volcano hazards; legal precedents for regulating volcanic risk areas; status of enabling legislation;
community attitudes toward adoption; and kinds of land uses
judged compatible, and not compatible, with certain volcanic
hazard situations. A research endeavor of this magnitude would
have a cost in the order of 12 person years over two years.

Insurance - Although there is evidence of a trend towards wider
availability of coverage under standard property policies, insurance against risk of volcanic eruption has been negligible
to date. However, there is a strong possibility that as the
nation moves closer to considering some forms of all-hazard
insurance, losses resulting from volcanic eruption will be
included in a more nearly comprehensive insurance program.
Looking toward the day when these possibilities could become
reality, the most fruitful application of research may be the
volcanic risk mapping and all investigations relevant to it.
In regard to more specific research into aspects of volcano
insurance per se, perhaps the best course of action would be
to wait and see what becomes of those trends. To do otherwise
might result either in duplication of effort or in unproduc-
tive kinds of research emphases.

Relief and rehabilitation - A well-established institutional framework for providing relief and rehabilitation to victims of natural disasters exists, and if the trends toward greater assumption of hazard costs by society as a whole are realized, the future may see this framework expanded. In the event of a major volcanic disaster, the Federal government, private relief organizations, and state and local governments would step in to lighten the burden of loss suffered by individuals and the affected communities. For minor volcanic disasters, the responsibility for relief and rehabilitation falls more squarely on the stricken state. The existing structure for relief and rehabilitation, therefore, probably would not warrant research aimed at expanding the present system.

A much needed research opportunity lies in the evaluation of the present system, focusing specifically upon the dynamic feedback relationships between relief and rehabilitation, alternative modes of adjustment, and other individual decisions. Such a volcano-related research effort should be combined with the same research focus on a range of hazards.

Other individual adjustments - Individuals can take a number of actions to prevent damage or injury from volcanic events, especially ash falls. Given the fact that ash fall from an eruption in either the Cascades or Alaska would be likely to affect the largest area and the greatest number of people, the potential for these adjustments to reduce loss appears large. However, inexperience with the hazard, particularly in the Cascades, probably causes the affected population to be unfamiliar with the actions available to it.

A worthwhile research opportunity would be an evaluation of effective sets of individual adjustments for specific volcano hazard locations, and the development of means to inform the population of their availability. For a preliminary analysis it is felt that two person years for one to two years would be justified.

All adjustments - In addition to the more specific kinds of research oriented towards particular types of adjustments, there are opportunities for research that are general enough to have importance in the whole adjustment process. Four such research opportunities top the list.

In comparing the volcano hazard situation in the world with that of the United States, it becomes quite apparent that the rest of the world has much to offer through experience with volcanic eruptions--experience which, especially for pyro-clastic-type eruption, the United States has yet to undergo. A program of cross-cultural research aimed at investigation and evaluation of the differential modes and conditions of human adjustment, adaptation, and response to volcano hazard, may well contribute greatly toward the understanding of, and adjustment to, volcano hazard in the United States. This research might take the form of an international enterprise in which the United States could play a leading role. A funding level of 15 person years over five years would seem reasonable.

There is need for a clearer understanding of the interaction between selected types of adjustment to volcano hazard. At present, our knowledge of these potential interactions is mea-ger. For example, an important question to be addressed in this regard is the possible effect that existing dams--if modi-fied to provide at least partial protection against volcanic mudflows and floods--could have on the adoption of land use management, insurance, and disaster preparedness in the Pacific Northwest. An initial expenditure of six person years over three years appears justified.

A valuable research effort would be to look into the

compatibility of other geophysical hazard adjustments to volcano hazard. The diversity of specific hazards associated with
volcanic eruption suggests that there might be some amount of
cross-over of the adjustment process to volcano hazard. An
example is the potential for some flood hazard adjustments to
serve simultaneously as adjustments to volcanically-generated
mudflows and floods. Perhaps in some cases only minor coordination of objectives would be necessary to allow an adjustment
to serve a dual purpose. Funding at a level of ten person
years over a five-year period is warranted.

Society is not accustomed to making explicit decisions about
potentially catastrophic, low probability events such as volcanic eruption. Only recently has the compounding of these
hazards as a product of complex technology made the need seem
acute. Such an evaluative framework is necessary in order to
utilize effectively basic data from research on the physical
characteristics and social consequences of volcanic eruptions
and to develop further some level of adjustment to the hazard
which is compatible with social aims and objectives. Encouragement of research directed toward these ends would prove
valuable not only for decision-making in the face of the risks
and uncertainties of volcano hazard, but for a wide range of
other geophysical and man-made hazards as well. Although similar research endeavors are underway in other fields (such as
nuclear reactor risk), additional expenditures of about 40
person years over five years directed specifically at the volcano hazard problem would be worthwhile.

Coordination of research - No single agency has major responsibility for volcano research and the work has been rather
restricted in outlook, and encumbered by the uncertainty of
occurrence of the next significant eruption. In these

circumstances, there would be merit in an agency taking the
lead in stimulating work which seems necessary upon the basis
of risk analysis, and also in encouraging exchange of information and viewpoints among concerned investigators and agencies.
Because of its experience with volcano hazard research and its
demonstration of flexibility and innovativeness in other hazard
fields, it is recommended that the U. S. Geological Survey take
this lead role.

New research initiated at a modest level of funding would
benefit from a systematic appraisal from time to time. This
function could be performed by the National Science Foundation,
or perhaps carried out jointly by NSF and the U.S.G.S. Its
role in the near future should be that of helping to stimulate
participation by nongovernmental groups in the research activities outlined above.

Summary

The new research activity outlined in the preceding sections
covers a wide range of scientific skills and interests. It is
described primarily to suggest the likely significance of the
needed work and its characteristics. Cost estimates are made
with the knowledge that, as in any research enterprise, they
may be far off the mark. The estimates are consistently con-
servative in taking lower limits of cost. They also assume
that much of the work will be exploratory and either will be
terminated after the suggested trial period or will be expanded
on the basis of favorable results. To emphasize the rough
character of the estimates they are stated as person years
rather than dollar units. They recognize that some work requiring heavy investment in equipment, such as in nighttime
tornado detection, will be far more costly per professional
worker than studies involving analysis of available data. The

person year is defined as comprising one professional worker
with support services and expenses, and at 1974 prices may run
$60,000 per year on the average.

Total new research work over a ten-year period would amount
to approximately 4,162 person years (see Table 11-20). Using
a mean cost of $60,000 per person year, this would involve
total new research expenditures of about $250 million. Annual
expenditures might be expected to run in the neighborhood of
$30 million in the early years and then either to slacken off
or expand, depending upon the demonstrated value of the various
projects.

Administrators familiar with national research programs may
regard the totals as far too modest in view of the needs. The
figures are set at that level not because of any anticipated
budget restraints but through prudence in recommending a large
number of new and unconventional starts. The opportunities are
stated cautiously rather than glowingly. The total amount of
effort proposed is less than 5% of the mean annual direct property losses from all 15 hazards. It is at least 2% of the
likely direct property losses from another 1906 magnitude
earthquake in San Francisco. The annual level of expenditure
is equivalent to one-half of recent annual research and development expenditures by the Forest Service or the U. S. Geological Survey, but would be widely distributed among Federal
and non-Federal agencies.

In arriving at the suggestions for each hazard, no attempt
is made to balance the level of expenditures among hazards on
the basis of current levels of activity or of burden of losses.
Thus, the suggested expenditures for frost are far below those
for hurricane because the opportunities are more promising for
one than the other. There have been no major volcanic eruptions in the continental United States, yet the possibility of

TABLE 11-20
SUMMARY OF RESEARCH OPPORTUNITIES IN RELATION TO CURRENT LEVELS OF FUNDING

HAZARD	RESEARCH OPPORTUNITIES SETS	CURRENT ANNUAL FUNDING LEVEL*	SUGGESTED ADDITIONAL PERSON YEARS TOTAL**	TIME HORIZON IN YEARS
Hurricane:	Land Use Management			
	Hazard mapping methods	1	20	5
	Adoption of new management	0	50	10
	Socioeconomic effects	0	50	10
	Hurricane-proofing: Technology	2	10	5
	Adoption	0	25	5
	Hurricane Modification			
	Hurricane dynamics	3	P	0
	Technology	2	P	0
	Socioeconomic effects	0	15	3
	Warning Systems			
	Evacuation methods	0	24	4
	Dissemination and response	0	50	10
	Relief and Rehabilitation			
	Trends, policy, socioeconomic effects	0	30	5
	Insurance			
	Policy formulation	0	3	3
	Adoption of insurance	1	16	4
			293	
Flood:	Control and Protection			
	Urban sewer and storm drainage	1	100	10
	Channel hydraulics	2	50	10
	Warning Systems and Flood-proofing			
	Forecasting methods	1	100	10
	Improving warning programs	1	60	10

* 0 = No expenditure or less than $10,000
1 = $10,000-$100,000
2 = $100,000-$1,000,000
3 = $1,000,000-$2,000,000
4 = Greater than $2,000,000

** Estimates are for the total number of person years over a period of 10 years: some projects may run only 1 year, others as long as 10 years.

P Program underway could include suggested work.

-continued

TABLE 11-20 continued

HAZARD	RESEARCH OPPORTUNITIES SETS	CURRENT ANNUAL FUNDING LEVEL*	SUGGESTED ADDI-TIONAL PERSON YEARS TOTAL**	TIME HORIZON IN YEARS
Flood: (continued)	Flood-proofing technology	0	40	10
	Physical and social aspects of proofing	0	10	5
	Feedback effects of flood-proofing	0	5	5
	Land Use Management			
	Adoption processes	0	30	10
	Social effectiveness	1	8	5
	Coordination of land measures	0	30	10
	Insurance, Relief and Rehabilitation			
	Hazard awareness and insurance purchase	1	P	10
	Linkage with land use	2		
	Compulsory flood insurance	0	5	5
	Influence on flood loss potential	0	10	5
	Relief and rehabilitation impacts	1	50	3-10
	Methods of providing relief	0	10	3
	Basic Data and Methods			
	Flood frequency estimation methods	3	100	10
	Hazard mapping methods	1	25	5
	Flood damage variables	1	100	5
	Public participation in choice	1	100	10
	Optimal mix of adjustments	1	60	5
			893	
Tornado:	Building Design and Codes			
	Design and code improvement	1	80	4
	Adoption of improved codes	0	20	3-4
	Warning Systems			
	Detection	1	100	10
	Dissemination	0	25	5
	Response	0	30	3
	Insurance Influence on Building Design	0	5	2
			260	

- continued

TABLE 11-20 continued

HAZARD	RESEARCH OPPORTUNITIES SETS	CURRENT ANNUAL FUNDING LEVEL*	SUGGESTED ADDITIONAL PERSON YEARS TOTAL**	TIME HORIZON IN YEARS
Lightning:	Electrical and Electronic Systems			
	Atmospheric electricity	2	40	10
	Protection technology	1	20	10
	Adoption of improved devices	0	3	2
	Forest Fire Management			
	Fire ecology	2	P	10
	Forest fire management program	0	20	10
	Management technology	3	P	10
	Adoption of improved methods	0	2	5
			85	
Hail:	Hail Suppression and Related Studies	3	150	10
	Insurance: Policy Formulation and Adoption	1	10	5
	Land Use Management	1	15	5
			175	
Windstorm:	Land Use Management			
	Data collection and dissemination	2	15	10
	Building technology for wind resistance	3	25	10
	Adoption of improved techniques	0	10	5
	Socioeconomic effects of management	0	5	5
	Insurance			
	Current trends	0	2	5
	Policy formulation	0	3	5
	Adoption of coverage	1	2	5
			62	

- continued

TABLE 11-20 continued

HAZARD	RESEARCH OPPORTUNITIES SETS	CURRENT ANNUAL FUNDING LEVEL*	SUGGESTED ADDITIONAL PERSON-YEARS TOTAL**	TIME HORIZON IN YEARS
Frost:	Improved Loss Data	1	30	5
	Aids to Selection of Adjustments	0	60	10
	Crop Insurance Operations and Effects	0	40	5
	Prediction and Forecasting	2	P	10
	Protection Methods	1	10	10
			140	
Urban Snow:	Local Government Finances and Management	0	2	2
	Prediction			
	Indicator of social mobility	0	3	3
	Performance of equipment	0	2	2
	Forecast accuracy	1	3	2
	Warning Dissemination--contingent	1	2	2
	Snowfest Experimentation	0	1	2
	Disruption Insurance	0	2	1
			15	
Earthquake:	Earthquake Reduction			
	Geophysical and engineering	3	P	10
	Adoption processes for new techniques	0	25	5
	Earthquake-resistant Construction			
	Analysis, design of building codes	4	200	10
	Code implementation	0	25	5
	Old building treatment	0	100	10
	Code adoption processes	0	30	5
	Land Use Management			
	Seismic risk zoning studies	1	200	10
	Zoning adoption processes	0	40	5
	Prediction and Warning			
	Geophysical aspects	4	P	10
	Warning system implementation	0	50	5
	Insurance			
	Adoption processes	1	10	5
	All-risk insurance	0	20	5

- continued

TABLE 11-20 continued

HAZARD	RESEARCH OPPORTUNITIES SETS	CURRENT ANNUAL FUNDING LEVEL*	SUGGESTED ADDITIONAL PERSON YEARS TOTAL**	TIME HORIZON IN YEARS
Earthquake (continued)	Community Preparedness, Relief and Rehabilitation			
	Micro-studies of vulnerability	1	30	5
	Preparedness studies	1	25	5
	Processes and socioeconomic effects	0	25	5
			780	
Tsunami:	Tsunami-resistant Construction			
	Analysis, design, building codes	0	5	5
	Adoption processes	0	2	5
	Land Use Management			
	Risk zoning studies	0	10	10
	Zoning adoption processes	0	2	5
	Warning Systems: Detection, Dissemination, Response	1	10	5
	Community Preparedness			
	Vulnerability studies	0	3	5
	Insurance and Tsunami History	1	3	5
			35	
Landslide:	Protection Works			
	Design	1	10	10
	Usage	1	2	3
	Prediction			
	Hazard region delimitation	0	2	1
	Case studies and regional methods	1	40	10
	Site-specific predictions	2	35	10
	Land Use Management			
	Codes and code adoption	0	15	5
	Insurance			
	Expansion of NFIP	0	1	2
	Adoption of insurance	1	3	2
	Information Program	0	50	10
			158	

- continued

TABLE 11-20 continued

HAZARD	RESEARCH OPPORTUNITIES SETS	CURRENT ANNUAL FUNDING LEVEL*	SUGGESTED ADDITIONAL PERSON YEARS TOTAL**	TIME HORIZON IN YEARS
Snow Avalanche:	Control and Protection			
	Prediction and Warning	2	100	10
	Land Use Management			
	Information Program			
			100	
Coastal Erosion:	Control and Protection Measures			
	Data coordination	0	2	2
	Data collection	2	40	10
	Loss evaluation procedures	0	5	2
	Sand resources evaluation	2	20	10
	Sand delivery system	1	5	2
	Environmental aspects of control	0	20	10
	Effects on littoral processes	0	40	10
	Broadening range of private action	0	10	10
	Land Use Management			
	Evaluation and adoption of land use controls	0	26	10
	Improved public participation	0	10	5
	Delineation of erosion risk zones	0	40	10
	Warning and Forecasting Systems	0	15	10
	Comprehensive Coastal Hazard Insurance	0	5	5
			238	
Drought-Rural:	Irrigation and Water Supply Conservation			
	Technical aspects of water supply conservation		P	5
	User efficiency	1	25	5
	Water laws/institutions	1	20	5
	Weather Modification			
	Technology evaluation	3	P	7-10
	Methods of social evaluation	0	P	5
	Legal and other social aspects of adoption	2	P	3-5

- continued

TABLE 11-20 continued

HAZARD	RESEARCH OPPORTUNITIES SETS	CURRENT ANNUAL FUNDING LEVEL*	SUGGESTED ADDITIONAL PERSON YEARS TOTAL**	TIME HORIZON IN YEARS
Drought-Rural (continued)	Land Use Regulation			
	Long-term land use alternatives	0	100	10
	Role of drought in emerging land use legislation	0	40	5
	Prediction and Forecast			
	Climatic modeling	3	P	10
	Use of information	1	P	
	Drought probability studies	2	P	10
	Operational Flexibility and Cultivation Practices			
	Drought-resistant, high-yield varieties	3	P	10
	Normative models of decision-making	1	40	5
	Financial Protection			
	Adoption processes	1	20	10
	Alternative policies	0	12	3
	Relief and Rehabilitation			
	Long-term system effects	0	20	5
	Food Supply Management			
	Drought contingency plans	0	100	5-7
	Alternative agricultural patterns	0	100	10
			477	
Drought-Urban:	Desalination and Recycling Technology Improvement	4	P	10
	Improving Conventional Water Supply Systems			
	Probability studies	1	P	10
	Institutional potential for furthering regional cooperation	0	20	2
	Altering Water Demand			
	Technologies of water-saving devices at user level	1	30	3-5
	Mix of Adjustments			
	Evaluative methods and criteria	1	20	2
			70	

- continued

TABLE 11-20 continued

HAZARD	RESEARCH OPPORTUNITIES SETS	CURRENT ANNUAL FUNDING LEVEL*	SUGGESTED ADDITIONAL PERSON YEARS TOTAL**	TIME HORIZON IN YEARS
Volcano:	Surveillance and Monitoring	2	80	10
	Geologic and Geophysical Risk Mapping	2	100	10
	Foreign Experience	1	40	10
	Lava Diversion Barriers	0	2	2
	Relation to Existing Reservoirs	0	10	5
	Social Consequences of Eruptions	0	40	10
	Behavioral Response to Warning	0	6	3
	Feedback Mechanisms in Adjustments	0	6	3
	Cross-cultural Investigations	0	15	5
	Evaluation of Land Use Management	0	12	2
	Compatability With Other Adjustments	0	10	5
	Means of Informing Public of Choice	0	2	2
	Warning System	0	10	3
	Effects of Relief and Rehabilitation	0	8	5
	Public Policy on Low Probability Events	2	40	5
			381	
Total:	All Hazards		4,162	

* 0 = No expenditure or less than $10,000
1 = $10,000-$100,000
2 = $100,000-$1,000,000
3 = $1,000,000-$2,000,000
4 = Greater than $2,000,000

** Estimates are for the total number of person years over a period of 10 years: some projects may run only 1 year, others as long as 10 years.

P Program underway could include suggested work.

one catastrophe weighs the balance in favor of undertaking an expanded program of studies on volcano hazard. The full array of opportunities reflects the assessment of likely returns for each hazard. It should be viewed as presenting the chief thrusts which deserve early attention in conjunction with the two related sets of activity described in Chapters 9 and 10 and summarized in Table 1-1.

The major conclusions from the assessment of the country's response to 15 geophysical hazards are implicit in the opportunities for research outlined in Tables 1-1 and 11-20. New emphasis needs to be infused in the nation's research effort to balance attention to technological solutions with attention to social measures. The new work would gain in value and relevance to national aims if it were organized around a few common themes of land use management, warning systems, hazard-resistant techniques, insurance and relief and rehabilitation. It would be strengthened by postaudits, longitudinal studies, clearinghouse services, immediate scientific assistance to states, and legislative overview which cut across all the hazards. Unless these changes take place, the national prospect is for rising property losses and increased vulnerability to catastrophe.

S. T. Algermissen
Branch of Seismicity and
  Risk Analysis
U. S. Geological Survey

John D. Alyea
Climatologist
State of Wyoming

D. R. Anderson
Washington State Department
  of Highways

William Anderson
Department of Sociology
Arizona State University

Richard Armstrong
Institute for Arctic and
  Alpine Research
University of Colorado

Montgomery Atwater
Avalanche Hazard Consultant

George W. Baker
National Science Foundation

Jerry Barnes
Salt Lake County Planner

Jack Barrows
Forest and Wood Sciences
Colorado State University

Duane Baumann
Department of Geography
Southern Illinois University

Jacquelyn Beyer
University of Colorado

Larry M. Boone
U. S. Department of
  Agriculture

Stewart W. Borland
National Center for Atmospheric Research

Charles Bradley
Department of Earth Sciences
Montana State University

Ian Burton
Department of Geography
University of Toronto

Joseph M. Caldwell
Coastal Hazard Consultant

Stanley A. Changnon
Illinois State Water Survey

Doak C. Cox
Environmental Center
University of Hawaii

Charles Culver
National Bureau of Standards

Ernest Dobrovolny
U. S. Geological Survey

Thomas E. Drabek
Department of Sociology
University of Denver

Fillmore C. Earney
Department of Geography
Northern Michigan University

Ted Fletcher
Public Service Company of
  Colorado

Don G. Friedman
Traveler's Insurance Company

Charles Fritz
NAS Advisory Committee on
  Emergency Planning

Tetsuya Fujita
Department of Geophysical
  Sciences
University of Chicago

Fred Glover
Thorne Ecological Institute

James E. Goddard
Consulting Engineer

Richard F. Gordon
American National Red Cross

Samuel O. Grimm, Jr.
Emergency Warning Branch
National Weather Service

Daniel Guice
Mayor of Biloxi, Mississippi

Vernon K. Hagen
Hydrologic Engineering Branch
U. S. Army Corps of Engineers

Keith Hart
Planner, City and Borough of
  Juneau, Alaska

L. M. Hartman
Department of Economics
Colorado State University

Charles Hertzberg
Small Business Administration

Leslie Hewes
Department of Geography
University of Nebraska

Marvin Hoover
Consultant

William Hotchkiss
National Ski Patrol System

George Housner
Earthquake Engineering
California Institute of
  Technology

Ed Jackson
Department of Geography
University of Toronto

Robert E. James
City Manager
San Fernando, California

Joseph W. Johnson
Department of Civil
  Engineering
University of California,
  Berkeley

Heinz W. Kasemir
Environmental Research
  Laboratory
National Oceanic and Atmos-
  pheric Administration

Robert W. Kates
Graduate School of Geography
Clark University

Edwin Kessler
National Severe Storms
  Laboratory
National Oceanic and Atmos-
  pheric Administration

Carl Kisslinger
Cooperative Institute for
  Research in Environmental
  Sciences
University of Colorado

Tom Koederitz
Water Superintendent
City of San Angelo, Texas

Edward R. LaChapelle
Department of Geophysics
University of Washington

James F. Lander
Environmental Data Service
National Oceanic and Atmos-
  pheric Administration

Theodore H. Levin
Federal Insurance
  Administration

John Lukens
State of Colorado Division
  of Emergency Services

Frank Manda
Federal Disaster Assistance
  Administration

Pete Martinelli
Rocky Mountain Forest and
  Range Experimental Station

John McGowan
American National Red Cross

Terry Minger
City Manager, Vail, Colorado

J. Kenneth Mitchell
Department of Environmental
  Resources
Rutgers University

Ugo Morelli
Federal Disaster Assistance
  Administration

William Napier
Ski Touring Groups

Robert Patton
Colorado Division of Highways

Carl F. Pawlass
State of Colorado Defense
  Civil Preparedness Agency

Allen Pearson
National Severe Storms
  Forecast Center
National Weather Service

George Phippen
Flood Plain Management
  Service
U. S. Army Corps of Engineers

Roy Popkin
American National Red Cross

Marshall Richards
National Weather Service

Clifford Russell
Resources for the Future, Inc.

Erling Rustad
State of Colorado Defense
  Civil Preparedness Agency

Thomas F. Saarinen
Department of Geography
University of Arizona

Marshall E. Sanders
Disaster Preparedness Division
Federal Disaster Assistance
  Administration

Robert Simpson
Department of Environmental
  Sciences
University of Virginia

Gary Soucie
Audubon Society

Karl V. Steinbrugge
Pacific Regional Insurance
  Services Office

Dick Stillman
U. S. Forest Service

Charles C. Thiel
National Science Foundation

Donald Thomas
Surface Water Branch
U. S. Geological Survey

Clem Todd
U. S. Bureau of Reclamation

Howard H. Waldron
U. S. Geological Survey

A. U. White
Commission on Man and
    Environment
International Geographical
    Union

Robert Whitman
Department of Civil
    Engineering
Massachusetts Institute of
    Technology

Clifford L. Williams
Soil Conservation Service

David Arey
Department of Geography
Southern Illinois University

Maurice D. Arnold
Bureau of Outdoor Recreation

William B. Barstow
Boulder County Engineer

Louis J. Battan
Institute of Atmospheric
   Physics
University of Arizona

Kurt W. Bauer
Southeastern Wisconsin
   Regional Planning
   Commission

John Bennett
Department of Sociology
   and Anthropology
Washington University

Sheldon G. Boone
Western U. S. Water Plan Unit
U. S. Department of
   Agriculture

John Borchert
Center for Urban and Regional
   Affairs
University of Minnesota

Earl E. Brabb
Branch of Western Environ-
   mental Geology
U. S. Geological Survey

Ian Campbell
Consulting Geologist
San Francisco

J. E. Cermak
College of Engineering
Colorado State University

George Cleveland
Division of Mines and Geology
California Polytechnical
   State University

Dwight Crandell
Engineering Geology Branch
U. S. Geological Survey

Robert Dolan
School of Environmental
   Sciences
University of Virginia

C. Martin Duke
Earthquake Engineering
   Research Institute
University of California,
   Los Angeles

Carlos R. Dunn
Scientific Services
National Weather Service

Edward S. Epstein
Environmental Monitoring
   and Prediction
National Oceanic and Atmospheric Administration

Virgil Eskew
Office of Intergovernmental
   Affairs
U. S. Department of
   Agriculture

Neal FitzSimons
Research Council on the
   Performance of Structures
   of the American Society
   of Civil Engineers

J. Ernest Flack
College of Engineering and
   Applied Science
University of Colorado

Louis Fong
National Aeronautics and
  Space Administration

George W. Griebenow
Upper Mississippi River
  Basin Commission

Warren A. Hall
Office of Water Resources
  Research
U. S. Department of the
  Interior

Irving Hand
Institute of State and
  Regional Affairs
Pennsylvania State University

William J. Hanna
College of Engineering and
  Applied Science
University of Colorado

Donald Henley, Jr.
Communications and Emergency
  Services
County of San Bernardino

Douglas Inman
Scripps Institute of
  Oceanography
University of California

Richard H. Jackson
Brigham Young University

Laurence Jahn
Wildlife Management Institute

L. Douglas James
Environmental Resources
  Center
Georgia Institute of
  Technology

Eugene F. Johnson
Rollins Burdick Hunter Co.

Mortimer Kaplan
Consulting Actuary

Carl Kindsvatter
U. S. Geological Survey

W. Kirby
U. S. Geological Survey

Samuel Kramer
National Bureau of Standards

Richard W. Krimm
Federal Insurance
  Administration, Flood
  Insurance Division

Howard Kunreuther
Wharton School of Finance
  and Commerce
University of Pennsylvania

Jon Kusler
Lawyer and Land Use
  Consultant

Helmut Landsberg
Graduate Committee on
  Meteorology
University of Maryland

Edward H. Lesesne
Tennessee Valley Authority

Ray K. Linsley
School of Engineering
Stanford University

Gordon A. Macdonald
Institute for Geophysics
University of Hawaii

Robert Martin
Defense Civil Preparedness
  Administration

Marion Marts
Department of Geography,
  Urban Planning
University of Washington

Alexander McBirney
Center for Volcanology
University of Oregon

Jerome Milliman
Center for Urban Affairs
University of Southern
  California

Keith Muckleston
Department of Geography
Oregon State University

Donald R. Mullineaux
U. S. Geological Survey

Clark F. Norton
Senate Committee on Public
  Works
United States Senate

Donald W. Peterson
Hawaii Volcano Observatory
U. S. Geological Survey

M. R. Peterson
Federal Crop Insurance
  Corporation
U. S. Department of
  Agriculture

M. X. Polk
Office of Telecommunications
  Policy

Ren Read
Defense Civil Preparedness
  Administration

Leslie E. Robertson
Skilling, Helle, Christiansen,
  Robertson
Consulting Structural and
  Civil Engineers

Gerald D. Robinson
The Center for the Environment
  and Man, Inc.

Steven O. Rosen
Case Western Reserve
  University

Herbert S. Saffir
Consulting Engineers

E. S. Savas
Graduate School of Business
Columbia University in the
  City of New York

Richard A. Schleusener
Institute of Atmospheric
  Sciences
South Dakota School of Mines
  and Technology

William J. Schneider
U. S. Geological Survey

C. F. Stewart Sharpe
Consulting Geologist

Lois Sharpe
Environmental Quality
  Department
League of Women Voters

Robert Shaw
Department of Climatology
  and Meteorology
Iowa State University

John Sims
Department of Psychology
George Williams College

Richard H. Sullivan
American Public Works
    Association

Herbert Thom
Consulting Climatologist
Labadieville, Louisiana

L. Scott Tucker
Urban Drainage and Flood
    Control District

Robert M. Ward
Department of Geography
East Michigan University

Fred Wells
National Oceanic and Atmos-
    pheric Administration

Ray Wilcox
U. S. Geological Survey

M. Gordon Wolman
Department of Geography and
    Environmental Engineering
Johns Hopkins University

Robert S. Ayre

Earl J. Baker

E. M. Beck

Mitchel J. Beville

Karen K. Bird

Waltraud A. R. Brinkmann

Anita Cochran

Harold C. Cochrane

Frederick W. Dauer

Barbara S. Dunn

Neil J. Ericksen

J. Eugene Haas

Daya Hewapathirane

Paul C. Huszar

Janice R. Hutton

Lee E. Kapaloski

Doris Knapp

Brian A. Knowles

Sigmund Krane

Michael K. Lindell

J. Gordon McPhee

Dennis S. Mileti

Allan Murphy

Jacque Myers

Sarah K. Nathe

Deanna J. Nervig

Madalyn M. Parsons

John H. Sorensen

Patricia B. Trainer

Hazel Visvader

Richard A. Warrick

Gilbert F. White

Maurice L. Albertson
Department of Civil
  Engineering
Colorado State University

S. T. Algermissen
Branch of Seismicity and
  Risk Analysis
U. S. Geological Survey

William Anderson
Department of Sociology
Arizona State University

David Jo Armor
The Rand Corporation

Holt Ashley
National Science Foundation

Charles Babendreier
National Science Foundation

George W. Baker
National Science Foundation

Harvey O. Banks
Consulting Engineer

Allen H. Barton
Bureau of Applied
  Sociological Research
Columbia University

Frederick L. Bates
Department of Sociology
University of Georgia

Louis J. Battan
Institute of Atmospheric
  Physics
University of Arizona

Duane Baumann
Department of Geography
Southern Illinois University

Curtis Beckmann
National Association of Radio
  & Television News Directors

Julie Bingham
National League of Cities and
  U. S. Conference of Mayors

Robert Blackwell
Mayor
Highland Park, Michigan

Robert Blair
Federal Disaster Assistance
  Administration

Stewart Borland
National Center for Atmospheric Research

Kenneth E. Boulding
Institute of Behavioral
  Science
University of Colorado

Robert Brown
San Francisco Bay Region
  Study
U. S. Geological Survey

Ian Burton
Department of Geography
University of Toronto

Dave Calfee
Environmental Policy Center

Emery N. Castle
Department of Economics
Oregon State University

Henry Caulfield, Jr.
Dept. of Political Science
Colorado State University

Robert Citron
Smithsonian Institution

Robert A. Clark
National Weather Service

Melvin Cohen
Labor's Community Agency, Inc.

Earl Cook
College of Geosciences
Texas A & M University

Walter Coward
Department of Rural
   Sociology
Cornell University

Doak C. Cox
Environmental Center
University of Hawaii

Charles Culver
Office of Federal Building
   Technology
National Bureau of Standards

Alvin Dalke
Alaska Disaster Office

Thomas E. Drabek
Department of Sociology
University of Denver

C. Martin Duke
Earthquake Engineering
   Research Institute
University of California

Thomas P. Dunne
Federal Disaster Assistance
   Administration

William M. Dye
State Farm Fire and
   Casualty Company

James J. Eagan
Mayor
Florissant, Missouri

Donald Eddy
Federal Disaster Assistance
   Administration

Alfred J. Eggers
National Science Foundation

Edward S. Epstein
Environmental Monitoring and
   Prediction
National Oceanic and Atmos-
   pheric Administration

Virgil M. Eskew
U. S. Department of
   Agriculture

J. Ernest Flack
Department of Civil
   Engineering
University of Colorado

Robert Fleagle
Department of Atmospheric
   Sciences
University of Washington

Olin H. Foehner
Bureau of Reclamation

James B. Foley
American National Red Cross

Don G. Friedman
Travelers Insurance Company

H. Paul Friesema
Department of Political
   Science
Northwestern University

Hubert R. Gallagher
Council of State Governments

Roger Gibbons
System Development
   Corporation

John M. Gibson
Emergency Preparedness Staff
Department of Housing and
  Urban Development

Lewis Grant
Department of Atmospheric
  Sciences
Colorado State University

George W. Griebenow
Upper Mississippi River
  Basin Commission

John Hadd
U. S. Army Corps of Engineers

William Haddon, Jr.
Insurance Institute for
  Highway Safety

Vernon K. Hagen
U. S. Army Corps of Engineers

C. Robert Hall
National Association of
  Independent Insurers

Walter P. Halstead
Hennepin County Office of
  Civil Defense and Disaster
  Planning

Bruce B. Hanshaw
U. S. Geological Survey

Thomas A. Heberlein
Department of Rural Sociology
University of Wisconsin

Robert Helmreich
Department of Psychology
University of Texas

Wilmot Hess
Environmental Research
  Laboratory
National Oceanic and Atmos-
  pheric Administration

Michael Holtz
American Institute of Architects Research Corporation

C. Nelson Hostetter
Mennonite Disaster Service

George Housner
Earthquake Engineering
California Institute of
  Technology

Charles Howe
Department of Economics
University of Colorado

Fred Ingham
American Society of Insurance
  Managers

Laurence Jahn
Wildlife Management Institute

L. Douglas James
Environmental Resources Center
Georgia Institute of Technology

Robert E. James
City Manager
City of San Fernando

Eugene F. Johnson
Rollins Burdick Hunter Company

Peter Jutro
U. S. House of Representatives
  Committee on Public Works

Archie M. Kahan
Bureau of Reclamation

David A. Katcher
National Advisory Committee
on Oceans and Atmosphere

Robert Kates
Graduate School of Geography
Clark University

Edwin Kessler
National Severe Storms
Laboratory
National Oceanic and Atmos-
pheric Administration

James Keysor
Joint Committee on Seismic
Safety
State of California

Carl Kisslinger
Cooperative Institute for
Research in Environmental
Sciences
University of Colorado

Robert W. Knecht
Office of Coastal Environment
National Oceanic and Atmospheric Administration

Richard W. Krimm
Federal Insurance
Administration

Howard Kunreuther
Department of Economics
Wharton School of Finance
and Commerce

Edward H. Lesesne
Tennessee Valley Authority

Robert Logan
Local Governmental Relations
Division
State of Oregon

Ruth P. Mack
Institute of Public
Administration

Richard F. Madole
Arctic and Alpine Research
Institute
University of Colorado

Robert J. Mahler
National Bureau of Standards

Frank Manda
Federal Disaster Assistance
Administration

Floyd Mann
Environmental Council
University of Colorado

Pete Martinelli
Rocky Mountain Forest and
Experimental Station

William Marty
Emergency Services
Organization

William G. McIntire
Coastal Studies Institute
Louisiana State University

Robert McNee
American Geographical
Society

James McQuigg
Environmental Data Service
National Oceanic and Atmos-
pheric Administration

Jerome W. Milliman
Center for Urban Affairs
University of Southern
  California

J. Kenneth Mitchell
Department of Environmental
  Resources
Rutgers University

F. W. Montanari
Parsons, Brinckerhoff,
  Quade & Douglas, Inc.

William R. Moore
Soil Conservation Service
U. S. Department of
  Agriculture

Ugo Morelli
Federal Disaster Assistance
  Administration

Allan Murphy
National Center for Atmospheric Research

Robert W. Newlon
Department of Public
  Utilities
City of Columbus

Clark F. Norton
U. S. Senate
Committee on Public Works

Roy E. Olson
College of Engineering
University of Texas at
  Austin

Harold Paulsen
Rocky Mountain Forest
  and Experimental Station

Allen Pearson
National Severe Storms Fore-
  cast Center
National Weather Service

Roy Popkin
American National Red Cross

Ramon Powell
United States Water Resources
  Council

Daniel Price
Department of Sociology
University of Texas at
  Austin

John E. Priest
Harza Engineering Company

E. L. Quarantelli
Disaster Research Center
Ohio State University

Ren F. Read
Defense Civil Preparedness
  Agency

Hale C. Reed
The Travelers Insurance
  Company

Will Reedy
Bureau of Reclamation

Leslie E. Robertson
Skilling, Helle, Christian-
  sen, Robertson
Consulting Structural &
  Civil Engineers

John Rold
Colorado Geological Survey

Douglas D. Rose
Department of Political
  Science
University of California

Richard L. Rudman
Electric Power Research
  Institute

Lois Sharpe
Environmental Quality
  Department
League of Women Voters

Lawrence A. Snell
Institute for Disaster
  Preparedness
University of Southern
  California

A. F. Spilhaus
American Geophysical Union

Ronald Stephenson
Commissioner, Pennington
  County

W. D. Swift
American Insurance Assn.

Lee M. Talbot
Council on Environmental
  Quality

Herbert Temple, Jr.
Office of Emergency Services
State of California

Frederick P. Thieme
Consultant to the Board of
  Regents
University of Colorado

John Townsend
National Oceanic & Atmos-
  pheric Administration

Patricia B. Trainer
Institute of Behavioral
  Science
University of Colorado

L. Scott Tucker
American Public Works Assn.

David J. Varnes
Engineering Geology Branch
U. S. Geological Survey

Stanton Ware
Office of Water Resources
  Research

Robert White
National Oceanic & Atmos-
  pheric Administration

Robert Whitman
Department of Civil
  Engineering
Massachusetts Institute of
  Technology

Thomas Whitman
U. S. Army Corps of
  Engineers

Charles W. Wiecking
U. S. Department of Housing
  & Urban Development

John H. Wiggins, Jr.
J. H. Wiggins Company
Research Engineers

William H. Wilcox
Department of Community
  Affairs
State of Pennsylvania

John M. Wilkinson
Arthur D. Little, Inc.

Robert Wolf
Congressional Research
  Service
Library of Congress

M. Gordon Wolman
Department of Geography
  & Environmental
  Engineering
Johns Hopkins University

Kenneth Wright
Wright Water Engineers, Inc.
Engineering Consultants

Arthur Zeizel
Office of the Assistant
  Secretary for Research
  & Technology
Department of Housing
  & Urban Development

Fred Zimmerman
Disaster Project
Council of State
  Governments

BIBLIOGRAPHY

Ad Hoc Panel on Earthquake Prediction
>1965   Earthquake Prediction: A Proposal for a Ten-Year Program of Research. Washington: Executive Office of the President, Office of Science and Technology.

Anderson, William A.
>1970   "Tsunami Warning in Crescent City, California and Hilo, Hawaii." Pages 116-124 in National Academy of Sciences, The Great Alaska Earthquake of 1964: Human Ecology. Washington: National Academy of Sciences.

Assessment of Research on Natural Hazards
>1973   Bibliography of Published Works on Natural Hazards Contributing to Social Scientific Knowledge. Boulder: University of Colorado Institute of Behavioral Science.

Baddeley, A. D.
>1972   "Selective Attention and Performance in Dangerous Environments." British Journal of Psychology 63, pp. 537-546.

Baker, Earl J., et al.
>1975   Land Use in Hazardous Places. Boulder: University of Colorado Institute of Behavioral Science (forthcoming).

Baker, George W. and D. W. Chapman (eds.)
>1962   Man and Society in Disaster. New York: Basic Books.

Barkley, Paul W. and David W. Seckler
>1972   Economic Growth and Environmental Decay: The Solution Becomes the Problem. New York: Harcourt, Brace, Jovanovich.

Barton, Allen H.
>1970   Communities in Disaster: A Sociological Analysis of Collective Stress Situations. New York: Anchor Books.

Batelle-Columbus Laboratories
>1973   Science, Technology, and Innovation. Prepared for the National Science Foundation. Washington.

Bates, F. L., *et al.*
    1963   The Social and Psychological Consequences of a
            Natural Disaster: A Longitudinal Study of
            Hurricane Audrey. National Academy of Sciences,
            National Research Council Disaster Study #18.
            Washington: National Academy of Sciences Printing
            Office.

Baumann, Duane D. and Clifford S. Russell
    1971   Urban Snow Hazard: Economic and Social Implica-
            tions. Urbana, Illinois: University of Illinois
            Water Resources Center.

Beck, Edward
    1954   Lightning Protection for Electrical Systems. New
            York: McGraw Hill.

Bennett, John
    1969   Northern Plainsmen. Chicago: Aldine.

Blanc, R. C. and G. B. Cleveland
    1968   Natural Slope Stability as Related to Geology,
            San Clemente Area, Orange and San Diego Counties,
            California. Special Report #98. Sacramento,
            California: California Division of Mines and
            Geology.

Blaufarb, H. and J. Levine
    1972   "Crisis Intervention in an Earthquake." Social
            Work 17, pp. 16-19.

Bodine, B. R.
    1969   Hurricane Surge Frequency Estimated for the Gulf
            Coast of Texas. Technical Memorandum #26.
            Coastal Engineering Research Center, Department of
            the Army. Washington: Corps of Engineers.

    1971   Storm Surge on the Open Coast: Fundamentals and
            Simplified Prediction. Technical Memorandum #35.
            Coastal Engineering Research Center, Department of
            the Army. Washington: Corps of Engineers.

Boone, Larry
    1974   Estimating Crop Losses Due to Hail. Economic
            Research Service. Lincoln, Nebraska: U. S.
            Department of Agriculture.

Borchert, John R.
1971 "The Dust Bowl in the 1970's." Annals of the
Association of American Geographers 61, pp. 1-22.

Bosselman, Fred and David Callies
1971 The Quiet Revolution in Land Use Control. Council
on Environmental Quality. Washington: U. S.
Government Printing Office.

Bowden, M. J. and Robert W. Kates
1974 "The Coming San Francisco Earthquake: After the
Disaster." In Harold C. Cochrane, J. Eugene Haas,
M. J. Bowden and Robert W. Kates Social Science
Perspectives on the Coming San Francisco Earth-
quake: Economic Impact, Prediction and Reconstruc-
tion. Natural Hazard Research Working Paper #25.
Boulder, Colorado: University of Colorado
Institute of Behavioral Science.

Bruun, Per
1968 "Beach Erosion and Coastal Protection." In Rhodes
W. Fairbridge (ed.) Encyclopedia of Geomorphology.
New York: Van Nostrand Reinhold.

Burton, Ian
1962 Types of Agricultural Occupance of Flood Plains in
the United States. Department of Geography
Research Paper #75. Chicago: University of
Chicago Press.

Burton, Ian and Robert W. Kates
1964 "The Perception of Natural Hazards in Resource
Management." Natural Resources Journal 3, pp. 412-
441.

Burton, Ian, Robert W. Kates and Rodman E. Snead
1969 The Human Ecology of Coastal Flood Hazard in
Megalopolis. Department of Geography Research
Paper #115. Chicago: University of Chicago Press.

Burton, Ian, Robert W. Kates and Gilbert F. White
1968 The Human Ecology of Extreme Geophysical Events.
Natural Hazards Research Working Paper #1.
Toronto: University of Toronto Department of
Geography.

Burton, Ian, Robert W. Kates and Gilbert F. White
    1975   The Environment as Hazard. New York: Oxford
            University Press (forthcoming).

California Division of Mines and Geology
    1973   Urban Geology: Master Plan for California.
            Bulletin #198. Sacramento, California.

Changnon, S. A., Jr.
    1972   "Examples of Economic Losses from Hail in the
            United States." Journal of Applied Meteorology 11,
            pp. 1128-1137.

Chase, Samuel B. (ed.)
    1968   Problems in Public Expenditure Analysis.
            Washington: The Brookings Institute.

City of Boulder
    1970   Analysis of Damage to Residential Properties from
            High Winds Occurring on January 7 and January 31,
            1969, in Boulder, Colorado. Boulder, Colorado:
            City Manager's Office.

    1972   Map: Boulder Generalized Land Use and Flood
            Hazard. Boulder, Colorado: City of Boulder
            Planning Department.

Clifford, R. A.
    1956   The Rio Grande Flood: A Comparative Study of
            Border Communities in Disaster. Disaster Study
            #7. National Academy of Sciences, National
            Research Council. Washington.

Cobb, William E.
    1971   Letter to David Ludlum (Editor, Weatherwise).
            October 22.

Cochran, Anita L.
    1972   A Selected, Annotated Bibliography on Natural
            Hazards. Natural Hazard Research Working Paper
            #22. Boulder, Colorado: University of Colorado
            Institute of Behavioral Science.

Cochrane, Harold C.
    1974   "Predicting the Economic Impact of Earthquakes."
            In Harold C. Cochrane, J. Eugene Haas, M. J.
            Bowden and Robert W. Kates Social Science Perspec-
            tives on the Coming San Francisco Earthquake:
            Economic Impact, Prediction and Reconstruction.
            Natural Hazard Research Working Paper #25.
            Boulder, Colorado: University of Colorado Insti-
            tute of Behavioral Science.

    1975   Natural Hazards: Their Distributional Impacts.
            Boulder, Colorado: University of Colorado Insti-
            tute of Behavioral Science.

Cochrane, Harold C., *et al.*
    1974   Social Science Perspectives on the Coming San
            Francisco Earthquake: Economic Impact, Prediction
            and Reconstruction. Natural Hazard Research
            Working Paper #25. Boulder, Colorado: University
            of Colorado Institute of Behavioral Science.

Committee on Public Engineering Policy
    1970   Priorities in Applied Research: An Initial
            Appraisal. Washington: National Academy of
            Engineering.

    1972   Perspectives on Benefit-Risk Decision Making.
            Washington: National Academy of Engineering.

    1973   Priorities for Research Applicable to National
            Needs. Panel of Natural Hazards. Washington:
            National Academy of Engineering.

Congressional Research Service
    1974   After Disaster Strikes: Federal Programs and
            Organizations. A Report to the Committee on
            Government Operations by the Congressional Re-
            search Service of the Library of Congress. July.
            Washington: U. S. Government Printing Office.

Cook, Neil R.
    1965   Effects of Upstream Flood Protection on Land Use,
            with Special Reference to the Upper Washita Basin
            of Oklahoma. Stillwater, Oklahoma: Oklahoma
            State University and Resource Development Econom-
            ics Division of Economic Research Service, U. S.
            Department of Agriculture.

Coomber, Nicholas H. and Asit K. Biswas
        1973   Evaluation of Environmental Intangibles. Bronx-
                ville, New York: Genera Press.

Corps of Engineers
        1971   Shore Management Guidelines: National Shoreline
                Study. Washington: U. S. Government Printing
                Office.

        1971a   Shore Protection Guidelines: National Shoreline
                Study. Washington: U. S. Government Printing
                Office.

Council of State Governments
        1972   Suggested State Legislation. Lexington, Kentucky.

Council on Environmental Quality
        1973   Report on Channel Modifications. Prepared by
                Arthur D. Little Incorporated. Washington: U. S.
                Government Printing Office.

Cox, Doak C.
        1963   Status of Tsunami Knowledge. Proceedings of the
                Tenth Pacific Science Congress. Monograph #24.
                Paris: International Union of Geodesy and
                Geophysics.

        1968   Performance of the Seismic Sea Wave Warning
                System, 1948-1967. Institute of Geo-
                physics. Honolulu: University of Hawaii.

Crandell, Dwight R. and D. R. Mullineaux
        1967   Volcanic Hazards at Mount Rainer, Washington.
                U. S. Geological Survey, U. S. Department of the
                Interior. Washington: U. S. Government Printing
                Office.

Dacy, Douglas C. and Howard Kunreuther
        1969   The Economics of Natural Disasters: Implications
                for Federal Policy. New York: The Free Press.

Daniel, Mann, Johnson and Mendelhall
        1972   Geophysical Hazards Investigation. Report to the
                City and Borough of Juneau, Alaska. Portland,
                Oregon.

Defense Civil Preparedness Agency
    1972   Protecting Mobile Homes from High Winds. DCPA
            #TR-75. U. S. Department of Defense. Washington:
            U. S. Government Printing Office.

Deutsch, Karl W., *et al.*
    1971   "Conditions Favoring Major Advances in Social
            Sciences." Science 171, pp. 450-459.

Directors of the Water Resources Research Centers of the South
    Atlantic-Gulf States
    1973   Coordinated Water-Land Management in Urban Areas:
            Definition of Research Needs and Priorities.
            N.p., mimeo.

Disaster Research Group
    1961   Field Studies of Disaster Behavior: An Inventory.
            National Academy of Sciences, National Research
            Council Disaster Study #14. Washington: National
            Academy of Sciences.

Dolan, Robert, Paul J. Godfrey and William E. Odum
    1973   "Man's Impact on the Barrier Islands of North
            Carolina." American Scientist 61 (March-April),
            pp. 152-166.

Drabek, Thomas E., *et al.*
    1968   Disaster in Aisle 13: A Case Study of the
            Coliseum Explosion, October 31, 1963. Disaster
            Research Center Series, College of Administrative
            Science Monograph #D1. Columbus, Ohio: The Ohio
            State University.

    1969   "Social Processes in Disaster: Family Evacuation."
            Social Problems 16, pp. 336-349.

    1973   "Longitudinal Impact of Disaster on Family
            Functioning: Final Progress Report." Denver,
            Colorado: University of Denver Department of
            Sociology.

Dynes, Russell R.
    1970   Organized Behavior in Disaster. Lexington,
            Massachusetts: D. C. Heath.

Dynes, R. R., J. E. Haas and E. L. Quarantelli
    1964   "Some Preliminary Observations in Organizational
            Responses in the Emergency Period After the
            Niigata, Japan Earthquake of June 16, 1964."
            Research Report #11. Columbus, Ohio: Disaster
            Research Center, Ohio State University.

Eagleman, Joe R. and Vincent U. Muirhead
    1971   "Observed Damage from Tornadoes and Safest
            Location in Houses." Preprints of the 7th Con-
            ference on Severe Local Storms. Kansas City,
            Missouri: American Meteorological Society.

Earthquake Engineering Research Institute
    1975   Learning from Earthquakes: Social Science Field
            Guide, Volume 4. Oakland, California.

Eckel, E. B. (ed.)
    1958   Landslides and Engineering Practice. Highway
            Research Board Special Report #29, NAS, NRC
            Publication #544. Washington: National Academy
            of Sciences.

Environmental Science Services Administration
    1966   ESSA Symposium on Earthquake Prediction. Washing-
            ton: U. S. Government Printing Office.

    1968   Tornado Preparedness Planning. Weather Bureau,
            U. S. Department of Commerce. Washington: U. S.
            Government Printing Office.

    1969   Studies in Seismicity and Earthquake Damage
            Statistics, 1969: Summary and Recommendations;
            Appendix A; Appendix B. U. S. Coast and Geodetic
            Survey. Washington: U. S. Department of Commerce.

Ericksen, Neil J.
    1975   Scenario Methodology in Natural Hazards Research.
            Boulder, Colorado: University of Colorado Insti-
            tute of Behavioral Science (forthcoming).

Farhar, Barbara C.
    1974   "The Impact of the Rapid City Flood on Public
            Opinion About Weather Modification." Bulletin of
            the American Meteorological Society 55, pp. 759-
            764.

Form, W. H. and S. Nosow
    1958   Community in Disaster. New York: Harper.

Friedman, D. G.
    1969   "Computer Simulation of the Earthquake Hazards."
            Pages 153-181 in Office of Emergency Preparedness
            Geologic Hazards and Public Problems, Conference
            Proceedings. Executive Office of the President.
            Washington: U. S. Government Printing Office.

    1971   The Storm Surge Hazard Along the Gulf and South
            Atlantic Coastlines. Unpublished Report. Hart-
            ford, Connecticut: The Travelers Insurance
            Company.

    1972   "Insurance and the Natural Hazards." International
            Journal of Actuarial Studies in Non-Life Insurance
            and Risk Theory 7 (part I), pp. 4-58. Amsterdam,
            the Netherlands.

    1973   "Computer Simulation of Natural Hazard Effects."
            Hartford, Connecticut: The Travelers Insurance
            Company.

    1973a   "Analysis for Earthquake Insurance." In Earth-
            quakes and Insurance. Pasadena, California:
            California Institute of Technology.

    1973b   "Prospective View of Natural Disasters in the
            United States." Paper presented at the First
            International Symposium of the System Safety
            Society on Safety and the Consumer. Denver,
            Colorado.

    1973c   Computer Simulation of the Natural Hazard Catas-
            trophe Potential. Hartford, Connecticut: The
            Travelers Insurance Company.

    1975   Computer Simulation Methodology and Natural
            Hazards Research. Boulder, Colorado: University
            of Colorado Institute of Behavioral Science
            (forthcoming).

Friedman, D. G. and T. S. Roy
    1966   Simulation of Total Flood Loss Experience on
            Dwellings on Inland and Coastal Flood Plains.
            Report prepared for the U. S. Department of
            Housing and Urban Development. Hartford, Connec-
            ticut: The Travelers Insurance Company.

Fritz, Charles
    1961   "Disaster." In R. K. Merton and R. A. Nisbet
            (eds.) Contemporary Social Problems. New York:
            Harcourt.

Fritz, C. E. and J. H. Mathewson
    1957   Convergence Behavior in Disasters: A Problem in
            Social Control. Washington: National Academy of
            Sciences/National Research Council.

Frutiger, Hans
    1972   Avalanche Hazard Inventory and Land Use Control
            for the City and Borough of Juneau, Alaska.
            Unpublished report. U. S. Forest Service. Fort
            Collins, Colorado: Rocky Mountain Forest and
            Range Experiment Station.

Garstang, M.
    1972   "A Review of Hurricane and Tropical Meteorology."
            Bulletin of the American Meteorological Society
            53, pp. 612-630.

Gentry, R. C.
    1966   "Nature and Scope of Hurricane Damage." Hurricane
            Symposium. American Society for Oceanography
            Publication #1, pp. 229-254.

Glaser, Edward M. and Samuel H. Taylor
    1973   "Factors Influencing the Success of Applied
            Research." American Psychologist 28 (February),
            pp. 140-146.

Glass, A. J.
    1970   "The Psychological Aspects of Emergency Situa-
            tions." In H. S. Abram (ed.) Psychological
            Aspects of Stress. Springfield, Illinois:
            Charles C. Thomas.

Goddard, James E.
    1973   An Evaluation of Urban Flood Plains. Unpublished
            report. New York: American Society of Civil
            Engineers.

Golant, Stephen
    1969   Human Behavior Before the Disaster: A Selected
            Annotated Bibliography. Natural Hazards Research
            Working Paper #9. Toronto: University of Toronto.

Great Plains Committee
    1937   The Future of the Great Plains. 75th Congress,
            1st Session. Document #114. Washington: U. S.
            Government Printing Office.

Grosser, George H., *et al.*
    1964   The Threat of Impending Disaster: Contributions
            to the Psychology of Stress. Cambridge, Massa-
            chusetts: MIT Press.

Haas, J. Eugene
    1971   Final Report on Effectiveness of Tsunami Warning
            System in Selected Coastal Towns in Alaska. Sub-
            mitted to the Environmental Science Services
            Administration. Boulder, Colorado: University
            of Colorado Institute of Behavioral Science.

    1973   "Social Aspects of Weather Modification." Bulletin
            of the American Meteorological Society 54, pp. 647-
            657.

    1973-1975 "Research Proposal on the Relation of Post-Disaster
            Community Policy Issues to Restoration, Reconstruc-
            tion and Future Vulnerability: A Comparison of
            Managua and Rapid City, South Dakota with Histori-
            cal Documentation from Anchorage, Alaska and San
            Francisco, California." Funded by the National
            Science Foundation, (May 1973-June 1975) under
            grant 39246. Boulder, Colorado: University of
            Colorado Institute of Behavioral Science.

    1974   "Sociological Aspects of Weather Modification."
            Pages 787-811 in Wilmot N. Hess (ed.) Weather and
            Climate Modification. New York: Wiley.

Haas, J. Eugene and William A. Anderson
    1974   "Coping with Socioeconomic Problems Following a
            Major Earthquake." Paper presented at Engineering
            Foundation Conference on Earthquakes and Lifelines,
            Pacific Grove, California.

Haas, J. Eugene and Robert S. Ayre
    1970   The Western Sicily Earthquake Disaster of 1968.
            National Academy of Engineering.

Haas, J. Eugene and Thomas E. Drabek
    1970   "Community Disaster and Systems Stress: A
            Sociological Perspective." Pages 264-286 in
            Joseph McGrath (ed.) Social and Psychological
            Factors in Stress. New York: Holt, Rinehart and
            Winston.

    1973   Complex Organizations: A Sociological Perspective.
            New York: Macmillan.

Haas, J. Eugene and Patricia B. Trainer
    1973   "Effectiveness of the Tsunami Warning System in
            Selected Coastal Towns in Alaska." In Proceedings
            of the 5th World Conference on Earthquake Engi-
            neering. Rome, Italy.

Hail Suppression Research Steering Committee
    1968   Outline of a Hail Suppression Test. Submitted to
            the National Science Foundation. N.p., mimeo.

Harbridge House, Incorporated
    1972   An Inquiry into the Long-term Economic Impact of
            Natural Disasters in the United States. Prepared
            for Office of Technical Assistance, Economic
            Development Administration, U. S. Department of
            Commerce. Boston: Harbridge House, Incorporated.

Harris, D. L.
    1963   Characteristics of the Hurricane Storm Surge.
            Technical Paper #48. U. S. Weather Bureau.
            Washington: U. S. Department of Commerce.

Hartman, L. M., D. Holland and M. Giddings
    1969   "Effects of Hurricane Storms on Agriculture."
            Water Resources Research 5, pp. 555-562.

Haveman, R. H. and Julius Margolis (eds.)
    1970   Public Expenditures and Policy Analysis. Chicago:
            Markham.

Higbee, K. L.
    1972   "Perceived Control and Military Riskiness."
            Perceptual and Motor Skills 34, pp. 95-100.

Higbee, K. L. and T. Lafferty
    1972   "Relationship Among Risk Preferences, Importance,
            and Control." Journal of Psychology 81, pp. 249-
            251.

Hollis, Edward P.
    1971   Bibliography of Earthquake Engineering. Oakland,
            California: Earthquake Engineering Research
            Institute.

Howard, R. A., J. E. Matheson and D. W. North
    1972   "The Decision to Seed Hurricanes." Science 176,
            pp. 1191-1202.

Institute for Defense Analyses
    1971   Some Guidelines for Developing an Office of
            Emergency Preparedness Clearing-House for
            Emergency-Related Research by Charles E. Fritz.
            Paper #P-824. Arlington, Virginia.

Institute for Local Self Government
    1972   Why the Wheels: The Immobile Home. Berkeley,
            California.

Instituut voor Sociaal Onderzoek van het Nederlandse Volk
    1955   Studies on Holland Flood Disaster 1953. 4
            Volumes. Washington: National Academy of
            Sciences, National Research Council.

International Association of Scientific Hydrology
    1966   International Symposium on Scientific Aspects of
            Snow and Ice Avalanches. Publication #69.
            Gentbrugge, Belgium.

Jackson, O. N., L. Hourany and N. J. Vidmar
    1972   "A Four-Dimensional Interpretation of Risk-
            Taking." Journal of Personality 40, pp. 483-501.

James, L. D.
     1964   A Time-Dependent Planning Process for Combining
               Structural Measures, Land Use, and Flood Proofing
               to Minimize the Economic Cost of Floods. Report
               #EEP-12. Palo Alto, California: Stanford Univer-
               sity Institute of Engineering-Economic Systems.

Janis, Irving L. and Seymour Feshbach
     1953   "Effects of Fear-Arousing Communications."
               Journal of Abnormal Social Psychology 48, pp. 78-
               92.

Jelesnianski, C. P.
     1967   "Numerical Computations of Storm Surges with
               Bottom Stress." Monthly Weather Review 95,
               pp. 740-756.

     1972   SPLASH (Special Program to List Amplitudes of
               Surges from Hurricane), 1: Landfall Storms.
               Publication #NOAA TM-NWS TDL-46. System Develop-
               ment Office. Silver Spring, Maryland: U. S.
               Department of Commerce.

Jelesnianski, C. P. and A. D. Taylor
     1973   A Preliminary View of Storm Surges Before and
               After Storm Modifications. Publication #ERL WMPO-
               3, NHRL-102. National Oceanic and Atmospheric
               Administration. Washington: U. S. Department of
               Commerce.

Joint Panel on the San Fernando Earthquake
     1971   The San Fernando Earthquake of February 9, 1971:
               Lessons From a Moderate Earthquake on the Fringe
               of a Densely Populated Region. Washington:
               National Academy of Sciences, National Academy
               of Engineering.

Jones, D. Earl, Jr. and Wesley Holtz
     1973   "Expansive Soils--The Hidden Disaster." Civil
               Engineering 43, pp. 49-51.

Kaplan, M.
     1971-1972 "Actuarial Aspects of Flood and Earthquake
               Insurance." Pages 474-511 in Proceedings of the
               Conference of Actuaries in Public Practice Volume
               21. Chicago: Association of Actuaries in Public
               Practice.

Kaplan, Stephen
    1972   "The Challenge of Environmental Psychology: A
               Proposal for a New Functionalism." American
               Psychologist 27, pp. 140-143.

Kates, Robert W.
    1962   Hazard and Choice Perception in Flood Plain
               Management. Department of Geography Research
               Paper #78. Chicago: University of Chicago Press.

    1971   "Natural Hazard in Human Ecological Perspective:
               Hypotheses and Models." Economic Geography 47,
               pp. 438-451.

Kates, Robert W., *et al.*
    1973   "Human Impact of the Managua Earthquake Disaster."
               Science 182, pp. 981-990.

Killian, L. M.
    1952   "The Significance of Multiple-Group Membership in
               Disaster." American Journal of Sociology 57,
               pp. 309-314.

Kogan, Nathan and Michael A. Wallach
    1967   "Risk Taking as a Function of the Situation, the
               Person, and the Group." In Theodore M. Newcomb
               (ed.) New Directions in Psychology Volume 3. New
               York: Holt, Rinehart and Winston.

Kraenzel, Carl Frederick
    1955   The Great Plains in Transition. Norman, Oklahoma:
               University of Oklahoma.

Krauskopf, Konrad B.
    1973   "History of the Committee on the Alaska Earth-
               quake." Pages 99-114 in National Academy of
               Sciences The Great Alaska Earthquake of 1964:
               Summary and Recommendations. Committee on the
               Alaska Earthquake. Washington: National Academy
               of Sciences.

Kunreuther, Howard
    1973   Recovery from Natural Disasters. Washington:
               American Enterprise Institute for Public Policy
               Research.

1973a   "Values and Costs." In Building Practices for
           Disaster Mitigation, Proceedings of a Workshop.
           National Bureau of Standards, Building Science
           Series #46. U. S. Department of Commerce.
           Washington: U. S. Government Printing Office.

LaChapelle, Edward R.
     1966   "Avalanche Forecasting - A Modern Synthesis." In
               International Symposium on Scientific Aspects of
               Snow and Ice Avalanches. Publication #69.
               Gentbrugge, Belgium: International Association
               of Scientific Hydrology.

Lachman, Roy, Maurice Tatsuoka and William Bonk
     1961   "Human Behavior During the Tsunami of May 1960."
               Science 133, pp. 1405-1409.

Lee, Robert R., Gerald A. Fleischer and Vincent J. Roggeveen
     1961   Engineering-Economic Planning of Water Resources:
               A selected Bibliography. Stanford, California:
               Stanford University Project on Engineering-
               Economic Planning.

Lemons, H.
     1942   "Hail in American Agriculture." Economic
               Geography 18, pp. 363-378.

Lucas, R. A.
     1971   "Social Behavior Under Conditions of Extreme
               Stress: A Study of Miners Entrapped by a Coal
               Mine Disaster." Dissertation Abstracts Inter-
               national 31 (9-A), p. 4906.

McGuire, William J.
     1968   "The Nature of Attitudes and Attitude Change."
               In Gardner Lindzey and Elliot Aronson, eds.
               Handbook of Social Psychology, 2nd edition,
               volume 3. Reading, Massachusetts: Addison Wesley.

McLuckie, Benjamin F.
     1970   The Warning System in Disaster Situations: A
               Selective Analysis. Research Report #9. Colum-
               bus, Ohio: The Ohio State University Disaster
               Research Center.

Mack, Raymond W. and George W. Baker
    1961   The Occasion Instant. Disaster Study #15. Na-
            tional Academy of Sciences, National Research
            Council. Washington.

Mader, G. G.
    1972   "Land Use Planning." In G. O. Gates (ed.) The
            San Fernando Earthquake of February 9, 1971 and
            Public Policy. Sacramento, California: Joint
            Committee on Seismic Safety, California Legisla-
            ture.

Mangen, George F. and Herbert A. Swenson
    1972   Urban Water Planning: A Bibliography. Water
            Resources Scientific Information Center, Office
            of Water Resources Research. Washington: U. S.
            Department of the Interior.

Melaragno, Michele G.
    1968   Tornado Forces and Their Effects on Buildings.
            Manhattan, Kansas: Kansas State University.

Mileti, Dennis S.
    1975   Natural Hazards Warning Systems in the United
            States: A Research Assessment. Boulder, Color-
            ado: University of Colorado Institute of Behav-
            ioral Science (forthcoming).

    1975a   Disaster Relief in the United States: A Research
            Assessment. Boulder, Colorado: University of
            Colorado Institute of Behavioral Science (forth-
            coming).

Mileti, Dennis S., Thomas Drabek and J. Eugene Haas
    1975   Human Systems in Extreme Environments: A Socio-
            logical Perspective. Boulder, Colorado: Univer-
            sity of Colorado Institute of Behavioral Science
            (forthcoming).

Miller, L. C., *et al.*
    1972   "Factor Structure of Childhood Fears." Journal
            of Consulting and Clinical Psychology 39, pp. 264-
            268.

Minor, Joseph E., *et al.*
    1972   Impact of the Lubbock Storm on Regional Systems.
            Final Report prepared for the Defense Civil Pre-
            paredness Agency. Washington: Department of
            Defense.

Mitchell, James Kenneth
    1968   A Selected Bibliography of Coastal Erosion,
            Protection, and Related Human Activity in North
            America and the British Isles. Natural Hazards
            Research Working Paper #4. Toronto: University
            of Toronto.

    1972   "Global Summary of Human Response to Coastal
            Erosion." 22nd International Geographical Con-
            gress, Paper #9. Boulder, Colorado: University
            of Colorado Institute of Behavioral Science.

    1974   Community Response to Coastal Erosion: Individual
            and Collective Adjustments to Hazard on the
            Atlantic Shore. Chicago: University of Chicago
            Press (forthcoming).

Moore, Harry Estill
    1958   Tornadoes Over Texas. Austin, Texas: University
            of Texas Press.

    1963   Before the Wind: A Study of the Response to
            Hurricane Carla. Disaster Study #19. National
            Academy of Sciences, National Research Council.
            Washington.

    1964   And the Winds Blew. The Hogg Foundation for
            Mental Health. Austin, Texas: University of
            Texas.

Murphy, F. C.
    1958   Regulating Flood Plain Development. Department
            of Geography Research Paper #56. Chicago: Uni-
            versity of Chicago Press.

Murton, Brian J. and Shinzo Shimabukuro
    1972   Human Adjustment to Volcanic Hazard in Puna
            District, Hawaii. International Geophysical
            Union Commission on Man and Environment Paper.
            Honolulu: University of Hawaii.

Nace, R. L. and E. J. Pluhowski
    1965   Drought of the 1950's with Special Reference to
            the Midcontinent. Geological Survey Water-Supply
            Paper #1804. Washington: U. S. Government
            Printing Office.

National Academy of Sciences
    1969   Toward Reduction of Losses from Earthquakes.
            Committee on the Alaska Earthquake. Washington.

    1970   The Great Alaska Earthquake of 1964: Human
            Ecology. Committee on Alaska Earthquake. Wash-
            ington: National Academy of Sciences Printing
            and Publishing Office.

National Academy of Sciences-National Research Council
    1969   Earthquake Engineering Research. A Report to the
            National Science Foundation prepared by the Com-
            mittee on Earthquake Engineering Research, Divi-
            sion of Engineering. Washington: National Acad-
            emy of Sciences.

    1971   The Atmospheric Sciences and Man's Needs:
            Priorities for the Future. NRC Committee on
            Atmospheric Sciences. Washington: National
            Academy of Sciences.

National Advisory Committee on Oceans and Atmosphere
    1972   The Agnes Floods: A Post-Audit of the Effective-
            ness of the Storm and Flood Warning System of
            NOAA. Washington: U. S. Government Printing
            Office.

National Bureau of Standards
    1970   Wind Loads on Buildings and Structures. Proceed-
            ings of Technical Meeting, Building Science
            Series #30. U. S. Department of Commerce. Wash-
            ington: U. S. Government Printing Office.

    1973   Building Practices for Disaster Mitigation. NBS
            Building Science Series #46. Washington: U. S.
            Government Printing Office.

National Oceanic and Atmospheric Administration
    1920-1972 Climatological Data: National Summaries. Ashe-
            ville, North Carolina: U. S. Department of Com-
            merce.

1934-1970   Climatological Data: National Summary. Monthly
            Issues. Asheville, North Carolina: U. S. Depart-
            ment of Commerce.

1970-1972   Storm Data 12, 13, 14. Asheville, North Carolina:
            Environmental Data Service.

1971   Climatological Data, National Summary 1971.
            Asheville, North Carolina: U. S. Department of
            Commerce.

1972   Climatological Data, National Summary 1972.
            Asheville, North Carolina: U. S. Department of
            Commerce.

1972a   A Study of Earthquake Losses in the San Francisco
            Bay Area: Data and Analysis. A Report prepared
            for the Office of Emergency Preparedness. Wash-
            ington: U. S. Department of Commerce.

1973   A Federal Plan for Natural Disaster Warning and
            Preparedness. U. S. Department of Commerce,
            Federal Committee for Meteorological Services and
            Supporting Research. Washington: U. S. Depart-
            ment of Commerce.

1973a   A Study of Earthquake Losses in the Los Angeles,
            California Area. Prepared for the Federal Disas-
            ter Assistance Administration, Department of
            Housing and Urban Development. Washington: U. S.
            Department of Commerce.

1973b   Summary Report: Weather Modification, Fiscal
            Year 1973. Rockville, Maryland: U. S. Depart-
            ment of Commerce.

National Science Board
    1971   Environmental Science: Challenge for the
            Seventies. Washington.

National Science Foundation
    1966   Weather and Climate Modification: Report of the
            Special Commission on Weather Modification.
            Washington.

National Water Commission
  1973   Water Policies for the Future. Washington: U. S.
          Government Printing Office.

Nichols, D. R. and J. M. Buchanan - Banks
  1974   Seismic Hazards and Land Use Planning. U. S.
          Geological Survey Circular 690. Washington:
          U. S. Government Printing Office.

Nichols, D. R. and C. C. Campbell (eds.)
  1969   Environmental Planning and Geology. Proceedings
          of the Symposium on Engineering Geology in the
          Urban Environment. San Francisco, October, 1969.
          Washington: U. S. Government Printing Office.

Nickerson, J. W.
  1971   Storm-Surge Forecasting. Navy Weather Research
          Facility Technical Paper #10-71. Norfolk,
          Virginia.

Nilsen, T. H. and E. E. Brabb
  1973   "Current Slope Stability Studies by the U. S.
          Geological Survey in the San Francisco Bay
          Region, California." Landslide 1 (Spring), pp. 2-
          10.

Nisan, M. and A. Minkowich
  1973   "The Effect of Expected Temporal Distance on Risk
          Taking." Journal of Personality and Social
          Psychology 25, pp. 375-380.

Office of Emergency Preparedness
  1972   Disaster Preparedness, Volumes 1, 2, and 3.
          Executive Office of the President. Washington:
          U. S. Government Printing Office.

Office of Science and Technology
  1970   Earthquake Hazard Reduction. Report on the Task
          Force on Earthquake Hazard Reduction. Executive
          Office of the President, Government Printing
          Office.

Ollier, Cliff
  1969   Volcanoes. Cambridge, Massachusetts: MIT Press.

Palmer, Wayne C. and Lyle M. Denny
     1971   Drought Bibliography. National Oceanic and
              Atmospheric Administration, NOAA Technical Memo-
              randum EDS 20. Silver Spring, Maryland.

Polenske, Karen R.
     1970   A Multiregional Input-Output Model for the United
              States. Report #COM-71-00943. Springfield,
              Virginia: National Technical Information Service.

Pollatsek, A. and A. Tversky
     1970   "A Theory of Risk." Journal of Mathematical
              Psychology 7, pp. 540-553.

Quarantelli, E. L.
     1970   "A Selected Annotated Bibliography of Social
              Science Studies on Disasters." American
              Behavioral Scientist 13, pp. 452-456.

Raker, J. W., et al.
     1956   Emergency Medical Care in Disasters. A Summary
              of Recorded Experience. National Academy of
              Sciences, National Research Council Disaster
              Study #6. Washington: National Academy of
              Sciences.

Rayner, Jeanette
     1957   "Annotated Bibliography on Disaster Research."
              Human Organization 16 (Summer), pp. 30-40.

Reilly, W. K.
     1973   The Use of Land: A Citizen's Policy Guide to
              Urban Growth. New York: Crowell.

Relph, E. C. and S. B. Goodwillie
     1968   Annotated Bibliography on Snow and Ice Problems.
              Natural Hazards Research Working Paper #2.
              Toronto: University of Toronto.

Reubin, D., et al.
     1974   A Rationale for Setting Priorities for New Energy
              Technology Research and Development. Livermore,
              California: Lawrence Livermore Laboratory.

Rogers, E. M. and F. F. Shoemaker (eds.)
     1971   Communication of Innovations. New York: The
              Free Press.

Rogers, George W.
    1970   "Economic Effects of the Earthquake." Pages 58-
            76 in National Academy of Sciences The Great Alaska
            Earthquake of 1964: Human Ecology. Washington:
            National Academy of Sciences.

Rogers, William J. and Harry L. Swift
    1970   Frost and the Prevention of Frost Damage.
            National Oceanic and Atmospheric Administration,
            U. S. Department of Commerce. Washington: U. S.
            Government Printing Office.

Rooney, John F., Jr.
    1969   "The Economic and Social Implications of Snow and
            Ice." In R. J. Chorley (ed.) Water, Earth, and
            Man. London: Methuen.

Rotter, J. B., M. Seeman and S. Liverant
    1962   "Internal versus External Control of Reinforce-
            ments: A Major Variable in Behavior Theory." In
            N. F. Washburne (ed.) Decisions, Values, and
            Groups, Volume 2. New York: Pergamon Press.

Russell, Clifford S., David G. Arey and Robert W. Kates
    1970   Drought and Water Supply: Implications of the
            Massachusetts Experiences for Municipal Planning.
            Baltimore: Johns Hopkins.

Saarinen, Thomas F.
    1966   Perception of Drought Hazard on the Great Plains.
            Department of Geography Research Paper #106.
            Chicago: University of Chicago.

Sadowski, A. F.
    1966   "Tornadoes with Hurricanes." Weatherwise 19,
            pp. 71-75.

Shaeffer, John R., et al.
    1967   Introduction to Flood Proofing. Center for Urban
            Studies. Chicago: University of Chicago Press.

Shepard, Francis P. and Harold R. Wanless
    1971   Our Changing Coastlines. New York: McGraw-Hill.

Simpson, R. H.
    1973   "Hurricane Prediction: Progress and Problem
            Areas." Science 181, pp. 899-907.

Simpson, R. H. and M. B. Lawrence
    1971   Atlantic Hurricane Frequencies Along the U. S.
           Coastline. NOAA Technical Memorandum #NWS SR-58.
           Washington: U. S. Department of Commerce.

Sims, John H. and Duane D. Baumann
    1972   "The Tornado Threat: Coping Styles of the North
           and South." Science 176, pp. 1386-1392.

Skaggs, Richard H.
    1969   "Analysis and Regionalization of the Diurnal
           Distribution of Tornadoes in the United States."
           Monthly Weather Review 97 (February), pp. 103-115.

Slosson, J.
    1969   "The Role of Engineering Geology in Urban
           Planning." Pages 8-14 in The Governor's Con-
           ference on Environmental Geology, April 30-May 2,
           1969. Sacramento, California.

Slovic, Paul
    1964   "Assessment of Risk Taking Behavior." Psycho-
           logical Bulletin 61, pp. 220-233.

Smith, Courtland L. and Thomas C. Hogg
    1971   "Benefits and Beneficiaries: Contrasting Economic
           and Cultural Distinctions." Water Resources
           Research 8, pp. 254-263.

Smith, R.
    1958   "Economic and Legal Aspects." Pages 6-19 in
           E. B. Eckel (ed.) Landslides and Engineering
           Practice. Washington: National Academy of
           Sciences.

Special Assistant to the President for Public Works Planning
    1958   Drouth: A Report. Washington: U. S. Government
           Printing Office.

Spence, H. E. and R. Moinpour
    1972   "Fear Appeals in Marketing: A Social Perspective."
           Journal of Marketing 36, pp. 39-43.

Starr, Chauncey
    1969   "Social Benefit versus Technological Risk."
           Science 165, pp. 1232-1238.

1972   "Benefit-Cost Studies in Socio-Technical Systems."
            Pages 17-42 in Committee on Public Engineering
            Policy Perspectives on Benefit-Risk Decision
            Making. Washington: National Academy of Engi-
            neering.

Steers, James A.
    1953   The Sea Coast. London: Collins.

Steinbrugge, Karl V.
    1968   Earthquake Hazard in the San Francisco Bay Area:
            A Continuing Problem in Public Policy. Berkeley,
            California: University of California Institute
            of Governmental Studies.

    1973   "Earthquake Insurance Losses for Single-Family
            Wood Frame Dwellings." Paper presented to the
            National Committee on Property Insurance. San
            Francisco: Earthquake Department of Insurance
            Services Office.

Stokol'nikov, I. S.
    1965   Study of Lightning and Lightning Protection.
            Joint Publications Research Service #29, 407.
            U. S. Department of Commerce. Washington: U. S.
            Government Printing Office.

Strumpfer, D. J.
    1970   "Fear and Affiliation During a Disaster." Journal
            of Social Psychology 82, pp. 263-268.

Sugg, Arnold L.
    1968   "Beneficial Aspects of the Tropical Cyclone."
            Journal of Applied Meteorology 7, pp. 39-45.

Summers, P. W.
    1973   "Project Hailstop: A Review of Accomplishments
            to Date." Journal of Weather Modification 5,
            pp. 43-55.

Tannehill, Ivan Ray
    1947   Drought: Its Causes and Effects. Princeton,
            New Jersey: Princeton University Press.

Task Force on Federal Flood Control Policy
    1966   A Unified National Program for Managing Flood
            Losses. House Document #465. Washington: U. S.
            Government Printing Office.

Taylor, James B., Louis A. Zurcher and William H. Key
    1970   Tornado: A Community Responds to Disaster.
            Seattle: University of Washington Press.

Taylors Digest
    1972   "Announcement of a Projected Study. To be con-
            ducted jointly by the American Insurance Associa-
            tion and McDonnell-Douglas." (July 29), p. 18.
            Indianapolis, Indiana.

Tennessee Valley Authority
    1962   Bibliography of Tennessee Valley Authority
            Projects. Knoxville, Tennessee.

Tennessee Valley Authority Technical Library
    1973   Flood Damage Prevention: An Indexed Bibliography.
            7th edition. Knoxville, Tennessee.

Thom, H. C. S.
    1968   "New Distributions of Extreme Winds in the United
            States." Journal of the Structural Division,
            Proceedings of the American Society of Civil
            Engineers 94 (July), pp. 1787-1801.

Thomas, H. E.
    1963   General Summary of Effects of the Drought in the
            Southwest. U. S. Geological Survey Professional
            Paper #372-H. Washington: U. S. Government
            Printing Office.

Thompson, J. Neils, et al.
    1970   The Lubbock Storm of May 11, 1970. A Report
            prepared for the Committee on Earthquake Inspec-
            tion of the National Academy of Engineering.
            Washington: National Academy of Sciences.

Uman, Martin A.
    1969   Lightning. New York: McGraw-Hill.

    1971   Understanding Lightning. Carnegie, Pennsylvania:
            Bek Technical Publications.

U.S. Bureau of the Census
    1961   U. S. Census of Population: 1960. U. S. Depart-
            ment of Commerce. Washington: U. S. Government
            Printing Office.

    1971   U. S. Census of Population: 1970. U. S. Depart-
            ment of Commerce. Washington: U. S. Government
            Printing Office.

U. S. Congress
    1966   "A Unified National Program for Managing Flood
            Losses." Report of the National Task Force for
            Flood Control, H.D. 465, 89th Congress, 2nd
            Session. Washington: U. S. Government Printing
            Office.

U. S. Department of Agriculture
    1927-1937 Yearbook of Agriculture. Washington: U. S.
            Government Printing Office.

    1936-1972 Agricultural Statistics, Yearly Reports. Washing-
            ton: U. S. Government Printing Office.

    1971   Farm Income; State Estimates 1949-1970.
            Economic Research Service. Washington: U.S.
            Government Printing Office.

    1972   Agricultural Statistics. Washington: U.S. Govern-
            ment Printing Office.

U. S. Department of Commerce
    1974   Construction Review. Table B-1. Washington:
            U. S. Government Printing Office.

U. S. Department of Housing and Urban Development
    1970   Environmental Planning and Geology. Washington:
            U. S. Government Printing Office.

U.S. Forest Service
    1968   Snow Avalanches: A Handbook of Forecasting and
            Control Measures. USDA Agricultural Handbook #194.
            Washington: U. S. Government Printing
            Office.

U. S. Geological Survey
    1966   Volcanoes of the United States. U. S. Department
            of the Interior. Washington: U. S. Government
            Printing Office.

U. S. Senate, Committee on Commerce
    1972   National Coastal Zone Management Act of 1972.
            Report of the Senate Committee on Commerce on S.
            3507. Senate Report #92-753. 92nd Congress,
            2nd Session. Washington: U. S. Government
            Printing Office.

U. S. Water Resources Council
    1968   The Nation's Water Resources. Washington: U. S.
            Government Printing Office.

    1971   Regulation of Flood Hazard Areas. Washington:
            U. S. Government Printing Office.

    1972   A Unified National Program for Flood Plain
            Management. Washington: U. S. Water Resources
            Council.

    1972a   Regulation of Flood Hazard Areas to Reduce Flood
            Losses. Washington.

Wallace, A. F. C.
    1956   Tornado in Worcester: An Exploratory Study of
            Individual and Community Behavior in an Extreme
            Situation. National Academy of Sciences, Nation-
            al Research Council Disaster Study #3. Washing-
            ton: National Academy of Sciences.

Wang, Jen Yu and Gerald L. Barger
    1962   Bibliography of Agricultural Meteorology.
            Madison, Wisconsin: University of Wisconsin.

Warrick, Richard A.
    1974   Personal communication to Gilbert F. White.
            Boulder, Colorado: University of Colorado Insti-
            tute of Behavioral Science.

Weisbecker, Leo W.
    1974   Snowpack, Cloud-Seeding, and the Colorado River:
            A Technology Assessment of Weather Modification.
            Norman, Oklahoma: University of Oklahoma Press.

White, Gilbert F.
    1945   Human Adjustment to Flood. Chicago: University
            of Chicago Press.

1964   Choice of Adjustment to Floods. Department of
        Geography Research Paper #93. Chicago: Univer-
        sity of Chicago Press.

1975   The Flood Hazard in the United States: A Research
        Assessment. Boulder, Colorado: University of
        Colorado Institute of Behavioral Science (forth-
        coming).

White, Gilbert F., *et al.*
    1958   Changes in Urban Occupance of Flood Plains in the
            United States. Department of Geography Research
            Paper #57. Chicago: University of Chicago Press.

Wiegel, Robert L. (ed.)
    1970   Earthquake Engineering. Englewood Cliffs, New
            Jersey: Prentice-Hall.

Wiggins, John H. Jr. and Donald F. Moran
    1971   Earthquake Safety in the City of Long Beach Based
            on the Concept of Balanced Risk. Palos Verdes
            Estates, California: J. H. Wiggins Company.

Williams, Harry B.
    1964   "Human Factors in Warning-and-Response Systems."
            Pages 79-104 in George H. Grosser, Henry Wechsler
            and Milton Grenblat (eds.) The Threat of Impending
            Disaster. Cambridge, Massachusetts: The MIT
            Press.

Wilson, Harold F.
    1964   The Story of the Jersey Shore, Volume 4. The
            New Jersey Historical Series. Princeton, New
            Jersey: D. Van Nostrand.

Wolfenstein, Martha
    1957   Disaster: A Psychological Essay. Glencoe,
            Illinois: Free Press.

Wolford, V. L.
    1960   Tornado Occurrences in the United States. U. S.
            Weather Bureau, U. S. Department of Commerce.
            Washington: U. S. Government Printing Office.

Yutzy, Daniel
    1970   "Priorities in Community Response." American
            Behavioral Scientist 13, pp. 344-353.

Zaruba, Q. and V. Mencl
     1969   Landslides and Their Control. New York: Elsevier.

Zegel, Ferdinand H.
     1967   "Lightning Deaths in the U.S.: A Seven-Year Survey
              from 1959 to 1965." Weatherwise 20, pp. 169-173.

Assessment of Research on Natural Hazards Publications

Computer Simulation in Natural Hazard Assessment. Don G. Friedman

Natural Hazards and Their Distributional Effects. Harold Cochrane

Drought Hazard in the United States. Richard A. Warrick

Earthquake and Tsunami Hazards in the United States. Robert Ayre

Flood Hazard in the United States. Gilbert F. White, et al.

Hurricane Hazard in the United States. Waltraud A.R. Brinkmann,
     et al.

Land Use Management and Regulation in Hazardous Areas. Earl J.
     Baker and Joe Gordon-Feldman McPhee

Disaster Relief and Rehabilitation in the United States. Dennis
     S. Mileti

Scenario Methodology in Natural Hazards Research. Neil Ericksen

Severe Local Storm Hazard in the United States. Waltraud A.R.
     Brinkmann, et al.

Volcano Hazard in the United States. Richard A. Warrick

Natural Hazard Warning Systems in the United States. Dennis S.
     Mileti

Coastal Erosion Hazard in the United States. John H. Sorensen
     and J. Kenneth Mitchell

Frost Hazard in the United States. Paul C. Huszar

Landslide Hazard in the United States. John H. Sorensen, Neil
     Ericksen and Dennis S. Mileti

Snow Avalanche Hazard in the United States. Project staff

Urban Snow Hazard in the United States. Harold Cochrane, et al.

Local Windstorm Hazard in the United States. Waltraud A.R.
     Brinkmann

Technological Adjustments to Natural Hazards. Robert Ayre